LONDON COUNTY

APS
AUXILIARY FIRE SERVICE
ENROL AT ANY FIRE STATION

COVER AT ONCE

If in the open
with no cover
-lie down

If your home is within
5 minutes-go there

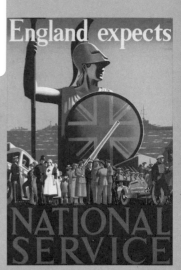

England expects

NATIONAL SERVICE

IN AN AIR RAID . . .

HOW TO FIGHT A FIRE

WANTED

Men for First Aid Parties

A REAL MAN'S JOB

ARP

APPLY TO YOUR LOCAL COUNCIL

**YOUR COURAGE
YOUR CHEERFULNESS
YOUR RESOLUTION
WILL BRING
US VICTORY**

FREEDOM IS
**IN PERIL
DEFEND IT
WITH ALL
YOUR MIGHT**

IN AN AIR RAID . . .

IF YOU ARE CAUGHT IN THE STREET

Don't stand and stare
at the sky

Take cover at once

**Air Raid Wardens
WANTED**

AND THEY ARE WANTED

NOW

GET INTO TOUCH WITH YOUR LOCAL COUNCIL

Outbreak 1939

By the Same Author

The German Home Front 1939–1945

Outbreak 1939

The World Goes to War

Terry Charman

To James Taylor

Published by Virgin Books 2009

2 4 6 8 10 9 7 5 3 1

Unless otherwise stated photographs and text © The Trustees of the Imperial War Museum 2009
Foreword © Melvyn Bragg 2009

The poster 'Take Your Gas Mask Everywhere' is reproduced with kind permission of RoSPA
(The Royal Society for the Prevention of Accidents)

The television programme *Outbreak* is an ITV Studios Production for ITV,
History Channel and France 3 in association with the Imperial War Museum
and ECPAD © ITV Studios Ltd 2009.

Extract on pages 142–143 © *Daily Express*

Terry Charman has asserted his right under the Copyright, Designs
and Patents Act 1988 to be identified as the author of this work.

First published in Great Britain in 2009 by
Virgin Books
Random House, 20 Vauxhall Bridge Road,
London SW1V 2SA

www.virginbooks.com
www.rbooks.co.uk

Addresses for companies within The Random House Group Limited can be found at:
www.randomhouse.co.uk/offices.htm

The Random House Group Limited Reg. No. 954009

A CIP catalogue record for this book
is available from the British Library.

Hardback ISBN 9781905264827
Trade Paperback ISBN 9780753519646

The Random House Group Limited supports the Forest Stewardship Council [FSC],
the leading international forest certification organisation. All our titles that are printed
on Greenpeace-approved FSC-certified paper carry the FSC logo.
Our paper procurement policy can be found at www.rbooks.co.uk/environment

Mixed Sources
Product group from well-managed
forests and other controlled sources
www.fsc.org Cert no. TT-COC-2139
© 1996 Forest Stewardship Council

FSC

Typeset in Sabon by Palimpsest Book Production Limited,
Grangemouth, Stirlingshire
Printed and bound in Great Britain by CPI Mackays, Chatham ME5 8TD

Contents

'Unless we heard from them by eleven o'clock that they were prepared at once to withdraw their troops from Poland, a state of war would exist between us.'
Neville Chamberlain, 3 September 1939.

FOREWORD

I just missed the start of the Second World War. On Sunday, 3 September 1939 I was not quite ready for landing. That happened on 6 October. Nevertheless the war was the landscape and currency of my childhood – its background noise, its daily prayers, the atmosphere of life both at that time and in some ways forever since.

Windows were blacked out nightly to give the German bombers no chink of light and even we children staggered rather drunkenly around the twisting alleys of the small town with weak pencil torches nervously flashed on and off but always pointed downwards. Rationing ruled the kitchen. Stories of war were our daily bread and games of war our childhood antidote. The wireless was the altar and news bulletins the daily service. It was a time when children conceived violent hatreds of nations and peoples they knew nothing of, when no propaganda was too black and yet the greatest tragedy of all was – to take my own experience – not even whispered in the streets. We did not know the depth of evil out there.

There were outings now and then, mainly to the seaside, to Silloth ten miles away, and the churches filled in social gaps with gaslit youth clubs. There would be dances in the blacked-out basement of a Congregational church where women, often in coats against the cold, danced with women or taught their children the steps of old ballroom dances.

And there were treats. Children whose fathers were in the war got a present now and then from sympathetic families doing their bit and felt very special because of it.

I lived in north Cumbria in the north-west of England, a borderland near Hadrian's Wall, a place both ruined and ripened in wars over the centuries – Romans, Vikings, Normans and in the Middle Ages 300 years of reiving border warfare with the Scots.

Then came the imperial wars with local regiments called up in heavy numbers to plant and to defend the flag. My grandfather and five of his brothers went through the First World War. My father and three of his brothers were in the Second.

Where I lived was involved in battles in the air not because it was on the aerial frontline but because it was so far from it. Fractured aeroplanes hedge-hopped from the south-east of England to a place thought to be out of range and out of sight of the German bombers. They were 'turned around' and sent back south into battle.

There were soldiers marching even in this small market town, Wigton, population 5,000. There were morale-boosting marches when the music played and little boys ran alongside in the gutters. There were soldiers and sailors and airmen on leave with the occasional story of combat and horror but those were tight-lipped days. And there were the casualties to men from the town and, early on, the growth of fear as the defeats could not be concealed and towards the end the birth of an even greater bottomless fear as the atom bomb entered into history.

And so when I realised that the seventieth anniversary of World War Two was all but on us, there were hundreds of iron filings which rushed to that magnet of the war in my past. You only rarely have a complete idea immediately. This was one of them.

I wanted to make a television programme about the day the Second World War broke out, the very day. To track through that day, to show what happened here in my own country and also in France, Germany, Poland, Australia, America, the Commonwealth and elsewhere. The proposition was accepted by ITV for an hour-long documentary.

You always want more and it would have been good to have two or three programmes which included a long and complex lead up to the war but others in print and in exhibitions will I'm sure do that. *Outbreak* stuck to the day.

There is something very satisfactory in the shape of a day. By concentrating on that we could embrace and contrast great acts of state with private mundane actions from members of the general public. There would be the grand drama unfolding but also, I hoped, the sense and evidence, the humour and personal fears in ordinary lives.

Above all I wanted the story to be told by those involved in the day either through archive (which was rich) or through finding people who could remember 3 September 1939.

That led the research team to some remarkable discoveries, not only in this country but in Germany, France, Poland, Australia and the West Indies.

We could go from a woman holding up a dress in which she had been christened on that Sunday, 3 September to a woman who had been on the SS *Athenia* sunk on the same day. We could go from the Dowager Duchess of Devonshire to words and recollections of Winston Churchill, from the memories of Richard Attenborough and children sent away from London to the countryside as evacuees to words from the Prime Minister of the day and from King George VI.

The team employed several telling strategies. For instance, descendants of the main players would read the words written about the time – Lady Soames quoted her father Winston Churchill. There was Neville Chamberlain's grandson. They played back the speech of King George to those who had listened to it at the time including George Cole, Betty Driver, Vera Lynn, Tony Benn and Nicholas Parsons, and their reactions were telling.

When the Imperial War Museum indicated interest, I was delighted. It was like being awarded a degree. The Museum had already drawn up its own plans to commemorate the seventieth anniversary with an exhibition and an accompanying book by its Senior Historian Terry Charman. With his immense knowledge of the period and his eye for detail, we were fortunate indeed to have Terry's services as historical consultant on the programme. In his thirty-five years at the Museum, he has assisted many eminent historians, including Asa Briggs, Sir Martin Gilbert and Professor Richard Holmes with their books. Now he has had the opportunity to write his own.

There cannot be many books that bring together both the vituperative diary entries of Dr Goebbels and the risqué jokes of Max Miller. Drawing on the immense and almost unrivalled collections at the Imperial War Museum, the book has skilfully woven together the stories of not only the Great and the Good, but also of ordinary people living through extraordinary times. We meet the vain and alcoholic Colonel Beck, Poland's foreign minister, who nonchalantly accepts Britain's guarantee to his doomed country between two flicks of his cigarette ash, and at the same time physiotherapist Joan Strange of Worthing, who perceives only too clearly the evil nature of the Nazi regime through her work for Jewish refugees.

Our programme dealt with just the one day, 3 September 1939, but the book goes on to cover the last months of 1939, and the first of what became known at the time as the 'Phoney War'. But while the RAF confined itself to dropping propaganda leaflets, *Outbreak* shows that there was no Phoney War at sea. Nor was it phoney in Poland, where right from the start the Nazis unleashed a campaign of racial terror that eventually led to the deaths of over six million Poles, Jewish and non-Jewish. Nor in Finland, a victim of aggression, not on Hitler's part this time, but from his new 'ally' Stalin. We learn how on 25 December 1939, while the British enjoyed a near-normal Christmas, the citizens of Helsinki spent most of it in air-raid shelters. We encounter both the sinister 'Lord Haw Haw', William Joyce, for whom the British people had such a morbid fascination during the war's first months, and 'Our Gracie' – Gracie Fields – still not recovered from a serious illness, but determined to entertain the 'boys' out in France.

The first day of the Second World War can without exaggeration be called one on which the world was changed. To have that day put on film and in an exhibition and in a book could not be more fitting. All of them give a salute to what the Allies undertook on Sunday, 3 September 1939.

In *Outbreak*, Terry Charman has produced a book that chronicles, in Evelyn Waugh's words, 'that odd, dead period before the Churchillian renaissance'. As Churchill himself used to say, you will read it with 'pleasure and profit'.

Melvyn Bragg

Introduction

'. . . a far-away country . . .'
– Neville Chamberlain, 27 September 1938

For the people of Britain, for her friends and for her enemies too, two-thirds of 1939 was spent in uneasy peace, one-third in a state of declared, but seemingly 'phoney', war. But for many, the years from 1933 had been a kind of 'phoney peace', full of 'wars and rumours of wars'.

1938, especially, had been a year of ever-increasingly serious crises. In February, Foreign Secretary Anthony Eden resigned over disagreements with Prime Minister Neville Chamberlain's policy of appeasing the dictators. On Eden's departure, one-third of Britons, when polled, said they expected there would be a war. Eden's resignation was soon followed by Hitler's 'bloodless' invasion and annexation of his Austrian homeland on 13 March 1938. Then, in May, came the first crisis over Czechoslovakia. Throughout the summer and autumn, Czechoslovakia and Hitler's demands for the German-speaking region of that country, the Sudetenland, dominated newspaper headlines in Britain. The Sudeten Crisis culminated on 29 September 1938 in the signing of the Munich Agreement. At Munich, in the words of a contemporary survey of the year:

The British and French Governments assented, in the hope of preventing war, to the mutilation of a free and democratic land, which Hitler's propaganda had covered with foul abuse. They handed over to Nazi Germany the Sudeten regions of Czechoslovakia, with all that country's chief fortifications, under threat that unless they did so Hitler would let loose a world war. He promised that this would be his last territorial claim in Europe.

Many believed, or professed to believe, him. Chamberlain flew back from Munich promising 'peace for our time', and the country's most popular columnist, Godfrey Winn, gushed in the *Sunday Express*, 'Praise be to God and to Mr Chamberlain. I find no sacrilege, no bathos, in coupling those names.'

In Britain there was an immense feeling of relief that war had been averted, but many entertained feelings of guilt too. Leslie Weatherhead, Britain's leading religious writer and broadcaster, spoke for many when he wrote, 'Do you feel a little uneasy, as though you had made friends with a burglar on condition that if he took nothing from you or your immediate friends, you would say nothing about what he took from somebody else? I feel like that.'

A Cambridge undergraduate put it more succinctly: 'I know we've let them down like hell, but then we're always swine, aren't we?'

In France, which, unlike Britain, had formal treaty obligations to Czechoslovakia, there was a similar feeling of euphoria that peace had been saved. Chamberlain's French opposite number, Edouard Daladier, had half expected to be lynched when he arrived back at Le Bourget airport from Munich. Instead, he was greeted by delirious crowds. But in France too there were those, like former premier Leon Blum, who confessed to a feeling of 'cowardly relief and shame'. Diplomat Alexis Leger, who had accompanied Daladier to Munich, put it more crudely: 'Oh yes, a relief! Like crapping in your pants.'

Six weeks after Munich, Britain and France, the victors of 1918, commemorated the twentieth anniversary of the signing of the

Armistice. Over 740,000 men from the British Isles had died in the Great War, and almost double that number of Frenchmen. Memories of 'The War To End War' were still vivid and all too painful for some. One ex-soldier said to a younger colleague: 'The average fellow who was in the thick of it wants to forget all about it.' But another, exasperated by the threat to peace posed by Hitler, told his workmates, 'We ought to have gone right into Germany and wiped them all out.' In Britain, forty million poppies were sold, and 80 per cent of people polled by the new Mass Observation public-opinion organisation observed the two minutes' silence. But Mass Observation also noted:

> The general attitude towards the Great War has changed. A new generation has grown up. Since 1918 the League of Nations has come into existence and then practically faded out again. The Versailles Treaty has been made and broken. The Great War is less in people's minds than the possibility of the next war.

That possibility was reinforced for many people in the New Year when the Government distributed twenty million National Service booklets. The booklet detailed the various organisations that Britons might volunteer to join in order 'to make us ready for war'. Foremost among them was Air Raid Precautions, for it was 'the shadow of the bomber' that dominated official and public thinking when it came to the prospect of a new war. In the 1914–18 war, Britain had been subjected to German air attacks by both airships and aeroplanes; 1,414 Britons had been killed and 3,416 seriously injured in these raids. These were small enough figures when compared to the enormous casualty figures on the Western Front. But it was the psychological effects of the raids that really mattered. They demonstrated that not only was Britain no longer an island, but that civilians, as well as the fighting forces, were now in the firing line. In 1935, Chamberlain's predecessor Stanley Baldwin had spoken of 'the tacit assumption on the part of all nations that the civil community will no longer be immune from the horrors of warfare as they have been since the barbarous ages until modern times'.

The following year, at the cinema, millions saw a celluloid depiction of the horrors of a new world war in Alexander Korda's *Things to Come*. The scenes of a devastating air raid on London, with high-explosive bombs and gas raining down on the practically defenceless city, shocked British picturegoers. So too did the newsreels of the bombing of Spanish and Chinese cities. Exaggerated accounts of the strength of Hitler's air force by, among others, the famous aviator Charles Lindbergh, did nothing to allay their fears. Nor did statements by politicians. In December 1938, Sir John Simon, Chamberlain's Chancellor of Exchequer told an audience, 'The Germans had it in their power to let loose 3,000 tons of bombs in a single day ... in the first week or two of war the Germans might do an amount of damage in London and other great cities which would amount in money to £500,000,000.'

A month later, on 28 January 1939, Chamberlain himself warned, 'If we should ever be involved in war we may well find that if we are not all in the firing line, we may all be in the line of fire.'

But despite all the official doom and gloom, and the darkening international situation, life for most Britons in 1939 went on much as before. The worst of the Great Depression was over, but of Britain's population of 47,762,000, over 1,270,000 were still registered as unemployed. The average weekly wage for a man in 1939 was £3.9s.0d (£3.45), while that of a woman's was a mere £1.12s.6d (£1.63). The average hours they worked to earn those wages were 46.5 and 43.5 respectively.

In 1939, Greater London, with a population of 8,650,000, was still the world's largest city, with Tokyo it nearest rival. The capital had a Jewish population of 210,000, and 313,900 foreigners, mainly French, Italians, Germans, Swiss and Americans, lived and worked in London. The capital's total working population was 2,749,000. Many lived in London's suburbs, where the price of a semi-detached house ranged from £400 to £600 (a similar house in the provinces fetched £100 less). Flats, such as ones in Hackney with deep balconies, advertised in early 1939, could be rented from as little as 10s (50p) per week, with larger ones at £1.1s.0d (£1.05).

To furnish them, there were bedroom suites from Fred Lawrence's of Westbourne Grove costing as little as £22.1s (£22.05), and half that in the sales. In the wardrobe there might be found, from Swan and Edgar's, a lady's sports jacket at £2.12s.6d (£2.63), trousers at £1.7s.6d (£1.38) and a matching shirt at 10s.9d (54p). The man of the house could buy a suit from Montague Burton, the Fifty Shilling Tailors, for £2.10s (£2.50). A three-piece drawing-room suite could be got for the same amount, while a dining-room set of table, four chairs, and sideboard cost £12.12s.0d (£12.60). For the dining room, an 84-piece canteen of cutlery could be bought for as little as £7.7s.0d (£7.35). Labour-saving devices were still coming into their own by 1939. Although few middle-class homes boasted a fridge, many now had a Hoover or Goblin vacuum cleaner which could be got from Southern Electrical Products of Kingston, Surrey, at £4.0s.0d (£4.00) and £2.9s.6d (£2.48) respectively, or weekly instalments of 3s.6d (18p) on the 'never-never'. In 1939, only 1,200,000 British homes had a telephone, and most people still relied on the Royal Mail for sending messages. A letter cost a penny-halfpenny (1p), while a telegram was sixpence (3p) for the first nine words and then a penny for each additional word.

In the bathroom, one could find a bar of Palmolive soap at three-pence (1p) or a tablet of Wright's Coal Tar soap costing sixpence (3p), the same price as a tube of Pepsodent or Kolynos toothpaste. In the medicine cupboard, to guard against coughs and colds, the household might have a large bottle of Galloway's Cough Syrup, 'equally effective for young and old' at 2s.6d (13p). There might also be DDD Prescription which had 'golden drops with miraculous powers to clear the skin of spots' at only 1s.3d (6p) a bottle. Most men still had wet shaves, but a Remington Electric Close Shaver could be bought for £3.7s.6d (£3.38). To keep his hair in place, the man of the house could buy Brylcreem at 1s.9d (9p) a jar. His wife or daughter's lipsticks cost from sixpence (3p) to 2s.6d (13p). A lot of British homes still did not have an inside, or separate, lavatory. But in those that did, one would probably find 'Bronco: the perforated toilet paper for economy, health, comfort and neatness', a 700-sheet roll for 1s (5p).

Downstairs in the lounge, or drawing room, the family's radio, or wireless set, took pride of place; 9,009,700 wireless licences at ten shillings (50p) were sold in 1939. A Bush all-wave radio set with ten push buttons, recommended by Britain's first disc jockey, Christopher Stone, cost £12.12s.0d (£12.60) cash, 'or on popular payments'. Also in the room might be the family's HMV portable wind-up gramophone, which retailed at £6. Records of some of the early hits of 1939, like 'And the Angels Sing' and 'If I Didn't Care', cost two shillings (10p). The room's cocktail cabinet would undoubtedly be stocked with whisky at 12s.6d (63p) a bottle, and a bottle of gin at just slightly less. A litre (1.76 pints) of Martini Dry cost 5s.6d (28p), the sweeter version a shilling (5p) less. A bottle of Gilbey's ready-made 'Odds On' wine cocktail retailed at 2s.6d (13p).

For those Britons who preferred to drink away from home, there was always the public house or pub. Bolton in Lancashire had no less than 304 pubs in 1939. In any of them one could buy a pint of mild for 5d (2p), India Pale Ale for 7d (3p) a pint and strong ale for 11d (5p). Whisky, rum and gin cost 6d (3p) a measure, while a Single Malt might cost as much as 10d (4p). A glass of port, sherry or Empire Wine was sold at threepence (1p) a time. In 1939, Britons sank 895 million gallons of beer and 10,098,000 proof gallons of spirits. The same year, they drank 887 million gallons of milk. Less healthily, they also smoked a lot too. A packet of twenty Player's Navy Medium Cut cost just under a shilling (5p) in 1939, while other brands like Woodbine, Piccadilly and De Reszke

Minors cost even less. To light them, a Ronson lighter could be got for £1.1s.0d (£1.05). Pipe tobacco cost a shilling (5p) an ounce, and five Manikin cigars were 11d (5p) a packet.

For those Britons with a sweet tooth, an extra large tin of Quality Street cost 4s.6d (23p), while a packet of Maltesers sold at twopence (1p), and Black Magic chocolates at 2s.10d (14p) a pound box. And if one over-indulged oneself there was always Beechams Pills and Powders at 1s.3d (6p) a packet, and Kelloggs All Bran, 'a food that brings normal "regularity" to constipation victims', retailing at 7½d (3p).

1939 saw the passing of the Holidays with Pay Act. Three million more Britons now received, for the first time, a fortnight's holiday with pay. Most people still went to British seaside resorts for their annual holidays. The majority went there by train or charabanc, but quite a number of Britain's 1,900,000 private-car owners packed up the family Morris Eight (£128) or the swisher Sunbeam Talbot (£285) and made for the coast. For those who wanted a more energetic holiday than sitting in a deckchair on the beach at Margate or Skegness, there were the Norfolk Broads, where the hire of an eight-berth cruiser for two weeks cost £18.

For those even more adventurous and with 15s (75p) for a passport, there were plenty of holidays advertised in Britain's ally, France. A room at the Hotel Opal near the Madeleine in Paris cost as little as 6s (30p) a night, while one with a bath at the smart resort of Deauville cost £1, and for an extra 12s (60p) one could get full board. To get away, if only physically, from Europe's troubles in 1939, a luxury cruise of fifty-six days to South America, the West Indies and Florida was being advertised at just 5s (25p) short of £100. For those Britons curious to see Nazi Germany at first hand, the London branch of the German Travel Bureau advertised an all-inclusive nine-day tour of the Reich for £6.16s.0d (£6.80). Ominously, as tension mounted that summer, the tour was advertised as being 'specially escorted'.

CHAPTER 1

Countdown to War

January–August 1939

January

1 January, LONDON
Gordon Cosmo Lang, Archbishop of Canterbury, broadcasts a New Year's Day message from Lambeth Palace. The archbishop tells listeners: 'In the dawn of a new year it is still a confused and troubled world that we see. Terrible wars are being waged in Spain and China. In Europe restless national ambitions are increasing the widespread sense of insecurity. No wonder it seems as if the whole world were going mad.'

1 January, WORTHING
'Everyone's wondering what can happen next!' (Miss Joan Colebrook Strange, aged thirty-four, a trained physiotherapist living with her widowed mother in Langton Road, Worthing. Joan Strange was a committed Christian who undertook a great deal of voluntary work amongst German and Austrian Jewish refugees.)

2 January, WORTHING
'The Archbishop of Canterbury broadcast last night a New Year's Sermon telling all "to hope for the best and prepare for the worst" – not very encouraging!' (Joan Strange)

5 January, OBERSALZBERG
On his way back from Monte Carlo, Polish foreign minister Colonel Jozef Beck pays a courtesy call on Hitler at the 'Berghof'. Hitler surprises the Pole by calling for Danzig's return to Germany. Under the terms of the 1919 Treaty of Versailles, Danzig has had the status of a 'Free City' with a League of Nations commissioner. The population is overwhelmingly German and the Nazis have control of the ruling Danzig Senate. Hitler tells Beck that Germany will guarantee Poland's frontiers if a 'final settlement' can be reached on Danzig, and other outstanding issues between the two countries. 'Danzig,' the Fuehrer reminds the Pole, 'was German, would always remain German, and sooner or later would return to Germany.' Beck, who has a reputation for deviousness, is evasive. He tells Hitler that Polish public opinion would be against any change in Danzig's status.

7 January, LONDON
Picture Post, Britain's largest-circulation illustrated weekly, features comedian Leslie Henson's humorous 'Outlook for 1939'. Henson warns readers: 'But to carry a rifle may at any time become compulsory, particularly in civilized countries.'

11 January, ROME
British Prime Minister Neville Chamberlain and his foreign secretary Lord Halifax visit Rome in an attempt to further the cause of peace. Chamberlain believes that Italian dictator Benito Mussolini is a moderating influence on Hitler. But nothing is accomplished by the visit. Mussolini tells his son-in-law and foreign minister Count

Galeazzo Ciano: 'These men are not made of the same stuff as Francis Drake and the other magnificent adventurers who created the empire. These, after all, are the tired sons of a long line of rich men and they will lose their empire.'

Ciano telephones his German opposite number Joachim von Ribbentrop and tells him that the visit has been a 'huge farce'.

11 January, WORTHING
'Mr Chamberlain and Lord Halifax have arrived in Rome this afternoon. Accorded a great welcome. Should we welcome Mussolini in a like manner, I wonder?' (Joan Strange)

15 January, BRITAIN
The Irish Republican Army starts a bombing campaign on mainland Britain. Targets in London, Manchester and Birmingham are attacked. The IRA demands the withdrawal of all British forces and officialdom from Ireland. The Nazi-orchestrated press in Germany reports the news with more than a touch of *Schadenfreude:*

> Five bombs went off, dreadful, my dear!
> Old England nearly choked with fear.

> When the overfed Englishman at his breakfast table heard this news
> he dropped his beefsteak from his fork in horror.

23 January, BERLIN
Anti-Nazi Admiral Wilhelm Canaris, head of German military intelligence, leaks misinformation that the Nazis are about to invade the Netherlands. They will seize Dutch airfields in order to use them to deliver a knockout blow on Britain. The leak is taken seriously in Whitehall. It is decided that 'an attack by Germany on Holland would be a first step to attack on us and must be regarded as a direct challenge'.

Hitler receives Polish foreign minister Colonel Jozef Beck at the Berghof, Obersalzberg, 5 January 1939. Beck told an English visitor, 'Hitler has power and charm and flair, but he is not a Colonel Beck.'

The British ministerial visit to Rome, January 1939. From left to right: Count Galeazzo Ciano; Lord Halifax; Neville Chamberlain and Benito Mussolini. As Chamberlain departed, British residents in Rome sang 'For He's a Jolly Good Fellow'. 'What is this little song?' Mussolini asked.

24 January, WORTHING
'In Spain, the Government's defence of Barcelona is giving in rapidly. Barcelona is bound to fall very soon. Hitler and Mussolini are reported to be preparing their manifesto on their colonial demands for January 30th. Can war possibly be avoided?' (Joan Strange)

26 January, BARCELONA
General Francisco Franco's Nationalist forces enter Barcelona. They encounter only sporadic resistance from the city's Republican defenders. Spain's civil war, which began in July 1936, and has cost over half a million lives, is now approaching its end.

26 January, WARSAW
Reich foreign minister Joachim von Ribbentrop pays an official visit to the Polish capital. He again brings up Hitler's proposals regarding Danzig and the Polish Corridor, the territory that separates East Prussia from Germany proper. Beck once again rebuffs the German offer. The vain and pompous von Ribbentrop returns empty-handed to Berlin. He has misled Hitler over the Poles' willingness to negotiate the future of Danzig and the Corridor.

26 January, PARIS
French foreign minister Georges Bonnet, regarded in Paris and London as an out-and-out appeaser, makes a speech reaffirming France's commitments in eastern Europe. Few believe that the Foreign Minister is being sincere. Bonnet is suspected of having told von Ribbentrop of France's disinterest in the region, when the Nazi visited Paris six weeks ago.

26 January, TEDDINGTON
'Barcelona fell to Franco at noon. Heigho!! I wish it could have offered the resistance Madrid has done.' (Mrs Helena Pare Lydia

Mott, aged sixty-six; a woman of independent means living in Teddington, Middlesex)

28 January, BIRMINGHAM

In a speech at Birmingham, Chamberlain defends the Munich Agreement: 'For myself looking back, I see nothing to regret nor any reason to suppose that another course would have been preferable.'

30 January, BERLIN

Adolf Hitler addresses the Reichstag on the sixth anniversary of his coming to power. He warns the deputies: 'If international Jewish finance inside and outside Europe should succeed in plunging the nations into a new world war, the result will not be the Bolshevization of the earth and thereby the victory of Jewry, but the annihilation of the Jewish race.' The Fuehrer's words are greeted with stormy applause.

30 January, TEDDINGTON

'Hitler's speech at seven. We had dinner early and he was in full blast when we had finished. Seemed to have a good reception – but his speech was much faster and much more clip style and varied very much in tone – high and biting . . . coughed at intervals. He went on bawling until 9.25pm then Goering. All sang "Deutschland, D- ueber alles in der Welt", "Horst Wessel". Heil! Heil! Heil! Damn!' (Helen Mott)

30 January, WORTHING

'While all Germany was listening to Hitler's broadcast on the sixth anniversary of the Third Reich, Worthing held a most interesting meeting in connection with the Jews. A Mr Davidson from Woburn House, London, gave a talk on the work of the refugee problem and a committee was formed to coordinate efforts being made here in Worthing. I got on!' (Joan Strange)

February

3 February, LONDON
The BBC broadcasts a radio programme entitled *Children in Flight*.
It consists of interviews made at the Dovercourt camp for German
Jewish refugee children. They have come to Britain under the
Kindertransport scheme, following the excesses of *Kristallnacht* last
November. The Nazi Party newspaper, the *Voelkischer Beobachter*,
attacks the broadcast. It accuses the BBC of 'making political capital
out of pity and at the same time agitating indirectly against
Germany'. The paper says the interviews with the children were
'cleverly selected to appeal to sentimentality'.

3 February, WORTHING
'In all the evening for once! Listened to excellent broadcast
"Children in Flight", a series of sound recordings of the German
child refugees taken about Xmas time. The little Laufen boy, Peter,
five and a half, was one of the little children at Dovercourt. His
father told me that Peter asked him if it were true that when he
came to England he would be allowed to go into a garden again.
In Austria and Germany Jews are not allowed in public gardens.
Their sufferings have been indescribable.' (Joan Strange)

6 February, LONDON
In a House of Commons speech, Chamberlain reaffirms that: 'Any
threat to the vital interests of France, from whatever quarter it
comes, must evoke the immediate co-operation of this country.'

9 February, LONDON
The Home Office, responsible for air-raid precautions, announces
plans to provide shelters to thousands of homes in areas thought
vulnerable to air attack. Families with an income of less than £250
a year will receive their shelters free. Other households may buy

them for £6.14s.0d (£6.70). The shelters are already being called 'Andersons' after Lord Privy Seal Sir John Anderson, the dour and rather pompous but ultra-efficient minister with responsibility for civilian defence. They are steel-built, tunnel-shaped shelters measuring 6 ft 6 in by 4 ft 4 in. They are made in sections and need only two people to put them up. It is reckoned that a million and a half 'Andersons' will be given out by the end of August. Last September at the height of the Sudeten Crisis, over thirty-eight million gas masks, costing 2s.6d (13p) each, were distributed to the civilian population.

10 February, VATICAN
Pope Pius XI dies. Although a Concordat was signed with Hitler back in July 1933, Pius XI has often spoken out against the Nazi regime and its persecution of the Roman Catholic Church. In May last year he deliberately and ostentatiously left Rome for Castel Gandolfo during Hitler's state visit.

10 February, WORTHING
'A remarkable character, and devoted to the cause of peace.' (Joan Strange on the Pope's death)

14 February, WILHELMSHAVEN
Germany's latest battleship, the 35,000-ton *Bismarck*, is launched. In his political testament *Mein Kampf*, Hitler wrote that it was a mistake on the part of the Kaiser's Germany to antagonise Britain by building a fleet to rival the Royal Navy. But it now looks as if he too is intending to challenge Britain's naval superiority.

15 February, TEDDINGTON
'£580,000,000 to be spent on defence for the year. What an abominable wicked thing due to one paltry Austrian paranoiac.' (Helena Mott)

25 February, LONDON
The first Anderson shelters are delivered in Tiber and Carlsbad Streets, Islington. Mrs Treadwell of Tiber Street tells the *Daily Telegraph*: 'I hope we shall never have to use it. Still if trouble does come, I'll feel safer there than in the house. In any case, we can always use it as a summer house!'

26 February, WORTHING
'And today we hear the British Government proposes to recognise Franco – blow!' (Joan Strange)

28 February, LONDON and PARIS
The British and French governments formally recognise General Franco's regime as the legitimate government of Spain. In the House of Commons, there is an Opposition vote of censure about the recognition. Amid angry scenes, in which there are shouts of '*Heil* Chamberlain', it is defeated by 344 votes to 137. In Paris, head of government Edouard Daladier persuades eighty-two-year-old Marshal Philippe Petain, the Hero of Verdun, to become France's first ambassador to Franco.

March

2 March, VATICAN
Cardinal Eugenio Pacelli, the Vatican Secretary of State, is elected pope and takes the title Pius XII. He was Papal Nuncio in Bavaria at the time of the Soviet republic there twenty years ago, and the experience has left him with a fear and loathing of communism. Many Vatican experts believe that this might make him turn a blind eye to the worst excesses of the Nazi regime.

10 March, LONDON
At Chelsea Town Hall, Home Secretary and staunch Chamberlain

'Well, I suppose we should feel safer, but I think I should stay in bed – until the guns began. I might go outside then.' Anderson shelters being loaded onto carts, ready for distribution at Wilbraham Road, Manchester, February 1939.

'It was always my fate to see him when he was under stress of some emotion or other.' British Ambassador Sir Nevile Henderson (left) and Hitler at a reception, 1 March 1939. Hitler's interpreter, Dr Paul Schmidt, translates for the two men.

supporter Sir Samuel Hoare delivers a speech to his constituents. He has asked the Prime Minister what tone he should adopt. 'Cheerful,' Chamberlain replied, 'there is every reason for it.' Now Hoare tells his audience that a Golden Age could be in the offing: 'Five men in Europe (Chamberlain, Daladier, Hitler, Mussolini, and Stalin), if they worked with a singleness of purpose and a unity of action, might in an incredibly short space of time transform the whole history of the world . . .'

10 March, MOSCOW

Soviet dictator Josef Stalin delivers a major speech on Soviet foreign policy. He tells the members of the Communist Party Congress that it is still Soviet policy to resist aggression and warns Britain and France against 'retreating and retreating', and making one concession after another to the dictators. This policy, Stalin tells the delegates, will in the end lead to war. But he then warns that the Soviet Union will not allow itself 'to be drawn into conflicts by warmongers who are accustomed to have others pull the chestnuts out of the fire for them'.

10 March, PRAGUE

In an attempt to preserve the unity of Czecho-Slovakia, the Prague government dismisses Monsignor Jozef Tiso, the premier of the autonomous Slovakian government. Ever since Munich, forces inside and outside the country have been intent on destabilising the administration of Emil Hacha, who became president after Eduard Benes resigned last October.

13 March, BERLIN

Hitler receives Tiso. He tells him, 'I am disappointed in Slovakia. The way your people have been behaving lately, they might almost be Czechs.' The Fuehrer then goes on to advise the Slovakian premier to declare his country's independence from Prague. Germany, Hitler assures Tiso, will guarantee that independence.

13 March, LONDON
At Holborn Town Hall there is a testing of gas helmets designed to protect babies and infants. The test proves successful and the Government announces that 1,400,000 gas helmets will be distributed within a few months.

14 March, BRATISLAVA
The Slovak Diet votes to break away from Prague and declares Slovakian independence.

14 March, BERLIN
At 11pm, sixty-six-year-old President Emil Hacha of Czecho-Slovakia, accompanied by his daughter and his foreign minister Frantisek Chvalkovsky, arrive in the German capital. The two Czech politicians have come to discuss the worsening situation in their country. The Czechs are taken to Germany's foremost hotel, the Adlon, where there is a large box of chocolates from the Fuehrer waiting for Hacha's daughter. At midnight, Hacha and Chvalkovsky set out for the Reich Chancellery where Hitler has just been watching a film called *A Hopeless Case*.

15 March, BERLIN
Just after midnight Hitler, accompanied by von Ribbentrop and Luftwaffe chief Hermann Goering, receive Hacha and Chvalkovsky. Hitler bluntly tells the two Czechs that 'in order to restore order' he has ordered the German Army to occupy the Czech provinces of Bohemia and Moravia. He tells them that any resistance will be useless and Goering threatens to bomb Prague ruthlessly if any is shown. Hacha, under great physical and mental stress, gives way. He telephones Prague and orders that no resistance is to be offered to the German invaders. He then signs a document stating that he has 'confidently placed the fate of the Czech people in the hands of the Fuehrer of the German Reich'. In the same document Hitler

accepts Hacha's declaration and 'expressed his intention of taking the Czech people under the protection of the German Reich and of guaranteeing them an autonomous development of their ethnic life as suited to their character'.

Ecstatic at his success, Hitler tells two of his female secretaries, pointing to his cheeks, 'So, children, each of you give me a kiss there and there . . . This is the happiest day of my life . . . I will go down as the greatest German in history.'

15 March, LONDON

In the House of Lords, Foreign Secretary Lord Halifax announces that Hitler's action in occupying Prague 'is inconsistent with the spirit of the Munich Agreement', while in the Commons, Chamberlain tells MPs: 'I bitterly regret what has now occurred. But do not let us on that account be deflected from our course . . . We will continue to pursue our policy of appeasement.'

In and outside Parliament, the Prime Minister's statement attracts a lot of unfavourable comment. He is accused of bringing 'humiliation and shame' on Britain. His personal shuttle diplomacy last September is now condemned as being 'a fatal mistake'. Even the faithful Chamberlain supporter and industrialist Lord Nuffield says, 'If it weren't for Neville Chamberlain's feelings, I would advocate the starting of war against Germany tomorrow.'

15 March, PRAGUE

Hitler arrives at Hradcany Castle to view his latest conquest. At a buffet in the castle's banqueting hall, the normally teetotal Hitler picks up a small glass of Pilsner lager and drains it dry. He grimaces and then laughs. Returning to Berlin he tells his entourage, 'marching into Prague pleased me more than all that shilly-shallying at Munich'.

15 March, WORTHING
'Another wretched crisis in Czecho-slovakia – Hitler appealed to, and off to Prague immediately. The whole state built up by Masaryk completely disrupted and Hitler snaps up all the valuable pieces. The whole world aghast at Hitler's arrogance. His flag hoisted on the wonderful old palace of Hungarian royalty. The Czechs humiliated to the dust – suicides, imprisonments, the Gestapo and all manner of dreadful things.' (Joan Strange)

15 March, TEDDINGTON
'Hitler's troops marched into Prague. The people hissed and booed and sang the Czech national anthem ... German troops entered Slovakia – in response to an appeal from the Slovak government. I wonder!!! So many lies are told and such atrocious deeds done that no reliance can be placed on any statement that comes out of Berlin. No words are fit for Hitler who, maniac though he is, is allowed to do anything without let or hindrance – much to our shame.' (Helena Mott)

16 March, TEDDINGTON
'Hitler (may he be damned) proclaims Czech state part of German empire. Bohemia and Moravia to be known as the Protectorate. He's taken Slovakia also ... 5,000 Czechs have been arrested by the Gestapo. Himmler is in Prague with Hitler (two fine specimens of cruel evil, ruthless brigands).' (Helena Mott)

17 March, LONDON
Virgil Tilea, Roumanian Minister in London, hears a rumour that his country is about to be attacked by Germany. He asks Lord Halifax if Roumania can expect British support if the Nazis invade. The next day, the Foreign Office hears officially from Bucharest that there is not a word of truth in the rumour.

17 March, BIRMINGHAM

Chamberlain is genuinely surprised at the vehemence of parliamentary and public opinion against Hitler's Prague coup. Now, on his home ground of Birmingham, the Prime Minister acknowledges, 'Public opinion in the world has received a sharper shock than has yet been administered to it, even by the present regime in Germany . . .' and asks, 'Is this the end of an old adventure or is it the beginning of a new? Is this the last attack upon a small state, or is it to be followed by others. Is this, in fact, a step in the direction of an attempt to dominate the world by force?' In *either* case, Chamberlain concludes, 'Others, too, knowing that we are not disinterested in what goes on in South-East Europe, will wish to have our counsel and advice.'

As a gesture of British disapproval, Ambassador Sir Nevile Henderson, who has only just returned to Berlin after an operation for throat cancer, is now recalled to London, 'to report'.

17 March, WORTHING

'The whole European situation looks almost as black as it did last September.' (Joan Strange)

18 March, BERLIN

French Ambassador Robert Coulondre delivers France's protest at the occupation of Prague. Like Sir Nevile, he too is recalled 'for consultations'.

18 March, PARIS

The Chamber of Deputies, followed by the Senate, votes full powers to Daladier, President of the Council of Ministers, to deal with the ongoing international crisis.

19 March, MOSCOW

The Soviet Government refuses to recognise the legality of Hitler's

Prague coup. It describes the latest German aggression as having 'dealt a fresh blow to the feeling of security of the peoples of Europe'.

21 March, WASHINGTON DC
The State Department strongly condemns the German occupation of the Czech lands and the 'temporary extinguishment of free and independent people'.

21 March, LONDON
French President Albert Lebrun arrives on a state visit to London to demonstrate the solidarity between France and Britain and the firmness of the *Entente Cordiale*. The visit is a great success, but disaster is only narrowly averted. At a reception at the Foreign Office, a sofa topples over and three British ministers are very nearly catapulted onto the King and Queen and their French guests. 'How Hitler would have laughed,' thinks Tory MP and devoted Chamberlainite Henry 'Chips' Channon.

21 March, BERLIN
Polish ambassador Jozef Lipski has an interview with von Ribbentrop. Beck has instructed Lipski to protest at Germany's recent move against Czecho-Slovakia. Poland is now threatened on three sides. Von Ribbentrop counters by saying that Hitler's patience with Poland is wearing thin. A solution to the problem of Danzig and the Polish Corridor must be found soon. This, von Ribbentrop tells Lipski, is a prerequisite for the peaceful future of German–Polish relations. Furthermore, Colonel Beck should himself come to Berlin to discuss the situation.

21 March, KAUNAS
The Lithuanian Government, under threat of German military action, are forced to agree to Hitler's demand to hand over the

port of Memel and its hinterland. Lithuania seized the German-inhabited territory back in 1923.

21 March, WORTHING
'Memel is about to return to Germany – the Jews there panic-stricken.' (Joan Strange)

21 March, TEDDINGTON
'Halifax states new policy. The Government has decided to take initiative in forming a powerful league against aggression . . . Russia, I do not think, will be cozened too easily. "Isvestia" [*sic*] says what is the value of lamentations like the British Premier's at Birmingham? French and British statesmen are not children. The authors of the dangerous non-aggression game are now reaping the new fruits of their policy.' (Helena Mott)

21 March, TEDDINGTON
'Franco sent a telegram of congratulation to Hitler on his raping of Czecho-slovakia and Hitler thanks him in a return message. Thieves' honour!!!' (Helena Mott)

22 March, BERLIN
From today, each evening at 8.15pm, German radio's *Reichssender* is to broadcast the news in English. This will, the Nazi press assures readers, 'give to the listener in foreign lands something quite new – the truth'.

22 March, TEDDINGTON
'Memel has been surrendered by Lithuania to Germany . . . Ribbentrop demanded absolute and immediate submission. And still we sit back and do not do anything, even protest.' (Helena Mott)

Dr Emile Hacha (left) *arrives in Berlin to receive, at Hitler's hands, 'the old tested methods of political tactics', 14 March 1939.*

'If you apply a bit of pressure, things happen.' Lithuanian and German foreign ministers, Juozas Urbsys and Joachim von Ribbentrop (seated left to right), *sign the formal agreement transferring Memel and district to the Reich, 22 March 1939.*

22 March, WORTHING
'Memel now under German Nazi rule. The ultimatum was delivered to Lithuania last night and accepted tonight – another "bloodless victory"(?)' (Joan Strange)

24 March, BERLIN
It is announced that any German who listens to foreign radio broadcasts and spreads the news contained in them is now liable to five years' imprisonment.

23 March, MEMEL
Hitler arrives in the port on the pocket battleship *Deutschland*. Since leaving Swinemuende yesterday, the Fuehrer has suffered from severe seasickness. He only spends three hours in the newly 'liberated' territory, before returning to Berlin. Hitler nonchalantly tells his SS manservant Heinz Linge, 'we now perform these trifles as a matter of course'.

27 March, LONDON
Chamberlain tells his cabinet that he is prepared to offer Poland a unilateral guarantee of her independence. The Prime Minister believes that Poland is going to be Hitler's next objective and he hopes that a guarantee will both deter the Fuehrer and stiffen the Poles in their resistance to Nazi demands.

28 March, MADRID
The Spanish capital finally falls to General Franco's forces. Throughout the Civil War, Franco has had the support of Italian 'volunteers' and Germany's Condor Legion of airmen and armoured troops.

28 March, WARSAW
Polish foreign minister Beck warns the German ambassador that

any attempt by Germany to use force to gain Danzig will lead to war.

28 March, TEDDINGTON

'Madrid surrendered at 2pm after two years and four months marvellous hold out. I only hope the treatment they receive may be free from cruelty. Poor things, they've suffered enough.' (Helena Mott)

29 March, LONDON

The Government announces plans to double Britain's Territorial Army to bring its strength up to 340,000 men. The move is seen as part recognition that, in the event of war, Britain will have to furnish extensive land forces as well as the Royal Navy and Royal Air Force. But one eager would-be recruit, on presenting himself at a recruiting office, is first asked, 'Could you come back tomorrow morning?' On doing so, he is told, 'Well, you see, we can't do anything until after Easter, but you'll certainly get a letter from us then.'

30 March, WARSAW

At the Foreign Ministry, British ambassador Sir Howard Kennard delivers the terms of Britain's guarantee to Poland. Colonel Beck accepts them 'between two flicks of his cigarette ash'.

31 March, LONDON

In the House of Commons, Chamberlain announces the news of the British guarantee to Poland. He tells MPs, 'In the event of any action which clearly threatened Polish independence, and which the Polish Government accordingly considered it vital to resist with their national forces, His Majesty's Government would feel them-selves bound at once to lend the Polish Government all support in their power.'

Labour's deputy leader Arthur Greenwood says, 'The Prime

Minister's statement may prove as momentous as any made in this House for a quarter of a century.' And anti-appeaser Alfred Duff Cooper, who resigned over Munich, is incredulous at Chamberlain's reversal of policy: 'Never before in our history have we left in the hands of one of the smaller powers the decision whether or not Great Britain goes to war.'

31 March, BERLIN
Hitler, on hearing of the British guarantee, falls into a terrible rage. 'I'll a brew them a devil's stew that they'll choke on,' he raves to his staff.

31 March, BUCHAREST
Roumanian foreign minister Grigore Gafencu, on hearing of the guarantee, says, 'The British must be mad. Poland is the least moral country in Europe.'

31 March, WORTHING
'Mr Chamberlain made an important announcement to the Commons which was specially broadcast at four o'clock, committing us definitely to Poland.' (Joan Strange)

31 March, TEDDINGTON
'Chamberlain three o'clock in the House – England will go to war for Poland – well! Well! Well! "Bound to give Polish government all the help in our power." Question . . . whether Russia and other powers will not join in a conference against aggression?' (Helena Mott)

April

1 April, WILHELMSHAVEN
Hitler attends the launching of the battleship *Tirpitz*. After the ceremony, the Fuehrer delivers a speech in which he makes thinly veiled

attacks on Poland and Britain's 'encirclement policy'. He tells the crowd, 'He who does not possess power loses the right to life.' And in a strange echo of Stalin's 10 March speech, Hitler says, 'Anyone who declares himself ready to snatch the chestnuts out of the fire for the Western Powers must expect to burn his fingers.'

1 April, MADRID
The Spanish Civil War is officially announced to be at an end.

3 April, BERLIN
Hitler is presented with the Wehrmacht's operational plans for 'Case White', the invasion of Poland and the destruction of its military forces. Hitler dictates a preamble to the directive which orders the armed forces to be ready to carry out 'Case White' at any time after 1 September 1939.

4 April, LONDON
Colonel Beck arrives in London for talks. An American reporter thinks Poland's foreign minister looks like a 'ham actor made up as the lean and hungry Cassius'. At the end of his discussions with British ministers, Chamberlain announces that Britain and Poland have agreed to sign a mutual assistance pact in the event of an attack 'by a European power'. France also issues a similar pledge.

5 April, LONDON
The Government's plans for civilian defence are debated in the House of Commons. Minister of Health Walter Elliot tells MPs that plans are being prepared for the immediate evacuation of 2,500,000 children in the event of war. It will be, Elliot tells them, 'a colossal task'. The Minister then goes on to say that 279,435 Anderson shelters, providing cover for 1,500,000 people, have already been distributed, and 80,000 are being delivered each week.

It is also revealed that twelve regional commissioners, 'men of national standing, capable of undertaking great responsibilities', are to be appointed. They will have sweeping powers in the event of their region being cut off from London by enemy action.

7 April, ROME
Mussolini, piqued at Hitler's foreign policy successes and bloodless conquests, occupies his own client state of Albania. King Zog, Queen Geraldine and their day-old son Prince Leka flee the country, and Italian King Victor Emmanuel is proclaimed King of Albania. Count Ciano notes in his diary that 'international reaction (is) almost non-existent' and that the British 'protest' note 'might have been written by our own offices'.

7 April, WORTHING
'On an extra news bulletin at one o'clock heard that Italy has "smashed and grabbed" Albania. Just like Hitler and his methods. What will result? The nine o'clock news reports fighting there.' (Joan Strange)

8 April, VATICAN
Much to the annoyance of Mussolini, the new Pope Pius XII denounces violations of international treaties.

8 April, LONDON
Picture Post publishes an article which argues that an Anglo-French alliance with Russia is now vital. It concludes, 'Let Mr Chamberlain fly there.'

8 April, TEDDINGTON
'20,000 Italians land simultaneously at four Albanian towns. Zog's queen had to travel to Greece two days after her baby was born. King Zog is expected to have gone too . . .' (Helena Mott)

13 April, BUCHAREST and ATHENS
Roumania and Greece accept British and French guarantees similar
to that already given to Poland.

15 April, WASHINGTON DC
President Franklin D. Roosevelt dispatches personal messages to both
Hitler and Mussolini. He proposes an exchange of pledges of non-
aggression pacts for ten or possibly twenty-five years between the
dictators and thirty-one states. The pledges would then be followed
by an international conference to discuss disarmament, raw materials
and international trade. Mussolini is contemptuous of FDR's proposal.
'A result of progressive paralysis,' he tells Count Ciano.

16 April, WORTHING
'Germany and Italy seem somewhat stunned by Roosevelt's proposal.
There is a very bitter anti-British press campaign going on in the
German press just now and now Roosevelt will be vilified too.'
(Joan Strange)

20 April, BERLIN
Hitler's fiftieth birthday is celebrated with a massive military parade.
The British, French and American ambassadors are all conspicuous
by their absence, but among the guests is Emil Hacha, now puppet
President of the Reich Protectorate of Bohemia and Moravia. The
parade goes on for nearly five hours, and propaganda minister Dr
Josef Goebbels enthuses, 'The Fuehrer is fêted like no other mortal
has ever been.' Among the telegrams of congratulations is a
restrained one from King George VI.

20 April, TEDDINGTON
'Hitler's birthday. He had an immense show of tanks, arms and
aeroplanes for five solid hours. I hope he enjoyed himself.' (Helena
Mott)

23 April, LONDON

Roumanian foreign minister Grigore Gafencu, on a tour of European capitals, arrives in Britain. At an audience at Buckingham Palace with the King and Queen, Queen Elizabeth asks Gafencu what Hitler is like. The foreign minister replies that he got the impression that the Fuehrer could be 'very simple in manner if he wished, but that made him all the more to be feared'. The Queen replies, 'If he is simple, it might be that he is really great, unless it should be greatness of another sort.' When Gafencu meets with Chamberlain, the Prime Minister is more forthright in his opinion of Hitler. 'He is a liar,' he tells the Roumanian statesman.

26 April, LONDON

Chamberlain announces to the Commons the introduction of compulsory military training. This is the first time that conscription has been introduced in peacetime in Britain, and the Prime Minister acknowledges that 'it is a departure from our cherished ideals'. But Chamberlain tells MPs, 'A very little weight one way or another might decide whether war is to come or not.' The Military Training Bill for all men between the ages of twenty and twenty-one will be introduced on 1 May.

28 April, BERLIN

Hitler addresses the Reichstag. He denounces both the 1934 Non-Aggression Pact with Poland and the 1935 Anglo-German Naval Agreement, 'since the British Prime Minister was not able to trust German assurances'. Hitler also sarcastically replies to President Roosevelt's proposals of a fortnight ago. None of the states named by the President, Hitler says, feels threatened by Germany. But he boastfully reminds Roosevelt: 'I have brought back to the Reich provinces stolen from us in 1919. I have led back to their native country millions of Germans who were torn away from us and

25

were in misery . . . and Mr Roosevelt, without spilling blood and without bringing to my people, and consequently to others, the misery of war . . .'

28 April, WORTHING

'Hitler made his two-and-a-quarter-hour speech in the Reichstag in answer to Pres. Roosevelt's Peace Statement. He demands Germany's former colonies, denounces the Anglo-German Naval Treaty, makes demands on Poland. But on the whole the situation is no worse.' (Joan Strange)

29 April, LONDON

Picture Post features a series of photographs of Prague under German rule. And in an article on economic appeasement, it argues strongly that 'it is wicked to dream of trade agreements with Germany'.

May

3 May, MOSCOW

Maxim Litvinov is replaced as Soviet foreign minister by Stalin's right-hand man Vyacheslav Molotov. Litvinov, a Jew, has always been regarded as pro-Western and has followed a policy aimed at 'collective security' with his slogan, 'Peace is Indivisible.' His abrupt dismissal is seen by many as indication that Soviet foreign policy may now take a new direction. Oliver Harvey, Lord Halifax's private secretary, wonders, 'Does it mean Russia will turn from the West towards isolation? And if so, won't she inevitably wobble into Germany's arms?'

4 May, TEDDINGTON

'Litvinov, foreign minister of USSR after ten years, is superseded by Mr Molotov. This may make all the difference to the negotiations with Russia.' (Helena Mott)

Soviet Dictator Josef Stalin, flanked by Vyacheslav Molotov (left) and Maxim Litvinov, walking in the Kremlin. Molotov replaced Litvinov as Soviet foreign minister, 3 May 1939. 'The last great friend of collective security is gone.'

5 May, WARSAW

Colonel Beck makes a firm but essentially non-provocative speech in Parliament. He rejects the Nazis' suggestion that the Anglo-Polish agreement presents any threat to Germany. Beck sees no reason why it should have led to Hitler cancelling the 1934 non-aggression pact.

5 May, LONDON

Picture Post publishes its first article in a series entitled 'Britain Prepares'. It features the Territorial Army and shows how 'Britain rebuilds her defences'. The same issue has examples of Nazi propaganda against Britain in the German press since Munich. Even 'The Lambeth Walk' has been attacked: 'A degenerate dance? – no, a degenerate people!'

5 May, LONDON

Chamberlain, 'looking like a turkey who has missed his Christmas', makes a statement on Anglo-Soviet relations. Former foreign secretary Anthony Eden, who resigned in February 1938 over Chamberlain's policy towards the dictators, is disturbed about the progress of Britain's negotiations with Russia. He believes that they lack boldness and imagination. Britain should be trying for a definite triple alliance with France and the Soviets. Eden met Stalin and other Soviet leaders on a trip to Russia back in 1935. He offers to go to Moscow as negotiator. His offer is not taken up.

7 May, VERDUN

From the First World War battlefield of Verdun, the Duke of Windsor, formerly King Edward VIII, broadcasts an appeal for peace. The BBC refuses to relay the Duke's speech, but it is heard by millions of Americans over the NBC network. The Duke tells his listeners, 'I speak simply as a soldier of the last war, whose most earnest prayer is that such a cruel and destructive madness shall never again overtake mankind.'

8 May, TEDDINGTON

'The Duke of Windsor, speaking at Verdun to America, gave an exceedingly wise, sensible and necessary speech against war and in favour of exercising the same spirit of give and take in international affairs as one carries on in a regulated daily intercourse with individuals. He spoke well, with assurance and feeling. We should be proud he could undertake to do this for humanity's sake.' (Helena Mott)

19 May, LONDON

The House of Commons debates Anglo-Soviet relations and the desirability of an alliance with the Russians. First World War Prime Minister David Lloyd George argues forcibly for such an alliance. If one is concluded, he tells MPs, then 'the chances against war would go up'. Churchill agrees, and addressing the Prime Minister tells Chamberlain, 'The question is how to make the system effective and effective in time.'

19 May, PARIS

At the conclusion of Franco-Polish staff talks, an agreement is reached. French commander-in-chief General Maurice Gamelin promises that, if the Germans invade Poland, 'France will launch an offensive against Germany with the main bodies of her forces, beginning on the fifteenth day from the first day of the French general mobilisation.'

22 May, BERLIN

Germany and Italy sign the Pact of Steel, a military and political alliance between the two powers. The amorous Count Ciano signs for Italy. At a banquet to celebrate the ceremony he sits between Frau Goering and Frau Goebbels, 'both of whom [find] it hard to cope with their table companion's pronounced sexuality'. Goering is literally in tears as von Ribbentrop, and not himself, is awarded Italy's highest order of chivalry. Ciano promises to try and obtain one for him.

French foreign minister, Georges Bonnet (right) receives his Roumanian opposite number, Grigore Gafencu, at the Quai d'Orsay, Paris, 28 April 1939. Bonnet explained 'the means by which he still steadfastly hoped to save the peace'.

Italian and German foreign ministers Count Ciano and von Ribbentrop sign the Pact of Steel, Berlin, 22 May 1939. 'As long as the Germans have need of us they will be courteous, and even servile, but at the first opportunity they will reveal themselves as the great rascals they really are,' was the prophetic comment of King Victor Emmanuel of Italy.

23 May, BERLIN
As Ciano leaves Berlin, Hitler meets with Goering and his military chiefs. He tells them, 'It is not Danzig that is at stake. For us it is a matter of expanding our living space in the East, and making food supplies secure.' To do this, the Fuehrer tells the others, Germany must, 'attack Poland at the first suitable opportunity. We cannot expect a repetition of Czechia. There will be war.'

24 May, WINNIPEG
King George VI delivers an Empire Day speech on the first visit by a King and Queen of England to North America: 'It is not in power or wealth alone, nor in dominion over other people, that the true greatness of an Empire consists. Those things are but the instrument; they are not the end, nor the ideal. The end is freedom, justice, and peace in equal measure for all, secure against attack from without and from within.'

26 May, LONDON
The Military Training Bill receives Royal Assent. Registration will now take place on 3 June, and the first conscripts, who will be known as 'Militiamen', are going to be called up on 1 July.

27 May, LONDON
Picture Post runs a feature entitled 'Danzig: The Danger Spot: Maybe The Cause of A World War'. The same issue has an article on Britain's volunteer firemen of the Auxiliary Fire Service in the magazine's 'Britain Prepares' series.

27 May, MOSCOW
New Anglo-French proposals for a three-power agreement on countering German aggression are sent to Moscow for consideration. The Foreign Office believes that they meet all previous Soviet requirements. But the Russians want guarantees to the Baltic states

to be included, and also a military agreement to come into force before a political one.

31 May, Moscow

Molotov delivers a speech on Soviet foreign policy. It is not well received in London. Oliver Harvey writes in his diary, 'Molotov has said in his speech that our proposals are so confused that he cannot make out whether we really want an agreement or not; and that in any case he is about to negotiate a Soviet-German commercial agreement.'

Meanwhile, Chamberlain is away fishing in Wales and Lord Halifax is on his estate in Yorkshire.

June

3 June, London

Peace campaigner Margery Corbett Ashby, writing to *Picture Post*, believes, 'perhaps, until after the harvest, we may be safe from war'.

8 June, Washington DC

King George VI and Queen Elizabeth arrive during the first-ever British state visit to the USA. The British sovereigns stay with the Roosevelts and are given hot dogs at a picnic lunch. The President shakes his famous Dry Martini cocktails for the King, and the two men discuss the international situation. FDR tells the King of his intention to try and get America's Neutrality Act revised in order to help Britain and France. He also says that if war comes then US warships will sink German U-boats on sight, 'and wait for the consequences . . . If London was bombed USA would come in.' The Royal visit is a great success at every level.

8 June, London

Lord Halifax tells peers that the Government hopes that German–Polish differences can still be settled by peaceful discussion. But he warns them, 'If an attempt were made to change the situation by force, in such a way [as] to threaten Polish independence, that would inevitably start a conflagration in which this country would be involved.'

9 June, TEDDINGTON

'Japs are threatening English and French settlements. Filthy little tricksters – thinking to carry out the same threats and scoundrelly behaviour as Hitler. But the world is getting tired of these methods.' (Helena Mott)

12 June, LONDON

William Strang of the Foreign Office's Central Department leaves for Moscow. He is to try and expedite the Anglo-French-Soviet negotiations that are in danger of stalling badly. The Russians are less than flattered that such a comparatively junior official is being sent to them. Unwelcome comparisons with Chamberlain's own three trips to Germany, on which Strang actually accompanied the Prime Minister, are being made in Moscow.

14 June, TIENTSIN

Tension rises between Britain and Japan following the alleged murder of a Japanese official by two Chinese citizens. The Japanese claim the Chinese have taken refuge in the International Concession, and launch a systematic campaign of harassment and humiliation of British residents of the Concession.

14 June, LONDON

National Gallery Director Sir Kenneth Clark and his wife Jane give a dinner party. American political pundit Walter Lippman tells the other guests that US ambassador Joseph Kennedy has told him that war is inevitable, and that Britain will be defeated. Guest of honour Winston Churchill is indignant and refutes the ambassador's claims.

Although at the outset of the 'almost inevitable war', Britain may very well suffer severe setbacks, Churchill tells the company: 'Yet these trials and disasters . . . will but serve to steel the resolution of the British people, and to enhance our will for victory . . . Yet supposing Mr Kennedy were correct in his tragic utterance, then I for one would willingly lay down my life in combat, rather than, in fear of defeat, surrender to the menaces of these most sinister men.'

14 June, TEDDINGTON
'The Japs blockaded Tiensin – British and French concession. Jap sentries are manning all the barbed wire fences and searching everyone. . . *Englishmen* received the same treatment as *coolies*! I have no words to denounce the policy that has placed our men abroad in such ambiguous positions. It is a disgusting and crying shame for Baldwin, MacDonald and Chamberlain, besides a lasting let down of our pride.' (Helena Mott)

15 June, LONDON
Lord Chatfield, Minister of Coordination of Defence, gives a speech in which he says that every day that war is postponed is of the greatest value to Britain in building up her defences.

17 June, MOSCOW
William Strang meets with Soviet foreign minister Molotov for the first time. Molotov is contemptuous of the British proposals for an Anglo-French-Soviet front against Hitler. He tells Strang, 'If you think that the Soviet Government is likely to accept these proposals, then you must think we are nitwits and nincompoops!'

18 June, DANZIG
Nazi propaganda minister Dr Josef Goebbels delivers a violent speech at the end of the Free City's Cultural Congress. He tells an

enthusiastic crowd, 'Danzig is German. It must return to Germany. It is our understandable clear, definite and sacred wish.' Throughout the Free City, there are huge banners proclaiming, 'We Want To Go Home To The Reich!'

24 June, LONDON
The Illustrated London News runs an advertisement from German Railways:

> Seeing is believing. Come and See Germany.
> Visitors from Britain are heartily welcomed at all times.
> They will find that friendliness and the sincere desire to help are the characteristics common to every German they meet.

25 June, DANZIG
Over 1,000 SS men from East Prussia have arrived in the Free City, ostensibly to take part in a sporting competition. This month has seen over fifty 'incidents' in which Danzig and Polish officials have clashed.

25 June, WORTHING
'News not good – the situation in Tiensin is very ugly – the Japs are behaving abominably, stripping Britons naked publicly and so on.' (Joan Strange)

29 June, TEDDINGTON
'Lord Halifax gave a speech in which no doubt is left in German minds that we are only to take action if she starts.' (Helena Mott)

30 June, BERLIN
Von Ribbentrop's deputy State Secretary Ernst von Weizacker tells the French ambassador, 'We are not on the eve of a tremendous eruption, unless it is provoked by Polish excesses.'

30 June, WARSAW
The Polish Government receives official notification that the German cruiser *Koenigsberg* will be making a courtesy visit to Danzig on 25 August.

30 June, WORTHING
'Everyone talking about Lord Halifax's speech last night. "All Britain's might behind her pledges – unchallengeable navy: air force to fear none." It sounds like 1914 over again. Hitler is expected to snatch up Danzig – will this let loose the "dogs of war"?' (Joan Strange)

30 June, TEDDINGTON
'German activity going on in Danzig. The Poles have been very patient and have handled the trouble in a statesman-like manner.' (Helena Mott)

July

1 July, PARIS
In an interview with the German ambassador, foreign minister Georges Bonnet reiterates France's 'firm determination' to fulfil its obligations to Poland.

2 July, LONDON
As a further measure of Britain's preparations for war, the formation of the Women's Auxiliary Air Force is given Royal Assent.

4 July, HAMBURG
The French consul general passes on to Paris some disturbing news that he has heard: 'If some agreement is not shortly concluded between London, Paris and Moscow, the Soviet Government will be prepared to sign a non-aggression pact with the Reich for a period of five years.'

4 July, LONDON
The *Daily Telegraph* begins a campaign to bring Churchill into the government. The *News Chronicle* and *Yorkshire Post* also call for Churchill's inclusion. Hoardings appear in London with the slogan, 'What Price Churchill?'

9 July, LONDON
Sir Nevile Henderson returns from Berlin to consult his specialist. On examination it is found that the ambassador's throat cancer is only in remission. At the Foreign Office, Oliver Harvey believes Sir Nevile is 'quite unfit to be in such a post at such a time. He ought, of course to be withdrawn at once – if only because the policy he was chosen to represent, appeasement, in which he passionately believes, has been reversed, and so long as he is there Germany and everybody else will never believe we may not have more appeasement.'

10 July, LONDON
In the House of Commons, Chamberlain reviews the situation developing in Danzig. The Premier tells MPs that if Poland felt obliged to use force to maintain the *status quo* in Danzig, then Britain will go to her assistance.

11 July: WASHINGTON DC
President Roosevelt's 'Cash and Carry' Neutrality Bill, which if passed would have greatly favoured Britain and France, fails in the Senate.

13 July, LONDON
Chancellor of the Exchequer Sir John Simon announces defence borrowings of £500 million.

14 July, PARIS
The French commemorate the 150th anniversary of the storming of the Bastille with a huge military parade. To demonstrate the

solidity of the *Entente Cordiale*, a contingent of Scots Guards take part in the march past and RAF Wellington bombers fly over the French capital. British war minister Leslie Hore-Belisha is one of the guests of honour, seated next to Premier Daladier.

16 July, MUNICH

As a deliberate counter-blast to the Bastille commemoration, the Nazis mount a four day 'Rally of German Art'. It is not entirely successful as it pours with rain on the main day of the festival. Hitler's rostrum is soaked and the Fuehrer is in a very bad temper, having already lent his raincoat to his mistress, Eva Braun.

16 July, LONDON

Sir Oswald Mosley, leader of the British Union of Fascists and National Socialists, holds a huge indoor rally at Earls Court exhibition hall. Mosley tells his audience: 'If any country in the world attacks Britain then every single member of this great audience of British Union would fight for Britain [. . .] but a million Britons shall never die in your Jews' quarrel. Why is it a moral duty to go to war if a German kicks a Jew across the Polish frontier . . .? We are going, if the power lies within us [. . .] to say that our generation and our children shall not die like rats in Polish holes.'

16 July, TEDDINGTON

'Hitler spoke for twenty minutes without mentioning the democracies, encirclement or the Jews. What's happened to him? Mosley suggested return of colonies to Germany and possessions in east. Does he know even the rudiments of the matter? He just wants to ride in on some popular ignorant slogan . . . his worst characteristic is his intolerance and dislike of the Jews – while his own fortune is derived from one.' (Helena Mott)

IWM Army Training Album Photo No. 28/12

'We had to join, we had to join, we had to join Belisha's army. Ten bob a week, bugger all to eat, great big boots and blisters on your feet.' Secretary of State for War, Leslie Hore-Belisha, addresses the first batch of Militiamen, July 1939.

IWM HU 39927

At Earls Court on 16 July 1939, British fascist leader Sir Oswald Mosley speaks to an audience of more than 20,000. 'I am told that Hitler is mad. What evidence have they got so far that this man, who has taken his country from the dust to the height . . . has gone suddenly mad?'

17 July, WARSAW

General Sir Edmund Ironside, the Inspector-General of British Overseas Forces, arrives in Warsaw. He tells the British military attaché that his main task is going to be to try 'to obtain a guarantee from the Poles that they will not precipitate a war through a corporal blowing up a bridge'.

20 July, LONDON

Birger Dahlerus, a Swedish businessman with connections both in Britain, where he worked as a young man, and in Germany, meets Lord Halifax. Dahlerus is setting himself up as unofficial peace broker between the two countries. He is on friendly terms with Goering and has arranged for Germany's second man to meet some British businessmen on 7 August to discuss how peace can be maintained.

22 July, LONDON

In this week's edition of *Picture Post* there appears a bi-lingual article 'We Want Peace – Britain Does Not Hate Germany'. The magazine urges its readers to cut it out and send it to friends in Germany.

29 July, LONDON

Picture Post features an article entitled 'And Still – War Clouds Over Danzig'. The magazine warns its readers: 'As we move towards the 25th anniversary of the Great War, events are shaping themselves with a terrible similarity.' In the same issue, the magazine's proprietor Edward Hulton contributes an article with the headline 'Mr Churchill Must Join the Cabinet'.

31 July, DANZIG

The Nazi-controlled Senate demands the withdrawal of all Polish customs officials from the Free City. Poland responds with economic reprisals and a refusal to withdraw the officials.

31 July, LONDON

Chamberlain announces that an Anglo-French military mission will be going to Moscow for staff talks with the Soviets. Molotov has told William Strang, 'If war comes with Germany, I wish to know exactly how many divisions each party will put into the field, and where they will be located.'

August

1 August, LONDON

A Government announcement is made stating that in the event of war, petrol rationing will begin immediately.

2 August, NEW YORK

German Jewish physicist émigré Albert Einstein writes a letter to President Roosevelt, alerting FDR to the military potential of the splitting of the atom. A single atomic bomb, Einstein tells the President, if dropped on a port, 'might destroy the whole port together with some surrounding territory'.

2 August, MOSCOW

British ambassador Sir William Seeds gives Molotov the names of the British military mission that is coming to Moscow. The Russians again feel insulted. None of the officers, headed by Admiral Sir Reginald Plunkett-Ernle-Erle Drax, compares in seniority or importance to General Ironside, who was sent to Warsaw in July. In reproach, Molotov asks Sir William and Strang, 'Do you not trust the Soviet Union? Do you not think we are interested in security too? It is a grave mistake. In time, you will realize how great a mistake it is to mistrust the government of the USSR.'

2 August, BERLIN
Foreign Minister Joachim von Ribbentrop meets informally with the Soviet chargé d'affaires. He tells the Russian, 'From the Baltic to the Black Sea, there was no problem which could not be solved to our mutual advantage.'

2 August, LONDON
Despite the growing crisis over Danzig, Chamberlain proposes that the Commons adjourn until 3 October. Churchill is both aghast and furious at the Prime Minister's complacency over the international situation. He tells the House, 'At this moment in its long history it would be disastrous, it would be pathetic, it would be shameful for the House of Commons to write itself off as an effective and potent factor . . .'

Churchill's view is echoed in a brave and passionate intervention by thirty-two-year-old Tory backbencher Ronald Cartland, who reminds MPs, 'We are in the situation that within a month we may be going to fight – and we may be going to die.'

Despite these warnings, Chamberlain's adjournment wins by 245 votes to 129.

4 August, DANZIG
Poland informs the Nazi-dominated Danzig Senate that in two days' time it will be arming its customs officials in the Free City. Any interference with their duties, the Poles warn the Senate, will be regarded as a violent act and will be treated accordingly. The Senate protests strongly at the arming of the men.

5 August, TILBURY
The Anglo-French military mission leaves for Leningrad (St Petersburg), on SS *City of Exeter*. The ship has a maximum speed of only eleven knots, and the journey will take over four days. Again, the Russians are not impressed. They have serious doubts

about the sincerity of the Western Allies in wishing to enter into a military alliance. On board, the British and French confer in the children's playroom. French captain André Beaufre notes how agreeable life is on the *City of Exeter* with 'copious repasts of curry served by Indian stewards in turbans'.

5 August, CHARTWELL (Westerham, Kent)
Churchill has written an article for this week's *Picture Post* on the outbreak of the Great War, twenty-five years ago this week. The magazine asks: 'Will There Be War Again?'

7 August, SOENKE-NISSEN-KOOG (German-Danish border)
Birger Dahlerus hosts a meeting between Goering and seven British businessmen. They tell the field marshal both orally and in a memorandum that Britain will stand by its obligations to Poland. Goering gives them his solemn assurance 'as a soldier and statesman' that he will do everything he can to avert war. Dahlerus will be continuing his unofficial peacemaking for the rest of the month, going backwards and forwards between Britain and Germany.

8 August, LONDON
Winston Churchill broadcasts to the United States. He tells his American listeners, 'If Herr Hitler does not make war, there will be no war. No one else is going to make war. Britain and France are determined to shed no blood except in self-defence or defence of their Allies.' He finishes by calling for a future system of human relations 'which will no longer leave the whole life of mankind dependent upon the virtues, caprice, or the wickedness of a single man'.

8 August, WORTHING
'News still bad from Danzig and Hitler ominously quiet – ugly!' (Joan Strange)

9 August, BERLIN

Luftwaffe chief Goering is reported as saying, 'The Ruhr will not be subjected to a single bomb. If an enemy bomber reaches the Ruhr, my name is not Goering: you can call me Meier.' (Meier is the German equivalent of Smith or Jones.)

9 August, MARGATE

Fifteen London holidaymakers take part in a snap poll on the international situation. 'Do you think we should go to war to defend Danzig?' they are asked. Seven say yes, four no, and four are undecided. They are then asked, 'Do you think there will be a war?' Eight say no, four yes and three are undecided. 'Do you think Hitler wants war, or is he bluffing?' is the final question and all fifteen reply, 'No, he's bluffing.'

9 August, WEYMOUTH

King George VI inspects 133 ships of the Royal Navy's Auxiliary Fleet. Many people are reminded that a similar review by the King's father took place just before war broke out in 1914.

9 August, LONDON

There is a practice blackout in the capital tonight. Superintendent Reginald Smith of the Metropolitan Police's 'K' Division goes to the top of Marble Arch to see how effective it is. The superintendent thinks London looks like 'a Gruyere cheese with a candle behind it'. In blacked-out Trafalgar Square a number of drunks splash in the fountains, bawling out the song, 'Show Me the Way to Go Home'.

10 August, BERLIN

Reinhard Heydrich gives orders to SS major Alfred Naujocks to simulate an attack on the Gleiwitz radio station near the border with Poland. It must look as if the attacking forces are Poles.

Heydrich tells Naujocks, 'Practical proof is needed for these attacks of the Poles for the foreign press as well as German propaganda.' Heydrich gives the operation the codename HIMMLER after his chief, the head of the SS.

11 August, OBERSALZBERG
League of Nations High Commissioner in Danzig, Swiss diplomat Carl Burckhardt, has an audience with Hitler, 'the most profoundly feminine man' he has ever encountered. Burckhardt has also never met before 'any human being capable of generating so terrific a condensation of envy, vituperation and malice' as Hitler does. The Fuehrer tells Burckhardt that 'the Polish army already has the mark of death stamped on its countenance'. Then Hitler, with astonishing frankness, tells the Swiss that everything he is undertaking is fundamentally aimed at Russia, just as he wrote in *Mein Kampf* back in 1925. If Britain and France are so stupid as not to recognise this, he tells the Swiss diplomat, then he will be forced to join with Russia in order to annihilate them. Then, he will turn on Russia and gain the *Lebensraum* (living space), so vital for the German race. Back home in Basle, Burckhardt reports the conversation to British and French diplomats. He fails, however, to mention Hitler's remarks about Russia because he believes 'a German-Soviet pact was simply too absurd to contemplate'.

11 August, WORTHING
'Danzig events look ugly – Herr Forster has been to see Hitler and made violent anti-British and anti-French speech to the Danzigers on his return.' (Joan Strange)

12 August, MOSCOW
The Anglo-French military mission begins their first formal discussions with the Soviets. The Russian delegation is headed by Soviet Commissar for Defence, Marshal Klementi Voroshilov, a crony of

Stalin's. Voroshilov is not over-endowed with brains. 'He would have made a good sergeant-major in anyone else's army' is the general opinion of him among Western military attachés. The talks get off to a bad start with suspicion on both sides. Captain André Beaufre of the French part of the military mission comments that the British and French strongly suspect 'The Soviet had organized the conference in order to obtain, on the eve of war, an idea of our plans, and then naturally, to pass them on to Germany.' The talks will continue inconclusively until a final meeting on 25 August. The great stumbling block is the Poles' refusal to have Red Army troops on their soil, even in the event of a German invasion. Their attitude is summed up by commander-in-chief Marshal Smigly-Rydz: 'With the Germans we risk the loss of our liberty, but with the Russians we lose our soul.'

12 August, OBERSALZBERG

Count Ciano has arrived from Rome for talks with von Ribbentrop and Hitler. Ciano is told quite frankly by von Ribbentrop that it is not a question of Germany wanting Danzig or the Polish Corridor. Hitler wants war. Ciano records in his diary, 'The decision to fight is implacable . . . I am certain that even if the Germans were given more than they ask for they would attack just the same, because they are possessed by the demon of destruction.' In between his meetings with Count Ciano, Hitler sets the date for the invasion of Poland. It will begin on Saturday, 26 August at 4.30am.

12 August, OBERSALZBERG

During the discussions with Count Ciano, von Ribbentrop is called to the telephone. The foreign ministry in Berlin tells him that the Russians are now prepared to open talks in Moscow.

14 August, MOSCOW

The German ambassador calls on the Soviet foreign ministry with a message that von Ribbentrop is willing to fly to Moscow, 'to lay the foundations for a final settlement of German-Russian relations'.

16 August, DOORN

Ex-Kaiser Wilhelm II of Germany, living in exile in Holland, receives two British visitors, John Wheeler-Bennett and Robert Bruce Lockhart. In discussing the present crisis he tells them, 'Don't go away with the idea that Russia and Germany will go to war.' And as they leave, Wilhelm ruefully comments, 'The machine is running with *him* as it ran away with *me*.'

16 August, LONDON

Registrar-General Sir Sylvanus Vivian announces that, in event of war, everyone in Britain will have their own National Registration number and an identity card.

19 August, ÖBERSALZBERG

Hitler receives from his ambassador in Moscow a message that the Russians are prepared to receive von Ribbentrop on 27 or 28 August to negotiate and sign a non-aggression pact. The Fuehrer is jubilant but because of the date set for the attack on Poland, he wants von Ribbentrop's visit to be brought forward.

20 August, OBERSALZBERG

From the Berghof, Hitler sends a personal message to Stalin. He proposes that 'in view of the international situation' von Ribbentrop should go to Moscow by 23 August at the latest.

20 August, OUTER MONGOLIA

In an undeclared war, Soviet forces under General Georgi Zhukov engage the Japanese in the biggest battle fought since the First World War. Over 150,000 troops are involved, and the Russians employ 690 tanks and 300 aircraft. The Japanese suffer their greatest military reverse to date, with over 18,000 casualties and the loss of 300 'planes.

21 August, WILHELMSHAVEN

Pocket battleship *Admiral Graf Spee* departs to take up its war station off the coast of Brazil.

21 August, HOLLYWOOD

Charlie Chaplin, born just four days before Hitler in April 1889, delays the production of his new film, tentatively called *The Dictators*. Chaplin 'hesitates to go before the cameras while the European situation remains so uncertain'. It is rumoured that the US State Department is also bringing pressure on the British-born Chaplin 'to avoid incensing Hitler and Mussolini in the present delicate state of international relationships'.

21 August, OBERSALZBERG

At 10.50pm, Stalin's reply arrives while Hitler, Eva Braun and their guests are having dinner. The Soviet dictator agrees to von Ribbentrop's coming to Moscow on 23 August. Hitler is overjoyed. He bangs the table so hard that the glasses and cutlery rattle, and exclaims, 'I have them! I have them!'

21 August, BERLIN

Just before midnight, German home service radio announces the news of the pact with Russia. Propaganda minister Dr Goebbels writes confidently in his diary, 'We're on top again. Now we can sleep more easily.' From Berlin, *The Times* correspondent notes that among ordinary Germans the initial reaction is: 'This means that nobody will dare fight against us, and we can do just as we please.' But many old Nazi Party members are dismayed at a pact with the Bolsheviks. The garden of the Brown House, the Nazi Party headquarters in Munich, is reportedly littered with the Party's swastika badges thrown there by disillusioned Nazis. Official and public opinion in Japan, Spain, Italy and Hungary is also aghast at Hitler's *volte face.*

21 August, TEDDINGTON

'Tension increasing – nurses called up, soldiers being inoculated – heavy troops being called up – Poland advises foreigners to leave.' (Helena Mott)

22 August, LONDON

The Cabinet meets to discuss the crisis. Lord Halifax rather airily dismisses the German–Soviet non-aggression pact as 'perhaps of not very great importance'. During the nine o'clock news this evening it is announced that Parliament is being recalled. This is the first time that this has been done over the radio. Chamberlain, mindful of the accusations levelled at Foreign Secretary Sir Edward Grey in August 1914, writes to Hitler:

> Whatever may prove to be the nature of the German-Soviet Agreement, it cannot alter Great Britain's obligation to Poland which His Majesty's Government have stated in public repeatedly and plainly and which they are determined to fulfil.
> It has been alleged that, if His Majesty's Government had made their position more clear in 1914, the great catastrophe would have been avoided. Whether or not there is any force in that allegation, His Majesty's Government are resolved that on this occasion there shall be no such tragic misunderstanding.

The Prime Minister's message is dispatched to the Berlin embassy for Sir Nevile Henderson to personally deliver to Hitler.

22 August, WILHELMSHAVEN

The German submarine *U-30* commanded by Oberleutnant Fritz-Julius Lemp leaves base to take up its war station in the Atlantic Ocean. Twenty other U-boats also leave this week.

22 August, OBERSALZBERG

Hitler addresses his military chiefs on the imminent invasion of Poland. He tells the generals that with the non-aggression pact with Russia, he now has Poland 'in the position in which I want her'. He is scornful of Chamberlain and Daladier: 'our enemies are small fry. I saw them in Munich.' Hitler goes on to say that he will provide a propaganda pretext, however implausible, for the invasion. In any case, 'The victor will not be asked afterwards whether he told the truth or not. When starting and waging war it is not right that matters, but victory. Close your hearts to pity. Act brutally. Eighty million people must obtain what is their right. Their existence must be secured. The stronger man is right. The greatest harshness.'

22 August, TEDDINGTON

'*Like a bombshell* the Russian news in the morning papers fell on us at breakfast. Well! We have asked for it and no doubt Germany has read books that have pointed out what an invincible combination these two powers would make . . . Still, we have nothing whatsoever of which to be proud nor has our policy been anything but weak and reprehensible. If Neville Chamberlain had no means of gauging the trend of events he is certainly not fit to hold the position of prime minister of an empire. To make us the laughing stock of the world is scarcely an accomplishment of which to be proud – to shilly shally as he has done is not only madness but criminal lunacy.

'I am listening to Mozart's "sinfonia concertante" for violin, viola and orchestra in E Flat. How lovely! It seems impossible to connect such beauty with this present age and time of bestiality, misery and war madness.' (Helena Mott)

22 August, WORTHING

'Crisis again. Amazing news of a Berlin–Moscow Pact. Sworn enemies but uniting in a non-aggression pact. "World shocked" say the placards.' (Joan Strange)

23 August, PARIS

The Council of Ministers hold an emergency meeting to discuss how the situation has been affected by the Nazi–Soviet pact. Foreign minister Georges Bonnet thinks that to avoid war France should put pressure on Poland to compromise. But Daladier, most of the other ministers and the military chiefs present, believe that France must stand by the Poles.

23 August, OBERSALZBERG

Ambassador Henderson arrives with Chamberlain's letter. Sir Nevile finds Hitler in a violent mood, and he attacks both the Poles for their intransigence and the British for giving them a 'blank cheque'. He tells Sir Nevile that he wants only friendship with Britain. Henderson is then dismissed only to be recalled shortly afterwards to receive Hitler's reply to Chamberlain's letter. The Fuehrer is calmer now, but tells the ambassador that he is fifty and prefers war now rather than in five or ten years' time. He finishes by saying that only a complete reversal of British policy towards the Reich would convince him of Britain's good faith. Sir Nevile leaves, and Hitler, having put on an act of rage for Henderson's benefit, laughingly tells his staff, 'Chamberlain won't survive this discussion. His cabinet will fall this evening.'

23 August, MOSCOW

Von Ribbentrop arrives by air to conclude the non-aggression pact, which he and Molotov sign. Under the terms of the pact's secret protocol, Germany and the Soviet Union carve out respective spheres of influence in central and eastern Europe. Finland, Estonia, Latvia, the Roumanian province of Bessarabia, and eastern Poland are all assigned to Russia, while Germany claims the rest of Poland and Lithuania. At the signing, Soviet champagne and vodka are served, and Stalin proposes a toast to Hitler: 'I know how much the German nation loves its Fuehrer. I should therefore like to drink his health.'

In preparation for the invasion of Poland, Hitler addresses his generals at the Berghof, 22 August 1939. A secret account of the meeting claimed that Goering, 'wild with enthusiasm, climbed on a table, rendered fervent thanks, and promised to carry out the blood-thirsty orders'.

Molotov signs the Nazi–Soviet Non-Aggression Pact, Moscow, 23 August 1939. 'Public opinion in our country, and probably in Germany too, will have to be prepared slowly for the change in our relations this treaty is to bring about,' was Stalin's comment after the signing.

At the British Embassy in Moscow, correspondents gather to hear a statement by Sir William Seeds on the future of Anglo-French-Soviet relations in the light of the new pact. While waiting for the ambassador, they ask press attaché John Russell what Sir William is going to say. Russell replies, 'I don't know what *he's* going to tell you, but it is my opinion that the British government has just been administered a considerable kick up the arse!'

23 August, DANZIG
The Senate decrees that thirty-seven-year-old Bavarian-born Nazi Party Gauleiter and former bank clerk Albert Forster is Danzig's head of state.

23 August, LONDON
The Imperial War Museum closes as usual for the day at 6pm. But later in the evening Ernest Blaikley, the Museum's Assistant in Charge of Pictures, is telephoned at home by the Office of Works to be told that the Museum is to close tomorrow and the evacuation of its works of art will begin at midday. The possibility of having to evacuate the Museum's most valuable contents in the event of another war was first considered way back in November 1933

23 August, WEST NORWOOD
'Things are working up to another serious crisis, almost identical with this time last year. We hope against hope, that even now war may be averted, but each day brings more dread news.' (Miss Nellie Violet Carver, Supervisor, Central Telegraph Office)

23 August, HUDDERSFIELD
'The Russo-German Pact is signed and the crisis begins. With the dramatic signature . . . Germany claims a diplomatic triumph which she declares will end resistance to her plans against Poland. She expects to get Danzig and the Polish Corridor without fighting.

She is confident Britain and France will not carry out their pledge to help Poland if she is attacked. Germany is wrong . . . The world begins to realize that war is dangerously near.' (Mrs Marjorie Gothard, wife of master butcher)

24 August, OBERSALZBERG
At 1am, von Ribbentrop telephones from Moscow and reports complete success. Once again, Hitler is both delighted and confident. Of Britain and France, he believes the signing of the pact 'will hit them like a bombshell'.

24 August, WILHELMSHAVEN
Pocket battleship *Deutschland* sails to take up position across the British sea lanes of the North Atlantic.

24 August, WASHINGTON DC
From the White House, President Roosevelt sends a personal appeal to Hitler. In it, the President calls for the settlement of the Danzig question by means of direct negotiation, arbitration or the appointment of an impartial mediator. Roosevelt concludes: 'I appeal to you in the name of the people of the United States, and I believe in the name of peace-loving men and women everywhere, to agree to the solution of the controversies existing between your government and that of Poland through the adoption of one of the alternative methods I have proposed.' A similar appeal is sent to President Ignace Moscicki of Poland. The Poles accept Roosevelt's offer. Hitler ignores it completely.

24 August, LONDON
Parliament reconvenes and immediately passes the Emergency Powers (Defence) Act, 1939. This will form the basis of the Defence Regulations to come into force in the now-likely event of war. The BBC broadcasts a Government announcement that all schoolteachers

are to return to their schools as soon as possible. This is a precaution in case evacuation has to take place.

At midday the first lorry arrives at the Imperial War Museum to evacuate the Museum's paintings. It is soon loaded and sets off for Colworth House, Sharnbrook. Another lorry arrives, is loaded, and routed to Penn House, Amersham. Across the river from Lambeth, at the Tate Gallery, Director John Rothenstein gives orders to close at midday. As the last of the public are ushered out, the Tate's staff start preparing for the evacuation of the Gallery's works of art. A similar exercise is also taking place under Sir Kenneth Clark at the National Gallery.

From the US Embassy, ambassador Joseph P. Kennedy cables the State Department. Kennedy is extremely pessimistic about the chances of peace. His son Jack has just arrived back from Berlin, where the US Chargé d'Affaires Alexander Kirk has told him that war will start within a week. Kennedy himself has just seen Chamberlain. He wires Washington that the Prime Minister 'says the futility of it all is the thing that is frightful. After all, they cannot save the Poles. They can merely carry on a war of revenge that will mean the destruction of all Europe.'

24 August, VATICAN

Pope Pius XII broadcasts an appeal for peace. But even devout Catholic convert Evelyn Waugh thinks that it was delivered 'in terms so general and trite that it passes unnoticed here, where no one doubts that peace is preferable to war'.

24 August, TEDDINGTON

'Halifax . . . spoke on Poland. "The British government do not go back on their obligations." A little late to make that observation, but steps back in the right direction . . . Forster is made Head of State and dictator in Danzig. The atrocity tales against Poland are very fierce in Berlin.' (Helena Mott)

24 August, WORTHING

'News blacker and blacker. Parliament recalled and the PM (Chamberlain) made a momentous statement our guarantee to Poland holds good. In this way the situation differs from that of last September over Czecho-slovakia.' (Joan Strange)

24 August, GERMANY

'Captain Wellmann gave a short address in which he informed us that the movement orders had been received. The situation is grave and we must do honour to the traditions of our battery. We gave another cheer for Fatherland and Fuehrer and marched off from the barrack square behind the battery colours, singing heartily. Our train started shortly after eight passing through Schoenebeck, we reached Magdeburg where we had to change. Everywhere one saw masses of men laden with trunks and parcels, making their way to the mobilisation points. Many of them wore medal ribbons from the Great War. Were those who had already experienced the horrors of 1914–18 to go campaigning once more? It was scarcely imaginable.' (Corporal Wilhelm Krey, 13th Artillery Observation Battery, German Army)

24 August, CITY OF LONDON

'New hats, frocks, coats, theatres and even holidays are forgotten and replaced by purchase of tinned foods, black curtains and adhesive tape.

'The railway stations had their blue anti-glare lights fixed, provision all over the country for a quick black-out is being made and everything is, apparently, ready for the "big bang".

'For twelve long weary months we have lived with the threat that on such-and-such a date war will be declared and as each date passes nerves become more strained, the tension grows tighter and we wait with a jagged dread for the next date. Of course, we carry on and live and eat and sleep and generally behave as though nothing was worrying us at all but all the time there is a little devil deep inside that whispers "what's the use of making this arrangement – we probably shalln't be here when the time comes to fulfil it."' (Miss Vivienne Hall, aged thirty-two, shorthand typist with the Northern Assurance Co. of Moorgate, London EC2, living with her mother in Putney)

25 August, LONDON
The BBC starts broadcasting news bulletins from 10.30am. Up until today the first news had gone out as late as 6pm. Britain and Poland sign a five-year military mutual assistance agreement. It is an unambiguous declaration that Britain will fight if Poland is invaded.

25 August, DANZIG
Instead of the cruiser *Koenigsberg* promised in June, the battleship *Schleswig-Holstein* arrives on a 'courtesy visit' to the Free City. The crew consists in the main of naval cadets. Three days ago, navy commander-in-chief Admiral Erich Raeder warned Hitler that Polish coastal batteries might very well sink the old battleship, with the loss of over 300 cadets. Hitler replied with a dismissive wave of his hand.

25 August, MUNICH
Because of the Nazi–Soviet Pact, Radio Munich abruptly cancels a scheduled talk entitled, 'I accuse Moscow – the Comintern Plan for World Dictatorship'. It is replaced by thirty minutes of Russian music.

25 August, NEW YORK
Despite the crisis, the Columbia Broadcasting System insists that its European correspondents, including William Shirer in Germany, go ahead with a programme *Europe Dances* featuring dance band music from Paris, London and Berlin. Shirer suggests calling it off as 'war's too imminent for that sort of thing'.

25 August, BERLIN

Sir Nevile Henderson is asked to meet with Hitler at 1.30pm. In an attempt to detach Britain from Poland, Hitler tells the ambassador that once the Polish 'question' has been settled, he is prepared to make Britain 'a large comprehensive offer' and to guarantee the British Empire. He puts an aeroplane at Sir Nevile's disposal to take the offer to London next morning.

Hitler receives a message from Mussolini. The Duce tells Hitler that Italy is in no position to render Germany any military assistance at the present time. This news, and the signing of the Anglo-Polish alliance, makes Hitler change his mind and at 7.45pm orders are sent to halt the attack on Poland scheduled to start at 4.30 tomorrow morning.

25 August, WORTHING

'News very bad but we are hopeful in this household that war will not come. Mother hasn't got any extra food in, any black stuff for black-outs or even a gas mask.' (Joan Strange)

25 August, TEDDINGTON

'Dull, some rain and *the* most oppressive day I've known. The sun did not break through once. One felt utterly exhausted. It couldn't have been a more appropriate setting for the news.' (Helena Mott)

25 August, CITY OF LONDON

'Another day of strain – last night there were the usual stories of "incidents" on the frontiers between Poland and Germany, speeches of determination from Hitler and Poland ... Britain (via Lord Halifax) issued her warning that we and France would stand by our obligations to help Poland – the Pope sent a message to the world to try and be reasonable and somehow stop the senseless slaughter of millions of people.

'We have been paid by the office and provision has been made for the paying of our salaries in the event of war, we are told to be in readiness to do nothing about work for three days after the actual outbreak of war and then our shift system is to try to start working – three days at a time for each shift – whether this will be possible remains to be seen.' (Vivienne Hall)

26 August, MOSTY (Polish Carpathian Mountains)
Not having received the orders to halt their attack, a special unit of the *Abwehr* (German military intelligence), made up of ethnic Germans, capture Mosty railway station to prevent the Poles from sabotaging it. They are then ordered to withdraw back into Slovakia. This they successfully manage to do. But their supporting engineer troops have killed two Poles and captured another forty in skirmishes around the strategically important railway line.

26 August, PARIS
Premier Daladier sends a personal message to Hitler, asking him to hold back from war. There is no question, Daladier tells the Fuehrer, that cannot be resolved peacefully. But 'If French and German blood is now to be spilled, as it was twenty-five years ago . . . then each of the two peoples will fight confident of its own victory. But surely Destruction and Barbarism will be the real victors.'

26 August, BERLIN
The commemoration ceremony to mark the twenty-fifth anniversary of the Battle of Tannenberg is cancelled. All German airports are closed, and apart from regular airline flights, the whole of the Reich becomes a prohibited zone for aircraft. German internal air services are also suspended.

26 August, LONDON
Sir Nevile Henderson arrives from Berlin at midday and is immediately taken to see Chamberlain at 10 Downing Street. For the

rest of the day, Foreign Office officials, Sir John Simon and Halifax's deputy R.A. Butler attempt to draft and redraft a satisfactory reply to Hitler's offer made to Sir Nevile yesterday.

26 August, TORQUAY
450 members of the Prudential Assurance Company's headquarters staff evacuate to previously hired hotels in the Devon resort.

26 August, TERIJOKI (Finnish-Russian border)
At 7pm, the Anglo-French military mission crosses into Finland. There is a collective sigh of relief on leaving Russia, and to his delighted surprise, Captain Beaufre sees Admiral Drax perform 'a little dance on the platform!'

26 August, TEDDINGTON
'Our Russian mission is returning – they were not accorded much courtesy and had difficulty in obtaining a compartment to themselves on the journey. Strange lack of manners on the Russians' part.

'Have more or less settled the ARP hangings [the blackout] but have not taken other precautions . . . I have never seen so few people at Hampton Court, or so little traffic . . . but a good number of soldiers about.' (Helena Mott)

26 August, CITY OF LONDON
'Everything seems easier. I am going to the pictures in the West End (Stoll – *Love Affair* with my favourite actor French Charles Boyer and *Jesse James* with everybody else's favourite Tyrone Power) so it can be seen that I am less nervous than I was. I sincerely hope this continues.' (Vivienne Hall)

26 August, WORTHING
'Our ambassador in Berlin flew to London and back to Berlin – our cabinet met at six o'clock. Great efforts being made to preserve peace. The Pope – the Scandinavian countries – President Roosevelt

and the King of the Belgians all doing what they can. We still feel that all will be well.

'Hitler must feel on the horns of a dilemma, especially as Japan's protested violently against the Russo-German Pact and Italy does not look favourably on it either.' (Joan Strange)

27 August, BERLIN
The annual September Nazi Party rally at Nuremberg is cancelled. The theme of this year's rally was to have been 'peace'.

27 August, CAP D'ANTIBES
The Duke of Windsor, 'as a citizen of the world', sends a telegram to Hitler, appealing for peace. The ex-King also cables King Victor Emmanuel of Italy asking him 'to use your influence to prevent the catastrophe which now seems imminent'.

27 August, LONDON
The Central War Room (now the Churchill Museum and Cabinet War Rooms) underneath Whitehall becomes operational. It has been constructed to provide safe accommodation for Chamberlain and his ministers and other officials in case of heavy bombing. The map keepers, called up from their civilian occupations, begin their first watch in the Map Room this afternoon.

27 August, BERLIN
Hitler replies to Daladier, regretting that France is intending to fight to 'maintain a wrong'. Germany must have Danzig and the Corridor returned to her. But, the Fuehrer writes, 'I see no possibility of persuading Poland, who deems herself safe from attack by virtue of guarantees given to her, to agree to a peaceful situation.'

The provisional rationing of certain foodstuffs and soap, starting tomorrow, is announced. Foreign observers note that it has come as a heavy blow to ordinary Germans. Sir Nevile Henderson describes it as 'a depressing measure'.

27 August, GERMANY
'Normally in the army Sunday is a free day. But this Sunday was one of the busiest ever. Live ammunition and gas masks were drawn from the stores, the issue of clothing was continued. I wrote once again to my loved ones at home. Orders were received from the battery that we were to be ready to march off at 18.00 hours on Tuesday ... No one knew where we were going and the wildest rumours flew around.' (Corporal Wilhelm Krey, 13th Artillery Observation Battery, German Army)

27 August, WORTHING
'News is as bad as ever – the Cabinet met this evening and our ambassador flies back to report to Hitler. What will the next three days bring forth? Mother still feels very strongly that it will be peace.' (Joan Strange)

27 August, CITY OF LONDON
'Sunday, the day of prayer; lurid newspapers with descriptions of demands by Poland, demands by Germany; state of Britain's defences, anxious listening to news bulletins ... all the tension has returned, our short-lived hope seems to have slipped away. Will this never end? These days of excitement and constant "keyed-up-ness" are very wearying.' (Vivienne Hall)

28 August, LONDON
Broadcasting today begins with the Daily Service. The introit for today is 'Blessed be the Peacemakers' and the hymn 'A Safe Strong-hold Our God Is Still' is sung. Later in the day, county cricket matches between Middlesex and Surrey, and Hampshire versus Yorkshire are broadcast.

28 August, BERLIN

Sir Nevile Henderson arrives back from London by 'plane at 8.30pm. After drinking a half bottle of champagne at the embassy, he sets off for the Reich Chancellery to deliver the British note. It rejects Hitler's offer to guarantee the British Empire. It also insists that if there are to be negotiations between Germany and Poland, the latter's interests must be safeguarded. Furthermore, any settlement should be the subject of an international guarantee. Hitler tells the ambassador that he will receive the German reply tomorrow. A crowd of less than 500 'grim and silent' Berliners stand outside the Chancellery, watching the diplomatic comings and goings.

28 August, WORTHING

'News worse and worse but the people feel everywhere that war will *not* come. The Mediterranean is closed to British shipping, Parliament's to be recalled tomorrow – all merchant and fishing boats under government orders and so on.' (Joan Strange)

28 August, TEDDINGTON

'Nevile Henderson flew back. Just arrived 9.05pm. I do not think Nevile H speaks German for Schmidt the interpreter was there with him and Hitler . . .. Hitler seems to have shot his bolt and missed. That of course may only make him more uncontrolled and one cannot think he'll have brought the horse to water and then refuse to let it drink.' (Helena Mott)

28 August, GERMANY

'In the afternoon we tested our masks in the gas chamber. Some of them didn't fit too well, and the owners got an eye full of tear gas.' (Corporal Wilhelm Krey, 13th Artillery Observation Battery, German Army)

28 August, CITY OF LONDON

'Personally I don't see why Poland should give up a vital piece of her land or free-land or whatever it is called just because Germany wants it – the German "Boo" tactics have lost their terror and have just become a nasty nuisance which must be stopped, I wish to God it needn't be necessary to kill and maim thousands upon thousands of well-built men and women in order to stop it. Poor Germany, poor weary world, what a mess we people have made of it.' (Vivienne Hall)

28 August, WEST NORWOOD

'Mum doesn't want us to have an Anderson in the garden. She says it would be better to be bombed in the warm than to get pneumonia.' (Nellie Violet Carver)

28 August, TAKELEY, ESSEX

'Nevile Henderson has just flown back to Berlin. We did not hear a word of his message but if Hitler's suggestion was anything like his suggestions to the French it isn't very peaceful. He will enter into any negociations [*sic*] with the provision that he gets his own way and annexes the Polish corridor, i.e. Poland. The Mediterranean has just been closed to merchant shipping. Well, well, war it must be, it seems.' (Miss Moyra Charlton)

29 August, LONDON

The crowd outside 10 Downing Street continues to grow. A middle-aged working-class woman announces to bystanders, 'What they come here to look at I don't know. Mr Chamberlain's fascist. They'll find that out before long. Don't look at me like that. I'm not Hitler's friend. All I said was that Chamberlain is as much a fascist as Hitler.' Her remarks are immediately repudiated by members of the crowd. An elderly woman tells her, 'I wouldn't like Mr Chamberlain's mind at the moment.'

29 August, TAKELEY
'Many notes passing between British cabinet and Hitler – we really feel war will be averted.' (Moyra Charlton)

29 August, TEDDINGTON
'Chamberlain . . . admitted there was no easing of the tension. He spoke as "we" but he meant "he only" for there is no doubt *he* steadfastly intends to be *England's saviour*, if such a phenomenon is likely to rise from the dead ashes after these four years' policy. We are just waiting for *one* maniac's decisive word – just a nut in the cracker, more shame to us.' (Helena Mott)

29 August, CITY OF LONDON
'Another tension-filled day. Will it be today or tomorrow, will the miracle, which is the only thing that can avert war, be performed; will the air raids be really as bad as we have been led to believe . . . Hospitals are being cleared, sandbags are being heaped up in front of buildings, all ARP people are being called up or told to be ready to go to their posts with forty-eight hours' supply of food.' (Vivienne Hall)

29 August, GERMANY
'We drove past the Volkswagen factory at Fallersleben, where thousands of Italian workers lined the streets, waved and shouted Italian battle cries.' (Corporal Wilhelm Krey, 13th Artillery Observation Battery, German Army)

29 August, TAKELEY
'We got back just after three, in time to hear of the Prime Minister's speech. They relayed it in strips between gramophone records of an offensively cheerful tone. He was very guarded but has not yet got Hitler's answer. I am afraid they will go through with Danzig however politely they beg our friendship.

65

'No news in the evening, except that Hitler has handed in his answer to Henderson. Everyone is thrusting the onus of war onto everyone else. England is indeed calm – in fact "fed up" and "browned off" with the whole crisis. I suppose we may be at war any day now. Oh dear.' (Moyra Charlton)

30 August, LONDON

In the early hours of the morning, Hitler's reply to yesterday's note reaches the Foreign Office. He is prepared to negotiate with the Poles, but they must send a plenipotentiary, with full negotiating powers, to Berlin by 30 August. London replies at once that it is impossible for any plenipotentiary to arrive today but the document is being studied carefully. A considered reply will be sent off later today for Sir Nevile to deliver to Hitler or von Ribbentrop tonight. The unofficial Swedish peace broker Birger Dahlerus is also active today. He contacts the Foreign Office on behalf of Goering, and urges that immediate negotiations take place between Berlin and Warsaw to prevent a German invasion.

30 August, GERMANY

Troops are massing on the Polish border. One of them, fanatical Nazi Wilhelm Prueller, still thinks Hitler might yet pull off another bloodless victory:

Personally, I think the 'Affaire Poland' will be settled peacefully; perhaps Daladier will at the last minute assume the function of a mediator. But if it does come to war, I am sure it won't last long. For the Poles won't be able to withstand our attack . . . it's unthinkable for us, too, as the greatest European power, to sit back and watch the persecution of the *Volksdeutsche* without doing something. It is our duty to rectify this wrong, which cries to Heaven. If we fight, then we know we are serving a rightful cause. We know, however, that the Fuehrer will do all he can to avoid war.

30 August, CITY OF LONDON

'The City is now a mass of sandbags and cellophane paper is being pasted on large windows . . . The whole point of this war business is that no one knows exactly how horrible it will be, how many nations will be ultimately involved, how much gas warfare will be used, where the battlefield will be, how long will it last, how strong we or the rather problematical enemy are.' (Vivienne Hall)

30 August, TAKELEY

'At one, four, six and nine as usual, we listened to the news. We got Hitler's answer (though it has not been made public) and he is now waiting for ours. The idea of writing and exchanging polite replies can't go on interminably and one wishes to goodness it could be decided one way or the other. This is a deadlock and one is bored and anxious of waiting.

'Tonight's news was more sinister. Hitler won't relinquish one jot of his Polish demands and troops are massing on the frontiers. Aircraft and searchlights very busy to-night but there is brilliant moonlight.' (Moyra Charlton)

31 August, BERLIN

Just after midnight, von Ribbentrop and Sir Nevile Henderson have a stormy interview. At one point, interpreter Paul Schmidt thinks that the two men are going to come to blows. Von Ribbentrop, despite his perfect English, reads out quickly in German to Sir Nevile sixteen proposals to be put to a Polish plenipotentiary. Hitler has been working on these for most of the day, although they are only intended to be a smokescreen for his real intention to invade Poland. Henderson's German is less than perfect, and he is unable to take them all down, but von Ribbentrop refuses to let him read them. He tells the ambassador that they are now out of date anyway, as no emissary arrived from Warsaw by midnight to negotiate. Sir Nevile, whose own diplomatic manners are faultless, reports to

London, 'Herr von Ribbentrop's whole demeanour during an unpleasant interview was aping Herr Hitler at his worst.'

Hitler sends a reply to the Duke of Windsor's telegram of 27 August. He tells the Duke, 'You may rest assured that my attitude towards Britain and my desire to avoid another war between our two peoples remain unchanged. It depends on Britain, however, whether my wishes for the future development of German–British relations can be realised.'

31 August, LONDON

At 11.17am, the Government issues orders that the evacuation from Britain's towns and cities of schoolchildren and other vulnerable groups is to begin tomorrow morning.

31 August, ROME

Count Ciano and Mussolini meet mid-morning and come up with a proposal that they hope might yet prevent war. The Italians suggest that there should be a five-power conference to be held on 5 September, perhaps at San Remo, 'for the purpose of reviewing those clauses of the Treaty of Versailles which disturb European life'. The proposal is sent to the British and French. Their initial reaction is favourable.

31 August, BERLIN

At 12.30pm, Hitler issues his Directive No. 1 for the Conduct of War. Its preamble reads, 'Now that every political possibility has been exhausted for ending by peaceful means the intolerable situation on Germany's eastern frontier I have determined on a solution by force. The date and time of the attack are now fixed: 1 September at 4.45am.'

31 August, ROME

Count Ciano calls in British ambassador Sir Percy Lorraine and commits 'an indiscretion'. Ciano tells Sir Percy that Italy, despite the Pact of Steel, will not be going to war at Germany's side. 'Can't you understand,' he asks Lorraine, 'that we shall never start a war against you and the French?' Lorraine is much moved and near to tears as he departs. Ciano then telephones Mussolini to tell him of the interview. To lessen the tension, the Duce has ordered that Rome's blackout be suspended.

31 August, LONDON

At 11pm, the Foreign Office receives a telegram from the embassy in Rome. In the telegram, Sir Percy Lorraine passes on Count Ciano's message. As he told Ciano earlier, Sir Percy has been aware for over a fortnight that Italy would not be marching with Germany. But the fact that the Italian foreign minister has now told him officially surely means that Germany is about to invade Poland.

31 August, GLEIWITZ

At 8pm, Alfred Naujocks's party of five SS men force their way into the Gleiwitz radio station and overpower the staff. Breaking into a relay broadcast from Radio Breslau, a Polish-speaking SS man takes over the microphone. Claiming to represent the 'High Command of Polish Volunteer Corps of Upper Silesia', he tells listeners that Gleiwitz is in Polish hands. He calls on local Poles to rise up against the Nazis. After four minutes, the broadcast ends with shouts of 'Long Live Poland!' To make the 'attack' sound authentic, revolver shots are fired in the air. A grislier touch is added when the body of a murdered anti-Nazi, Silesian Franciszek Honiok, is left on the scene to provide 'proof' of the Polish 'attack' to foreign correspondents. Two similar 'incursions' take place near Gleiwitz at Pitschen and at Hochlinden. At Hochlinden, 'Polish' soldiers and irregulars storm the customs house and hold it for an hour and a half before it is 'recaptured' by German border guards. Six concentration-camp inmates, dressed in Polish uniforms, drugged and then shot, are left by the building to demonstrate

Polish 'guilt'. Heydrich has given them the cynical codename CANNED GOODS.

31 August, BERLIN
At 9pm the German home service radio broadcasts the sixteen proposals that von Ribbentrop so rudely read out to Sir Nevile Henderson nine hours ago. But as 'the Fuehrer and the German government have now waited for two days in vain for the arrival of a Polish plenipotentiary', they are considered to have now been rejected by Poland. A quarter of an hour after they are broadcast, at the foreign ministry State Secretary Ernst von Weizsacker hands Sir Nevile Henderson a copy of the sixteen proposals. When Sir Nevile asks why they are being given to him only at this late stage, von Weizsacker tells the ambassador that he is only obeying orders.

31 August, ROME
At midnight, Count Ciano receives a 'phone call from Berlin. It is his brother-in-law and embassy counsellor Massimo Magistrati on the line. Magistrati tells Ciano that newspapers are now being distributed free in the German capital. Their headlines read, 'Poland Refuses! Attack About To Begin!'

31 August, BERLIN
Sunday Times special correspondent, American Virginia Cowles, is in Berlin on a flying visit. After a hectic day, she dines at Horcher's, Goering's favourite restaurant. On the way back to her hotel she passes Hitler's Chancellery and reflects that, 'Only twenty years before ten million had died in the most savage conflict the world had ever known. They had died violently: burnt, suffocated, gassed, drowned, bayoneted and blown to atoms. Now once again the German nation was going to unloose the same, and even greater horrors. Any hour now, one man would give the signal.'

31 August, HUDDERSFIELD
'We think in our hearts that peace will prevail.' (Marjorie Gothard)

31 August, GERMANY
'After an uninterrupted journey we reached the frontier at Kreuzburg in the morning and took our position in a wood near the town. In the wood we shaved in coffee, because not even the cooks had water. We wondered how long we should stay there. I couldn't sleep the whole night long in the wood; for along all the roads and paths the German Army was rattling and clattering its way towards the frontier. We were lying only eight kilometres from the Polish boundary. At 2am we heard the news that the infantry was to cross the border at quarter to five in the morning. After hearing this news, there was no more sleep for us. Everyone was speculating on what the day would bring forth. We all knew now that it was serious, and the guns would soon be rolling forward.' (Corporal Wilhelm Krey, 13th Artillery Observation Battery, German Army)

31 August, TAKELEY
'It looks as if we are "for it"! One doesn't evacuate three million children and then halt, maim and blind just for the fun of it. Heigho! God must be sick of this world of ours.' (Moyra Charlton)

31 August, WORTHING
'Wireless news at one o'clock told us that London school children will be evacuated tomorrow. Worthing is to expect 13,000 and me two! Terrible, as it makes war seem nearer. Surely it *can't* happen. It's dreadful to think that the "victors" will be those who use most effectively the most diabolical instruments of death as quickly as possible ... The papers are very depressing – all the pictures are of soldiers – sandbags – ARP city girls evacuating from their offices – guns, aeroplanes and so on.' (Joan Strange)

'In spite of the Polish warmongers' arrogant provocations, supported by the British, the Fuehrer still tries to avoid war. Late at night the English ambassador, Sir Neville [sic] Henderson (second from left), brings the Fuhrer an answer from the English government' was the original German caption to this photograph, taken on 28 August 1939.

'If only this waiting were over. If only something would happen. One way or the other.' Men of an SS signals battalion at Knipprode, East Prussia, 31 August 1939.

31 August, CITY OF LONDON
'We heard yesterday from one of the boys ... that he had been digging for days, digging trenches for the soldiers and, having finished, they have been put to digging trenches in a nearby park for civilians – I notice as I passed the signals barracks yesterday that the "Terriers" there were stripped to the waist and shovelling sand into the bags as hard as they could go, placing the full bags against their barracks. They all seem to be growing moustaches and are now very "tough!!"' (Vivienne Hall)

31 August, TEDDINGTON
'This month has been an unbroken series of incidents to goad Poland to war, culminating in the Russia–German Pact which was ratified last night but which failed in its object of making us give in to German demands. "Demands" has become about the most stinking word in the whole German vocabulary, though many run it close for the honour. Justice! Race! Kultur!' (Helena Mott)

CHAPTER 2

Friday, 1 September 1939

Introduction: resumé of 31 August

Europe now stood on the brink of war. All day long, on 31 August, crowds had gathered in London, Paris, Berlin and Warsaw, watching the comings and goings of statesmen and diplomats. Everywhere people hoped against hope that peace might still be preserved.

In Britain, the general mood on that last day of August was still one of unwarranted optimism. Only 18 per cent of people when polled admitted that they expected war to break out. A large majority, when asked whether they thought Hitler was bluffing or not, answered Yes. But the announcement that the official evacuation of schoolchildren and others was to begin the next day seemed to many an ominous sign: 'War seems nearer after the evacuation news,' recorded one thirty-year-old man in the diary he was keeping for Mass Observation. Another diarist, a woman of twenty-four, thought, 'Every day gained makes one still hope. Strain is very great. Evacuation seems to imply the worst.'

In Germany, there was still the hope that, having successfully brought off so many bloodless 'victories', the Fuehrer would do it again. Other Germans were not so sure, and American correspondent William Shirer recorded in his diary, 'optimism in official circles [is] melting away this morning'. At the same time many Germans wondered why there was any crisis at all. 'The Corridor?' one man remarked to Shirer, 'Hell, we haven't heard about *that* for twenty years. Why bring it up now?'

In France, the mood of ordinary people was perhaps more pessimistic than in Britain. There was a widespread feeling of resigned acceptance that war would come. Already one could hear the slogan '*Il faut en finir*' (We've got to put a stop to it) among the public and the mobilised soldiers. Some in official circles clung to the hope that Mussolini's conference plan would yet preserve peace. Minister Anatole de Monzie urged its acceptance on his colleague Georges Bonnet: 'Georges . . . if the project for a conference fails . . . we will be caught up and pulverised in the wheels of war . . .'

In Poland, the people faced the prospect of war with a stolidity which amazed every foreigner. One reported, 'The crowds in Warsaw showed no emotion whatever. I suppose it was fatalism.' Some Poles still talked of riding in victory into Berlin, but most thought that if war came, it would be a long and arduous conflict. Only a very few realists were doubtful that resistance could last for very long without effective aid from Britain and France. Warsaw newspaperman Wladyslaw Besterman told his American colleague Ed Beattie, 'Poland is going to fight if she has to. No government could possibly give in to Hitler. But make no mistake, either. We are going to need every last ounce of pressure that Britain and France can bring to bear . . . They must come in at once, and when they do come in, they must hit Germany hard in the west.'

Beattie had been in Warsaw for a week, staying at the Europejski

Hotel. 'At dinner', he wrote, 'someone had the straight tip that war would start the next morning. Everyone at the table laughed. Setting dates for "Hitler's next move" had been a favourite sport in Europe for years. For once, the date was right.'

3.17am (4.17am), DANZIG

German forces, including the locally raised Danzig Heimwehr, have just started firing on Polish-occupied positions in the Free City of Danzig.

3.45am (4.45am), DANZIG

The old German battleship *Schleswig-Holstein*, in Danzig on a 'courtesy visit', starts bombarding the Polish military garrison on the small peninsula of Westerplatte.

4.00am (5.00am), DANZIG

Expectant mother Sybil Bannister, the English wife of a German doctor, wakes up to the sound of gunfire. 'This is the end,' Sybil thinks as she dresses quickly. She is trembling so violently that she can scarcely grasp her clothes or stand on her shaking legs. She rushes downstairs and runs into the caretaker. He tells her that Gauleiter Albert Forster has broadcast a proclamation that Danzig has returned to the 'Greater German Reich'. He also says that the shooting and explosions are coming from the Polish Post Office on the Heveliusplatz in the city and Westerplatte.

4.00am (5.00am), KATOWICE

Daily Telegraph string correspondent Clare Hollingworth wakes up suddenly. She hears what sounds like doors slamming and then the roar of aeroplanes. Clare runs to the window and sees the 'planes high in the sky and below them bursts of anti-aircraft fire. She also sees what she thinks are incendiary bombs falling in a nearby park. 'It's the beginning of war!' Clare is told. Without

waiting for confirmation, she telephones *Daily Telegraph* correspondent Hugh Carleton Greene in Warsaw with the news. Clare
sets out for the British Consulate. She is now having doubts and
is afraid that she has made the gaffe of her life by reporting a non-
existing war. But at the Consulate the news is confirmed. One of
the German employees weeps at the news. She tells Clare, 'This is
the end of poor Germany.'

4.20am (5.20am), WARSAW

The Times' correspondent Patrick Maitland is fast asleep when
the telephone rings. It is his colleague Hugh Carleton Greene of the
Daily Telegraph on the line. Greene tells Maitland that he has just
heard from Clare Hollingworth in Katowice. Clare has woken up
to the sound of bombing and shelling. It looks as if war has begun.
More than half asleep still, Maitland puts the receiver down and
totters back to bed and drops off to sleep again.

4.30am (5.30am), UNITED STATES EMBASSY, BERLIN

Embassy clerk William Russell is on night duty in the office of the
Chargé d'Affaires Alexander Kirk when the telephone rings. Kirk
appears and takes the phone from Russell. He listens and then puts
the phone down without a word. 'Russell, will you wake the code
clerk?' he asks quietly. 'That was the British Embassy calling. The
first German bombers left for Poland ten minutes ago.'

4.35am (5.35am), WARSAW

Patrick Maitland wakes up with a start. Has he really been phoned
up by Greene with news that war has begun? He rings Greene, who
confirms the news, as does the British Embassy who have just heard
the news from the Consulate in Katowice.

4.40am (5.40am), ALL GERMAN RADIO STATIONS

Hitler's proclamation to the Wehrmacht is read out over the radio:

The Polish state has refused the peaceful settlement of relations which I desired and has resorted to arms. Germans in Poland are persecuted with bloody terror and driven from their homes. A series of violations of the frontier, intolerable to a great power, prove that Poland is no longer willing to respect the frontier of the Reich. In order to put an end to this lunacy I have no choice than to meet force with force; the German Army will fight for the honour and rights of a new-born Germany ...

5.00am (6.00am), KUTNO, EAST OF WARSAW

A thirty-coach passenger train from the Baltic port of Gdynia to Warsaw is just leaving Kutno station. On board the train, which left Gdynia yesterday, are the wives and children of civil servants, officers and railway officials. A few soldiers and reservists are also passengers on the train. Suddenly six two-engine bombers appear. They fly low over the railway line. The passengers watch the 'planes calmly. They believe that they are Polish bombers on an exercise. Then equally suddenly, they hear an explosion and a shower of machine-gun bullets hits the sides and roofs of the carriages. Many of the passengers are hit, while others in a panic jump through the doors into a ploughed field. The German 'planes fly over, circle and return, sending another shower of machine-gun fire into the crowd before flying off. Near the end of the train in a third-class Pullman, survivors can hear the moans of badly wounded Polish soldiers. They have been literally cut to pieces by bullets and flying glass. Further on, a goods van has been split into two and the bodies of eight soldiers thrown out on the roof by the effects of blast. A stunned woman sits on the ground by the train, staring at the bodies of her two dead daughters and son.

5.15am (6.15am), WARSAW

Patrick Maitland has just finished telephoning when the sirens sound the air-raid warning. He and his housemates, some grabbing gas masks, make for the shelter.

5.30am (6.30am), WARSAW
British military attaché Lieutenant-Colonel Edward Roland Sword
is woken by the telephone ringing. His colleague Robin Hankey is
on the line. He tells Sword that the Germans have just started
bombing Katowice. The military attaché rings a Polish staff officer
who confirms the news.

6.00am (7.00am), MOABIT, BERLIN
John 'Jack' McCutcheon Raleigh of the *Chicago Tribune* is called
to the telephone in his *pension*. Because of the crisis, he has had
only two hours' sleep. Picking up the receiver, his boss, Sigrid Schlutz,
tells him, 'The Germans have marched into Poland. Early this
morning – 5.45am. It's really war. Get down to the office quickly.'
Raleigh rushes back to his room to dress. His landlady follows him.
She asks the correspondent what's the latest news. She is very worried
as she has two sons in the army. 'War,' Raleigh tells her briefly. He
gets a taxi and makes for the city centre. Berlin looks the same.
Passers-by seem calm enough.

6.00am (7.00am), ZRARDOW, WARSAW DISTRICT
Fourteen year old Zbigniew Leon wakes up in bed. He is on the
country estate of a friend of his father's. He hears air-raid sirens,
but thinks that it is an emergency drill. There have been several in
the last few days. But when he gets up and goes outside, Zbigniew
sees two large and strange-looking aeroplanes. They do not look like
Polish 'planes. Suddenly, two smaller 'planes appear. They are Polish
fighters and they start shooting at the larger aircraft. Zbigniew is
completely taken by surprise and it dawns on him that something
is not right.

7.28am, FOREIGN OFFICE, WHITEHALL
The first news of the German invasion of Poland reaches the British
Government via a Reuter's News Agency report.

8.00am (9.00am), Europejski Hotel, Warsaw

The sirens sound as United Press correspondent Ed Beattie is on the 'phone to Amsterdam. The morning is hazy and overcast. Beattie cannot see the German raiders, but he hears 'the bark of anti-aircraft in the distance' as it moves gradually closer. Then the American sees 'little puffs from the shell-bursts, showing black against the white cloud layer'. From the suburbs of the city, Beattie hears 'a sound different from the sharp AA fire, a sort of heavy *c-r-r-r-rumph*'. He realises that the sounds that he is hearing are the first bombs falling on the Polish capital. Smoke emerges from the west of the city. Beattie's hotel window overlooks Pilsudski Square, which is rapidly emptying. A peasant, in for Friday market, dutifully turns his horse round in its harness. He dumps some hay in the road for feed and then makes his way to the nearest shelter. After a while the gunfire ceases, and the All Clear sounds. The peasant re-emerges, turns his horse around again and calmly drives off.

8.30am, Head Office, Granada Theatres Ltd, Golden Square, London

Managers of the Granada cinemas in the London area have just received the following announcement to be read out if war is declared:

> Ladies and gentlemen,
> I want you to listen very quietly to what I have to say and I want you to remain in your seats until I have finished. We have just received orders from the authorities that a state of emergency has arisen and that all theatres are to be closed immediately. There is no cause for undue alarm. Will you please leave the theatre quietly. Attendants at the exits will issue readmission tickets to all who care to ask for them. The authorities advise you to go home. Thank you.

8.30am, FOREIGN OFFICE, WHITEHALL
A telegram arrives from the British Embassy in Warsaw, reporting that Poland has been invaded and bombing is taking place.

8.45am (9.45am), GERMAN-POLISH BORDER
Twenty-three-year-old Viennese Wilhelm Prueller is with the 10th Rifle Regiment of the 4th Light Division. He just has time to jot in his diary, '9.45: We've crossed the border. We're in Poland. *Deutschland, Deutschland ueber alles!*'

8.50am (9.50am), BRITISH EMBASSY, BERLIN
Birger Dahlerus, the Swedish businessman and friend of Goering, telephones with an offer to fly to Britain to try to end the fighting. He repeats what Goering has told him earlier: 'The Poles are sabotaging everything . . . The Poles do not want to negotiate . . .'

9.00am (10.00am), KROLL OPERA HOUSE, BERLIN
Hitler arrives to address a special sitting of the Reichstag. Before leaving the Reich Chancellery, his doctor Theodor Morell has injected him with a stimulant. It is very hot and humid in the opera house as Hitler, in a new field-grey tunic, mounts the podium. He tells the deputies that Poland has not only intensified the campaign of atrocities against ethnic Germans, but 'for the first time Polish regular soldiers fired on our territory'. Now, Germany is being forced to retaliate: 'Bombs will be met by bombs. Whoever fights with poison gas will be fought with poison gas. Whoever departs from the rules of humane warfare can only expect that we shall do the same.' But, the Fuehrer tells the Reichstag: 'I will not wage war against women and children. I have ordered my air force to restrict itself to attacks on military objectives.' Hitler goes on to say that if he should fall in battle, then Goering is to be his successor, and if Goering too should fall, then Deputy Fuehrer Rudolf Hess will take over. Referring to his new uniform, Hitler says, 'I am from

now on just the First Soldier of the German Reich. I have once more put on that coat that was most sacred and dear to me. I will not take it off again until victory is secured or I will not survive the outcome . . .'

9.30am (10.30am), United States Embassy, Berlin

William Russell and other embassy staff listen to Hitler's speech on the radio. Russell expects 'something terrific to happen immediately' but nothing does. And opposite the embassy a group of workmen continue moving concrete blocks, 'undisturbed by the declaration of war'. And why not? After all, Russell muses, nobody has asked their opinion about it.

10.00am, City of London

'Evacuation of the children to the country. The children (I saw some of them at Waterloo on my way to work) are all labelled, carry packets of food and their gas masks and are taking a change of clothing and essentials for carrying on for a day or two. All roads and railways are requisitioned for today, from nine until 5.30 and as we have, most of us, managed to get up to the City early, heaven knows what will happen to us if there is a war before we get home.' (Vivienne Hall)

10.00am, Highgate Hospital, London

Nursing Sister Gwyneth Thomas is supervising the last patients to be evacuated. All this week, she has been busy either getting them ready for evacuation, or preparing strips of cardboard for the sides of the windows as a precaution against bomb blast. Everybody is pitching in, and even the Medical Superintendent is helping to fill sandbags. One of the last patients to leave is a little boy, 'clutching his gas mask as if it were a toy'. Sister Thomas fervently hopes that 'it will not mean any more than that to him'. Another patient, Paul, only nine months old, has been very

'*Wish me luck as you wave me goodbye.*' *Teachers and children from the Robert Montefiore School, Hanbury Street, Whitechapel on their way to evacuation, 1 September 1939.*

ill in the hospital's isolation ward. Now he too has to go. Sister Thomas hopes 'they will be kind to him in the hospital he is going to – but how silly of me to worry about that. He is such a darling, they couldn't help loving him.' Amidst all the turmoil of the hospital's evacuation, Sister Thomas wonders, 'What type of lunatic is this man Hitler to cause such an upheaval in our lives?'

10.00am (11.00am), POLISH POST OFFICE, HEVELIUSPLATZ, DANZIG
The defenders of the Polish Post Office are forced to surrender. Six have been killed in the fighting and another six are mortally wounded. Four others have managed to escape. The rest are going to be shot as *francs-tireurs*.

10.15am, WHITEHALL
With the news of the German invasion of Poland confirmed, the Defence Policy Plans Committee of the Cabinet decide on the total mobilisation of the British armed forces.

10.15am, CITY OF LONDON
'We have just heard that the Free City of Danzig has just returned to the Reich. If this is true there is no more to say. We are in it to the neck and over . . . the beastly and disgusting machinery of war is slowly turning, and I expect we will be in full blast almost immediately. Well, we have, we are told, brought it on ourselves by our evil and careless living, by our disregard of everything and everyone, our lack of thought, but I feel that we haven't had much of a chance! The last war, so pathetically labelled the war to end war; what did it bring to either side? Nothing of value, only a legacy of misery and uncertainty. And what of this one – will it really be as bad as we are led to believe? Can't any of us hope for some future? It seems not.' (Vivienne Hall)

At the end of his speech to the Reichstag on 1 September 1939, the deputies 'declare their unshakeable loyalty to the Fuehrer in the name of the German people'.

The beginning of Blitzkrieg. *Men of the German 76th Motorised Infantry Regiment attacking the village of Lichnowy, 10.00am, Friday, 1 September 1939.*

10.30am, Elysée Palace, Paris
The French Council of Ministers meet. They agree to ask the National Assembly for a declaration of war and for a vote of funds to fight it. Foreign minister Georges Bonnet then meets with Polish ambassador Juliusz Lukasiewicz and tells him, without going into specifics, 'France will fulfil all her obligations.'

10.30am, Broadcasting House, Langham Place
In the day's first news bulletin, the BBC reports the German invasion of Poland.

10.30am, Foreign Office, Whitehall
Oliver Harvey, private secretary to Lord Halifax, hears that the chiefs of staff want to declare tonight, 'and get at Germany as soon as possible'. By 6pm, Harvey learns, 'the children will have been evacuated'.

Foreign Secretary Lord Halifax receives Polish ambassador Count Edward Raczynski. The ambassador tells Halifax that German troops have crossed the frontier at a number of places. Polish towns have also been bombed. Raczynski also tells the Foreign Secretary that, in his opinion, British should now implement its guarantee to his country. Halifax replies cautiously. Provided the facts are as stated he does not suppose the Government will differ from the Polish ambassador's conclusion.

11.00am (12.00pm), Reich Chancellery, Berlin
Hitler returns after delivering his speech to the Reichstag. He is exhausted and bathed in sweat. He takes a hot bath and Dr Morrell prescribes him an Ultraseptyl for the relief of inflammation.

11.00am, Phoenix Theatre, Charing Cross Road
The cast of Noël Coward's two new plays, *This Happy Breed* and *Present Laughter*, due to open in just over a week's time, assemble

French premier Edouard Daladier (third from the right, holding a cigarette) *and his ministers emerge from the Elysée Palace, 1 September 1939. They have decided on general mobilisation, and have just heard that Italy will not be joining the war on Germany's side.*

on the stage. They have known that, if war came, the plays would not open. But, 'like everybody else, they had been hoping all along for a miracle to happen'. Now they all say goodbye to each other and make 'cheerful false prophecies for the future'.

11.00am, BISHOP'S STORTFORD, HERTFORDSHIRE
Moyra Charlton motors in from Takeley to have her car oiled and greased. She finds the town 'is very crowded and glum with news that has just come through that Germany has bombed Poland. They started at 5.30 this morning. Oh, that insufferable Hitler.'

11.00–11.40am, TEDDINGTON
'Dull morning, bright eleven o'clock. Dull again 11.40. German Embassy in London burnt their secret papers. I should say they need to – they must be pretty damning evidence of Hitler's diabolic intentions.' (Helena Mott)

11.00am (12.00pm), ADLON HOTEL, UNTER DEN LINDEN, BERLIN
American radio correspondent Max Jordan is in the Adlon bar at the table with a group of Germans. All are less-than-enthusiastic Nazis. One, an officer on the general staff, tells Jordan that the invasion of Poland this morning is just 'the beginning of World War II'. Another, a countess whose husband is in von Ribbentrop's ministry, is 'almost beside herself'. Without bothering to keep her voice down, she tells the American, 'Oh, if the British would only come tonight and destroy this whole city! Smash everything and us, too! What would it matter, if only these mad dogs could be stopped!'

11.00am (12.00pm), REICH CHANCELLERY, BERLIN
Outside the Chancellery there is a crowd of only fifty or sixty Berliners. There are a few shouts from them for the Fuehrer to come out on the balcony. Hitler does not appear, but two windows

away, in a part of the building being decorated, three painters in white caps lean out of the window and stare inanely at the crowd.

11.30am, OXFORD STREET, LONDON

Fashion writer Florence Speed sees newspaper placards announcing the German invasion of Poland. 'For half a second' she feels relieved, but then full realisation of what it means begins to sink in.

11.30am, 10 DOWNING STREET, WHITEHALL

The Cabinet meets. Chamberlain tells his ministers that they are meeting under 'the gravest possible conditions ... the event against which we had fought so long and so earnestly had come upon us. But our consciences are clear, and there could be no possible question now where our duty lies.' The Cabinet orders initial preparations for war to be put in operation. Among them are the decentralisation of Smithfield meat and Billingsgate fish markets.

11.30am, BOLTON TOWN HALL, LANCASHIRE

A woman passer-by has just heard the news that Hitler has invaded Poland. She tells an observer from Mass Observation: 'Well, I hope we knock hell out of him now. They said he couldn't start a war. You don't know what to expect when a madman is at the head of affairs.'

12.00pm, BOLTON

A group of building workers discuss the news from Poland. All are agreed that 'Hitler is a villain.' One of them believes, 'There won't be a scrap of Germany left after the war. All the countries will get a bit.' Another agrees, 'Yes, this treaty will be worse than Versailles.' But one of them keeps reiterating, 'But the German people don't want war, we must help them to get rid of Hitler.'

12.00pm, RADIOLYMPIA, OLYMPIA EXHIBITION HALL
A Mickey Mouse cartoon is being televised. Mickey, imitating Greta Garbo, has just said, 'Ah tink ah go home,' but now, without warning, the screens have gone blank.

12.00pm, GOODWOOD GOLF COURSE
Alfred Duff Cooper, who resigned from the Cabinet over Munich last September, has finished a round of golf. In the bar, the club secretary calmly tells him that 'Hitler started on Poland this morning.' To Duff Cooper the news comes as a relief. Back home in Bognor, he receives a message that the Commons will be meeting at 6pm this evening. 'In pretty good spirits', he then enjoys 'an excellent luncheon of lobster and cold grouse', washed down with Montrachet 1924 and Château Yquem 1921.

12.00pm, BBC TELEVISION STUDIOS, ALEXANDRA PALACE
Val Gielgud, the Head of Drama, is rehearsing James Mason and the rest of the cast of Somerset Maugham's *The Circle*. It is due to be broadcast live on Sunday night. The telephone rings, and Gielgud learns that, due to the 'emergency', the television service has been suspended.

12.00pm, CITY OF LONDON
'Rumours, posters announcing "Poland attacked by Germany". Rumours of the bombing of Warsaw with 3,000 casualties. God, what a world to live in. The highest drama in films and plays about the last war is not exaggerated. The sight of a newspaper brings a rush to read it, newspaper men are running round the streets, reaping a harvest, everyone feels sick but we are making even more jokes about the whole business. Here we are stuck in the City with very little chance of getting home as the evacuation will, I suppose, be in full swing all day. Someone wished me a happy month, this 1st September!!' (Vivienne Hall)

12.00pm (1.00pm), POLSKIE RADIO, WARSAW
President of the Republic Ignace Moscicki broadcasts to the Polish people. He tells them that war with Germany has broken out.

12.00pm (1.00pm), ZYRARDOW, WARSAW DISTRICT
Zbigniew Leon listens on a primitive wireless set to his president's broadcast. It comes as a real shock to Zbigniew and the others listening. They feel numb and the general mood is sombre and tense.

12.00pm (1.00pm), ADLON HOTEL, BERLIN
American correspondent Virginia Cowles with her friend Jane Leslie is on a flying visit to the German capital. Virginia bluntly asks a desk clerk how he feels about a world war. Virginia is astonished at the man's reply. 'What do you mean, a world war? Poland is Germany's affair. What's it got to with anyone else?'

12.05pm, PRINCE'S DOCK, THE CLYDE
SS *Athenia*, a 13,500-ton ship of the Donaldson Line, is about to leave the Clyde. She is making her way first to Belfast, and then to Liverpool before crossing the Atlantic to Montreal. On board at present are 735 people, including 315 crew. There are 143 Americans among the passengers. As the ship leaves dock, New Yorker Belle Maranov hears shipyard workers shout out, 'Cowards! Cowards!'

12.15pm (1.15pm), BROACASTING HOUSE, BERLIN-CHARLOTTENBURG
NBC correspondent Max Jordan is in the midst of a heated argument with the German radio censor. In his broadcast to New York, Jordan was going to say, 'Hitler today spoke to the Reichstag almost exactly in the same vein as the Kaiser did to that body twenty-five years ago', but the censor has cut it. He appeals to Dr Karl Boehmer of the Propaganda Ministry. But Boehmer is adamant. He asks Jordan how he can compare 'Hitler to the Kaiser, to a Kaiser who

suffered defeat?' Jordan tells the foreign press chief that it is his honest opinion. But Boehmer is unimpressed: 'I don't care how honest it is. You can't say it. This time it isn't a Kaiser! This time we won't crack!'

12.30pm, VICTORIA STATION, LONDON
A party of elementary schoolchildren have just arrived at the terminus. There are about 200 people to see them off, the vast majority women. The children are belting out 'The Chestnut Tree' as they pass down the platform. The sound of their singing fills the station. But the mothers watching the children are quiet, and although some smile, there is a good deal of wiping of eyes with handkerchiefs.

12.30pm (1.30pm), ADLON HOTEL, BERLIN
Virginia Cowles and Jane Leslie are having lunch in the hotel's courtyard with Sir George Ogilvie Forbes of the British Embassy. Virginia sees that at the next table there are a group of German officials. They stare curiously at Sir George and seem perplexed at the diplomat's smiling and impervious expression. He has received no news yet about the British declaration of war, but it is expected at any moment.

12.30pm, THE IVY, ST MARTIN'S LANE
Noël Coward, with friends, lunches at The Ivy as usual. They are all downcast by the news of the German invasion of Poland, which has meant the abandonment of Coward's two new plays. But to tide themselves over, at lunch they joke and gossip becoming 'over-bright and jocular'. Coward is expecting to be employed in propaganda work, possibly with the French.

12.35pm, VICTORIA STATION, LONDON
Pupils and teachers from Buckingham Gate School arrive ready for evacuation. One of the older girls is carrying a banner, on which is

written 'L.C.C. Buckingham Gate'. The children are greeted by their parents as they march in twos into the terminus. They are carrying bulging shoe-bags, and have haversacks on their backs. Some of the children have paper parcels and one is clutching a net bag full of tennis balls. All the children are carrying their gas masks in cardboard boxes slung round their necks with string. They, and their teachers, all have red and white LCC armlets and some of them have other pieces of cloth giving their name and school sewn or pinned on their sleeves as well. The children are mostly smiling and look happy. They are quite unselfconscious. Many are looking round for their parents, but there is no attempt to break ranks to meet up with them.

The parents, too, do not try to butt in on the procession that is now being waved on by the police. Children and parents call out to each other; 'Ta-ta', 'Good-bye, dear', 'Cheerio, Mum', 'Bye-Bye', but there is no stopping for a farewell kiss and embrace. The teachers are mostly smiling too. Occasionally, some stop for a second or so to reassure anxious parents. 'They'll be all right,' says one to a mother as the children pass through the barrier. As the last children go through, the police close the barrier. Parents move up and stand close against the railings. The children have stopped near the other end of the platform and are sitting on seats or their cases. They wave to their parents, who wave back at them. 'Well, we can't do any more,' says one mother. 'Thank God they've gone.'

2.00pm, FOREIGN OFFICE, WHITEHALL

A telegram is received from Sir Howard Kennard, the British ambassador in Warsaw. In it he includes the request from Polish foreign minister Colonel Beck that the RAF should mount 'some military action from the air this afternoon'.

2.00pm (3.00pm), UNITED STATES EMBASSY, WARSAW

Correspondent Edward Beattie is at his country's embassy when the sirens sound again. The sky is now deep blue with occasional high-piled banks of cloud. For the first time, Beattie sees the German raiders. There about sixty of them, and he is struck by the beauty of them as the sun silvers them against the blue sky. Puffs of AA bursts show white around them. Now the formation breaks up, and the German 'planes swing singly or in pairs in great circles over Warsaw. Three or four Polish fighters appear and chase ineffectually after them. While Beattie hears some heavy muffled explosions from across the Vistula, no bombs are dropped on the city centre. An embassy official comes up with an explanation. The German machines are just reconnaissance aircraft. This afternoon, the diplomat tells Beattie, they are pinpointing and photographing objectives for future raids.

2.30pm, 10 DOWNING STREET
At Chamberlain's invitation, Winston Churchill, out of office since 1929, arrives at the Prime Minister's residence. Chamberlain tells Churchill that he sees no hope of war being averted. He proposes to form a small War Cabinet of ministers without departmental responsibilities to conduct it. Chamberlain says that while the Labour Party is not willing to share in a national coalition government, he has hopes that the Liberals will join. Chamberlain then swallows his pride, and invites Churchill to become a member of the War Cabinet. Without comment, Churchill agrees, and the two men begin to discuss 'men and measures'. Churchill urges the Prime Minister that Anthony Eden should also be given a cabinet post. Chamberlain agrees. 'Yes, certainly, one of the major offices of state,' he tells Churchill.

2.30pm, THREADNEEDLE STREET, CITY OF LONDON
An observer from Mass Observation asks two workmen what they think about the crisis. The first tells him, 'Berlin was never bombed before, but it will sure get it now. It'll get a taste of what we got. No one is getting settled with these affairs. You can't settle.' While

the other says, 'People are fed up with it that they want to have done with it. Get it over.'

2.30pm, BOLTON

A Mass Observation observer hears two women what they would like to do to Hitler. One says, 'I would just like to get Hitler on this field at the top of the street just to give him some punishment. First thing I would do, saw his feet at the ankles, sharpen the shin bones and force him down into the earth, down to his shoulders, then I would just hammer the top of his head with my big saucepan until I'd driven him down out of sight.' But her friend says, 'I wouldn't give you that chance. I should take him on the same field, warn all the women of the estate to come and see the fun, then I would strip him naked and pluck every hair from his body, from head to toe.'

3.00pm (4.00pm), ADLON HOTEL, BERLIN

Virginia Cowles finds out what more of the hotel staff think about war with Poland. A waiter tells her, 'The Poles provoked Germany too far. Now they can pay the price.' When Virginia asks him about what happens if Britain and France intervene, he replies, 'Who says we are going to fight Great Britain and France? Poland is no one's concern but Germany's. We couldn't sit back and let Poles shoot down German women and children. Why should anyone else interfere?' A receptionist agrees. But an elderly porter, when asked if he thinks it will result in a world war, tells Virginia, 'My God, I hope not. I had four years in the last one and that was enough.'

4.00pm, TAKELEY

Moyra Charlton and her parents are spending the afternoon preparing their house for war. They empty the attic of junk in case of incendiary bombs, and fit black discs onto the sidelights of the

95

Crowds in Downing Street, 1 September 1939. A diarist recorded 'most people fairly resigned and determined, but desperately disappointed. False cheerfulness and jokes'.

The changing of the guard. Irish Guardsmen in khaki service dress take over from their ceremonially attired comrades at Buckingham Palace, 1 September 1939.

family cars. Moyra has volunteered for the First Aid Nursing Yeomanry [FANY], but up to now has had no orders from them. But she is going to help out at home when the evacuees arrive. Taking a quick bath, she ponders on her hatred for Hitler, 'for bringing this terrible thing on us all. How could he do it?'

4.00pm, BOLTON

At a mill in the town, some of the younger hands get their calling-up papers. They change into uniform immediately and then line up to get their pay. The other mill hands give the lads, the oldest of whom is only twenty-four, a hearty send-off. They depart, 'with a mixture of bravado and fear on their faces'.

4.00–4.30pm, BOBROWA

'Precisely at four in the afternoon we crossed the Polish frontier at Bobrowa. It was a strange feeling to leave the last German farmhouse behind. I have crossed many frontiers in my life to enjoy the pleasures of travel. This time I was crossing to do battle with an enemy. We reached Bobrowa at 4.30 in the afternoon. The population was unreliable. In the evening ... after a short halt for a wash we went into position at Zsarski with twelve vehicles. Zsarski is a larger village so far untouched by the army. Crucifixes bear witness to fanatical Catholicism.

'The Polish territory we were invading was a purely Polish district, which had belonged to Russia before the Great War. So we had to be prepared for anything.

'We are reinforcements and at a distance from the main body. Lorry drivers keeping in touch with the forward troops are being sniped by civilians. One wonders how these people can aim, let alone shoot, when they can hardly see out of their eyes for dirt.' (Corporal Wilhelm Krey, 13th Artillery Observation Battery, German Army)

5.00pm, FOREIGN OFFICE, WHITEHALL
Lord Halifax telephones Paris. He suggests to his French opposite number Georges Bonnet that as a gesture Britain and France withdraw their ambassadors from Berlin. Bonnet demurs saying, 'A hope remains of saving peace and I do not wish to destroy that hope.'

5.45pm, FOREIGN OFFICE, WHITEHALL
Sir Nevile Henderson at the embassy in Berlin is telephoned with instructions to deliver 'a severe warning' to the German Government. Sir Nevile is told too that the next stage will be an ultimatum with a time limit or an immediate declaration of war. He is instructed to seek a meeting with Foreign Minister von Ribbentrop as soon as possible to hand over the warning. Sir Nevile telephones the Foreign Ministry to arrange an immediate meeting, but is put off until 9.30pm (10.30pm Berlin time). In the meantime, Henderson gets in contact with the United States Embassy. America has had no ambassador in Berlin since President Roosevelt withdrew Hugh Wilson last November in disgust over *Kristallnacht*. Now, Sir Nevile speaks with Chargé d'Affaires Kirk. He asks the American diplomat to take over responsibility for British affairs in the event of war. Both men now realise that this is only a matter of time.

6.00pm, BROADCASTING HOUSE
The BBC tells listeners that it is merging its national and regional programmes and will in future broadcast only one programme – the Home Service. The mobilisation of Air Raid Precautions personnel is also announced in the news this evening.

6.00pm, HOUSE OF COMMONS, WESTMINSTER
The Speaker arrives and prayers are said. The House's chaplain adds one of his own today, 'Let us this day pray for wisdom and courage to defend the right.'

6.00pm (7.00pm), ADLON HOTEL, UNTER DEN LINDEN, BERLIN
Air-raid sirens sound the warning. Virginia Cowles's first thought
is that it is the Royal Air Force coming over. From her balcony she
sees cars stopping and people running in every direction. People
hurry into the hotel lobby from the street to find shelter. An elderly
German asks Virginia if she has been in an air raid before. She tells
him that she was bombed several times by German 'planes during
the Spanish Civil War. He relapses into silence.

6.00pm (7.00pm), ESPLANADE HOTEL, BERLIN
Jack Raleigh is working in the *Chicago Tribune* bureau as the
alert sounds. Not relishing the thought of being buried alive, he
decides not to go to the shelter in the hotel's sub-basement. He
carries on working. Raleigh hears two air-raid wardens talking.
One tells the other that this is no practice alarm. A Luftwaffe
officer has told the warden that seventy Polish bombers are on
their way to Berlin. Raleigh carries on working, but confesses to
himself that he wants to hear 'the All Clear signal more than
anything else in life'.

6.00pm (7.00pm), BERLIN-STEGLITZ
Ruth Andreas-Friederich is having tea with a judge who has been
pensioned off by the Nazis. Both Ruth and her host loathe Hitler
and his regime, and they are speculating on what will now happen.
Then suddenly they hear 'a strange sound . . . up and down, down
and up, a long drawn howl'. It is the air-raid warning. They quickly
go downstairs to cellar

6.15pm, FOREIGN OFFICE, WHITEHALL
Lord Halifax has just finished composing his statement for the
House of Lords at 6.30pm. Walking over to Parliament, the deeply
religious Foreign Secretary asks Oliver Harvey, 'How can a man
be so wicked to launch this?'

6.15pm, HOUSE OF COMMONS

The Prime Minister and Labour's acting leader Arthur Greenwood enter the chamber together and receive a cheer from MPs. Chamberlain rises immediately. In a voice full of emotion he reminds MPs, 'About eighteen months ago in this House I prayed that the responsibility might not fall upon me to ask this country to accept the awful arbitrament of war.' The Prime Minister then tells the House how the Government has made it crystal clear to Nazis that, if they use force, then, 'we were resolved to oppose by them force'. Raising his voice and striking the despatch box in front of him with a clenched fist, Chamberlain continues, 'We shall stand at the bar of history knowing that the responsibility for this terrible catastrophe lies on the shoulders of one man. The German Chancellor has not hesitated to plunge the world into misery to serve his own senseless ambition.'

The Prime Minister now explains the course of events over the last few days. When he slowly reads the text of the warning note that Sir Nevile Henderson has been instructed to hand to von Ribbentrop, it is clear that Chamberlain is 'in real moral agony'. There is a feeling of deep sympathy for him in the House. Recovering, the Prime Minister ends on a defiant note: 'Now it only remains for us to set our teeth and to enter upon this struggle, which we have so earnestly endeavoured to avoid, with determination to see it through to the end. We shall enter it with a clear conscience, with the support of the Dominions and the British Empire, and with the moral approval of the greater part of the world.'

Making his way to the Savoy Hotel for dinner, Duff Cooper thinks that Chamberlain was unimpressive. And fellow anti-appeaser Harold Nicolson is afraid that, 'lobby opinion is rather defeatist and they all realize that we have in front of us a very terrible task'.

6.30pm (7.30pm), HOTEL EUROPEJSKI, WARSAW

In the courtyard of the hotel, diners sit at tables lit by well-shaded lights and eat their meals just 'as usual in the peaceful summer air'. Warsaw has had seven air-raid warnings today, but there has been little excitement and no bombing of the city centre.

6.45pm (7.45pm), BERLIN-STEGLITZ

The 'All Clear' sounds. It has been a practice alarm. Ruth and her fellow shelterers emerge from the cellar. Nobody says anything 'about this new experience; it's disagreeable and almost makes us feel as if we'd disgraced ourselves'.

7.47pm, BRITAIN

The blackout comes into force tonight.

9.30pm, SAVOY HOTEL GRILL, THE STRAND

Duff Cooper and his wife Lady Diana are dining with Churchill, his son-in-law Duncan Sandys, and Lord Lloyd. Churchill confides to Lady Diana that this afternoon Chamberlain asked him to join the War Cabinet. He also tells her that he will try to get her husband a government post. But Duff Cooper is not at all sure that he wants to serve again under Chamberlain. Or indeed if the Prime Minister wants him back.

9.30pm (10.30pm), FOREIGN MINISTRY, WILHEMSTRASSE, BERLIN

Sir Nevile Henderson arrives to deliver the written British warning. Von Ribbentrop receives it without comment, but tells the ambassador that sole blame rests with the Poles. It was they who mobilised first, and invaded German territory. French ambassador Robert Coulondre has also arrived with a similar communication from Paris. Both men are told by von Ribbentrop that their notes will be submitted to Hitler for a response. When von Ribbentrop takes him the notes, the Fuehrer is derisory. 'We will now see if they come to Poland's aid,' he tells his staff. Hitler is supremely confident that 'they'll chicken out again'.

10.00pm, SS ATHENIA OFF BLACK HEAD, BELFAST
136 more passengers, including sixty-seven Americans, have just joined the ship. The *Athenia* weighs anchor and sets course for Liverpool.

10.00pm, SAVOY HOTEL, THE STRAND
In the blackout, the Coopers leave the hotel. They cannot find a taxi, but the Duke of Westminster, the fabulously rich 'Bendor', offers them a lift to Victoria in his Rolls-Royce. As they drive to the station, the Duke inveighs against the Jews and rejoices that Britain is not at war with Germany. Hitler, 'Bendor' tells the Coopers, 'knows that we are his best friends'. Duff Cooper, whose violent temper is notorious, explodes and tells the Duke that he hopes the Fuehrer will 'soon find out that we are his most implacable and remorseless enemies'.

10.00pm, WORTHING
'Blackouts have started – no one must show a glimmer of light anywhere. Cars have the merest glimmer left and have to be painted white in front, rear or on running boards – the roads have a white centre line and the kerb whitened.' (Joan Strange)

10.00pm (11.00pm), FOREIGN MINISTRY, BERLIN
Some foreign correspondents, including NBC's Max Jordan, are hanging about the press department, waiting for any news. They discuss the announcement that has just been made, forbidding Germans to listen to foreign radio broadcasts. Correspondents may still listen, and earlier today Jordan heard a broadcast on the BBC of evacuees, all cheerfully singing 'The Lambeth Walk', leaving Waterloo Station.

10.30pm, TAKELEY

Moyra Charlton is getting ready for bed. The family home is blacked out and the Charltons 'move like unhappy wraiths in a queer half light'. Before turning in, Moyra brings her diary up to date: 'Within the next few days we will be at war. It is still even now hardly believable. I think I shall be scared stiff of an air raid. Anyhow, if we live through it, it will be "copy" for the budding author – seeing life with a vengeance, and perhaps death too. Surely a nation has never gone to war so grim and disillusioned and coldly resentful as we are now.'

10.30pm (11.30pm), FOREIGN MINISTRY, BERLIN

Max Jordan and some other correspondents are still waiting around in the press department to see if there is any hope that peace can be preserved. A diplomat tells them, off the record: 'Yes, there is still hope, but it's as when a mouse nears a trap – the only hope is that the trap won't work!'

11.00pm (12.00 midnight), BERLIN-STEGLITZ

Anti-Nazi Ruth Andreas-Friederich is on her way home from a meeting with like-minded friends. She reflects on the blacked-out city: 'On our way we see stars over Berlin for the first time – not paling sadly behind gaudy electric signs, but sparkling with clear solemnity. The moon casts a milky gleam over the roofs of the town. Not a spark of electric light falls upon the street.'

11.30pm, FOREIGN OFFICE, WHITEHALL

Lord Halifax returns from seeing Chamberlain. He tells his staff that the Prime Minister has said that nothing can now be done before 9.30 next morning. The Foreign Secretary himself then decides to go to bed.

CHAPTER 3

Saturday,
2 September 1939

Introduction: resumé of 1 September

As the full force of the German *Blitzkrieg* hit Poland, her allies
Britain and France remained in a state of uneasy peace. Only the
day before (31 August), a poll in Britain had shown that a large
majority of people still thought Hitler was bluffing. Now the mood
had changed. With the BBC's morning bulletins announcing news
of the German invasion, the commonest remarks heard were, 'Let's
get started,' or 'Let us strike and get right into Germany'.

Mass Observation diarists recorded their own emotions and those
of friends and family. A twenty-five-year-old woman wrote: 'Had
been expecting it. Whole world turned upside down. Everybody
grey and serious, but making cynical jokes. Didn't sleep very well.'
A seventeen-year-old boy noted, 'All decided very little hope left.
All very worried. Go on working as usual. Parents have anti-German
outburst.'

Throughout Britain's town and cities, the evacuation of schoolchildren and others took place. There was a good deal of forced

cheerfulness, and also a lot of tears, but for many children it was all a glorious lark.

French radio stations announced the news of the German invasion of Poland at 10am on 1 September. Already towns, cities and localities were being evacuated. In Paris, Simone de Beauvoir saw 'an endless procession of cars crammed with luggage and children'. She noted, 'the disturbing nature of the news is not overemphasized, but no one takes a hopeful line, either.' Most French people were only too conscious of the fact that their country had been invaded by Germans three times in the last 125 years, and that the last time France had lost nearly 1,400,000 dead. At railway stations, conscripts, on the way to rejoin their regiments, mingled with refugees. At the Quai d'Orsay, Foreign Minister Georges Bonnet persisted in his increasingly futile efforts to preserve the peace by pushing for the conference proposed by the Italians. Like many Parisians, Simone de Beauvoir found sleep difficult that night, experiencing, 'a feeling of unfathomable horror'.

In Berlin, anti-Nazi Ruth Andreas-Friederich recorded the events of 1 September in her diary:

'At 4.45 German troops crossed the Polish frontier on a broad front. The government has popped up with an abundance of new decrees. Streets, shops and dwellings to be blacked out. Compulsory air-raid duty. As of today listening to foreign radio stations is forbidden under severe penalties.'

Many Germans believed that the invasion of Poland would be only a 'localised police action', and that Britain and France would not fulfil their obligations and go to war. 'They are afraid to fight Germany,' a Berlin policeman told US Embassy official William Russell. Hitler's speech to the Reichstag was a 'weak one', according to former ambassador Ulrich von Hassell, received with only 'official enthusiasm'. At night, Berlin's restaurants, cafés and beer halls were all packed, but many Berliners feared that the Poles might attempt a bombing raid.

The Polish air force began 1 September with 392 serviceable aircraft. Facing them were 1941 'planes of the Luftwaffe. The Germans flew 2700 sorties over Poland in the course of the day, attacking airfields and bombing over 100 cities and towns. The ancient town of Ciechanow was attacked three times; twenty-two civilians including one child and four soldiers were killed and over fifty injured. In the capital, Ed Beattie noted, 'Warsaw was taking the start of the war with the same stolidity and the same fatalism she had shown in the summer months of tension.' At the same time, Poles waited impatiently for some positive action from Britain and France. 'Do they know in the west how quickly and hard they must attack?' a newspaper editor asked Beattie. 'We can do our part with help, but there must be two fronts.'

12.00 midnight, BERLIN–COLOGNE TRAIN

Virginia Cowles and her friend Jane Leslie are making their way to Holland before the borders close. They decide to find out what their travelling companions think of the situation, and what they believe Britain and France will do. 'Germany is only taking police action,' one *Hausfrau* assures the two Americans. 'No one will go to war for that.' A musician from Duesseldorf agrees. 'After we cut Poland's throat,' he tells them, drawing his finger across his own throat, 'we'll settle down to peace again.' Everybody laughs, and Virginia and Jane marvel that everyone is so confident that Hitler is going to pull it off again.

1.00am (2.00am), POLSKIE RADIO BUILDING, WARSAW

Patrick Maitland is just finishing a broadcast on the first day's fighting. Earlier tonight, he had dinner with Hugh Carleton Greene and American correspondent Alex Small. To take their minds off the war, the three men discussed classical Greek literature. Leaving his two friends, on the way to the studio Patrick passed cheerful Polish soldiers having a last fling before they set off for the front.

There seem to be hundreds of girls about, 'flirting, ogling in the moonlight', with the soldiers.

4.45am (5.45am), BOLESLAWIEC, GERMAN-POLISH BORDER
Men of the *SS Leibstandarte Adolf Hitler,* Hitler's own bodyguard troops serving with the army's XIII Corps, have just arrived in the village and are pulling Poles and Jews from their homes. They shoot dead the father of Franciszek Lizon at his workbench. An SS trooper also shoots elderly Antoni Czubowicz in the back at point-blank range.

7.00am (8.00am), CIECHANOW, NEAR EAST-PRUSSIAN BORDER
German 'planes again bomb the town; twenty-one civilians are killed and thirty-six wounded, including nine women and four children.

9.00am, LIVERPOOL
Popular author Cecil Roberts is leaving for London after receiving a summons from the War Office last night. The weather over Liverpool is grey and overcast as Roberts starts his journey. He is soon held up by 'a pathetic procession of schoolchildren led by their teachers'. They are all tagged and are carrying drinking mugs, gas masks and hand baggage. Roberts was a war correspondent on the Western Front in the last war. Today, he reflects on seeing the evacuees: 'So this was modern war in the progressive age, children were in it as much as the men in trenches. There was no "front" any more.'

9.00am (10.00am), STETTINER STATION, BERLIN
US embassy clerk William Russell is seeing off a Canadian friend. In an effort to cheer up his friend, Russell says, 'Maybe it will blow over. Maybe you'll be back in a few days.' But the Canadian replies, 'I wouldn't come back. If we don't keep our word this time I would be ashamed to be seen here.'

107

9.00am, Melton, Suffolk

Author and psychologist Anthony Weymouth and his family are just finishing breakfast. They listen to the news, but find it puzzling, 'Germany is invading Poland and in spite of our guarantee we seem to be doing nothing.' Nonetheless, the threat of war hangs over the Weymouths' holiday home. Anthony believes, 'Nothing but a miracle or the breaking of our word can prevent us being at war in a few hours, at most.' But the tension lifts, if only momentarily, when his daughter Yvonne asks, 'Of course, Hitler would be much better if he were married, wouldn't he, Pop?'

9.30am, Tolleshunt D'Arcy, Essex

Popular crime writer Margery Allingham is just setting about assembling 'about three hundredweight of depressing books'. She is going to make a wall of them halfway across the breakfast-room windows to offset the effects of bomb blast. Her friend and neighbour Christine is furious with her. She tells Margery, 'If you go on like that, you'll *make* it happen.'

10.00am (11.00am), British Embassy, Warsaw

Patrick Maitland has come to the Embassy to see if there is any news. He finds the place cluttered with packing cases. Papers and files are being burnt. It is obvious that preparations for evacuation are already taking place. 'Peter' Norton, the highly efficient and practical wife of the Embassy's Counsellor, has managed to scrounge a lorry from the Polish Army for the move. Meanwhile, in the Chancery, the *Times* correspondent comes across a typist still typing out menu cards for a dinner that ambassador Sir Howard Kennard is due to give next week.

10.30am, Piers Court, Stinchcombe, Gloucestershire

Novelist Evelyn Waugh is awaiting the arrival of the evacuees expected yesterday. As a precaution, he has removed all the valuable objects from the rooms that he is going to let them have. Except for an hour and a half's delay on the telephone to London, Waugh thinks every-thing else seems normal today. He fills in his time waiting for the evacuees by writing to offer his services for the war effort.

11.00am, HUDDERSFIELD, YORKSHIRE
Master Butcher George Gothard and his wife Marjorie are converting their garage into an air-raid shelter. With the help of neighbours, they dig holes in the garden to fill protective sacks with dirt. Marjorie acknowledges, 'It is very hard work, but everybody is willing to help and [her sons] Guy who is six and George Junior nearly five are quite enjoying themselves and think it is great fun.' Despite everyone's efforts, Marjorie knows, 'We shall have to work many days before there are enough sacks filled, and we are having very warm weather, which makes it harder still.'

11.00am, PIERS COURT, STINCHCOMBE, GLOUCESTERSHIRE
Evelyn Waugh is told that due to an administrative error, no evacuees are coming to him today. And yet, he reflects, last night on the radio it was announced that 'the evacuation was working like clockwork'.

12.00pm (1.00pm), HOTEL EUROPEJSKI, WARSAW
US ambassador Anthony J. Drexel Biddle Jr and his family are having lunch in the hotel's courtyard restaurant. German 'planes are over the city, but the ambassador notes that his fellow guests evince nothing more than 'calm interest'. And the waiters, 'aside from an occasional glance upwards to note the progress of the aerial action', continue to serve as if an air raid is an everyday occurrence.

12.00pm (1.00pm), MINISTRY OF PROPAGANDA, BERLIN
An official statement is released to the press and foreign correspondents. It reiterates that Germany is confining her bombing in Poland to purely military targets.

12.00pm (1.00pm), WARSAW

Patrick Maitland and other correspondents leave the capital to see how the city's suburbs have fared in the bombing. In one village, a blazing cottage stands alone. A peasant woman sits outside it. She is cradling a dead child. The woman just stares apathetically at the flames. She has given up trying to put them out with pails of water. Her husband is dead, machine-gunned on his land. Her son is also dead.

1.00pm (2.00pm), GERMAN-POLISH BORDER

Austrian soldier Wilhelm Prueller hurriedly jots down in his diary: '14.00: we've climbed a big hill. Hours it took. In front of us the guns boom, also light machine gun-fire. For the past two hours they've been under fire from our artillery and trench mortars, but they wouldn't give in. We're lying ready in a wood. Banging of rifle shots. We learn there are five civilians behind our back shooting at us. I go with two others, and in five minutes these five civilians have had it.'

1.00pm, BOLTON

A women tells an observer from Mass Observation, 'My nerves have completely gone; we've been waiting for a whole year, not knowing if there'll be a war or not. I want a knock at Hitler.'

1.30pm (2.30pm), GERMAN-POLISH BORDER

During a brief lull in the fighting, Wilhelm Prueller catches up with his war diary, '14.30: the first Polish reconnaissance aircraft. He shot a few rounds at us and disappeared. Our flak saw him, shot at him, and I hope, got him. The Poles seem to be well entrenched, but our artillery clears the way for us. Over hills and valleys, through burning villages we continue to attack. We take some civilians with us, and they have to carry our heavy things.'

2.00pm (3.00pm), RYBNIK, SILESIA
Polish soldiers of 12th Infantry Regiment surrender to the Germans. They are thrown to the ground by their captors and tanks are driven over them.

2.45pm, PARIS
New Zealander Geoffrey Cox, *Daily Express* correspondent in the French capital, is rushing to get to hear Premier Daladier's speech. He has been held up queuing for a gas mask from a stock that the British Embassy has made available for Britons in Paris. The chief of the volunteers distributing the masks is a bank clerk. Cox recalls that his manner has always verged on the obsequious. But, 'now, dressed in the alas none too brief authority which war confers', he has great pleasure in ordering about the correspondent and the others waiting for their masks.

2.00pm (3.00pm), TIVOLI GARDENS, COPENHAGEN
Impatient at Britain's delay in honouring her pledge to Poland, Ewan Butler, *The Times* correspondent in Berlin until the day before yesterday, comes up with a novel idea. He decides to launch his own propaganda raid on Germany. With a colleague, he buys several dozen balloons and then composes offensive messages to the Fuehrer'. These they attach to the balloons and launch them. There is a brisk breeze blowing and the two men see their missives bowling southwards towards the Reich.

2.30pm (3.30pm), FOREIGN MINISTRY, ROME
Count Ciano puts through a call to Lord Halifax in London. The Count tells the Foreign Secretary that he believes Hitler might yet agree to a five-power conference on the understanding of an immediate armistice being signed. Halifax tells his Italian opposite number, who has just also telephoned Georges Bonnet with the same news, that Britain cannot contemplate a conference with German troops

on Polish soil. They must withdraw before any negotiations can take place.

3.00pm, CHAMBER OF DEPUTIES, PARIS

Premier Edouard Daladier mounts the tribune. He first reads a message from President Lebrun, and then addresses the deputies and senators. He tells them that 'if measures of reconciliation are renewed, we are still ready to join them'. 'But,' Daladier continues, 'time presses. France and Britain will not stand by and witness the destruction of a friendly people . . .' The premier says that France must fulfil her obligations, because if she does not, then she would be 'despised, isolated and discredited, without allies and without support'. He warns them, 'At the cost of our honour we should purchase only a precarious, revocable peace and, tomorrow, when we had to fight, having lost the esteem of our Allies and of other nations, we should be nothing but an abject people, doomed to defeat and servitude.' Daladier finishes his speech by telling the parliamentarians, 'Our duty is to finish with aggression and violence. By peaceful means, if we still can, and we will keep on trying to that end. By using our force, if all moral decency and reason have disappeared from the aggressors.'

The premier is given a standing ovation as he leaves the tribune. There is a brief recess and then the Finance Committee approve the Government request for seventy billion francs of war credits to help finance France's military effort. Both houses then vote on the war credits. In the Senate, former premier Pierre Laval tries to speak. He demands that the Government work with Italy to keep the peace. He is shouted down. In the Chamber, Deputy Gaston Bergery calls for a secret session to debate on France going to war. He too is shouted down. Both houses vote on the war credits. They pass unanimously. Daladier considers this as good as a declaration of war, and decides it will not be necessary to seek an actual vote on going to war. But outside the Chamber, Verdun veteran and newspaper editor Emil Bure tells Geoffrey Cox, 'They are talking to the Italians, and hope to get a conference tomorrow. We will yet see a sell-out.'

3.00pm, St James's Park, London
Florence Speed notes that there is still no concrete news on what Britain and France intend to do. In the park, Florence finds it much quieter than usual. It dawns on her that, because of the evacuation, there are no children playing there.

3.00pm, 'Villa Volpone', South Hampstead
Critic James Agate brings his journal up to date: '3pm: Nothing yet. I hear that we are waiting for the evacuation of the children to be completed. No excitement. No flag-waving. Only, last night in the pubs, all the old war songs except "Tipperary".' Thinking back to the last war and the Treaty of Versailles, Agate wonders today, 'what the shades of Clemenceau and Foch are thinking'.

3.00pm, Teddington
'Dull, then bright but terribly oppressive, then dull and cloudy again but pleasantly breezy. 3pm: No news. So far *we* have heard nothing. That fool Hitler says that the present hostilities are not to be considered a state of War. It is merely to "rectify the Eastern Frontier". He has given his word (!!) to Roosevelt not to bomb civilian towns & has already bombed refugee train. Lord Halifax has had no reply from Hitler. It may be that Italy is trying for peace. Greenwood spoke well and for action. The only man worth his salt. Chamberlain shuffling as usual. Strange noise in studio – sounded like booing or anger while his speech was being read out.' (Helena Mott)

3.00pm (4.00pm), WARSAW

Patrick Maitland returns to the city. He finds that there is still no news of Britain and France honouring their pledges to Poland. He senses that the Poles are beginning to be badly shaken at the lack of any positive action by London and Paris. And his American colleague Ed Beattie is constantly being asked, 'are England and France going to sell us out too?'

4.00pm, WORTHING

'Worthing, being a safe zone, has had over 10,000 evacuees billeted on the inhabitants from London. On Saturday afternoon Schofield and I helped billet some Bermondsey blind people. We both felt how terrible it was that so much money, time and trouble was taken to help these poor, old, ill, blind people, while we send healthy, young, virile people to be killed.' (Joan Strange)

4.00pm (5.00pm), POLAND

'We couldn't think of sleep last night, we felt too insecure. Death might lurk anywhere. We drove all the men out of their hovels at the point of the bayonet. To call them dwellings would be going too far. I was lucky enough to get the job of searching all the inhabitants for arms. At the end of the job I shuddered at my own fingers. After the search we shut all the men in a large barn and posted a strong guard. We found no weapons. The Pole is a cowardly fanatic. This sounds like a contradiction in terms, but it is none the less true.

'The Pole' homes are almost all filthy and utterly neglected. Open a door to search for weapons and you meet a solid wall of stench. One's gas mask comes in useful when searching these houses. This afternoon the attack continued . . . in a nearby place twenty soldiers were murdered by the inhabitants. The order was given to set fire to all the villages. We are not putting up with any more nonsense from the Polès.' (Corporal Wilhelm Krey, 13th Artillery Observation Battery, German Army)

4.15pm, ELYSÉE PALACE, PARIS

Jean Zay, Daladier's thirty-five-year-old education minister, announces his intention of resigning his cabinet post to rejoin his regiment. His colleague, the pugnacious Minister of Finance, Paul Reynaud, is dead set against the Italian proposal for a five-power conference. It was first mooted two days ago, and Count Ciano's 'phone call to Bonnet an hour or so ago has breathed new life into it. Reynaud, in forthright language, tells the Council of Ministers, 'If we go crawling to Rome on our knees, we'll be docile sheep offering our necks to the butcher's knife. For one of two things might happen: either we'll be defeated without a war, or much worse, we shall have lost our honour without winning the peace. If there is still time left, the only way to avoid a slap on the face is to put up our fists instead of turning the cheek.'

4.15pm, 10 DOWNING STREET

Chamberlain and his ministers meet. They are told of the proposal from Mussolini for a five-power conference to try and settle the current crisis. But the British attitude is that there must be a withdrawal of German forces from Polish soil before any such conference can take place. This they are all agreed upon. The ministers also discuss a French proposal to postpone sending an ultimatum to the Germans for another forty-eight hours. The British chiefs of staff are firmly against such a delay. So too is Secretary of State for War Leslie Hore-Belisha, who thinks any delay 'might result in breaking the unity of the country' as 'public opinion was against yielding an inch'. He also thinks that Italy is acting in collusion with Germany and that various troop movements lend support to this view. Colonial Secretary Malcolm MacDonald agrees with the War Minister. Lord Halifax, however, still thinks the time limit should be extended to midnight on 3/4 September, 'if this would facilitate consideration of a conference'. But he is in a minority of one. The Cabinet decide that the ultimatum should expire at midnight tonight.

4.30pm, LIVERPOOL

The SS *Athenia* slips anchor and begins the hour-long run down the Mersey on the first stage of her 2,625-mile voyage to Canada. She is now carrying 1,102 passengers; 469 Canadians, 311 Americans, some 150 European refugees and the rest British and Irish citizens. Among the Europeans are thirty-four Germans, including a handful of Jews, escaping from persecution to seek a new life in North America. The *Athenia* is carrying a cargo of 880 tons, including 472 tons of bricks. There are also fifty pairs of curling stones and a batch of text-books for Toronto schoolchildren.

4.30pm, OLYMPIA EXHIBITION HALL, KENSINGTON

Anti-Nazi German Jewish refugee Eugen Spier has just been arrested at his flat by two plain-clothes Scotland Yard officers and brought here by car. No charge has been made against him and no judicial warrant for his arrest has been issued. The police officers, who arrived at Spier's flat just as he was writing to the Home Office to offer his services to the British Government, tell him that his arrest is 'required under Royal Prerogative'. He is mystified as to why he has been arrested.

5.00pm, BOLTON

A local dance-band leader tells an observer from Mass Observation, 'I've been calm all week, but yesterday I listened to the news bulletin and I got a bad dose of the jitters. I read somewhere that they're going to move London to Canada, and I can well believe it.'

5.00pm, NATIONAL GALLERY, TRAFALGAR SQUARE

The last of the Gallery's paintings have just left, evacuated to Aberystwyth. In view of the expected devastating air raid on London, Director Sir Kenneth Clark suggests to his remaining staff that it might be appropriate to go to St Paul's. Two taxis are flagged down and the small party make their way to the Cathedral. On arrival, they are greeted by a posse of vergers shouting, 'All out! All out!' Sir Kenneth tries to remonstrate with them. As war is almost upon us, he tells the vergers, many people will want to visit the Cathedral for prayer and solemn meditation. In a few hours St Paul's itself may be destroyed by bombs. His words cut no ice. The vergers carry on shouting, 'All out! All out!' And it dawns on Sir Kenneth that they are not acting out panic. It is simply the Cathedral's official closing time. 'It would have been,' Clark believes, 'different in the Middle Ages.'

5.00pm, ARSENAL FOOTBALL STADIUM, HIGHBURY
Daily Express Editor Arthur Christiansen, finding nothing to do at the office, has come to see Arsenal play Sunderland. Arsenal thrash Sunderland five goals to two, with Ted Drake scoring four of their goals.

5.00pm, TAKELEY
Moyra Charlton and her mother are at the village hall. All afternoon they have been busy buttering bread, slicing cake, and generally getting ready for the evacuees' arrival. There has been no shortage of helpers and 'people are willing and generous to the extreme'. But the Charltons keep getting conflicting reports as to when the evacuees will be arriving. Moyra and Mrs Charlton decide to have tea themselves. Just as they do, a rumour goes round that no children will be coming today. But at that very moment, two buses roll into the village with sixty-five children on board. They are fed and then allotted to homes in the village. Moyra is told that another 206 will be coming tomorrow. If they do come, she thinks, 'we will have our work cut out'.

5.00pm (6.00pm), POLSKIE RADIO STATION, WARSAW
Polish radio broadcasts a denial that the Germans have suspended military operations. This refutes the rumour that the Poles have heard is going round the French Chamber of Deputies, and which threatens to weaken France's resolve to help Poland.

Pictures and empty frames lying on the floor, awaiting evacuation at the National Gallery. The last of the Gallery's paintings left on the afternoon of 2 September 1939. During this time 3,453 commercial firms also left London.

A column of German tanks advancing in Poland. Six Panzer (armoured) Divisions, employing over 2,000 tanks, took part in the German invasion.

5.00pm (6.00pm), Mieleszyn, German-Polish border
In the main street of the small village, SS men first shoot and then bayonet sixty-year-old Tomasz Pasek. Moving on, they now force Jan Maczka, the village storekeeper, to open up his shop. He is then bayoneted to death.

6.00pm, French Foreign Office, Quai d'Orsay, Paris
Foreign Minister Georges Bonnet receives Polish ambassador Juliusz Lukasiewicz. The emotionally pent-up diplomat demands to know when France will honour its obligations to his country. Bonnet comes up with the excuse that nothing can be done as yet. The evacuation of women and children from Paris has not been completed, he tells the Pole. 'Do you then want the women and children of Paris to be massacred?' Bonnet asks the ambassador. Lukasiewicz, only too aware that Polish towns and cities are already being bombed, protests indignantly. He tells Bonnet that the French air force and anti-aircraft defences are surely strong enough to protect Paris. Each hour's delay is only helping the Germans in their invasion. Bonnet fobs off the ambassador with a promise to speed things up.

6.00pm, House of Commons
MPs gather to hear Chamberlain make a statement. Every seat is occupied and many MPs have to stand. All the galleries are packed. But the Prime Minister fails to appear and MPs are told that he will now make his statement at 7.30pm. Many adjourn to the members' bars for 'Dutch courage'.

6.30pm (7.30pm), Foreign Ministry, Rome
Count Ciano receives a 'phone call from the Foreign Office in London. The Italian foreign minister is told that Britain cannot agree to the five-power conference taking place unless German forces withdraw completely from Poland. In his diary, the Count writes, 'the last glimmer of hope has died'. He also notes that Mussolini

is convinced of the need to remain neutral, but the Duce is not at all pleased about it. The Italian people, however, are 'unequivocally happy' that their country is not marching at Hitler's side. And so too is Ciano himself.

7.00pm, BRITISH EMBASSY, PARIS

Ambassador Sir Eric Phipps is telephoned by Lord Halifax. The Foreign Secretary tells Sir Eric to circumvent Bonnet and see Daladier himself. He is to impress on the French premier the need to act quickly. Britain and France must be seen to be acting in concert. Sir Eric agrees to do so, but warns Halifax that the French will say any action is impossible until both their mobilisation and evacuation are completed.

7.30pm, THE ELYSÉE PALACE, PARIS

The Council of Ministers meet. They agree with Commander-in-Chief General Gamelin's request for more time to complete mobilisation, but there is dissension among them. Some, like Paul Reynaud and the tough colonial minister Georges Mandel, are all for immediate and concerted action with the British. They deplore the ongoing disagreement with London over the timing of the ultimatum. Others, like the pro-Italian and fervent appeaser Minister of Public Works Anatole de Monzie think, 'For once we can afford the luxury of being a step behind the British.'

7.30pm, SS ATHENIA, SIXTY-TWO MILES OUT FROM LIVERPOOL

The liner is being blacked out as dinner is served. Passenger Barbara Bailey tells Chief Radio Officer D. Don that she thinks the liner is too crowded. 'Don't worry,' he reassures her, 'there'll be a lifebelt for you.'

7.30pm, THE NEW THEATRE, ST MARTIN'S LANE, LONDON

Chelsea teenager Joan Wyndham has heard the news that because of the danger of air raids, the Government is going to close all

Mothers with babies and children waiting to be evacuated from Victoria Station, London, 2 September 1939. Chamberlain's Minister of Health, Walter Elliot, proclaimed that evacuation showed what a democratic nation could do.

places of entertainment, so she has rushed here to get a gallery seat to see John Gielgud and Edith Evans in *The Importance of Being Earnest*. Joan thinks that the people in the streets seem quite cheerful. She is struck too by the fact that those in the gallery queue are all talking to each other, 'which is very unusual for the English!'

7.30pm (8.30pm), PODZAMCZE, LODZ DISTRICT, POLAND

Soldiers from the German 17th Infantry Division break into the home of wheelwright Kazimierz Hoffmann. They force Hoffmann, his wife, six children and neighbour Maria Domalga into the yard and gun them down. At the same time four other men from the town are first beaten and then bayoneted to death.

7.44pm, HOUSE OF COMMONS

The Prime Minister arrives with acting Labour leader Arthur Greenwood. Chamberlain rises to make his statement. It only lasts four minutes. Half of it is given over to the Italian conference proposal which the Cabinet discussed earlier this afternoon:

> While appreciating the efforts of the Italian Government, His Majesty's Government for their part would find it impossible to take part in a conference while Poland is being subjected to invasion . . . If the German Government should be ready to withdraw their forces then His Majesty's Government would be willing to regard the position as the same as it was before the German forces crossed the Polish frontier. That is to say, the way would be open to discussion between the German and Polish Governments on the matters at issue between them . . .

MPs are horrified at the Prime Minister's bland and vacillating statement. To many it smacks of another Munich. Two MPs are said to be physically sick on hearing it. Arthur Greenwood now rises to his feet. From the Government back benches, Tory grandee Leopold Amery calls out, 'Speak for England, Arthur!' And rebel Conservative MP Bob Boothby also shouts out, '*You* speak for Britain!' Chamberlain goes white, and at least one MP thinks that he is going to collapse. Flushed, but rising magnificently to the occasion, Greenwood tells MPs:

> I am gravely disturbed . . . I wonder how long we are prepared to vacillate at a time when Britain and all that Britain stands for, and human civilization, are at peril . . . I should have preferred the Prime Minister to have been able to say tonight definitely, 'It is either peace or war.' Tomorrow we meet at twelve. I hope the Prime Minister then – well, he must be in a position to make some further statement. And I must point out to him, every minute's delay now means loss of life, imperilling our national honour . . . The moment we look like weakening, at that moment dictatorship knows we are beaten. We are not beaten. We shall not be beaten. We cannot be beaten; but delay is dangerous . . .

Greenwood sits down to resounding cheers. Even Chamberlain's most loyal supporters are cheering him. The Prime Minister looks as if he has been slapped in the face. Hore-Belisha believes that Greenwood has acted with great patriotism and statesmanship. Had he turned on the Government just now, he would undoubtedly have had Tory support. And it might have meant Chamberlain's fall. The Prime Minister now gets up again and attempts a conciliatory speech to calm the House down. He tells MPs, 'I should be horrified if the House thought for one moment that the statement that I have made to them betrayed the slightest weakening either of this Government or of the French Government . . .'

But this does nothing to assure the House. Hore-Belisha thinks that, on the contrary, it gives the impression that Britain is weakening in its undertaking to Poland, and that the French are 'ratting'.

Harold Nicolson agrees and notes that Chamberlain 'must know very well that the better-informed among us already know about Georges Bonnet. He is not telling the truth, and we know it.' In the Press Gallery, lobby correspondent J.E. Sewell is seized by the lapels by a man he scarcely knows. In an agonised voice, the man shouts in Sewell's face, 'the French have ratted; it's another sell-out!'

7.45pm (8.45pm), WIERUSZOW, NEAR THE GERMAN-POLISH BORDER

In Main Street, SS men from *Leibstandarte Adolf Hitler* murder three Jews, two men and a woman – all members of the Lewi family.

8.00pm (9.00pm), FOREIGN MINISTRY, WARSAW

Ed Beattie and other foreign correspondents gather to hear the latest news. They are told that poisoned chocolates have been scattered from German 'planes for Polish children to pick up. There are also stories of small balloons, containing some form of poison gas, being found here and there. Beattie is sceptical, believing what is actually happening is 'bad enough, without all the improbable fairy tales'.

8.00pm (9.00pm), OSTROWEK, LODZ DISTRICT

German troops begin to set fire to houses in the village. Aniela Hess and her seventy-seven-year-old father Wojciech Goralski try to escape. But he is shot and dies as he attempts to run past the burning houses. Their neighbour Michal Dulski is also murdered tonight, and so too is Anilela's married sister Jozefa Binkowska.

8.30pm, HOUSE OF COMMONS

Ten members of Chamberlain's cabinet meet in Chancellor Sir John Simon's room. They are all aghast at what they have just heard in the House, and demand that the Cabinet meet again. Sir John, up till now a staunch supporter of appeasement, is deputed to see

Chamberlain. He is to tell the Prime Minister of their profound disquiet at the turn of events. Some MPs at Westminster suspect that Sir John has his eye on toppling Chamberlain with a view to replacing him as Prime Minister.

8.40pm, HOUSE OF COMMONS
Chamberlain agrees to see not just Sir John but the other cabinet 'rebels' as well. They file into the Prime Minister's room where they are met by Chamberlain and his loyal supporter, air minister Sir Kingsley Wood. Simon puts their case very forcibly. He tells Chamberlain that his announcement tonight has taken them completely by surprise. It seems to be going back on what was decided in Cabinet this afternoon, the ultimatum to expire at midnight tonight, irrespective of what the French intend to do. Chamberlain tells his ministers that the problem is indeed with the French. It has proved impossible to get them to agree to synchronise their ultimatum with Britain's. Earlier today, Paris had told London that it must have a further forty-eight hours to complete French evacuation and mobilisation processes. The Prime Minister tells his colleagues that he wants to banish the impression he has just made in the House. They tell him that a statement should be made forthwith, and not to bother about the French. Chamberlain leaves for Number 10, and the 'rebels' go back to Simon's room. There they draw up a letter to the Prime Minister, summarising points made just now and send it over to Downing Street.

9.00pm, RMS *ATHLONE CASTLE*, SOUTH ATLANTIC
As the liner makes its way from Cape Town back to Britain, ship's steward Paine writes up his diary entry for today: 'We receive news that Germany are become [*sic*] more aggressive to Poland, also that England and France are still talking. Why are they hesitating? It is impossible to retract now with honour ... As the day wears on speculation is high; it must be war, there is no alternative. We are

125

eagerly waiting the news on the loudspeakers at seven o'clock. The time comes, and all we hear is that the Irish Prime Minister de Valera, says "Although a lot of Irishmen sympathize with England, they have to look after their country first." What do you expect from pigs but grunts? Why are we not getting any news? Has England already declared war? The suspense is getting worse.'

Preparations for war are already being made on the ship. The Captain asks passengers to come forward to fill sandbags. The response is good. Among the volunteers are the Cambridge University boat crew, who have been touring South Africa.

9.00pm, House of Commons
Sir John Simon, Hore-Belisha and two other 'rebels' dine with Chamberlain supporter Sir Kingsley Wood. As the ministers eat, no further word comes from Number 10.

9.15pm, 10 Downing Street
The Prime Minister 'phones Lord Halifax. The Foreign Secretary has never heard Chamberlain sound so disturbed before. Halifax joins him for dinner, and Chamberlain recounts this evening's events and the cabinet 'revolt'. He also tells Halifax that Churchill is getting restless. But this is hardly surprising. Chamberlain has not made any contact with Churchill since offering him a post in the War Cabinet yesterday.

9.45pm, French Embassy, London
Ambassador Charles Corbin is rung up by a furious Winston Churchill. His 'ear-splitting voice' makes the telephone vibrate. In no uncertain terms, Churchill, who has always been a passionate Francophile, tells Corbin that, if France goes back on her word now, he will be entirely indifferent to her fate. In an effort to pacify Churchill, the ambassador starts to explain about technical difficulties. 'Technical difficulties be damned!' growls Churchill,

rudely interrupting. 'I suppose you would call it a technical difficulty for a Pole if a German bomb dropped on his head.'

9.50pm, 10 DOWNING STREET

Chamberlain puts through a call to Daladier. He tells his French colleague of the angry scene in the Commons tonight. Furthermore, the Prime Minister tells Daladier, if the French persist in a time limit of forty-eight hours to run from midday tomorrow, it will be impossible for Chamberlain 'to hold the situation here'. Daladier is still clinging to the hope that the Italian proposal for a five-power conference might yet save the peace. Moreover, he reminds the British Prime Minister, it will be France which will have to bear the immediate brunt of a German attack. Daladier tells Chamberlain, 'Unless British bombers were ready to act at once, it would be better for France to delay, if possible, for some hours, attacks on the German armies.' On that note the two heads of government break off the conversation.

10.00pm, HOUSE OF COMMONS

The cabinet 'rebels' meet again in Sir John Simon's room. He and Lord Privy Seal Sir John Anderson decide to go to Downing Street to once again confront the Prime Minister. Hore-Belisha thinks that they should go *en masse*, but he is overruled by the others.

10.00pm, TAKELEY

Moyra Charlton and her family listen to the news on the BBC's new Home Service. They are not at all reassured at what they hear: 'From Halifax's and Chamberlain's speeches tonight we gather that England is taking no immediate action against Germany . . . We send no ultimatum, in fact we hem and haw and talk of negotiation. Meanwhile Germany bombs Poland and hurls her man-power against Polish defences. We are mad, mad. Before we know where we are Danzig and the Corridor will be German. Hitler will declare his objective gained and the crisis will be over, and there will be crisis on crisis again and the agony of suspense, the German faith in the Fuehrer will be forever unshakeable and no one will believe our word again ... We can't, *can't* back out now.'

10.00pm (11.00pm), PODZAMCZE, LODZ DISTRICT, POLAND
German soldiers arrest Mayor Tomasz Monka and two other elderly men. They are taken to a brickyard where they are beaten so savagely that Monka receives fatal injuries.

10.30pm, FOREIGN OFFICE, WHITEHALL
Lord Halifax telephones Georges Bonnet at the Quai d'Orsay. He urges the French foreign minister that their two countries should present a united front to Hitler. Both their ambassadors in Berlin should call on von Ribbentrop at 8am tomorrow. They should tell him that if no satisfactory reply is made by midday then 'we should be free to take action to fulfil our obligations to Poland'. But, Halifax tells Bonnet, if the French will not agree to that, then Britain will go it alone, providing that France follows suit within twenty-four hours. Bonnet is still reluctant to go ahead on such terms. He tells the Foreign Secretary that more time is needed for the evacuation of women and children from Paris. He has been to the Gare d'Orsay, where there are 'long lines of women, with their infants in their arms'. If there is a German air raid on the French capital, Bonnet tells Halifax, there will be 'a frightful massacre'. The two men finally agree that the British will deliver their ultimatum in Berlin at 8am, and the French theirs at midday.

10.30pm, TRAVELLERS CLUB, LONDON
Harold Nicolson comes out of the club to find London's blackout is complete. Nicolson walks home, creeping carefully. Glumly, he foresees 'that once the habit of order leaves us, there will be a recrudescence of footpads and highway robbery'.

10.30pm, BOLTON
A Mass Observation diarist encounters a drunk leaving a pub at closing time. 'Heil Hitler,' the drunk says, 'Och, dinna listen to me – I dinna mean it.'

10.30pm (11.30pm), GERMAN-POLISH BORDER
Wilhelm Prueller and his company receive tea and are issued with fifteen cigarettes each. They suffered their first fatality at 5pm this afternoon. Prueller now beds down for the night.

10.45pm, HOUSE OF COMMONS
Sir John Anderson returns from Downing Street. He tells Hore-Belisha and the others that the ultimatum will now be given tomorrow morning at 8am to expire at midday. The war minister thinks the interval too long. Another message now arrives from Number 10. The Cabinet is to meet at 11pm.

10.45pm, 10 DOWNING STREET
Chamberlain receives French ambassador Charles Corbin. The Prime Minister does not beat about the bush. He tells the French diplomat, 'Public opinion unanimously considers the Italian offer a trap, intended to favour the advance of the German armies in Poland by immobilizing the Allied forces. Britain is definitely united now, but the country is beginning to be seriously disturbed by the delays due to the vacillating attitude of the French Government. We cannot wait any longer. If necessary, we shall act alone.'

11.00pm, PLACE DE LA CONCORDE, PARIS
Hubert Earle of the US Embassy is walking home to his apartment in the pitch dark. The blackout is so complete with 'not a suspicion of the moon', that Hubert walks right into a fountain and is soaked to the skin.

11.00pm, CABINET ROOM, 10 DOWNING STREET

Ministers begin to assemble, some in white tie and tails, others in dinner jackets or ordinary suits. To Minister of Agriculture Reginald Dorman-Smith, Chamberlain is like 'a stag at bay', with his ministers angrily demanding action and 'if necessary to destroy him'. But things calm down rapidly as Chamberlain acknowledges his colleagues' strength of feeling. Hore-Belisha puts forward his view that the ultimatum should be given in three hours' time at 2am to expire at 6am, 'The less time involved the better.' Chamberlain tells his colleagues of the trouble both he and Lord Halifax have had with the French over delivering a joint ultimatum. And it is now reluctantly acknowledged that the two allies will hand in separate ultimatums tomorrow morning.

11.00pm, TAKELEY

The Charlton family discuss the latest radio news of the crisis. Moyra has never felt so angry or worked up before. She believes that 'Mr Greenwood, in a concise and excellent speech, voiced some of the points which express surely, not only Opposition views, but the views of anyone with any foresight in England. War is ghastly, but what of the future if we let this go? What security, what peace would there be? Damn it all, we still have the guts to face it, even if Mr Chamberlain has not.' The Charltons decide that there must be some definite reason for the apparent change in the Government's policy. Moyra records 'two fascinating suggestions: (a) that Hitler has shot himself. (b) That there is a revolt in Germany.' She goes to bed, 'very worried ... I hope to Heaven we know soon one way or the other.'

11.00pm, BOLTON

In the street, a loud voice is heard shouting, 'T' war cancelled for twenty-four hours.'

11.30pm, WEST NORWOOD

Nellie Carver, a supervisor at the Central Telegraph Office in the City, has had a busy day. Writing up her diary tonight she reflects on how the telegraph service always seems to thrive in crises. 'Well, I've seen a few myself. Coal strikes, General Strike, two Kings' deaths & funerals, a war, an Abdication & now another war! In each of these we appeared to be the centre of the whirlpool, but this beyond everything yet seen.' Nellie is unable to sleep because of a violent thunderstorm breaking over the capital. It seems to 'put the lid on a ghastly situation'. She tries to imagine what the future might hold but her imagination fails and she just writes in her diary, 'Germany has been given until 11am tomorrow (an ominous hour in our History), but we know what her answer will be – they will not withdraw now.'

11.55pm, BROADCASTING HOUSE

Chief BBC Announcer Stuart Hibberd is exhausted. He has been on duty all day, although there has been virtually no news. About to leave, Hibberd reflects that today has been 'A glorious summer day. Why is it,' he asks himself, 'that at this, the most lovely time of the year, men should start thinking about killing their own kind?'

12.00 midnight, PUTNEY

'As I write there is raging outside a terrific storm, almost continuous lightning and thunder. Nature is providing the finishing touches to these poignant, horrible days. The waiting, listening to news bulletins every hour, the instructions for complete blackout at night, general mobilisation yesterday – khaki-clad boys everywhere – the speeded up evacuation of three million children and invalids from the cities, all these have come to us – a supposed civilised people! Warsaw has been bombed, German tanks and aeroplanes have been shot down and war is once more striding across our world.

'This storm makes one feel that perhaps God is wishful of reminding us that our little wars are as nothing compared with his awful power, but it is too late now, we are too deeply immersed in it. The blackness in the streets is so strange, one feels one must be quiet and secret all the time and walk upon one's toes. What a state to come to – darkness and fear – a vast organised army of people wondering if all the fighting, first aid, ARP and other services for which they have trained, rather amusedly in most cases, for the past months, will be used in the worst manner they have conceived . . . Here's the storm again tearing its way across the sky above us – I wish it would stop and we could have some sleep, as we should be able to do, without fear of raids for tonight at any rate!' (Vivienne Hall)

CHAPTER 4

Sunday,
3 September 1939

Introduction: resumé of 2 September

For twenty-four hours Poland had been under attack. But there was still no positive news of Britain and France coming to her aid. Huddersfield housewife Marjorie Gothard wrote in her diary, 'the people of Britain wake up to hear that no reply to the British ultimatum has come from Hitler'. People were perplexed at the lack of action on Britain's part. There was a genuine concern that the Government was still trying to appease Hitler and wriggle out of its obligations to Poland. A Mass Observation diarist, a woman of twenty-four, 'woke up feeling flattened and weak. News in evening bewildering. What is the reason for delaying the decision? Afraid of letting down Poland.' In Bolton, a woman told Mass Observation, 'No one would stand another Munich.' In her diary, Helena Mott, a persistent critic of Chamberlain and appeasement, wrote with increasing frustration: 'WHY HAVE WE NOT STARTED?!!'

In France too, there was uneasy feeling that the Poles were going to be abandoned, just as the Czechs had been the year before.

Despite Daladier's brave words in the Chamber, there were many deputies who believed that 'Bolshevism is our first enemy. Let us not forget it,' and that the Nazis posed no threat to France. After all, said one deputy, 'Hitler declared that he will not claim Alsace Lorraine!' The ordinary people displayed more resolution, but nothing like the enthusiasm that had been seen in 1914. Captain Daniel Barlone noted of his men that, if ordered, 'Of course they will go, and return home to peace and quietness after handing Hitler a good drubbing. The men's great hope is that Hitler will be assassinated.' In Paris, reservists were still arriving at the Gare de l'Est and other stations. Writer Jean Malaquais, a naturalised Polish Jew, described the scene: 'You know how stations are on general mobilisation days: sniffles, tears, promises that a stray bullet can break.'

On the morning of 2 September, Berlin's Stettiner Bahnhof was full of small children, wearing blue tags, ready to be evacuated to the countryside. William Shirer noted that in general Berliners 'seemed to be a little more cheery' as no Polish bombers had got through to the capital, which had 'a fairly normal aspect today'. Berliners appeared to have quickly 'settled down to a dazed war routine'. All German papers reported the initial successes in Poland, and the High Command confirmed that the advance was going according to schedule. 'The people were cheered. They did not expect that England and France would enter the conflict,' one of Shirer's colleagues reported. At the British and French embassies, the diplomats' bags were packed ready for departure, but their American colleague William Russell still 'wondered fearfully if they would break their word again'.

As the British and French continued to vacillate, Poland was not only bearing the full brunt of Germany's military machine but also the consequences of Nazi racial propaganda. Corporal Willi Krey wrote in his war diary: 'The houses in these Polish villages are crammed with filth . . . the folk who stand outside and gape at us appear to be totally uncivilised: they all look dirty and bedraggled, the women as well as the men. These so-called representatives of civilisation seem to me to be competing as to who can be the dirtiest.'

Later the same day, 2 September, his unit came under fire from a house. They stormed it and found, as Krey wrote, 'Two Poles lay in their blood, one dead, the other wounded in the arm and stomach ... Our German doctors refused to treat the wounded Pole. We placed him on pile of straw ... and left him to rot. He took seven hours to die.'

12.00 midnight, Harwich–Liverpool Street boat train

Virginia Cowles and her friend Jane are only just back from the Continent. Before boarding the train they ask a docker whether war has been declared. 'Not yet,' comes the reply, 'But I hope it won't be long now. This waiting around is making us all nervous.' The two young Americans now hear the sound of far-away explosions. They lean out the train window and see 'the sky lighting up with sharp spasmodic flashes – obviously bursts from anti-aircraft fire,' thinks Virginia. She and Jane are still hanging out of the window when they reach the outskirts of London. Suddenly, they feel torrential rain coming down. And only now does it dawn on them that the 'explosions' they heard, and 'anti-aircraft fire' they saw, were just a thunderstorm.

12.00 midnight, Hampstead, London

A violent and frightening thunderstorm breaks over the capital. Verily Anderson, a member of the First Aid Nursing Yeomanry [FANY], is shivering in her bed. But she manages to ask her friends jokingly, 'Perhaps it could be Hitler's secret weapon?'

12.00 midnight, Savage Club, London

Britain's leading theatre critic James Agate watches the storm from the Club's steps. 'One moment there is complete darkness: the next a sheet of vivid green showing Westminster cut out in cardboard like the scenery in a toy theatre.' The lightning flashes last so long that Agate can count the surrounding buildings.

12.00 midnight, 10 DOWNING STREET

Alec Douglas-Home, Chamberlain's Parliamentary Private Secretary, and Tory MP Henry 'Chips' Channon are standing on the steps of Number 10 when the heavens open and rain deluges down. To both men simultaneously comes the thought that this is the gods weeping for the folly of man.

12.00 midnight, SCOTT'S RESTAURANT, PICCADILLY

Daily Express Editor Arthur Christiansen has been to see Arsenal play this afternoon. Now, coming out of the restaurant, he sees the lightning bringing daylight to the blacked-out streets. The thunder, Christiansen thinks, sounds like 'the noise of a million guns, as though God Himself were rumbling in rage at human folly'.

12.00 midnight, WATCHET, SOMERSET

Regular soldier Second Lieutenant Peter Parton of the Royal Artillery is now back in camp. He's just been to the local cinema to see a late showing of *Wuthering Heights*, starring Merle Oberon and Laurence Olivier. The film was only halfway through when a notice was flashed on the screen: 'ALL OFFICERS AND SOLDIERS RETURN TO YOUR BARRACKS IMMEDIATELY.' Silently, the cinema rapidly emptied. Parton has spent most of the last few weeks training men of the Territorial Army's anti-aircraft regiments. His own unit has now been brought up to full strength and they are all awaiting the inevitable. The cinema notice seems to indicate that things are coming to a head. Parton knows that his unit will be among the first to go out to France, 'when the balloon goes up'.

12.00am (1.00am), WARSAW CENTRAL STATION

The first hospital trains arrived about an hour ago in the Polish capital. One eyewitness sees 'the wounded men, looking very long and flat, [they] lay on stretchers roughly covered with blankets. Horribly wounded. The first fruits of the Great Mechanised War.' Civilian volunteers and boy scouts have come to the station to help out the overstretched Polish Army medical personnel and Red Cross. They go up and down the platforms, offering the wounded men cigarettes, snacks and hot soup. The men on the stretchers have heard no real news for the past two days. They ask the helpers what is happening in the outside world. Their most urgent enquiry is to find out if Britain and France are honouring their pledges. They all want to know if fighting has started on the Western Front.

12.00am (1.00am), Foreign Minister's residence, Warsaw

As the hospital trains are being unloaded, France's ambassador Leon Noël is having an awkward conversation with Foreign Minister Jozef Beck and his wife Jadwiga. Poland has now been under attack since Friday morning, and still France has made no move to assist its ally. Noël tries to allay Beck's suspicion that France is attempting to wriggle out of her obligations. But the ambassador himself is torn by conflicting emotions. On one hand, he hopes that France will stand by Poland and come to her aid. On the other, he remembers that in the last war France lost over 1,300,000 men and that she cannot bear to stand such a catastrophic loss again this time. Noël knows too that even at this late hour Georges Bonnet, his foreign minister, is attempting to find a way of France getting out of honouring her word.

1.30am, Cabinet Room, 10 Downing Street

Neville Chamberlain's cabinet have been in session for the past two hours. The meeting is a fraught one and nerves are getting frayed. The French are insisting on further delay in presenting the Germans with an ultimatum to withdraw their troops from Poland. But Britain's service chiefs oppose any further delay. War minister Leslie Hore-Belisha wants the ultimatum to expire at 6am, which is in

less than five hours' time. Chamberlain replies that this is imprac-
tical. Eventually agreement is reached. Lord Halifax is to instruct
Sir Nevile Henderson in Berlin to present the Germans with the
British ultimatum, which will expire at 11am this morning. The
ministers now disperse into Downing Street where they are met by
blinding rain. In the mêlée, Government Chief Whip David
Margesson tells 'Chips' Channon, 'It must be War, "Chips", old
boy. There's no other way out.'

1.30am, FOREIGN OFFICE, WHITEHALL
A cluster of Foreign Office officials and Dr Hugh Dalton, Labour's
spokesman on foreign affairs, are watching the activity in Downing
Street as the rain pelts down. Dalton sees that the cabinet meeting
is breaking up and intends to buttonhole Lord Halifax to find out
what the situation now is regarding a declaration of war. As Dalton
makes to leave, Ivone Kirkpatrick, who has served in the Berlin
embassy under Henderson, tells him, 'If we rat on the Poles now,
we are absolutely sunk, whatever the French do. We shall have no
chance against Hitler. But if we go ahead, we shall have two chances.
First, we may shame the French into coming in, even though they
would not have moved unless we had; second, even if the French
stay out, we shall have the opinion of the world behind us, and we
at least have the Poles on our side with a chance that the United
States and others will come in before we are beaten.'

Dalton is a fervent anti-appeaser who has many friends in Poland.
He agrees with Kirkpatrick's prognosis. As he goes down the Foreign
Office's wide central staircase, Dalton bumps into Sir William
Malkin, the FO's chief legal adviser. Sir William tells Dalton that
he's only just come from 10 Downing Street. The Labour politician
asks him, 'How are things going?' and Sir William replies, 'I have
got the declaration in the bag now. It's settled now.' Slightly relieved,
Dalton leaves to accost the Foreign Secretary.

1.40am, 10 Downing Street

Dalton approaches Halifax and asks him what the British position is now and what the French are intending to do. The abrasive Dalton sternly tells Halifax, 'I warn you that if the House of Commons meets again without our pledge to Poland having been fulfilled, there will be such an explosion as you in the House of Lords may not be able to imagine. It may well blow up the Government altogether.' Halifax is put out by Dalton's hectoring tone. But he assures the Labour politician 'that we shall be at war in ten hours'. The delay has been caused by the French wanting more time to get their mobilisation completed, he tells Dalton. 'We may have to go in a few hours before the French,' Halifax continues, 'but they will follow all right now.' The two men part. Dalton is now much relieved.

2.00am, Foreign Office, Whitehall

Now the decision has been taken, there is a general feeling of relief and a lightening of tension. Lord Halifax calls for beer. And bottles are brought to the Foreign Secretary's office by one of the resident clerks, who only looks half awake. Jokes are cracked. Kirkpatrick tells Halifax that news has just come in that Dr Goebbels has forbidden listening to foreign broadcasts. The Foreign Secretary quips, 'He ought to pay me to listen to his.'

2.00am, Polish Embassy, London

Mentally and physically exhausted ambassador Count Edward Raczynski receives a telephone call from Hugh Dalton. Dalton tells the ambassador, 'Today both we and France shall be on your side. I hope this news will help you to get a little sleep tonight.' Raczynski replies that he is indeed grateful. 'Yes,' he tells the Labour politician, 'it's true, it makes me feel just a little less unhappy.' The ambassador then tells Dalton of the speeches made yesterday in the Polish parliament: 'They were all brave speeches, but one thing was missing. None of the speakers felt able to make any reference to our friends.'

3.00am, FOREIGN OFFICE, WHITEHALL

In anticipation of Britain and France going to war later today, officials have already drawn up a joint Anglo-French declaration on their proposed conduct of that war. It begins, 'The Governments of the United Kingdom and France solemnly and publicly affirm their intention, should a war be forced upon them, to conduct hostilities with a firm desire to spare the civilian population and preserve in every way possible those monuments of human achievement which are treasured in all civilized countries.'

3.00am (4.00am), BRITISH EMBASSY, BERLIN

Sir Nevile Henderson receives instructions that he is to seek an interview with Foreign Minister von Ribbentrop to present the British ultimatum at 9am. The text of it is being prepared now. It will be sent to Henderson within the hour. The embassy now tries to get through to the Foreign Ministry to arrange the ambassador's interview with von Ribbentrop. The obtuse Foreign Minister is with interpreter Dr Paul Schmidt when he receives Henderson's request. Von Ribbentrop correctly suspects that the ambassador's communication 'could contain nothing agreeable'. He turns to Schmidt and says, 'Really, you could receive the Ambassador in my place. Just ask the English whether that will suit them, and say the Foreign Minister is not available at 9am.' Schmidt gets back to the embassy and it is agreed that Henderson will see him in five hours' time.

3.40am, SS *ATHENIA*, ATLANTIC OCEAN

The liner passes Inishtrahull, on the north-western corner of Ireland, as she sails into the Eastern Atlantic.

3.50am (4.50am), FOREIGN MINISTRY, BERLIN

Already, there is a great deal of German criticism of Italy 'ratting' on the Pact of Steel, which was signed less than four months ago. It is 1914 all over again. To defuse such criticism, von Ribbentrop sends a message to all German missions abroad, 'German-Italian policy is based on complete and clear agreement between the Fuehrer and the Duce. In case you are addressed on the subject, you should adopt this point of view. There must be no criticism of the Italian attitude and, if made, it will be severely punished.'

5.00am, FOREIGN MINISTRY, QUAI D'ORSAY, PARIS

Georges Bonnet hears from André François-Poncet, his ambassador in Rome. The ambassador reports on the collapse of the Italian proposal for a five-power conference. Any hopes of pulling off another Munich are now dead. Realising now that war is inevitable, Bonnet's mind goes back to August 1914: 'the mobilisation drums, the departure for the front of trains covered with slogans, carrying away friends and brothers'. Having been a soldier in 1914–18, and decorated for bravery, Bonnet knows only too well the horrors of war. He has hoped to spare France from those horrors this time. Reluctantly, he now accepts that war with Germany is just a matter of hours away.

5.00am (6.00am), GERMAN-POLISH BORDER

Fervent Nazi Wilhelm Prueller writes an anniversary letter in his diary to his wife Henny: 'Today our first anniversary! How can we celebrate it? I: in the woods ready to attack. You: thinking of me, not knowing where I am. Sad, isn't it? But there's nothing to do about it, is there? It's war! Just what is war? A compilation of sacrifices and exhaustion, of thirst and occasionally hunger, of heat and cold. I hope it's finished soon.'

6.16am, BRITAIN: It is sunrise, British Summer Time and therefore the official end of last night's blackout.

7.00am, BRITAIN: All over the country, newspaper boys are delivering the Sunday newspapers. In them are the first eyewitness accounts of the German invasion of Poland, now entering its third

day. The *Sunday Express* carries a vivid description by special correspondent Denis Sefton Delmer of the first raids on the outskirts of
Warsaw:

I was driving out to Modlin, twenty miles from Warsaw, to check
up on the casualties and damage of the morning's raid there. Just
across the Vistula I sighted the first group of raiders, four German
bombers, being headed off from the bridge by Polish fighters. The
fighters were driving them on to Polish anti-aircraft fire.

Truly it was superb shooting the Polish batteries were putting up,
and sure enough it told. I saw one German machine come heading
earthwards like a great black arrow. A moment later a second followed
on the left. Two black clouds of smoke half a mile from each other
showed where they'd fallen.

More and more German bombers came over. Though I still do
not think it was the real mass stuff, there was one group of triple-
engine bombers with three escort planes above and behind them.
They tried to fly through a barrage of black anti-aircraft shrapnel –
then suddenly the guns were silent and high out of the skies silver-
glinting Polish fighters swooped down, machine guns going full out.
They swept past the Germans. The Germans opened formation, then
as the anti-aircraft fire started up again, they wheeled and bombs
dropped harmlessly, judged by the cloud of smoke I saw coming up
from riverside fields.

Farther on a cottage was burning. A bomb had set it on fire.
Behind this group had come another group of planes diving in circus.
There was furious bombing. What they were after I do not know.
Perhaps it was the bridge. But within a second the fighters were on
their tail and the circus was forced to beat it. By the roadside stood
a fair-haired girl weeping beside her two little blond children, a boy
and a girl. She frantically waved at us. 'Take me back to Warsaw, I
can't stand it here any longer,' she pleaded.

Somehow we piled them all in. The burning house was their

country cottage. She had come out with them in the four o'clock bus this afternoon to have them safe outside Warsaw.

As I put them down at the first waiting tram, an air raid warden rushed up to show us a 'bit of bomb', his first. It was a fragment of shrapnel.

Driving back to Warsaw an hour and a half after the raid began, the alarm was still on. Behind us out in the country, the anti-aircraft firing away stopped the last wave of German afternoon raiders.

No bomb had fallen in Warsaw. Fire brigades and ambulances were standing by unwanted . . .

And the paper also features another story from the Polish capital that surely stretches the reader's credulity this Sunday morning. It smacks of the rumours twenty-five years ago of Russian soldiers on the way to France with snow on their boots. 'It has been reported that two out of three of the bombs used in the first air raids on Warsaw did not explode. On examination they were found to contain, instead of high explosive, slips of paper bearing the words, "We are with you in spirit," and signed, "Workers of the Skoda Arms Factory, Czecho-Slovakia".'

8.00am, Foreign Ministry, Quai d'Orsay, Paris
Foreign Minister Georges Bonnet, looking, an American reporter thinks, 'how Pinnochio would have looked at forty-nine', leaves the Foreign Ministry. He is driven to the Ministry of National Defence. He is going to meet Premier Edouard Daladier, who is also defence minister, to confer about the time limit in the French ultimatum Ambassador Coulondre is going to present in Berlin at midday. Daladier tells Bonnet to set the opening of hostilities for Monday, 4 September at 5am. The premier, who is highly distrustful of his foreign minister, tells Bonnet that the general staff refuse to accept a shorter delay. Bonnet now returns to the Quai d'Orsay and starts to draft the ultimatum, 'weighing each word of this historic dispatch'.

8.00am (9.00am), KONSTANCIN, WARSAW DISTRICT

United States ambassador to Poland, the urbane Anthony J. Drexel Biddle Jr is at his emergency residence at Konstancin. It is about twelve miles south of Warsaw on the left bank of the Vistula. With Mrs Biddle, his daughter and some guests and staff, the ambassador left the capital last night to try and get some rest. Konstancin is a small town which has a dozen or so villas like the Biddles', and also a brick factory. As his guests enjoy the morning sunshine, the ambassador is in the bathroom shaving. Suddenly a lone Dornier bomber dives out of the clouds. The 'plane straightens up and releases its load of eleven bombs. One hits a neighbouring villa and six fail to explode; they are either time bombs or duds. The Biddles are lucky. They receive no direct hits, but the windows of the ambassadorial villa have been blown in. And their Great Dane 'Okay' is badly shaken by the bomb blasts.

8.00am (9.00am), LEKI DUZE, LODZ DISTRICT, POLAND

Men of SS *Leibstandarte Adolf Hitler* enter the small village. They shoot a number of unarmed civilians. Among the dead are Anna Ostrycharz, her small child and brother Stanislaw. The SS men then set fire to Anna's home. Moving on through the village they also murder Jozefa Wysota and Leon Kowalski. The villagers are at a loss to know why these indiscriminate killings are taking place because no one has fired on or attacked the Germans.

8.00am (9.00am), FOREIGN MINISTRY, WILHELMSTRASSE, BERLIN

Today of all days, Dr Schmidt has overslept. He has had to dash by taxi to get to the Foreign Ministry in time for his meeting with Sir Nevile Henderson. As he is driving across the Wilhelmplatz, Schmidt sees the elegant British envoy entering the building. By using a side entrance, he manages to catch up with himself. And he is in von Ribbentrop's office when, punctually at 9am, Sir Nevile is shown in. Schmidt sees immediately that the ambassador is in a very serious frame of mind. The two men shake hands, but Sir Nevile declines Schmidt's offer of a seat.

'I regret,' says Henderson in a voice of deep emotion, 'that on the instructions of my government I have to hand you an ultimatum for the German Government. Still standing in the middle of the room, Sir Nevile reads out to Schmidt the British ultimatum:

Sir

In the communication which I had the honour to make to make to you on 1st September, I informed you on the instructions of His Majesty's Principal Secretary of State for Foreign Affairs that unless the German Government were prepared to give His Majesty's Government in the United Kingdom satisfactory assurances that the German Government had suspended all aggressive action against Poland and were prepared promptly to withdraw their forces from Polish territory His Majesty's Government in the United Kingdom would without hesitation, fulfil our obligations to Poland.

Although now it is more than twenty-four hours ago no reply has been received, and German attacks upon Poland have intensified.

I have, therefore, to inform you that unless not later than 11am British Summer Time today, 3rd September, satisfactory assurances to the above effect have been given by the German Government and have reached His Majesty's Government in London, a state of war would exist between the two countries as from that hour.

Henderson finishes reading the ultimatum and hands it to the normally jovial Schmidt, a popular figure with foreign diplomats in Berlin. The ambassador tells him, 'I am sincerely sorry that I must hand such a document to you in particular, as you have always been most anxious to help.' Schmidt too expresses his regret and adds a few heartfelt words. He has the highest regard for Sir Nevile, who, despite all his many failings, has been pathetically sincere in his mission to bring peace and understanding between Britain and Germany. The two men shake hands in parting, and Henderson returns to the embassy. Schmidt hurriedly makes his way down the Wilhelmstrasse to the Reich Chancellery.

8.20am (9.20am), REICH CHANCELLERY, VOSS-STRASSE, BERLIN
Schmidt arrives at the Chancellery. It has been designed and built by Hitler's favourite architect Albert Speer. The Fuehrer only moved into it this January. Schmidt has to virtually fight his way through a crowd of Government and Nazi Party officials that have collected in the room next to Hitler's study.

'What's the news?' Schmidt is asked, to which he can only reply, 'Classroom dismissed', before he is ushered into the Fuehrer's presence. The study measures 400 square metres. Speer has placed the furniture, groups of chairs, map table and a huge globe, all of which he has designed himself, near the walls. This is in order to heighten the sense of size and spaciousness. Hitler's desk, at which he is sitting as Schmidt enters, is decorated with a wooden inlay depicting a sword half drawn from the scabbard. 'Good, good,' Hitler had said when he first inspected it, 'when the diplomats sitting in front of me at this desk see this, they'll learn to shiver and shake.'

But today the only other person present as Schmidt delivers the British ultimatum is von Ribbentrop, standing by the window. Both men look up expectantly as the interpreter comes in. Stopping at some distance from Hitler's desk, Schmidt slowly translates the British ultimatum. When he finishes there is complete silence in the enormous room. Hitler sits immobile, gazing before him, completely silent and unmoving. After an interval that seems like eternity, Hitler turns to his foreign minister, still standing by the window, and with a savage look on his face asks von Ribbentrop, 'What now?'

To which von Ribbentrop quietly replies, 'I assume that the French will hand in a similar ultimatum within the hour.'

Schmidt now withdraws, and in the anteroom tells the waiting throng, 'The English have just handed us an ultimatum. In two hours a state of war will exist between England and Germany.' Just as in Hitler's study a few minutes ago, the news is met by stunned silence. Goering turns to Schmidt and says, 'If we lose this war, then God have mercy on us!' And as he is about to make his way back to the Foreign Ministry, Schmidt sees Dr Goebbels standing in a corner. Hitler's propaganda genius, he notices, looks downcast and self-absorbed, 'like the proverbial drenched poodle'. So far today Hitler has retained his self-control, but now in the Chancellery's conservatory in front of von Ribbentrop, Hess, Himmler and Dr Goebbels, he verbally savages the British:

'The Poles are a miserable, good-for-nothing, loud-mouthed rabble. The British understand that as well as we do; the British gentlemen understand that might is right. When it comes to inferior races they were our first schoolmasters. It is disgraceful to present Czechs and Poles as sovereign states when this rabble is not a jot better than the Sudanese or the Indians – and only because on this occasion, it is about German interests and not British ones. My entire policy towards Britain has been based on recognising the natural realities as they exist on both sides, and now they want to put me in the pillory. That is an unspeakable vilification.'

9.15am, OLYMPIA EXHIBITION HALL, LONDON
Anti-Nazi activist Eugen Spier, a German Jewish refugee, wakes up after an incredible sixteen-hour sleep. He has been in detention since yesterday afternoon, and at Olympia is registered as Prisoner of War No. 1. Among his fellow prisoners are the Jewish former Police Vice-President of Berlin Bernhard Weiss and Ernst 'Putzi' Hanfstaengl. Up until two years ago, 'Putzi' was the Nazi Party's Foreign Press Chief.

9.15am (10.15am), Bydoszcz (Bromberg)

Polish troops are withdrawing through the western parts of the city when they are suddenly fired upon. The shooting comes from members of the German minority, the *Volksdeutsche,* who have featured so heavily in Dr Goebbels's propaganda over the last few weeks. One eyewitness to the shootings is Lucy Baker-Beall. She is an English schoolteacher who has taught in Polish schools for the past thirty-two years. Today's attacks on Poles by ethnic Germans are not the first. Miss Baker-Beall heard the first shots on Friday, and she herself has been fired on twice while in the street. Today, she has heard the firing intensify with the Germans using machine guns against the Poles. Among the Polish victims that Miss Baker-Beall sees is an unarmed air-raid warden shot dead with a bullet in his head. Two other wardens, a man and a women, who live in the same house as Miss Baker-Beall, have also been wounded. A nearby first-aid post is under constant fire from a German-inhabited house. The Poles are taking strong counter-measures. Any German caught with a weapon in his hand is shot. An official Polish count puts the fatalities today, 'Bloody Sunday', at 238 Poles and 223 Germans.

9.20am, Foreign Ministry, Quai d'Orsay, Paris

Georges Bonnet telephones the text of the French ultimatum to his ambassador in Berlin, Robert Coulondre. He tells his ambassador, 'If the reply . . . is negative . . . you will notify the German Minister of Foreign Affairs, or his representative, that from 5am, tomorrow September 4, France will be obliged to fulfil her obligations to Poland, which are known to the German government. You may then ask for your passports.'

10.00am, 10 Downing Street

Over the BBC's new Home Service, announcer Alvar Lidell broadcasts a statement from the Prime Minister's residence: 'Following the midnight meeting of the Cabinet, the British ambassador at 9.00am this morning gave the German Government two further hours in which to decide whether they would at once withdraw their troops from Poland. This ultimatum expires at 11.00am. The Prime Minister will broadcast to the nation at 11.15am.'

10.00am, OXFORD

Dorothy Bartlett is at her parents' home when she hears the BBC announcement that Chamberlain is going to speak at 11.15am. The family are all out in the garden. The day has started off rather chilly, but the sun has gradually risen: it is now fine and rather warm. But the announcement has put them all in a strange mood. They all know or strongly suspect what Chamberlain is going to tell them. Dorothy notices that everybody finds it difficult to settle to the simplest of tasks. Her young sister Mary says, 'Well, it is a good job that it is Sunday and time doesn't really matter. We should be thankful that we have a few hours in which to get used to the idea.'

10.00am (11.00am), GERMAN-POLISH BORDER

Wilhelm Prueller's unit is just about to go into action when the attack is called off. In his diary, he notes down the latest rumour: '11am: The Fuehrer is said is said to have issued an ultimatum to the Poles that they should give us the land we've taken. If there's no satisfactory answer by 12.00, 2,000 of our planes will take off at 12.01 and destroy cities and villages. That would mean practically the end of Poland. The Poles ought to accept.'

10.00am (11.00am), MUNICH

Unity Mitford, twenty-five-year-old daughter of Lord Redesdale, and a passionate admirer of Hitler and all things German, drives up to the Bavarian Ministry of the Interior. She is promptly shown into the office of Munich Gauleiter Adolf Wagner. She hands Wagner

149

a heavy envelope with the words, 'I should like to give you this.' She then abruptly leaves. The Gauleiter, with so much else on his plate today, puts the envelope to one side, and carries on dealing with official correspondence.

10.15am (11.15am), GERMAN-POLISH BORDER

Wilhelm Prueller and his comrades are still mulling over the rumour about the Fuehrer's ultimatum to the Poles. Suddenly, Polish planes are spotted: 'Plenty of excitement. Polish flyers appear and shoot at us, the flak goes into action. One, two, three, they are all shot down.'

10.30am (11.30am), KONSTANCIN, WARSAW DISTRICT

Hearing of the attack on the American ambassador's villa, foreign correspondents have dashed from Warsaw to view the damage. They are now clamouring to interview Biddle. He puts on a brave front and jokingly tells them, 'I am sure Hermann Goering knew my address but I hardly believed he would send a calling card so soon. As an American husband and father I'm proud of the way the women took the experience. They stood it like soldiers and never quivered.' The Poles are naturally anxious for the popular ambassador's safety. But they are delighted that such a leading foreign envoy can now be cited as a witness to the fact that the Germans, despite their promises, are deliberately bombing non-military targets. Biddle now motors back to Warsaw. There he cables Secretary of State Cordell Hull in Washington an account of the bombing.

10.30am (11.30am), GERMAN-POLISH BORDER

After the excitement of the air attack, Wilhelm Prueller's company receives orders to prepare to march on Krakow, Poland's second-largest city. Prueller writes, 'It's supposed to be a forced march ... Perhaps Poland is already done for today.'

10.45am (11.45am), FRENCH EMBASSY, BERLIN

Foreign Minister Bonnet's urgent telephone call from Paris is taken by Robert Coulondre. He has been ambassador in Berlin since last October. Bonnet tells him of the change in expiry times, and Coulondre alters the text with his own fountain pen. But suddenly the ambassador is seized with doubts. Perhaps it is not Bonnet on the line but an impostor? Coulondre calls for verification. Alexis Leger, the permanent head of the Quai d'Orsay, comes on the line. He confirms to the ambassador that it is indeed France's foreign minister to whom Coulondre has been speaking. Reassured, the ambassador prepares to leave for the Wilhelmstrasse.

10.55am (11.55am), FRENCH EMBASSY, BERLIN

Ambassador Coulondre leaves the embassy to make the short drive to the Foreign Ministry to present France's final ultimatum. Like Henderson, Coulondre has tried to make an appointment to see von Ribbentrop himself. But the ambassador is told that the foreign minister is not available. Instead, Coulondre will be received by von Ribbentrop's more sympathetic and congenial deputy, State Secretary Ernst von Weizsacker.

A small crowd has gathered on the Pariser Platz outside the embassy. It has been drawn perhaps by the smoke billowing from the embassy chimneys. Inside, Coulondre's staff are frantically burning the last secret documents, codes and ciphers. Just as the dapper French envoy is about to get into his car, a teenage boy approaches him from the crowd. For an instant Coulondre wonders if he is going to be physically or verbally attacked. But the teenager just wants the ambassador's autograph, which Coulondre willingly gives.

Arriving at the Foreign Office, Coulondre is greeted by von Weizsacker. He is an ex-naval officer and most of Berlin's diplomatic colony much prefer to deal with him, rather than his boss, the bumptious von Ribbentrop. But the ambassador is now dismayed when von Weizsacker tells him that he himself can give no reply to the French ultimatum. Coulondre must wait for von Ribbentrop. The French diplomat considers this to be a deliberate snub and he is annoyed to be kept waiting. But von Ribbentrop soon appears. He has been at the Reich Chancellery with Hitler to receive the new Soviet ambassador.

Getting straight to the point, Coulondre asks the Foreign Minister if he can give him a satisfactory reply to the French note presented on Friday. Von Ribbentrop is evasive and tells the ambassador, 'The delay in replying was due to Mussolini's initiative taken on 2 September. The Duce had offered to mediate and we were prepared for a compromise if we had French agreement. Later Mussolini informed us that the compromise had failed owing to British intransigence.'

Deliberately speaking in German, despite having faultless French, von Ribbentrop continues, 'This morning, the ambassador of Great Britain gave us an unacceptable ultimatum which was rejected. If the French Government considers itself bound, because of all its engagements towards Poland, to enter the conflict, I can only regret it. We shall only fight France if she attacks us, and it would be on her part a war of aggression.'

Having heard all the German's lame excuses in silence, Coulondre now asks, 'Must I conclude from this that the German Government's reply to my letter of 1 September is negative?'

'Yes,' von Ribbentrop curtly replies.

Coulondre now reads out to the Foreign Minister and von Weizsacker the terms of the French ultimatum:

Your Excellency

Not having received by noon on 3rd September a satisfactory reply from the Government of the Reich to the letter which I presented to you on 1st September at 10pm, I have the honour, on the instructions of my Government, to make the following communication to you.

The Government of the French Republic consider it their duty to point out for the last time the heavy responsibility assumed by the Government of the Reich in opening hostilities against Poland without a declaration of war and in not taking up the suggestion made by the Governments of the French Republic and of His Britannic Majesty to suspend all aggressive action against Poland and to declare themselves ready promptly to withdraw their forces from Polish territory.

In consequence, the Government of the French Republic have the honour to inform the Government of the Reich that they find themselves obliged to fulfil, as from today, 3rd September at 5pm, the obligations which France has entered towards Poland and which are known to the German Government.

Pray accept, Your Excellency, the assurance of my highest consideration.

On hearing the terms of the ultimatum, von Ribbentrop says in a cold voice, 'Very well, France will be the aggressor.'

To which Coulondre replies, 'History will be the judge of that.'

The diplomatic formalities over, the French ambassador makes to take his leave. He gives von Weizsacker a firm farewell handshake, but does not offer his hand to von Ribbentrop. Instead Coulondre gives the despised Foreign Minister a sharp look and returns to his embassy, feeling now 'a little like a robot'. There is still a small crowd outside the embassy. But the ambassador observes there is 'no patriotic fever, none of the bellicose enthusiasm which accompanied the war of 1914. If the war with Poland was popular among Nazi and military leaders, it did not seem to be with the man in the street.'

11.00am, SS ATHENIA, ATLANTIC OCEAN

Because of the swell, especially the cross currents of the Devil's Hole, the great Atlantic chasm off Ireland, there are fewer passengers this morning at the ship's church service. Those who have felt up to attending sing the traditional seamen's hymns, 'Eternal Father, Strong to Save' and 'Oh God, Our Help in Ages Past.'

11.00am, HMS SUFFOLK, PORTSMOUTH

Fifteen minutes ago, the order was given to 'clear lower deck' and now naval pilot Hugo Bracken and the rest of the ship's company are assembled on the parade ground of the Royal Naval Air Station at Lee-on-Solent. As the hour strikes, the Captain tells the crew that Britain is now at war with Germany. He makes a speech and then calls for three cheers for the King. Nobody is surprised by the news. Hugo has been expecting it since Hitler broke the Munich Agreement back in March when he occupied Prague. As the parade is dismissed and the men begin to disperse, the air-raid sirens sound and the men go to their allotted air-raid shelters.

11.00am, PUTNEY

'No reply from Germany so at eleven o'clock this country declared war. Almost immediately the sirens screeched forth their warning – I looked up from my window and found everyone down the road hanging out of theirs. In my loud carrying voice I shouted, "That's the warning, you know" and it was most comical to see the heads disappearing and the windows slamming as they all rushed to shelter. Nothing happened and quite soon the "all clear" sounded.' (Vivienne Hall)

11.00am (12.00pm), REICH CHANCELLERY, VOSS-STRASSE, BERLIN

Just as the British ultimatum expires, Adolf Hitler, in his capacity as head of state, receives the new Soviet ambassador. For the ceremony, the Fuehrer is wearing his new field-grey uniform. But with the addition of a gold-embroidered sword-belt, which seems to be more Goering's style than Hitler's. The ambassador, Alexander Shkvartsev, is accompanied by his military attaché, Maxim Purkayev.

Von Ribbentrop is on hand to assist Hitler with the ceremony. Unthinkable only a month ago, a guard of honour is drawn up in the courtyard to salute Stalin's envoy and his party on arrival and departure.

11.00am (12.00pm), BRITISH EMBASSY, BERLIN
As the British ultimatum expires, staff of the Berlin embassy gather together in the Chancery. Among the assembled diplomats the feeling is one of relief that the waiting is now over. For a long time they have all thought that nothing would prevent Hitler from going ahead and invading Poland. They now stop the ornate Chancery clock with its hands exactly on 11.00am. Third Secretary Geoffrey Harrison pastes a piece of paper over its glass face. On it is written a note that says that the clock has been stopped on purpose at the hour that Britain went to war with Germany. It will not be restarted until Hitler is defeated.

11.00am (12.00pm), BAVARIAN MINISTRY OF THE INTERIOR, MUNICH
Hard-drinking Gauleiter Adolf Wagner, who lost a leg in the last war, and whose voice sounds just like Hitler's finally picks up the envelope that Unity Mitford left earlier this morning. On opening it, he is horrified to find a suicide note from Unity, together with her signed portrait of the Fuehrer and Nazi Party badge. The note says that as she cannot bear a war between Britain and her beloved Germany, 'she must put an end to herself'. Aware of Unity's place in Hitler's intimate circle, Wagner is now thoroughly alarmed. He puts through an emergency call to the Munich Police Department with orders to find the English aristocrat before she goes ahead with her suicide plan.

11.05am, FRENCH EMBASSY, LONDON
France's Ambassador to the Court of St James Charles Corbin is meeting with Hugh Dalton and fellow Labour frontbencher and

defence expert A.V. Alexander. Corbin is angry. He has heard rumours that around Westminster there are stories current that France is going to dodge out of her obligations to Poland. Nothing could be further from the truth, Corbin tells the two Labour leaders. But Dalton remains sceptical. He looks at his watch and pointedly remarks to the ambassador, 'My country is at war *now* in fulfilment of *our* pledge to Poland.' Corbin comes back with the reply, 'And *my* country will be at war in a few hours' time.' Corbin also reminds Dalton and Alexander that France has now got three million men under arms and 'soon she will have six million'. And he rams home the point that 'it is upon my country that the heaviest blows will fall'.

11.10am, CITY OF LONDON

Daily Express columnist Tom Driberg is in a taxi on the way to Fleet Street. Seeing Driberg's gas mask, the driver chuckles. 'You won't need that, sir,' he tells the journalist. 'I have had two campaigns; I know.' But Driberg tells him that he isn't allowed in the *Daily Express* building without it.

11.10am, GERMAN EMBASSY, CARLTON HOUSE TERACE, LONDON

Robert Dunbar, forty-four-year-old head of the Treaty Department of the Foreign Office, leaves his office and makes for the German Embassy, which in the absence of ambassador Herbert von Dirksen, is headed by the chargé d'affaires Dr Theodor Kordt. In his briefcase, as he crosses Horse Guards Parade and the Mall, Dunbar is carrying Britain's formal declaration of war. As soon as he arrives at the embassy, Dunbar, a Military Cross winner in the last war, is taken to Dr Kordt, who is secretly an anti-Nazi. Dunbar has met with Kordt a number of times, and both men respect each other. The British diplomat hands over to the chargé d'affaires Britain's declaration of war. He also gives him a listing of Germans resident in London whom the British Government consider entitled to have diplomatic protection. The absence of certain names on the list causes Kordt to challenge the validity of the list. He and Dunbar then politely argue backwards and forward about the list for the next three-quarters of an hour.

11.14am, 10 DOWNING STREET

Chamberlain gets up from his chair and makes his way to the Cabinet Room, where a microphone has been installed. Outside Number 10 is a large crowd, spreading into the road itself, but they are not making any noise. Nor are they showing any signs of obvious excitement. Waiting in the Cabinet Room is BBC announcer Alvar Lidell who has the job of introducing the Prime Minister. Lidell looks up as Chamberlain enters. His shoulders are hunched and to Lidell he looks 'very, very serious'. Chamberlain sits in front of the microphone and Lidell leans over his shoulder to make his introduction: 'This is London. The Prime Minister.' As Chamberlain begins to speak, Lidell registers how 'crumpled, despondent and old' he looks.

This morning the British Ambassador in Berlin handed the German Government a final note stating that unless we heard from them by eleven o'clock that they were prepared at once to withdraw their troops from Poland, a state of war would exist between us.

I have to tell you now that no such undertaking has been received and that consequently this country is at war with Germany.

You can imagine what a bitter blow it is to me that all my long struggle to win peace has failed. Yet I cannot believe that there is anything more, or anything different that I could have done that would have been more successful.

Up to the very last it would have been quite possible to have arranged a peaceful and honourable settlement between Germany and Poland, but Hitler would not have it.

He had evidently made up his mind to attack Poland whatever happened, and although he now says he put forward reasonable proposals which were rejected by Poland, that is not a true statement.

The proposals were never shown to the Poles, nor to us, and though they were announced in a German broadcast on Thursday night, Hitler did not wait to hear comments on them, but ordered his troops to cross the Polish frontier. His action shows convincingly that there is no chance of expecting that this man will ever give up his practice of using force to gain his will. He can only be stopped by force.

We and France are today, in fulfilment of our obligations, going to the aid of Poland, who is so bravely resisting this wicked and unprovoked attack on her people.

We have a clear conscience. We have done all that any country could do to establish peace.

The situation in which no word given by Germany's ruler could be trusted and no people or country could feel themselves safe has become intolerable.

And now we have resolved to finish it I know that you will play your part with calmness and courage.

At such a moment as this the assurances of support that we have received from the Empire are a source of profound encouragement to us.

When I have finished speaking certain detailed announcements will be made on behalf of the Government. Give these your closest attention.

The Government have made plans under which it will be possible to carry out the work of the nation in the days of stress and strain that may be ahead. But these plans need your help.

You may be taking your part in the fighting services or as a volunteer in one of the branches of civil defence. If so, you will report for duty in accordance with the instructions you have received.

You may be engaged in work essential to the prosecution of the war, for the maintenance of the life of the people – in factories, in transport, in public utility concerns, or in the supply of other necessaries of life.

If so, it is of vital importance that you should carry on with your jobs.

Now may God bless you all. May He defend the right. It is the evil things that we shall be fighting against – brute force, bad faith, injustice, oppression and persecution – and against them I am certain that the right will prevail.

11.15am, Queen Charlotte's Hospital, London

As Chamberlain begins to speak, twenty-eight-year-old Mrs Frank Mooney gives birth to a baby boy. Milkman Frank and his wife have intended to name the baby Michael, but in view of what is happening today, it looks as if the baby is now going to be called Neville after the Prime Minister.

11.15am, Great Britain

All over the country, volunteer diarists of the Mass Observation organisation are recording their thoughts and emotions as they listen to the Prime Minister's broadcast. Mass Observation was set up just over two and a half years ago. Its aim is to record and report in minute detail, across as wide a spectrum as possible, the thoughts and behaviour of the British people.

11.15am, TEDDINGTON

'Clear, bright, breezy – a lovely morning with white clouds in a blue sky after the most violent storm in the night that sounded like a bombardment. Prime Minister at 11.15 . . . "This Country is at War with Germany".' (Helena Mott)

11.15am, SHEFFIELD

A twenty-one-year-old female office worker is listening to the wireless with her parents. It is a glorious morning outside, but the family are glued to the radio, avidly catching every BBC news bulletin. As Chamberlain announces that war is declared, the diarist has a 'funny feeling inside me, and yet all three stood at attention for "The King", and I know that we were all in the same mind, that we shall and must win'.

11.15am, UNNAMED SMALL COUNTRY TOWN

The diarist here is a forty-eight-year-old schoolmistress. As Chamberlain makes his broadcast, she notes, 'I held my chin high and kept back the tears at the thought of all the slaughter ahead. When "God Save the King" was played we stood.'

11.15am, LEEDS

A young housewife writes, 'The milkman told me about the ultimatum to Germany expiring at 11am. We could eat no breakfast hardly and just waited with sweating palms and despair for eleven o'clock. When the announcement was made, "This country is at war with Germany", I leant against my husband and went quite dead for a minute or two.'

11.15am, ESSEX

In her Mass Observation diary a 'gentlewoman' records, 'I had been told by the gardener that an important announcement would be given out on the wireless. It would be either peace or war, and anxiety increased as the time drew near. Then it was the latter. I stood up for "God Save the King" and my little dog got out of her basket and stood beside me. I took her on my lap for comfort.'

11.15am, ETON COLLEGE, BERKSHIRE

Sixteen-year-old Eileen Donald is an evacuee from Wandsworth. She has just taken her Matriculation exams and hopes to get into the sixth form and then go to university. She came to Eton on Friday, and yesterday was at Windsor station helping with the arrival of new evacuees. With her friends, she hears Chamberlain speak on the wireless, and then goes for a walk on the playing fields of Eton, where the Duke of Wellington is supposed to have said the Battle of Waterloo was won. Eileen thinks to herself how beautiful they and the weather are today and how strange it is 'to be conscious of so much beauty and at the same time to be so horrified at the thought of war'.

11.15am, THE COTSWOLDS

Crispin Tickell, nine-year-old son of writer Jerrard Tickell, is staying at his grandmother's house on the banks of the River Windrush. Just before Chamberlain is due to speak, Crispin and his brother are called into the dining room to hear the broadcast. Crispin is both 'vaguely disturbed and depressed' as he listens to the Prime Minister's announcement. He thinks Chamberlain sounds so sad. But Crispin's grandmother calls the Prime Minister 'a damned fool', just as she did at the time of Munich last year. She then goes out to snip flowers. Cheered up by his grandmother's forthright response, Crispin follows her out into the garden.

11.15am, CITY OF LONDON

Tom Driberg and his taxi driver have pulled up at a City church to hear the broadcast. Together with the congregation they learn that Britain is once again at war. 'That's that,' the vicar says slowly. Driberg thinks this 'an extremely, characteristically English way of acknowledging the news'.

11.15am, TAKELEY

In the village hall, Moyra Charlton's mother has assembled a group of volunteer helpers to assist with the arrival of evacuees from London. They were due soon after 10.00am, but still have not turned up. Moyra and the others, 'Women Institute members, farmers, all the good solid Takeley faces', now listen impassively to the Charltons' portable radio set as Chamberlain speaks. Moyra's eyes fill with tears as she looks around and sees 'those grave, ruddy faces … and the golden country outside, with the church in the trees and the harvest not yet in'. But, thinks Moyra, 'thank Heaven the suspense is over'.

11.15am, GOLDERS GREEN ROAD, LONDON

Britain's leading radio and variety comedian, Arthur 'Big-Hearted' Askey, star of the hit show *Band Waggon*, turns on his radio. Arthur has had a hectic week filming and then appearing twice nightly at the London Palladium, and has not had time to catch up with the news. Now, he is shocked to hear the Prime Minister announce that we are at war. As Chamberlain finishes and sirens begin to sound, Arthur looks out of the window to see a patrolling air-raid warden. The warden, on hearing the sirens, manages to blow his own whistle. But then, without warning, he faints on the pavement.

11.15am, CHICHESTER, SUSSEX

Pamela Mountbatten, fifteen-year-old daughter of Royal Navy Captain Lord Louis Mountbatten and his wife Edwina, is out riding

IWM D 2771

An air-raid siren situated by a police public call-box. 'The first air-raid warning symbolised the end of the war of nerves and the start of the war of arms, above all the war from the air.'

this morning. She has ridden up to the top of one of the ancient burial sites that overlooks the countryside. Knowing that Britain is now at war, she thinks, 'How *extraordinary* that from now on, and who knows for *how* long, we are going to be at war, with all that that means.'

11.15am, North Cheam, Surrey

Sixteen-year-old Iris Cutbush has just washed her hair and rolled it up in pipe cleaners so that when combed it will come out 'all lovely and frizzy'. She hears Chamberlain's broadcast and then the sirens. Iris is sure that the Germans are going to use poison gas, so she puts on her gas mask, still with the pipe cleaners in her hair. Mr Cutbush, a 1914–18 veteran, comes in from the garden, where he's been mowing the lawn. He sees Iris and says, 'What do you think you're doing? You're not going to be gassed. Take it off.' Iris struggles with the mask, but try as she might, she cannot get it off. Eventually she pulls the mask off, but tears the rubber. Iris now ruefully reflects that it will not be 'any good in a gas attack after that'.

11.15am, Piers Court, Stinchcombe, Gloucestershire

Novelist Evelyn Waugh, a Roman Catholic convert, has attended Mass and taken communion early this morning. After returning home, he has breakfast and listens to Chamberlain's broadcast. 'He did it very well' is Waugh's opinion.

11.15am, London

Writer and former secret agent Compton Mackenzie hears the Prime Minister's broadcast and registers Chamberlain's 'tired sad voice'. Last Sunday, Mackenzie returned early from abroad because of the crisis. He is still rather shocked at the way his porter at Victoria Station praised Hitler: 'It's a pity we haven't got anybody as good as him here. What I mean is, look what he has done for his own people. Well, he comes from the people himself. He knows what they want.'

Mackenzie is also surprised to be told by an official at the Air Ministry: 'We are not going to drop bombs on Germany. We are going to drop propaganda leaflets. Don't you think that's a wonderful idea?'

11.15am, CAMBRIDGE

German Jewish refugee Hans Koenigsberger is a student at Caius College, reading History. He has been in Britain since 1934, but his mother Kaethe only got out of Germany earlier this year. Together with Hans's landlady they listen to the Prime Minister on an old radio set in the sitting room of his digs. The declaration of war comes as no surprise to the Koenigsbergers. They know only too well that the Hitler is not going to give in tamely to the British ultimatum and withdraw his troops from Poland. But the landlady has retained hopes that peace could be preserved. Now, as she hears that the country is at war, she keeps repeating over and over again, 'They are wicked . . . they are wicked . . . they are wicked.'

11.15am, GLASGOW, SCOTLAND

As Chamberlain delivers his broadcast there is a huge rumble of thunder, and lightning flashes across the sky.

11.15am, CROYDON

Twelve-year-old convent schoolgirl Sheila Ward is getting ready to be evacuated as she and her family wait for Chamberlain to speak. Sheila and her brother have spent the morning packing up their books and stamp collections to be stored away 'for the duration'. Their father has already written out their evacuation labels with their names, school addresses and identity numbers. Sheila's is CDE 64/5.

11.15am, HAMPSTEAD

FANY Verily Anderson hears Chamberlain's broadcast at a friend's house. From it one can look down on all of London. Hearing the sirens go after the broadcast, Verily and her friends Phyl and Portia tear upstairs to the top window to see what is happening. From all over the London they can see 'from the green of squares, the gardens, the parks, silver barrage balloons shining in the morning sun . . . floating silently up into the sky'.

Verily says to her friends, 'If this is war, it's much prettier than I expected.' To which Portia replies, 'It is the war. The Prime Minister said so.' The 'All Clear' sounds and the girls soon learn that it has been a false alarm. Verily picks up on a false rumour that is soon going the rounds: 'It was only the Duke of Windsor flying in. He wanted to be there at the start.'

11.15am, CAMBRIDGESHIRE

In a farmhouse kitchen, trainee Land Girl Edith Barraud listens to Chamberlain's announcement with farmer Ted and his mother. Edith notes how tired the Prime Minister's voice sounds. On hearing Chamberlain say, 'this country is at war with Germany', Ted's mother exclaims, 'Oh Ted, that means war!' 'Ah!' Ted laconically replies. He then gets up and goes out to mix the cows' grub for the afternoon feed.

11.15am, OXFORD

Dorothy Bartlett and her family are sitting round the radio set. It has been tuned in for some time when Chamberlain finally comes on the air. Dorothy and the others hear the Prime Minister's 'tired, almost exhausted' voice tell them that they are now at war. After Chamberlain finishes speaking, they turn the radio off and each speculates what the news will mean to them. Already, Dorothy has received an official notification from the Territorial Nursing Service. It tells her to hold herself 'in readiness for an emergency'.

11.15am, CHELTENHAM, GLOUCESTERSHIRE

Nan Wise, a fifteen-year-old pupil at Birmingham's King Edward High School, has been in Cheltenham since Friday. She fears today that Chamberlain is going to let the Poles down, just as the Czechs were abandoned last year. But now Nan hears that the Prime Minister has announced that Britain is at war. She is tremendously relieved that Britain has honoured her pledge, but relieved too that she and her schoolfriends can now 'settle down to enjoy their new-found world'. She is glad that they will not 'have to return, tails between our legs, to the old familiar rut'.

11.15am, Ashford, Kent

Schoolboy Rodney Giesler, of mixed English and German parentage, hears Chamberlain's broadcast and is 'absolutely inconsolable' at the news.

11.15am, The King and Queen Public House, Harrow Road, Paddington

Peter Coats, a Territorial Army officer in the Middlesex Yeomanry, is going the rounds of his unit's various posts in Paddington. One of them is located in the vestry of St Mary's Church, where the actress Mrs Siddons is buried. At 11.00am, an hour before opening time, Coats and his sergeant enter the pub to hear the prime-ministerial broadcast. Coats is a close friend of the Chamberlain admiring Conservative MP, Henry 'Chips' Channon. He does not, however, share his friend's blind enthusiasm for the Prime Minister. But now as Coats listens to Chamberlain's 'sad old voice on the wireless', he feels sorry for him. Coats and the sergeant start making their way back to St Mary's when the sirens sound. Coats experiences mixed emotions: slight panic, exhilaration 'and a desire, at all costs, not to seem afraid'. The thought flashes through his mind that in the space of a few minutes London would be sharing the fate of Warsaw, turned into blazing rubble. Instead, the 'All Clear' sounds. Coats has been frightened. But he hopes that he has not shown it. He hopes too that 'perhaps it would be easier the next time'.

11.15am, CARN, INISHOWEN, SOUTHERN IRELAND

Glasgow schoolboy Bob Crampsey is on an extended holiday at his aunt and uncle's. But he is homesick. With war threatening he wants to go back to Glasgow. Fortunately, Bob's father has arrived earlier this morning to take him back. Mr Crampsey came over on the *Royal Ulsterman*, which was 'crammed to the rails with evacuees'. He then motored down from Belfast. Now Bob, his father, aunt and uncle sit in the stone-floored kitchen, listening to the battery radio as Chamberlain announces that Britain is at war with Germany. As they hear the Prime Minister's words, Bob sees his father and uncle exchange glances. Instantly, he knows they are thinking back to the Great War, in which both men fought. Then quietly, as 'God Save the King' dies away, Mr Crampsey tells Bob to get ready for the journey home.

11.15am, CHARING CROSS ROAD, LONDON

Sir Kenneth Clark listens to the Prime Minister in a café not far from the National Gallery. Finally, Clark thinks, Chamberlain has come to acknowledge 'the reality of evil', which the British people have 'dumbly recognised for the last two or three years'.

11.15am, BALCOMBE STREET, MARYLEBONE

Barrister and volunteer ARP stretcher-bearer Robert Bayne-Powell records his reflections on hearing Chamberlain speak: 'Chamberlain spoke shortly and well. So it has come as I feared it would. God grant us victory and, after it, the wisdom to make a treaty which will not seem to the vanquished so necessary to be revised as the "Versailles *Diktat*". Germany, in the event of our victory, should be helped economically, but crushed politically, perhaps by dismemberment into the pre-1870 states.'

11.15am, EVESHAM, GLOUCESTERSHIRE

Popular travel writer and novelist Cecil Roberts is motoring back to London from Liverpool. Last night he broke his journey in the attractive Cotswolds town of Evesham. Going out this 'sweet and clear' morning to get a Sunday newspaper, he hears the sound of Chamberlain broadcasting from an open window. He is invited in by the young housewife, who has a baby in her arms. Ten people are crammed in the little parlour, listening to the Prime Minister. Among them is the young husband, a railway porter, sitting with a little girl evacuee on his knee. Chamberlain finishes and the National Anthem is played. Everybody stands and looks gravely at each other. Roberts catches the eye of the husband. He seems to be saying, 'I know this means that in a few weeks I shall be a soldier. Next year at this time my wife may be a widow and my girl have no father.' As the last bars of 'God Save the King' fade away, his wife turns off the radio. 'Mr Chamberlain spoke beautifully,' she says, her voice choking with tears.

11.15am, MINISTRY OF ECONOMIC WARFARE, LONDON SCHOOL OF ECONOMICS BUILDING, LONDON

Twenty-four-year-old junior Foreign Office official John Colville has just arrived at the LSE building. He is being seconded from the FO to work at the new ministry. But as yet he and his new colleagues have nothing to do. A radio is produced and switched on. Colville and the others listen to Chamberlain's broadcast. Colville thinks it is made 'with slow, solemn dignity'. On hearing the news that Britain is now at war, Colville experiences a sense of numbness. But, the young civil servant is soon 'rudely revived by the sirens moaning out the war's first air-raid warning'.

11.15am, BIRMINGHAM

Frank T. Lockwood is a commercial artist with Cadbury Brothers Ltd at Bournville. He has only just got back from holiday at Fairbourne, where fifty evacuees arrived yesterday. With his family, Frank, who served with the Royal Flying Corps and the RAF during the Kaiser's War, listens to the Prime Minister's broadcast. Frank has the overriding impression of Chamberlain's 'genuine sadness' as he hears the Premier announce, 'with emotion', that Hitler has rejected the British ultimatum. Frank considers that Chamberlain has given 'a reasoned and memorable speech'. But even today, with Britain at war, Frank thinks it seems very strange to hear the Prime Minister speaking of 'Hitler' and not '*Herr* Hitler'. After Chamberlain finishes, Frank decides to carry on improving domestic air-raid precautions. As he works at the back of the house, Frank can see 'a considerable number of barrage balloons' up in the blue sky.

11.15am, JERSEY, CHANNEL ISLANDS

Writer Norman Scarlyn Wilson, author of some of the bestselling 'Teach Yourself' books, listens to the Prime Minister in the lounge of his hotel. Wilson is struck by the effectiveness of Chamberlain's simple words. 'Here was no great oratory, no sonorous periods, no phrasemaking, but words one could understand, words born of sincerity and honesty of purpose.' As the Prime Minister finishes, Wilson and his fellow guests stand for the National Anthem.

11.15am, SS *ATHENIA*, ATLANTIC OCEAN

Second Radio Officer Donald McRae picks up the news of Britain's declaration of war from the radio station at Valentia.

11.15am, BARKING, EAST LONDON

Twenty-two-year-old dance-band vocalist Vera Lynn is at home with her parents. Today is her father's birthday and the family are sitting out in the garden, enjoying the sunshine, when they hear on a portable radio that Britain is now at war. Over the last three or four years, Vera has done well, and she is now appearing with Britain's top dance band, Ambrose and His Orchestra. Today, with war declared and all places of entertainment due to be closed indefinitely, Vera is worried about the future and thinks, 'Just as I'm beginning to get well-known, bang goes my career.'

11.15am, ESSEX

Anthony Wedgwood-Benn, fourteen-year-old son of a Labour MP, is on holiday with his family. The day before yesterday, his father had to leave the holiday home to return to Parliament. Now Tony and his brothers listen to Chamberlain on a radio set they have hired for the holiday. Tony thinks Chamberlain is much too self-pitying. Today, he has no sympathy for the Prime Minister, nor for his policy of appeasement. Tony is very politically aware for a teenager, and for some time now has regarded war as inevitable. Last year he even bought his own gas mask for five shillings (25p).

11.15am, MITCHAM, SURREY

Dorothy Tyler is a nineteen-year-old athlete who competed in the Berlin Olympics three years ago. Usually on Sundays she trains at the News of the World track at Mitcham. But this morning she is at home with her mother and two brothers to hear the Prime Minister's broadcast. Dorothy's first reaction is a selfish one. She won't now be able to go to Helsinki to take part in the 1940 Games. This is a great disappointment as she is a world-record holder and favourite for a gold medal.

11.15am, CHESHAM BOIS, BUCKINGHAMSHIRE

Thirty-nine-year-old Great War veteran Derek Barnes listens to 'Chamberlain's tired, heart-broken voice telling us that we were at war with Germany for the second time in twenty-five years'. As the Prime Minister speaks, Derek looks round his quiet, sunny, green garden. His two-year-old baby son 'is staggering about the lawn, picking daisies with the podgy earnestness of the two year adventurer'. Derek remembers how, in August 1914, as a teenager he had 'cheered and cheered and prayed only that the war might last enough for me to join the army'. 'And,' he sombrely recalls, 'it did.' Now he and his wife blink back the tears. Their immediate reaction this morning is 'entirely selfish, entirely personal'. Derek's own overriding emotion is that of anger. He is inflamed 'with fury at the futility of governments which had failed to give realization to the universal longing of their inarticulate peoples for peace and gentleness'. Pacing up and down the garden he shouts to his wife, 'You couldn't find a single German man or woman who doesn't want peace. Not a soul in all of England or France, either! And yet these bloody governments, with their blasted politics, land us all in *this*!' But even as he sounds off, to his own intense amazement and forgetting his age, Derek recognises in a flash, 'I must go to this war – leaving all that I loved behind me – precisely because I loved it.'

11.15am (12.15pm), Hotel Angleterre, Copenhagen
Ewan Butler and the other correspondents who have managed to get out of Germany in time, gather in a colleague's hotel room. There, they hear on his radio, 'the tired, sad voice of Neville Chamberlain', announce that Britain is at war. The correspondents open champagne and drink a toast to victory. Butler then goes down to the bar, where he encounters two stout prosperous Danish businessmen he met there last night. 'Ah!' they cry out cheerfully, 'so you are at war! Come and have a drink!' And Butler, relieved that the waiting is now over, gratefully joins them.

11.15am (12.15pm), Englischer Garten, Munich
Atomic scientist Professor Hoenigschmitt is taking a Sunday-morning stroll in Munich's English Garden. He is only a hundred or so yards inside the park when he hears what sounds like a shot. He sees a figure slumped on a park bench quite near to the entrance by Hitler's prized House of German Art. Rushing up to the bench, the Professor immediately recognises the slumped figure as that of Unity Mitford. He has met her in the past at the house of a mutual friend. He urgently calls for help and the police arrive. They flag down a Luftwaffe car and order the driver to

rush Unity to Munich's university clinic. Unity is hovering between life and death, 'very white and corpse-like', when she arrives at the clinic.

11.15am (12.15pm), WARSAW

Patrick Maitland and some others are crowding around a radio set, trying to pick up Chamberlain's broadcast, but the Germans are jamming it. At the Foreign Office, correspondent Ed Beattie is waiting with one of Colonel Beck's officials when suddenly the door opens and in bursts another Pole who tells them that Britain has just declared war, and the French are going to follow suit this afternoon. Beattie's companion breaks down and cries, 'It has been quite a strain, this waiting,' he explains.

11.15am (12.15pm), ESPLANADE HOTEL, BERLIN

In the *Chicago Tribune* bureau office, correspondents Sigrid Schultz and John 'Jack' M. Raleigh listen to Chamberlain's speech on the radio. They both gasp as they hear the Prime Minister announce that Britain is at war. As soon as Chamberlain finishes, Raleigh dashes out of the office and into the hotel lobby. He is on his way to the Propaganda Ministry to get more information. One of the hotel desk clerks asks the hurrying correspondent if there is any news and Raleigh shouts back in reply 'You are at war with France and England!' The clerk is absolutely stunned. He recoils and turns white, his hands grasping the edge of the counter. Mumbling 'God in Heaven', the man stumbles into the manager's office to pass on the bad news.

11.15am (12.15pm), WILHELMSHAVEN

Commodore Karl Doenitz, head of the German Navy's U-boat arm, is told of Britain's declaration of war. He is stunned and keeps repeating, 'My God! So it's war against England again!'

11.15am (1.15pm), German Embassy, Ankara

Ambassador Franz von Papen has only just received official notification of the British ultimatum. With his staff, he now hears on the embassy's radio Chamberlain announcing that Britain is at war with Germany. Von Papen, a former Reich Chancellor, was one of those responsible for helping Hitler into power six years ago. Today he is both distraught and horrified at the news. In the safety of the embassy's garden, he confides in Fraulein Maria Rose, his personal secretary. 'Mark my words,' von Papen tells her, 'this war is the worst crime and the greatest madness that Hitler and his clique have ever committed. Germany can never win this war. Nothing will be left but ruins.' Despite this, the lightweight, foppish von Papen decides to remain as Hitler's ambassador to the Turks. He hopes that he may have a chance to 'deflect the coming catastrophe' or at least 'limit the conflict'.

11.17am, Admiralty, Whitehall

The signal goes out to all Royal Naval warships to commence hostilities against Germany.

11.17am, HMS Cornwall, at sea off Singapore

Eighteen-year-old Midshipman Peter Austin and the crew are fallen in on the quarter deck listening to a talk by the ship's captain. The men have already been told that the British ultimatum is going to expire at 18.00 hours, Singapore time. The captain tells his men 'that we realise that it was now a question of time before we went to war. The object of this war was not to smash the German people themselves, but to uproot Hitlerism and destroy it completely.' Just as he finishes speaking, the Admiralty signal to commence hostilities is received. On hearing the news, Austin turns and 'examines the horizon expecting to see the enemy waiting to attack us'. There is of course, as Austin soon realises, nothing in sight at all.

11.17am, HMS CICADA, HONG KONG

Lieutenant Patrick Bayly and the other members of the crew of the river gunboat listen to the captain read out the Admiralty signal, adding, 'God Save the King and keep safe all our families.' For Bayly and the other men it is 'a highly emotional moment'.

11.17am, HMS DELIGHT, INDIAN OCEAN

Radio operator Bernard Campion is coming to the end of his first 'dog watch'. The sea is very rough, and in the cramped and stuffy radio compartment the lead-covered codebooks are being constantly flung about by the destroyer's pitching and rolling. The seasick Campion is counting the minutes to the time he can turn over to his relief. He desperately wants to get back to his hammock. But a new signal arrives. Unusually, it is in plain language, not code. It is the Admiralty signal to commence hostilities. Campion admires its 'Nelsonian simplicity'. He senses that he is turning over a page of history as he bawls the message up the voice-pipe to the bridge.

11.25am (12.25pm), BERLIN

Although Britain and Germany have been at war for the last half hour, from the British Embassy Sir Nevile Henderson sets out for the Foreign Ministry. He has just received a message from von Ribbentrop, requesting an interview. The pavement outside the embassy is completely deserted with just a single Berlin policeman pacing up and down. Sir Nevile is reminded that, on 4 August 1914, the embassy was besieged by a howling mob that smashed the windows and 'hurled abuse at its inmates and at Great Britain'.

11.28am, LONDON

Backbench Tory MP Victor Cazalet, once an early protégé of Churchill's, comes up to London to attend today's midday sitting of the Commons. He arrives just as the sirens are sounding and people running to the shelters. At first, Cazalet and fellow MPs joke about the warning, but then he experiences 'a sort of sinking feeling'.

11.28am, CITY OF LONDON

High Anglican Driberg has decided to stay on and attend morning service. Just as it is beginning, the sirens go. For Driberg it is a 'blood-curdling, spine-shivering sound'. He last heard the sound of sirens in February this year during the last days of the Spanish Civil War. He recalls that then the sirens were followed 'within five minutes or so by the drone of German bombers, by ear-shattering explosions, by crumbling houses and gutters streaming blood'. Now the young vicar quietly says, 'People must do what they like – what they think best.' No one leaves, but Driberg and a few others prudently move to a windowless aisle. The service continues with the parable of the Good Samaritan.

11.28am, 10 DOWNING STREET

As soon as Chamberlain finishes, some of his colleagues enter the Cabinet Room. R.A. Butler, Lord Halifax's deputy at the Foreign Office and a leading appeaser, thinks the Prime Minister's speech 'pathetically moving, but scarcely a tocsin ringing to arms'. Just as the Prime Minister is asking his colleagues how they liked his speech, there is a terrible wailing sound. 'That is an air-raid warning,' Chamberlain tells them. He is quite calm, Butler notices. Somebody says, 'It would be funny if it were,' but Chamberlain keeps on repeating the phrase 'That is an air-raid warning.' He reminds Butler of a schoolmaster dinning a lesson into a class of late developers. Then Mrs Chamberlain appears in the doorway. She is carrying a large basket which contains books, thermos flasks and gas masks. Her appearance galvanises everybody into action, and there is a general move towards the underground cabinet war rooms through the basement of Number 10. Butler sees some people scurrying across Horse Guards to take shelter, but he decides to return to the Foreign Office and shelter in the basement there. When he arrives there, Butler finds that he has to sit on the floor, as no furniture has been provided. An officious air-raid warden starts telling Butler and his fellow shelterers that he is not expecting the Germans to use poison gas immediately. Just as he doing so the 'All Clear' sounds, and Butler and the others return to their offices.

11.28am, Snack bar, Clarendon Road, Notting Hill

As the sirens start, a customer leaves hurriedly to take shelter. 'There's my bacon and eggs gone wallop,' he tells a passer-by. As the sirens wails, twenty-year-old Doris, the proprietor's daughter confesses to a 'funny feeling' in her stomach, 'as though it was all upside down'. Her hand is trembling as she offers a customer a cigarette. Doris's mother looking out sees pedestrians hurrying to take shelter and says, 'Look! There must be something wrong. They are running. It must be a raid. It's awful, isn't it?' No one in the snack bar seems to have a very clear idea as to the meaning of the air-raid signals being given. But they do see a warden riding around on a bicycle with placards front and back with 'Take Cover' on them, just like during the German daylight raids back in 1917.

11.28am, Bloomsbury, London

Teenager Nina Masel is playing the piano in her parents' semi-detached house when her mother suddenly bursts in. 'Stop that noise,' Mrs Masel tells Nina as she flings open a window to let in the sound of the sirens. Nina's father takes charge and tells the family. 'All get your gas masks . . . Steady, no panicking! . . . Every man for himself . . . Keep in the passage.' Nan's eleven-year-old sister begins to sob. She keeps asking, 'Will it be alright? Will it be alright?' Nina's own heart keeps beating hard but it soon calms down. As the Masels have not got an air-raid shelter, the family gather in the passage of the house and sit on the stairs. Then, as nothing seems to be happening, Nina, her father and brother, go out to the front gate. Nina hears some babies crying and sees air-raid wardens wearing gas masks and steel helmets running up and down the road. Finally, to everyone's immense relief, the 'All Clear' sounds.

11.28am, MORPETH MANSIONS, WESTMINSTER

Winston Churchill is at his Westminster flat as Chamberlain finishes and the sirens sound. With a nice touch of ironic humour, Mrs Churchill comments 'favourably upon German promptitude and precision'. The Churchills then decide to go up to the flat top of the building to see what is going on. Churchill sees thirty or forty barrage balloons beginning to slowly rise and he gives his new colleagues a good mark for this 'evident sign of preparation'. The Churchills leave the roof and make for their nearest shelter, a hundred yards down the street. They are 'armed with a bottle of brandy and other appropriate medical comforts'. Arriving at the shelter, Churchill sees that everyone is cheerful and jocular, 'as is the English manner when about to encounter the unknown'. Standing at the doorway, Churchill has an apocalyptic vision of 'ruin and carnage and vast explosions shaking the ground; of buildings clattering down in dust and rubble, of fire brigades and ambulances scurrying through the smoke, beneath drone of hostile aeroplanes'. Instead, the 'All Clear' sounds, and an air-raid warden appears shouting the same message. The Churchills and their fellow shelterers disperse. Churchill sets out for the House of Commons.

11.28am, LONDON

Conservative MP Beverley Baxter starts making his way to the Houses of Parliament. Like Churchill, he looks up to the sky and sees, 'high up, in the almost Mediterranean sky, the grotesque defence balloons . . . like distorted, silver boxing gloves'. As he does so, the sirens begin to wail. Like Clementine Churchill, Baxter admits a sneaking admiration for the Nazis' promptitude: 'Our ultimatum had expired at eleven o' clock; now, barely half an hour later, 5,000 machines were bringing their answer . . . at any minute now, that which we had all foreseen would come to pass'.

11.28am, CHELSEA, LONDON

Bohemian teenager Joan Wyndham and her family have just heard Chamberlain. As they are sitting around, feeling rather sick, the air-raid warning goes. For a moment, Joan and the others cannot believe their ears. It has not really sunk in yet that Britain is now at war. But they soon recover, and go down to the cellar which they have prepared as a gasproof room. There, they start damping blankets with pails of water as a measure to keep poison gas out. That done, Joan goes and sits on the front doorstep to wait for the first sounds of gunfire. She looks up and sees the barrage balloons that are 'too lovely in the sun against the blue skies, like iridescent silver fish swimming in blue water'.

11.28am, BALCOMBE STREET, MARYLEBONE

Robert Baynes-Powell and his wife Nancy hear the air-raid warning and make for the bathroom, their flat's safest room in the event of an air raid. They sit there wearing their gas masks and feeling 'very queasy' until the 'All Clear' sounds.

11.28am, HARROW, WEST LONDON

As the sirens sound, writer George Beardmore experiences a sensation of utter panic. He, like so many others, has seen the film *Things to Come*, and now remembers all 'the dire prophecies of scientists, journalists and even politicians of the devastation and disease that would follow the first air raid'. He pictures the Houses of Parliament one heap of rubble and St Paul's Cathedral in ruins.

11.28am, ST PAUL'S CATHEDRAL

The boys of the St Paul's Choir School have already been evacuated to Truro. But even without them, this morning's congregation is unusually large. They are singing:

> 'O God of Love. O King of Peace
> Make wars throughout the world to cease!'

Londoners taking cover as air-raid sirens sounded shortly after war was declared, 3 September 1939. Chamberlain had said earlier in the year, 'If we should ever be involved in war we may well find that if we are not all in the firing line, we may all be in the line of fire.'

just as the air-raid warning is given. The Bishop of Willesden is taking this morning's service. He calmly leads the worshippers down to the crypt to take shelter.

11.28am, GRANADA CINEMA, NORTH CHEAM, SURREY

The staff have just heard Chamberlain's broadcast. They are now listening to cinema manager Watson as he gives them a pep talk. 'And above all,' Watson is telling them, 'we must at all times keep calm,' as the air-raid sirens sound the warning. Before Watson knows what is happening, he is swept aside as most of the staff fly down the stairs into the cinema's foyer and out into the street. Two or three of the cleaners are on top of the circle steps, clinging to the hand-rails and screaming at the tops of their voices. Despite Watson's entreaties they refuse to come down, and the manager ruefully reflects that it must be the effect of his speech.

11.28am, ST JOHN'S WOOD, LONDON

As the sirens begin to wail, Noel Coward is driving up to Woburn Abbey, the 'Hush Hush' headquarters of Britain's secret propaganda organisation. He has already heard Chamberlain's 'lachrymose' announcement, and is now on his way to hear confirmation of a propaganda liaison job with the French in Paris. As the warning sounds, Coward feels 'a sudden coldness in the heart' and an 'automatic tensing of the muscles'. An air-raid warden appears and waves Coward to take cover immediately. He is ushered into a large apartment building and into the basement. Everybody is calm, except for one young woman carrying a baby, who is in tears. Coward wonders if this 'is going to be the real knockout blow, a carefully prepared surprise attack by Hitler within the first hour of war being declared'. More and more people are arriving in the already crowded basement. Coward decides that if he is going to die, 'I would rather die in the open and not suffocate slowly with a load of strangers at the bottom of a lift shaft.' Thus resolved, Coward makes his way up the stairs to the hall. There he runs into theatrical costumier Morris Angel. Angel is delighted to meet Coward and says, 'I think this calls for a bottle of bubbly!' They go up to the Angels' flat on the third floor to find the electricity is turned off and the Sunday joint ruined. Nevertheless, a bottle of champagne is opened and they toast 'the King, each other, and a speedy victory for the Allies'.

11.28am, LONDON

Virginia Cowles hears the sirens sound. Only two days ago she was in Germany, and on Friday evening had heard similar sirens during an air-raid drill in Berlin. Virginia soon learns that this too is a false alarm. She is told that Captain de Brantes, French assistant military attaché in London, has flown in on a private plane, and been mistaken for a German. She also gets an early example of war neurosis. A fellow journalist assures her that he has heard bomb explosions, and that his own building has even rocked – 'ever so slightly'.

11.28am, CROYDON

As the sirens begin to wail, the Ward family all think they are about to die. But then the 'All Clear' sounds and they make tea, 'that great English panacea'. Sheila and her brother are now really excited at the prospect of being evacuated. They have never been away from home before except for the family's annual fortnight's holiday at Broadstairs. But 'this is going to be different, without our parents'. And now it is finally happening, Sheila finds 'it is difficult not to enjoy it'.

11.28am, MINISTRY OF ECONOMIC WARFARE, LONDON SCHOOL OF ECONOMICS

John Colville and three others are playing bridge in the shelter of the London School of Economics. Colville has visions of London being reduced to rubble as in the 1936 film of H.G. Wells's *Things to Come*. But he tries to preserve 'a semblance of nonchalance' while playing cards. He and the others are just finishing the first rubber when the 'All Clear' goes.

11.28am, ASHFORD, KENT

Rodney Giesler hears the siren and thinks, 'Oh, My God, they're *coming*.' The family rush down to the cellar to await the bombs, only to emerge when the 'All Clear' is sounded.

11.28am, EALING, WEST LONDON

Elsie Warren, a volunteer in the Auxiliary Fire Service, has just been listening to the Prime Minister on the wireless. She thinks Chamberlain delivered 'a wonderful speech to the Empire', but 'sounded very unhappy'. Now, just as she is going out, the siren sounds. Seeing a friend, Elsie tells her, 'Hurry up inside . . . that's the air-raid warning.' But her friend replies, 'No, it's just a test.' As they begin to argue, a warden comes rushing up the street, blowing his whistle, and people start scurrying off to shelter. Elsie gets on her bicycle and pedals furiously off to Ealing Fire Station. There, she takes up her place by the telephone, but the news soon comes through that 'it was only a friendly plane that caused the excitement'.

11.28am, MITCHAM, SURREY

After Chamberlain finishes, Dorothy Tyler's two brothers decide to go and see some friends to talk things over. Dorothy goes with them. They are just driving off when the siren goes. They turn the car round, and quickly drive back home. Rushing indoors, they grab and put on their gas masks. They then sit down at the kitchen table to wait and see what happens next. Dorothy is worrying about her fiancé, who is in the army. She thinks that he might be sent to fight in Poland.

11.28am, Smith Square, Westminster

Home Office civil servant Peter Allen and his wife have just driven up to Westminster to attend morning service when they hear an air-raid warning. An air-raid warden, 'suddenly conscious of his grave new responsibilities', ushers the Allens, dutifully clutching their gas masks, into a nearby office block to take shelter. From an upstairs window they can see a barrage balloon going up and then down beyond the roof of Westminster Abbey, 'rather like a slow moving and inverted yo-yo'. Although he realises that German bombers may very well be on their way, Allen experiences a feeling of relief rather than apprehension. The 'long preliminaries' are over at last, and Britain is now engaged 'in a clear-cut contest in which the end, however distant that might be, would surely result in the destruction of the evil regime which held the world in jeopardy'.

11.28am, Brixton, South London

Britain's most popular newspaper columnist Godfrey Winn of the *Sunday Express* is in Brixton, intending to buy a motorcycle. He hopes that by having one, with war coming and petrol rationing inevitable, he will still be able to 'stay mobile'. He is trying out the machine when he hears the 'first sound of that wailing of the banshee'. Winn, startled and nervous, looks up at the sky, half expecting it to be black with enemy bombers. He promptly falls off straight into the gutter.

11.28am, London

Twenty-six-year-old schoolteacher Mary Custance is sitting with her elderly headmistress in the school's small kitchen-cum-staffroom. They are the only two teachers on the staff, and have been told to report to school each day of the crisis to await further orders. Mary's headmistress 'is in great distress of mind about the possibility of war' and feels that she cannot face the anxiety. Just as she is unburdening herself to Mary, the school caretaker/cleaner joins them. She tells the two teachers that war has just been declared. No sooner are the words out of her mouth than the sirens begin to sound. Mary's immediate thought is that they are going to die. But they hurry over to the air-raid shelters, built during the last war, in a nearby works. Like so many others in London today, Mary's mind has been 'influenced by science fiction and H.G. Wells's *The Shape of Things to Come*'. She imagines 'that everything and everybody will have disappeared into bomb-strewn rubble when they finally emerge.' But then the 'All Clear' sounds, and Mary and her companions emerge into an unscathed London.

11.30am, 'La Croe', Côte d'Azur

At his villa in the south of France, Britain's former king, Edward VIII, now Duke of Windsor, is impatiently waiting to hear from London. He is anxious to learn how he can best serve his country, just as he had promised he would do in his Abdication speech almost three years ago. The Duke served throughout the Great War. Because of his status he was denied frontline service, but he has always keenly identified with ex-servicemen and they with him. In May this year he launched an eloquent plea for peace and understanding from the former battlefield of Verdun.

And just a few days ago, on 29 August, as 'a citizen of the world', he sent a telegram to Hitler, urging him not to plunge the world into war. Now, hearing nothing from London, the Duke and Duchess decide to go for a swim. But just as they are setting off, a servant hurries after them. Sir Eric Phipps, the British ambassador in Paris, is on the telephone, urgently wanting to speak with the Duke. The Duke now hurries back to the house. He is back in a few minutes, rejoins the Duchess and announces, 'Great Britain has just declared war on Germany, and I'm afraid in the end this may open the way for world Communism.' He then dives into the pool.

11.30am, FOREIGN MINISTRY, QUAI D'ORSAY, PARIS
The 'phone rings on Georges Bonnet's desk. It is Daladier tele-phoning from the Ministry of National Defence. He tells Bonnet that the Army Chief of General Staff General Colson has agreed to advance the opening of hostilities by twelve hours to five o'clock this afternoon. Bonnet now has to telephone Ambassador Coulondre in Berlin with fresh instructions.

11.30am, TEDDINGTON
'Sirens went off at 11.30. Guns going off. All Clear 11.55.' (Helena Mott)

11.30am (12.30pm), WARSAW
The news has broken that Britain has declared war on Germany. Crowds are swarming out of church after Mass and emptying the city's cafés. They make their way up Nowy Swiat, Warsaw's Piccadilly, towards the British Embassy. The crowds are delirious, singing their own versions of 'God Save the King' and 'Tipperary' as they snatch up one-sheet special editions of the papers that carry blazing headlines announcing Britain's declaration of war. Union Jacks appear and a group of students carry a huge banner embla-zoned with the slogan 'Cheers for England!' When the embassy is reached, crowds surge into the shabby little court where grey plaster is peeling off the walls. Boys and young men clamber up the walls and drainpipes and shout for Britain and for France. Ambassador Sir Howard Kennard is not the most demonstrative of men, but he allows himself to appear on the balcony to acknowledge the cheering crowds. Military attaché Lieutenant-Colonel Edward Sword also appears on the balcony several times and raises a glass of cham-pagne to toast the assembled crowd, which now seems to stretch miles down Nowy Swiat.

Flowers are thrown at embassy staff, and anyone British, and also a few Americans, are being slapped on the backs and their hands pumped by enthusiastic Poles, supremely happy that their country is now no longer alone. Sir Howard is obliged to show himself time and time again on the balcony. Each time he appears he is greeted with prolonged cheering and shouts of 'Long live Britain!' and 'Long live the fight for liberty!'

Suddenly, there is a fresh outburst of cheering as Foreign Minister Colonel Beck arrives. He has come to convey his personal thanks to Britain's ambassador. The Foreign Minister's car can barely negotiate its way through the dense crowds. For ten minutes Beck and Sir Howard have to salute each other across a sea of upturned faces, until the Colonel finally manages to enter the embassy building. Beck is offered a drink. But he refuses, saying in French, '*Non, le moment est trop triste pour ma patrie.*' ('No, this is too sad a moment for my country.') But he and Kennard appear on the balcony together and shake hands. This sets off the ecstatic crowds again. Sir Howard, in Polish, tells the crowd, 'Long live Poland. We will fight side by side against aggression and injustice.' A great roar of approval greets the phlegmatic diplomat's words. Colonel Beck now tells his fellow countrymen, 'Britain and Poland have locked hands in a fight for freedom and justice. Britain will not be disappointed in Poland and Poland will not be disappointed in Britain.'

11.30am (6.30pm), HOLLYWOOD

After a decidedly alcoholic night at the Balboa Yacht Club, David Niven and fellow actor Robert Coote are sleeping it off on their small sloop, the *Huralu*. They are due to join other members of Hollywood's British colony, including Laurence Olivier and Vivien Leigh, on Douglas Fairbanks Jr's yacht. Niven and Coote awake to hear a man banging on the side of their boat. He asks them, 'You guys English?'

Well and truly hung over, the two actors reply, 'Yes'.

'Well, lotsa luck – you've just declared war on Germany,' he tells them.

'Police on bicycles ride up from the police station down the road . . . wearing "Take Cover" placards on chest and back and shout "Take cover", and "Take cover" is echoed by people in cafés and streets.' The scene in Whitehall, 11.30am, 3 September 1939.

Not speaking a word to each other, Niven and Coote go below and fill two tea cups with warm gin.

11.42am, HMS WALKER, ST GEORGE'S CHANNEL

Second Officer of the Watch John Adams is given the Admiralty signal, sent out at 11.17am, to 'commence hostilities at once with Germany'. Adams senses the feeling of immense relief that goes round the bridge of the destroyer at the news. He and the others are all pleased that the decision has at last been made. Now help can be sent to the Poles.

11.45am, OLYMPIA EXHIBITION HALL, LONDON

Eugen Spier and his fellow internees are told by a German-speaking British officer that Britain has been at war with Germany since 11.00am. He tells them that they must elect a camp leader who will act as their spokesman. 'Putzi' Hanfstaengl tries to engineer the unanimous election of a known Nazi to the post. He tells his fellow internees, 'Comrades, we want to show these Englishmen that we are well disciplined Germans. We want, above all, to keep order and to display the strictest discipline like true German soldiers on the parade ground.' But Spier steps forward and manages to thwart Hanfstaengl's ploy. He suggests that they hold a truly democratic election with an alternate candidate. Spier puts forward Dr Weiss as that candidate. The vote takes place and, much to the disgust of the Nazi internees, Weiss duly wins the election.

11.45am, LIVERPOOL TO LEEDS TRAIN

Ninette de Valois and the Sadler's Wells Ballet Company are travelling from Liverpool to Leeds. En route they pass through a small village station without stopping, but see stuck up on the platform a placard which reads, 'WAR DECLARED.' On reaching Leeds, the Company find that the theatre is closed by Government order, and so they now have to return to London.

11.45pm, PARIS

Daily Express staff reporter Geoffrey Cox is making his way by taxi to the *Express* offices in the Rue du Louvre. Cox has already heard that Britain has declared war from an American colleague, Edwin Hartrich. Now he tells his taxi driver of the French ultimatum. The driver reacts with fury. He pours out a stream of obscenities and oaths against Hitler and the Nazis. In his terrible rage, the driving has now become so erratic that Cox has to plead with him, 'Take it easy. There are eighty million Germans trying to kill us now. There's no need for you to do the job for them.'

11.48am, RAF STATION WYTON

Blenheim bomber N6215 of No. 139 Squadron takes off on the Royal Air Force's first operation of the war. The two-engine bomber is piloted by Flying Officer Andrew McPherson and crewed by an air gunner, Corporal Vincent Arrowsmith, together with an observer from the Royal Navy, Commander Thompson. Its mission is to make a reconnaissance of the German naval base at Wilhelmshaven. This will prepare the way for a later bombing raid. Though reluctant to order attacks on German land targets for fear of killing civilians, the Government are agreed that the German fleet is a legitimate target. Even so there are still a number of provisos in place. The ships may only be attacked if on the high seas, or in the open waters of their bases, but definitely not while still in dockyards.

11.50am, PARLIAMENT SQUARE, WHITEHALL

A member of the Mass Observation organisation joins a group of working-class men in Parliament Square to hear what they have to say about the air-raid warning. One remarks, 'They didn't lose any time attacking.' To which another replies, 'Course he didn't – he meant it all along.' A third member of the group adds, 'I wonder how they got on in Paris.' Surprised at this mention of France, the Mass Observer asks if the French have been attacked. 'Yes,' replies the first speaker, 'so've we. They turned 'em back off Southend.' The second speaker 'confirms' this: 'That's right, isn't it? Perhaps we've already bombed Berlin – no one knows. We're too much for 'em. We'll split Berlin so they won't know it again.'

11.52am, HMS WALPOLE, St George's Channel
HMS *Walker*'s sister ship gets a good ASDIC contact, and carries out the Royal Navy's first depth-charge attack of the war against a suspected U-boat. But the attack brings not a U-boat to the surface but a shoal of dead fish. From the bridge of HMS *Walker*, Sub-Lieutenant John Adams sees the fish. Their bladders have been forced through their mouths from the shock of the explosions.

12.00pm, HMS SUFFOLK, Portsmouth
Hugo Bracken and other members of the ship's company wearing beards are ordered to shave them off in order that their gas masks will fit properly.

12.00pm, Takeley
London buses full of child evacuees from Wood Green pull up on their way to Felstead. Myra Charlton watches as the children, 'hundreds of rather gay little things', swarm to the nearest lavatory.

12.00pm, German Embassy, Carlton House Terrace
Robert Dunbar and Dr Kordt have reached an *impasse* over who should or should not receive diplomatic status and protection from among London's German colony. They decide to call a halt and Dunbar prepares to return to the Foreign Office. As he leaves he wishes Kordt 'goodbye', but remembers just in time not to add 'good luck'. The Chargé d'Affaires likewise wishes the British diplomat a plain 'goodbye'. Dunbar retraces his steps back to his office. There he sets about working on the details of the German diplomats' departure from London.

12.00pm, 'VILLA VOLPONE', SOUTH HAMPSTEAD

James Agate hears the 'All Clear' sound and emerges from his 'dug-out', as he calls his air-raid shelter. Curious, he goes out into the street and sees a man look at his watch. It is now midday and the man joyfully exclaims, 'They're open!'

12.00pm, SS *ATHENIA*, ATLANTIC OCEAN

Captain Cook orders Chief Officer Barnet Copland and Chief Purser Wotherspoon to draw up a notice to tell the passengers that war has been declared. 'The important thing, of course,' Cook tells the two men, 'is not to alarm the passengers. Try to avoid discussing the matter with them; but if you have to, be reassuring. Make certain they understand that our preparations are precautionary.'

12.00pm, HOUSE OF COMMONS

The House is crowded. There has not been a Sunday sitting since 30 January 1820, when King George IV came to the throne on the death of his father George III. As usual, there is the Speaker's procession and the ritual of prayers. To MP Beverley Baxter they appear to give a secure sense of permanence to a world that seems already collapsing. He too notices a complete absence of emotion. Members know that they are witnessing a great historic scene and yet the element of drama is missing completely. Because everybody has heard the Prime Minister's broadcast, Baxter cannot get over the feeling that he and his fellow MPs are like mummers performing in a play which the audience have already seen. But already a subtle change has taken place in the appearance of the Commons. About half a dozen members are now in uniform. One young MP, booted and spurred, is already wearing the badges of rank of a colonel, while another is in Royal Air Force blue. An older MP is wearing Other Ranks uniform with a single lance-corporal's stripe on each sleeve.

Those in the gallery are equally devoid of emotion. The ambassadors give the appearance of 'a board of directors attending the

'You can imagine what a bitter blow it is to me that all my long struggle to win peace has failed.' Neville Chamberlain, accompanied by his Parliamentary Private Secretary, Lord Dunglass (later Sir Alec Douglas-Home), leaves 10 Downing Street for the midday sitting of the House of Commons.

liquidation of a business that once had promised well'. French ambassador Charles Corbin is in his usual place, 'his fine, pale face is utterly impassive, his delicate hands are always still,' Baxter notes. Next to Corbin is Poland's representative to the Court of St James, grim-faced Count Edward Raczynski, who is clearly showing the effects of the enormous pressures that have been on him over the last few days. Near him is the immensely popular American ambassador Joseph Kennedy. Kennedy too is not looking his usual ebullient self. Even more than Racyznski's, Baxter thinks that Kennedy's face is showing the marks of suffering. The MP hears a report that the ambassador has just now been to see Chamberlain at Number 10. Both men broke down and wept unashamedly. For today's historic Sunday sitting, Kennedy has brought his wife Rose with him, together with their two eldest sons, Joe Jr and twenty-two-year-old Jack. Harvard student Jack senses today 'a feeling of grim determination among the Government and the people'.

The Duke of Alba, representing Franco's Spain, is also in the diplomatic gallery, and so too, much to the surprise and disgust of many, is Stalin's ambassador, Ivan Maisky, 'smiling his Cheshire-cat smile'. Baxter reflects that the ambassador, like his country's reputation, has shrunk. For a few brief months this year, 'While the flirtation of Russia and the Allies had been on, Maisky had experienced something of the exhilaration of Cinderella. He had been taken from the kitchen to the ball. Flattery had been poured upon him and Russia praised as a civilizing influence . . . now he was an outcast again . . . Russia had sold the pass, and Russia's ambassador reverted to his permanent position of diplomatic outsider.'

The King's younger brothers, the Dukes of Gloucester and Kent are also sitting in the gallery directly behind the clock. Like the diplomats, their faces are earnest but impassive as they look down on the Commons waiting for the Prime Minister to appear. Making

*Foreign Secretary Lord Halifax, with his Private Secretary Oliver Harvey
and followed by his Under-Secretary R.A. Butler, leaving the Foreign Office,
3 September 1939. Harvey recorded in his diary, 'Halifax and I then walked
across to the House of Lords where Halifax announced a state of war with
Germany.'*

his way to the chamber, David Lloyd George, Britain's victorious First World War leader, tells a lobby correspondent in a cheerful voice, 'There's nothing new in all this to me. I've been through it all before.'

12.00pm, Daily Express Building: Fleet Street
Editor Christiansen's phone rings. It's Parliamentary Lobby correspondent William Barkley on the line. He's at the Palace of Westminster and has just seen how the 'Mother of Parliaments' has reacted to the first air-raid warning. Barkley tells Christiansen that it's all been a great joke: 'Chris, you should have seen all the MPs squashed together in the terrace corridor. If anything had happened, my dear, we'd all have been crushed to death or drowned in the Thames.' Christiansen, rather exasperated, asks, 'Go on, Willie, where's the joke in that?'

'Well,' Willie replies, 'it suddenly occurred to me that the whole thing must be a false alarm organised by Neville Chamberlain.'

'Why, Willie?'

'Because, my dear, he's afraid to face the House!'

12.00pm (1.00pm), German-Polish border
Wilhelm Prueller's company is again attacked by Polish aircraft. Of the five attacking planes, three are brought down by flak. Soon after this, Polish troops, hiding in nearby woods, fire on the company, causing a number of casualties, both in killed and wounded.

12.00pm (1.00pm), Zloczew, Lodz District, Poland
SS men from the SS *Leibstandarte Adolf Hitler* and soldiers from the 95th Infantry Regiment are terrorising the town. Without any reason, they set buildings on fire, and indiscriminately shoot civilians on the street. Zofia Zasina's husband Michal is one of the victims of a random shooting by the German troops. Janina Modrzewska witnesses some frightful scenes. She sees the disembowelled body

of a ten-year-old girl lying in the street. The girl has been shot through the back. Janina also sees a German soldier crush the skull of an infant with the butt of his rifle. Jozefa Blachowa is shot in the arm and then thrown into a blazing house, where she burns to death. A wagon carrying refugees is ordered off the road so that German units can get pass. As they do so, they turn their machine guns on the refugees and slaughter them. Nearly 200 civilians are murdered today in Zloclew.

12.05pm, PARIS

In the French capital civil-defence preparations are still taking place. The early-morning heavy rain has now stopped, but the sky above Paris is still distinctly murky as workmen place sandbags around the city's statues. Those around the base of the Obelisk give it, correspondent Alexander Werth thinks, 'an even more phallic look than usual'. The enormous Hotel Continental on the Rue Castiglione is in the process of being taken over by the Commissariat of Information. Premier Daladier has already asked Jean Giraudoux, one of France's greatest living playwrights, to head the Commissariat. It will be responsible for France's propaganda effort and media censorship.

12.05pm, HOUSE OF COMMONS

Chamberlain enters the crowded chamber and is greeted with cheers from the Government benches. Although almost dapper in dress, he looks utterly haggard. His hands are shaking as he fingers the notes which are to be the basis of the speech he is about to make. Opposite sits Lloyd George, 'The Man Who Won The War'. Lloyd George loathes and despises Chamberlain, whom he sacked as Director of National Service back in August 1917. The feeling is mutual. Beside the Prime Minister on the front bench sits Sir John Simon. He is in exactly the same place he was twenty-five years ago, when Foreign Secretary Sir Edward Grey

Neville Mooney, the first baby born in London after the declaration of war, wearing a new type of gas helmet specially made for babies and infants.

described the British ultimatum to Germany on 4 August 1914. Another member of that government, Winston Churchill, is sitting in his usual place on a corner seat below the gangway. He has not sat on the Government front bench for ten years now. In a slow, weary voice that sometimes appears to falters, the Prime Minister tells the House:

> When I spoke to the House last night I could not but be aware that in some parts of the House there were doubts and some bewilderment as to whether there had been any weakening, hesitation or vacillation on the part of the Government.
>
> In the circumstances I make no reproaches, for if I had been in the same position as Hon. Members on those benches and not been in a position of having the information which we have I might have felt the same.
>
> The statement that I have to make this morning will show that there is no ground for those doubts. We were in consultation all day yesterday with the French Government, and we felt that the intensified action which the Germans were taking against Poland allowed of no delay in making our position clear.
>
> Accordingly we decided to send our Ambassador in Berlin instructions which he was to hand to the German Foreign Secretary.

Chamberlain reads out the ultimatum that Sir Nevile Henderson handed to Dr Schmidt earlier this morning, and continues:

> Sir, that was the final Note. No such undertaking was received by the time stipulated, and consequently this country is now at war with Germany.
>
> I am in a position to inform the House that according to arrangements made between the British and French Governments the French Ambassador in Berlin is at this moment making a similar *démarche* also accompanied by a definite time-limit.

Polish civilians who had taken up arms against the German invaders are rounded up by a reconnaissance patrol of the 76th Motorised Regiment during the Battle of the Tucheler Heide, 1–5 September 1939.

As the British ultimatum runs out at midday, Hitler receives the new Soviet ambassador Alexander Shkvartsev (second from left) *at the Reich Chancellery.*

The House has already been made aware of our plans, and, as I said the other day, we are ready.

The Prime Minister ends his statement on perhaps a too highly personal note:

> It is a sad day for all of us. For none is it sadder than for me. Everything that I have worked for, everything that I hoped for, everything that I believed in during my public life has crashed into ruins this morning. There is only one thing left for me, and that is to devote what strength and powers I have to forwarding the victory of the cause for which we have to sacrifice so much.
>
> I cannot tell what part I may be allowed to play myself, but I trust I may live to see the day when Hitlerism has been destroyed and a restored and liberated Europe has been re-established.

12.15pm, LONDON

Chamberlain sits down to sympathetic cheers from all sides of the House. Victor Cazalet thinks the speech 'very dramatic. No overstatement, no appeal to emotion or sentiment. Just a heartfelt cry against the stupidity of it all.' The Prime Minister is followed by Arthur Greenwood and Sir Archibald Sinclair, the leader of the Liberal Party. Both the tone and content of the two leaders' speeches demonstrate the unity of all the parties today in their determination to have the war prosecuted successfully. Greenwood speaks of how 'The intolerable agony of suspense from which all of us have suffered is over; we now know the worst. The hated word "war" has been spoken by Britain, in fulfilment of her pledged and unbreakable intention to defend Poland and so to defend the liberties of Europe. We have heard more than the word spoken. We have heard the war begin, within the precincts of this House.'

Labour's acting leader then goes on to praise the Poles, 'who for fifty-four hours had stood alone, at the portals of civilization, defending us and all free nations'. He finishes with a call that 'Nazism must be finally overthrown'. To this end he promises Labour's 'wholehearted support to the measures necessary to equip this State with the powers that are desired'. But he warns Chamberlain and his ministers that should they not prove up to the job, should there be inefficiency or wavering, then 'other men must be called to take their place'.

Sir Archibald Sinclair also rises to the occasion. But he warns MPs:

> Great advances have been made in our organization for war, but in individual preparation, in the contributions which the men and women of the two countries are making to the common cause, I say that France at this moment is ahead of us. If you go to France and meet ten people in the streets you may be sure that eight of them have their places and parts to play. Our people will do the same as time goes on, but let us have no doubts as to the determination with which the French people are facing this crisis.

As Sir Archibald speaks, there are still nearly one and a half million registered unemployed men in Britain. The Liberal leader concludes on a fine rhetorical flourish. 'Let me only say in conclusion: let the world know that the British people are inexorably determined, as the Prime Minister said, to end this Nazi domination forever and build a word based on justice and freedom.'

As Sir Archibald sits down, his old commanding officer from the Great War then rises to make his statement. At last, Winston Churchill knows that he is now to be given an important government post. Chamberlain has asked to see him just as soon as the debate dies down. To the House he now says:

> In this solemn hour it is a consolation to recall and dwell upon our repeated efforts for peace. All have been ill-starred, but all have been

faithful and sincere. That is of the highest moral value – and not only moral value, but practical value – at the present time, because the wholehearted concurrence of scores of millions of men and women, whose co-operation is indispensable and whose comrade-ship and brotherhood are indispensable, is the only foundation upon which the trial and tribulation of modern war can be endured and surmounted.

This moral conviction alone affords that ever-fresh resilience which renews the strength and energy of people in long, doubtful and dark days. Outside the storms of war may blow and the lands may be lashed with the fury of its gales, but in our own hearts this Sunday there is peace. Our hands may be active, but our consciences are at rest.

We must not underrate the gravity of the task which lies before us or the temerity of the ordeal, to which we shall not be found unequal. We must expect many disappointments and many unpleasant surprises, but we may be sure that the task which we have freely accepted is not beyond the compass and the strength of the British Empire and the French Republic.

The Prime Minister said it was a sad day, and that is indeed true, but at the present time there is another note which may be present, and that is a feeling of thankfulness that if these great trials were to come upon our island, there is a generation of Britons here now ready to prove itself not unworthy of those great men, the fathers of our land, who laid the foundations of our laws and shaped the greatness of our country.

This is not a question of fighting for Danzig or for fighting for Poland. We are fighting to save the whole world from the pestilence of Nazi tyranny and in defence of all that is most sacred to man. This is no war for domination or imperial aggrandisement or mate-rial gain; no war to shut any country out of its sunlight and means of progress.

It is a war, viewed in its inherent quality, to establish on impreg-nable rocks the rights of the individual, and it is a war to establish and revive the stature of man. Perhaps it might seem a paradox that a war undertaken in the name of liberty and right should require as a necessary part of its processes, the surrender for the time being of so many of the dearly valued liberties and rights. In these last few days the House of Commons has been voting dozens of Bills which hand over to the executive our most dearly valued traditional liberties.

We are sure that these liberties will be in hands which will not abuse them, which will use them for no class or party interests, which will cherish and guard them, and we look forward to the day, when our liberties and rights will be restored to us, and when we shall be able to share them with the peoples to whom such blessings are unknown.

Churchill, the man who has now been proved so devastatingly correct in his warnings, receives a generous and enthusiastic reception from all sides of the House. But, Beverley Baxter is not one of the speech's admirers today. He thinks it far below Churchill's usual high standard. Baxter believes this is because Churchill has put too much preparation in it. It smacks, thinks Baxter, too much 'of the professional orator, the too conscientious pupil of Pericles. The language too colourful, the sentiment too significant, the style too momentous.' But, Baxter concedes, 'Perhaps history will record his efforts ... as a triumph.' Others share Baxter's view. Harold Nicolson thinks Churchill's speech misfires as it sounds too much like one of his newspaper articles. On the other hand 'Chips' Channon, a devoted Chamberlainite, considers that Churchill has spoken well. And in the Press Gallery, lobby correspondent J.E. Sewell thinks as he listens, 'That's it! That's just it!' Churchill, he believes, has just given a brilliant and succinct definition of Britain's war aims, encapsulated in the one Churchillian sentence, 'it is a war to establish and revive the stature of man'.

Former Labour leader George Lansbury, a passionate pacifist, also speaks. But it is Lloyd George who wins outright the parliamentary plaudits this afternoon. Britain's great wartime leader tells his fellow MPs:

> I am one of those who, with Hon. and Right Hon. Friends on this side of the House, have from time to time challenged the handling of foreign affairs by the Government, but this is a different matter. The Government are now confronted with the latest, but I am afraid not the last, of a series of acts of brigandage by a very formidable military power, which if they are left unchallenged will undermine the whole foundation of civilisation throughout the world. The Government could do no other than what they have done. I am one out of ten million in this country who will back any government that is in power in fighting this struggle through, in however humble a capacity we may be called upon to render service to our country. I have been through this before, and there is only one word I want to say about that. We had very bad moments, moments when brave men were rather quailing and doubting, but the nation was firm right through, from beginning to end. One thing that struck me then was that it was in moments of disaster, and in some of the worst disasters with which we were confronted in the War, that I found the greatest union among all classes, the greatest disappearance of discontent and disaffection, and of the grabbing for rights and privileges. The nation closed its ranks then. By that means we went right through to the end, and after four and a half years, terrible years, we won victory for right. We will do it again.

A great cheer sweeps through the House as the seventy-six-year-old former premier resumes his seat. Even the acerbic Baxter believes that the 'Welsh Wizard's' speech has exactly caught both the spirit of the occasion and the mood of the House. And one of Churchill's supporters, Major-General Sir Edward Spears, the MP for Carlisle, thinks it the best speech that he has heard today.

12.15pm, SS ATHENIA, ATLANTIC OCEAN

Passengers crowd around the notice board to read the announcement that Copland and Wotherspoon have just drawn up. In the main the news is greeted in silence. Some feel a sense of relief. Others notice that there is a 'sudden cessation of laughter and gaiety' among the younger people on board. Texan college student Rowena Simpson confesses to feeling butterflies in her stomach, and so do some of her friends. Most passengers, however, are sure that nothing will happen to the liner, now 296 miles from Liverpool. But Judith Evelyn, travelling to Toronto with her Canadian fiancé Andrew and his father, feels the 'surge of a strong presentiment'. All morning she has been 'conscious of a dull, oppressive sense of disaster'.

12.15pm, GRANADA CINEMA, GREENWICH

On hearing the Government announcement that all places of entertainment are now to be closed indefinitely, assistant cinema manager Clulow tells his staff to change the canopy lettering. From advertising the film *You Can't Get Away with Murder*, it now reads 'SORRY, WE'RE CLOSED, FOLKS. HOPE TO REOPEN SOON. GOOD LUCK TO YOU ALL'.

12.20pm (1.20pm), BRITISH EMBASSY, BERLIN

Dozing in a comfortable red leather armchair in the Chancery, assistant air attaché Alex Adams is woken up. He is told that he and his colleagues are about to be moved next door to the Adlon Hotel, prior to their repatriation. There, at the bar, they are joined by American friends, including CBS radio correspondent William Shirer, for cocktails before lunch. Shirer, although no great lover of the British Empire, cannot help but admire the sang-froid of the embassy contingent as they sip their Dry Martinis and talk 'about dogs and such stuff'. Cocktails drunk, Adams, the other British diplomats and the Americans go into lunch at the Adlon's courtyard restaurant, mixing freely with the other hotel guests.

12.25pm (9.25pm), MELBOURNE

Forty-four-year-old Robert Menzies, who has only been Prime Minister and Federal Treasurer since April, announces to the Australian people that once again they are at war with Germany. The genial Prime Minister and his ministers are meeting at the Commonwealth Offices in Melbourne. There they hear Chamberlain's broadcast on a short-wave radio. In the absence of an official telegram from London, Menzies and his ministers decide to take Chamberlain's broadcast as official news that Britain is now at war. This is soon confirmed by a telegram from the Admiralty in London which the Navy Office in Melbourne passes on to Menzies.

The Prime Minister now summons the Executive Council, which approves an already prepared proclamation that declares a state of war exists between Australia and Germany. Menzies knows he has the backing of the vast majority of Australians. Like him they believe that the strength of the British Empire and Commonwealth rests in unity to a common loyalty to the Crown. Menzies has said publicly that any idea that the King could be at war in one part of his empire and at peace in another is 'a metaphysical notion that quite eludes me'. He also believes that an immediate declar-ation of war by Australia will give the Allied cause a tremendous morale boost. He is perhaps conscious too of the criticism levelled at him for not having done his patriotic duty and fought in the Great War. A war in which over 59,000 young Australians died. Sitting at the microphone in the Postmaster-General's room in the Commonwealth Offices, he now tells listeners on a nationwide radio hook-up:

> It is my melancholy duty to inform you that, in consequence of Germany's persistence in her invasion of Poland, Great Britain has declared war, and that as a result Australia is also at war. No harder task can fall to the lot of a democratic leader than to make such an announcement.

Great Britain and France, with the co-operation of the British Dominions, have struggled to avoid this tragedy. They have, as I firmly believe, been patient. They have kept the door of negotiation open; they have given no cause for aggression. But in the result their efforts have failed and we are, therefore, as a great family of nations involved in a struggle which we must at all costs win, and which we believe in our hearts we will win . . .

It is plain, indeed it is brutally plain, that the Hitler ambition has been, not as he once said, to unite the German peoples under one rule, but to bring under that rule as many European countries, even of alien race, as can be subdued by force. If such a policy were allowed to go unchecked there could be no security in Europe and there could be no peace for the world.

A halt has been called. Force has had to be resorted to to check the march of force. Honest dealing, the peaceful adjustment of differences, the rights of independent peoples to live their own lives, the honouring of international obligations and promises – all these things are at stake. There never was any doubt as to where Great Britain stood in relation to them. There can be no doubt that where Great Britain stands, there stands the entire British world.

Bitter as we may feel at this wanton crime, this is not a moment for rhetoric. Prompt as the action of many thousands must be, it is for the rest of us a moment for quiet thinking, for that calm fortitude which rests not upon the beating of drums but upon the unconquerable spirit of man, created by God in his own image. What may be before us we do not know, nor how long the journey. But this we do know: that truth is with us in the battle, and that truth must win.

Before I end, may I say this to you; in the bitter months that are to come, calmness, resoluteness, confidence and hard work will be required as never before. The war will involve not only soldiers and sailors and airmen, but supplies, foodstuffs, money. Our staying power, and particularly the staying power of the

Mother Country, will be best assisted by keeping our production going; by continuing our avocations and our business as we fully can; by maintaining employment, and with it our strength. I know that, in spite of the emotions we are all feeling, you will show that Australia is ready to see it through. May God in His mercy and compassion grant that the world may soon be delivered from this agony.

12.25pm (9.25pm), SWAN HILL, VICTORIA

When Menzies tells the Australian people they are at war, the parents of nine-year-old Margaret Maxwell both burst into tears.

12.25pm (9.25pm), SYDNEY

As she hears the broadcast from Melbourne, pacifist Margaret Holmes begins to feel 'absolutely terrible'. She has the sensation of the world dropping to pieces, and her 'whole life . . . going down the drain'. She is 'terribly depressed and terribly worried'.

12.25pm (9.25pm), LEEDERVILLE, PERTH

Twelve-year-old schoolboy Maurie Jones, his parents and fourteen-year-old brother are coming home from a church function when they hear the news that Australia is now once again at war. His mother is very upset. Maurie's father tries to reassure her by saying, 'It's alright, Kate. It'll be over long before the boys are of military age.'

12.25pm (9.25pm), NEW SOUTH WALES

After a hard day's sheep-shearing, Bob Bahnsen has only just gone to bed. Now he is rudely woken up by the farmer's son, who tells him, 'They've declared the bloody war.' Bob cannot take it in. He just cannot believe 'that Hitler would be such a maniac as to launch the world into war. But he did it just like that, thought nothing of it.'

12.25pm (9.25pm), SYDNEY
Army sergeant Sandy Rayward is on leave, and staying at a friend's place, where he hears Menzies tells the nation that Australia is at war. As soon as the Prime Minister finishes his broadcast, Sandy rushes back to barracks. When he arrives, he finds every one of his friends also there, eager and ready for orders.

12.25pm (9.25pm), MELBOURNE
University student Niall Brennan's family are in the drawing room, listening to Menzies announce that, as Britain is at war, so too is Australia. As Niall's cousin bursts into tears, his father jumps up 'like a firecracker' and shouts out, 'That's constitutionally wrong!' But for the Brennan family it is 'the end of possibly two or three years of fearing that there would be a war', and their overriding feeling is that of relief.

12.25pm (9.25pm), MOUNT GAMBIER, SOUTH AUSTRALIA
Tonight, after hearing the Prime Minister's broadcast, schoolboy Charles Janeway's father, a Great War veteran, has nightmares. But nevertheless, he, his brother and cousin, all army reservists, are keen 'to do their bit' again this time.

12.25pm (9.25pm), MELBOURNE
Ralph Doig, a civil servant in the Prime Minister's Department, sums up the feelings of most Australians as they hear that for the second time in twenty-five years they are at war: 'Britain's in it and so we're in it as a matter of course.'

12.30pm (12.00 midnight), WELLINGTON
New Zealand Prime Minister and Labour Party leader Michael Joseph Savage is terminally ill. But he rises from his sick bed to issue an announcement that New Zealand is once again at Britain's side in the war against Germany. Twenty-five years ago, during the

Great War, out of a population of just over a million New Zealand raised forces totalling 124,211 of whom 16,711 died. Now Prime Minister Savage's announcement reads:

> With reference to the intimation just received that a state of war exists between the United Kingdom and Germany, His Majesty's Government in New Zealand desire immediately to associate themselves with His Majesty's Government in the United Kingdom in honouring their pledged word.
>
> They entirely concur with the action taken, which they regard as inevitably enforced upon the British Commonwealth if the cause of justice, freedom and democracy is to endure in this world ...
>
> The New Zealand Government wish to offer to the British Government the fullest assurance of all possible support. They are convinced that the step that has been taken will meet with the approval of the people of this Dominion, and they will give the fullest consideration in due course to any suggestion of the British Government as to the method or methods by which the Dominion can best assist in the common cause.

The Premier is too weak to undertake more today, so it is Savage's deputy Peter Fraser who will broadcast the news that New Zealand is standing by Britain for the second time in twenty-five years.

12.30pm (12.00 midnight), WANGANUI
Pacifist Merv Brown hears that New Zealand is once more at war. On Friday night he was at the pictures when the news of the German invasion of Poland was flashed on the screen. Leaving the cinema, he had looked up into sky, 'quite expecting there to be bombers coming over'. Today, he has reaffirmed that, for moral reasons, he cannot fight and will register as a conscientious objector.

211

12.30pm (12.00 midnight), Auckland
Nineteen-year-old Maisie Younger has been praying that there will not be a war. Both her uncles fought last time and she has heard their dreadful stories of 1914–18. Today she is very worried, as once again young New Zealanders, including her three brothers and her fiancé Ken, are intending to join up. Ken is not really keen to go, but recognises it as his duty to do so.

12.30pm (12.00 midnight), Mount Eden, Auckland
Teenager Gwen Pollard's father is a regular listener to the BBC. Tonight they have heard from London that Britain has declared war on Germany. To the Pollard family it doesn't seem so long since the end of the last war, in which Gwen's Uncle Norman was killed. Now Gwen's brother, named after their uncle, is keen to join up. Mr Pollard is not very happy about Norman enlisting, but recognises that it is his patriotic duty to do so.

12.30pm (12.00 midnight), Gisborne, NZ
High-school student sixteen-year-old George Judge hears the news that war has been declared today. Over the last couple of years, he has been avidly following the news of the crises in Europe, first Czecho-slovakia, and now Poland. As New Zealand is so far away, he admits, the events unfolding in Europe seem very remote. Nevertheless, he is keen to help the war effort before reaching call-up age. He intends to volunteer to help out at the local Territorial Army headquarters.

12.30pm (12.00 midnight), Hastings, NZ
Baker's roundsman Harry Spencer is with a group of friends at a party when the phone rings with the news that war has been declared. The party continues, 'but in a very gloomy sort of way'. Harry and the others are 'knocked flat' by the news and after a while the party breaks up. Tonight, 'after giving it lots and lots of thought', Harry decides to join the Army.

12.20pm (1.20pm), FOREIGN MINISTRY, BERLIN
On reaching the Foreign Ministry, Sir Nevile is met by von Ribbentrop. He hands Henderson a copy of the German reply to the British ultimatum. Sir Nevile reads the opening sentence: 'The Reich Government and the German nation refuse to accept, or even to satisfy, the demands in the form of an ultimatum from the British Government.'

The rest of the lengthy memorandum is an attack on Britain for giving the Poles a 'blank cheque', and promising 'military help to the Polish Government unreservedly in the event of Germany's defending herself against any provocation or attack'.

Sir Nevile considers the document pure propaganda. It is designed for both domestic consumption and to convince world opinion that Britain, not Germany, is responsible for war. The ambassador tells von Ribbentrop, 'It will be left to history to judge where the blame really lies.' The Foreign Minister replies that history has already proved the facts. Nobody, von Ribbentrop tells an incredulous Sir Nevile, has striven for peace and friendship between Germany and Britain more than Hitler himself. Von Ribbentrop ends the interview by extending to Sir Nevile his personal good wishes. The ambassador replies that he regrets that his own efforts for peace have failed, but he bears no grudge against the German people. He then leaves, after first presenting a last note to the German Government. It asks if it is their intention to abide by the 1925 Geneva Protocol. This prohibits the use in war of asphyxiating, poisonous, or other gases, and of bacteriological warfare. This task completed, Sir Nevile returns to the embassy. Strangely enough, he finds that its telephone lines are still functioning.

12.22pm (1.22pm), BERLIN
It is a still, hot and sunny afternoon in the German capital. On *Deutschlandsender,* the German home-service radio, the Hamburg Radio Orchestra is playing Lizst's 'First Hungarian Rhapsody'. Suddenly and without any warning the music fades out. Listeners

213

now hear the announcer's voice. He calls them to attention and says, 'In a few minutes we shall make an important announcement.' The music then fades in again.

12.29pm (1.29pm), BERLIN
On the radio Lizst's 'Hungarian Rhapsody' finishes and the announcement promised seven minutes ago is read over the air:

> The British government, in a note to the Reich government, has made a demand that the German troops which have advanced into Polish territory be withdrawn to their original positions. At nine o'clock this morning the British Ambassador in Berlin informed the Reich government in a provocative note that if a satisfactory answer was not received by eleven o'clock, England would consider itself in a state of war with Germany ...

Just like the British, Germans now hear that they are at war through the medium of radio.

12.29pm (1.29pm), ROT-WEISS TENNIS CLUB, BERLIN
Life magazine's Berlin correspondent William D. Bayles hears the news at the capital's exclusive 'Rot-Weiss' Lawn Tennis Club, which numbers Goering, von Ribbentrop and former Chancellor Franz von Papen among its members. He has gone there with Norwegian diplomat Carsten Helgeby to play a game and to try and take their minds off the crisis. Instead they have to listen to a German naval officer who assures them that 'the Fuehrer knows what he is doing; there will be no war with England'. Helgeby is sure that Britain will honour its obligations to Poland. If it does not, he tells the American, 'it will be the end of the British Empire'. Bayles is not so sure. He still doubts whether 'the men who had played so selfishly and recklessly with the reputation of the Empire through the bitter years of appeasement would realise that the day of the

show-down had at last arrived'. The German sailor has no such doubts. 'We Germans', he tells Bayles and Helgeby, 'are born fighters and wars bring out the best in us. But the English have dissipated their blood through their Empire and now they are exhausted. They want only an old man's peaceful world. They won't fight.' Just as the German finishes speaking, and as if deliberately on cue to contradict him, the radio announces that Britain is at war with Germany. Bayles is overcome with emotion. His heart seems to fill his throat. He avoids looking at his Norwegian friend because he is barely able to hold himself in check and knows that even a single sign of enthusiasm or understanding from Helgeby might start anything – even tears. At last, Bayles rejoices, 'The British Empire had come through. The miserable voice of appeasement . . . was dead and the mighty voice of historic England had spoken.'

Looking around the clubhouse, Bayles sees that the news of Britain's declaration of war has shocked the Germans. Even the supremely confident naval officer is deflated. But he recovers enough to tell the two foreigners in a peevish and reproachful tone, 'Again and without cause, England has declared war on us. England is in the wrong. The Fuehrer wanted only peace, but England struck away his outstretched hand. This time England will be condemned by the world.' Afraid that he is not going to be able to suppress the sensation of gloating that is pushing out of his chest, Bayles leaves the glum Germans and makes for home.

12.30pm (1.30pm), BERLIN

William Joyce, a former member of the British Union of Fascists, and his wife Margaret are at temporary lodgings in the German capital. Joyce has 'an absolute belief in National Socialism' and admires 'Hitler's superhuman heroism'. Realising that as 'England was going to war . . . I must give her up forever', the Joyces came to Germany last week. Now their landlady rushes into the room

215

and exclaims, 'It's war now with England!' Her husband enters the room behind her and shakes hands with the Joyces. He tells them, 'Whatever happens, we remain friends.'

12.30pm, 'Villa Volpone', South Hampstead

James Agate's secretary, Alan 'Jock' Dent, arrives to look for his gas mask. He tells his employer two things. Firstly, that the Irish navvies in Camden Town refuse to leave London, even though Eire has declared herself neutral. One of them has told Dent, 'Oi don't mind dying for Ireland, but Oi won't live in it!' Secondly, this morning's sirens caught him eating breakfast at Lyons Strand Corner House. With the other customers, Dent is shepherded to the basement. There, he tells Agate, 'His first and chief emotion took the form of the angry exclamation, "What a very unattractive crowd of people to die with!"'

12.30pm, Lyons Corner House, Charing Cross

Home Office civil servant Peter Allen and a group of colleagues have come up from Whitehall. They are enjoying an extravagant and hilarious lunch. All share the same feeling of relief that at last the decision has been taken and everything now seems simpler.

12.30pm, Balcombe Street, Marylebone

The Bayne-Powells decide to lunch at The Sussex, a local pub, and then take a walk in Kensington Gardens. They are struck by the beauty of the gardens, 'the sun and the green trees and the bright pink and white hibiscus flowers'. The only reminders they have that Britain is now at war are 'the barrage balloons shining silver in the afternoon sunlight'. Robert and Nancy walk to Paddington Station to see if there are crowds of people leaving London. But they only encounter a slightly larger crowd than normal, mostly made up of women and children. They walk back home, as the No. 27 bus does not seem to be running this afternoon.

12.30pm (1.30pm), Bugaj, Radom District

A Polish two-seat plane is brought down by ground fire from the 4th Panzer Division. The crew are taken prisoner by German soldiers. One of the Poles is tortured by them. His tongue, ears and nose are cut off. He is then murdered by his captors.

12.30pm (1.30pm), Warsaw

News of the French ultimatum has reached the Polish capital. Crowds now surge towards the French Embassy to acclaim Ambassador Leon Noël and his staff. On their way, they pass the British Consulate-General, where Consul-General Frank Savery, who has been a Warsaw fixture for nearly twenty years, greets the crowds. On the balcony he appears waving the Union Jack and the crowd goes mad with joy. An old pump organ is brought out and someone starts playing 'Tipperary'. The crowd bellows its approval. Savery leads shouts of 'Long Live Poland!' In turn, a Pole steps up and shouts, 'Long Live King George!', 'Long Live England!', 'Long Live British Democracy and twentieth-century civilisation!' *Times* correspondent Patrick Maitland and his colleague Hugh Carleton Greene of the *Daily Telegraph* receive their share of acclamation from a wildly enthusiastic band of students.

The crowd then cross the street to the United States Embassy to cheer Ambassador Biddle and President Roosevelt. Pushing his way past the crowds, Ed Beattie manages to get into the embassy. He goes upstairs to see the American military attaché Major William Colbern. Beattie asks the Major how Britain and France can now help the Poles. Colbern tells the reporter, 'They must draw the pressure from here. They must strike in the west with everything they've got and force the Germans to pull back their tanks and planes. But,' the military attaché insists, 'they must strike now.'

1.00pm, SS *Athenia*, Atlantic Ocean

All of the liner's twenty-six lifeboats are now ready for launching. Two are swung out in case of an 'abrupt emergency'.

1.00pm (2.00pm), WILHELMSHAVEN
Commodore Doenitz signals his U-boat crews: 'U-boats to make war on merchant shipping in accordance with operations order.'

1.00pm (2.00pm), U-30, ATLANTIC OCEAN
Oberleutnant Fritz-Julius Lemp, twenty-six-year-old commander of the 650-ton submarine, receives signal confirmation from Wilhelmshaven that Britain has declared war on Germany. He gives orders for the U-boat to make for its operational area.

1.10pm (2.10pm), U-30, ATLANTIC OCEAN
Radio operator Georg Hoehgel is asleep in his bunk. Suddenly, he is roughly woken up by a shipmate who tells him, 'My God, Georg, England has declared war on Germany!'

2.00pm (3.00pm), BERLIN
Even before the French ultimatum expires, orders are issued to the inhabitants of the threatened Red Zone of Saar-Pfalz to start the evacuation of their area. Already, two days ago, the sick and infirm, old people and children were evacuated on special trains, but now everyone between the ages of ten and sixty must leave. They are only being given two hours' notice to lock up their homes and make for the evacuation assembly points. Nearly half a million civilians are on the move. A rumour is going the rounds that of the thirty-four 'Hitlers' in a Saarland lunatic asylum, only twelve still maintain this identity after being evacuated.

2.00pm, WESTMINSTER
Winston Churchill and wife Clementine are guests at the flat of their son-in-law, the Austrian-born entertainer Vic Oliver. Their daughter Sarah married the much older Oliver against their will nearly three years ago. Although there is still tension over the marriage, the Churchills, Sarah and Oliver today are as one as they raise their champagne glasses to toast 'Victory'.

2.00pm, EALING FIRE STATION, WEST LONDON
Elsie Warren finishes her shift and goes to Westbourne Park. Elsie reflects that 'the past few days have been very morbid' under the shadow of war. Now in the park with the sun shining, 'the folly of war seems so stupid'.

2.00pm (3.00pm), ADLON HOTEL, BERLIN
Alex Adams and the rest of the British Embassy staff are now incarcerated on the first floor of the Adlon. For their own protection, they are assured by the Berlin police. The second floor is already reserved for the staff of the French Embassy. The British diplomats find that they can still use the hotel telephone to ring numbers within Berlin, and so they get some of their essential belongings sent to them at the hotel. Naval attaché 'Tommy' Troubridge even manages to have a case of champagne delivered for an impromptu celebration. As he waits for 'Tommy's' party to begin, Adams is relaxing on his bed, reading a John Buchan novel. Suddenly, there is a knock on the door and the sound of heavy breathing. A burly German enters, and Adams sees in the reflection of the wardrobe mirror that he is carrying an axe. In a flash, Adams is off the bed and gripping the back of a chair. He is determined to keep it between himself and the intruder. Adams's voice is unsteady as he asks the German what he is going to do with the axe. 'I have been sent to open a wooden case,' comes back the simple reply. Adams gives a sigh of relief, and directs the German to the naval attaché's room, where the case of champagne awaits. Adams follows on not far behind, keen now 'to slake an anxious thirst'.

2.00pm, FOREIGN OFFICE, WHITEHALL
Oliver Harvey, Lord Halifax's Private Secretary, notices the 'strange silence' in the Foreign Office after all this morning's excitement. Halifax gives orders that the Office is to close this afternoon, and Harvey thankfully goes home and drops exhausted into bed.

2.15pm, WILHELMSHAVEN, GERMANY

Flying Officer McPherson's Blenheim bomber has successfully completed its mission. Unfortunately, flying at 24,000 feet, the aircraft's radio has iced up. McPherson is thus unable to send back to base immediate information as to the disposition of the German warships. But they have taken seventy-five valuable reconnaissance photographs. McPherson can proudly write in the 'plane's logbook: 'Duty successful . . . the first RAF aircraft to cross the German frontier.'

2.30pm, EALING, WEST LONDON

Elsie Warren arrives home to find that her Sunday dinner has got cold. Her mother is in good spirits and believes that despite the declaration of war, 'it can't come to much'.

2.30pm (3.30pm), BERLIN

Seventeen-year-old schoolgirl Else Danielowski is travelling on the 'S' Bahn suburban railway. She and her fellow passengers have heard of Britain's declaration of war. Looking across the carriage she senses that everyone is sharing the same feeling that 'a huge thick cloud was bearing down upon us'. Nobody is the least bit cheerful, let alone defiant.

2.30pm (3.30pm), WARSAW

The weather is changing, and not for the better, and with it the mood of the capital's inhabitants. The feeling of exultation has passed. It is drizzling now, the wind has risen and it is turning cold. A party of foreign correspondents are being taken out to view the Jewish children's home and hospital that was bombed yesterday evening. It is situated at Otwock, a few miles from Warsaw. The flimsy building has been blown into matchwood, while part of it is still smoking from the fire caused by incendiary bombs. The correspondents are told that eight Jewish children between the ages of three and seven were burnt to death in their beds. They are shown one of the bodies, completely carbonised, still in the twisted metal of a bed. Reporter Cedric Salter, looking down on the body, thinks that it does not look as though it could ever have been human, and is not therefore particularly terrible unless you permit yourself 'to imagine the agony that it must have suffered before it was reduced to this handless, footless, hairless, faceless blob looking more like a badly overcooked joint of lamb than a human being'.

3.00pm, TRENT PARK

John Colville and his brother Philip, who is awaiting his call-up to the Grenadier Guards, have motored over to Sir Philip Sassoon's former home. Sir Philip died only three months ago and left Trent Park to his cousin Mrs Gubay. Trent Park has an excellent private twelve-hole golf course which the Colville brothers are now going round. John reflects what a peaceful way it is to spend the first afternoon of a new world war.

3.00pm, OLYMPIA EXHIBITION HALL, LONDON

Eugen Spier and his fellow internees are now joined by Captain Siebert and his crew from the German merchant vessel *Pomona*. They have tried to scuttle their ship in the Port of London after being refused permission to sail. Their arrival now means that anti-Nazis like Spier and Weiss are outnumbered. The newcomers strut around giving the 'Heil Hitler' salute and taunt the Jewish internees 'with the foulest anti-semitic and anti-religious insults'. They boast that the war will be won by Christmas and they will all sail home in ships of the surrendered Royal Navy.

3.00pm, BELFAST

In East Bridge Street, a Territorial Army soldier of the 8th (Belfast) Heavy Anti-Aircraft Regiment is set upon by six armed members of the Irish Republican Army. They strip him of his khaki uniform and burn it before running off.

3.30pm, CITY OF LONDON

'I reported at 3.30 at the [ARP report] centre, passing through unfamiliar streets. Every person had his or her gas mask slung across their shoulders and fireman, policemen and air raid wardens had tin hats and very smart uniforms. Soldiers passed in lorries and the little world I have known so long has disappeared.' (Vivienne Hall)

3.45pm, BELFAST

Another Territorial Army soldier is attacked by the same IRA gang. This time they shoot him in the stomach and he is seriously injured. He is the first British serviceman to be injured in the Second World War.

4.00pm, 10 DOWNING STREET

Neville Chamberlain has now put together his new administration. Running Britain's war effort will be the nine-strong War Cabinet. Apart from the Prime Minister himself, it consists of Churchill, now back in office as First Lord of Admiralty, and the two other service ministers, Leslie Hore-Belisha at the War Office and Sir Kingsley Wood, the Secretary of State for Air. Chamberlain's three closest pre-war colleagues are all also included; Lord Halifax at the Foreign Office, Sir John Simon at the Treasury and Sir Samuel Hoare, who now leaves the Home Office to become Lord Privy Seal. Completing the team are two non-party experts, Admiral of the Fleet Lord Chatfield as Minister for Coordination of Defence and Lord Hankey, Secretary to the War Cabinet in the last war, as Minister without Portfolio. Anthony Eden, now back in office as Dominions Secretary, and Home Secretary Sir John Anderson are also going to be regular attendees.

'Aren't we a very old team?' Chamberlain's War Cabinet. From left to right (standing): *Lord Hankey (Minister without Portfolio); Leslie Hore-Belisha (Secretary of State for War); Winston Churchill (First Lord of the Admiralty); Sir Kingsley Wood (Secretary of State for Air).* From left to right (seated): *Lord Chatfield (Minister for the Co-ordination of Defence); Sir Samuel Hoare (Lord Privy Seal); Neville Chamberlain (Prime Minister); Sir John Simon (Chancellor of the Exchequer) and Lord Halifax (Foreign Secretary).*

Apart from Churchill, and, to a lesser extent, Hore-Belisha, it is not a very inspiring collection of personalities to galvanise Britain's war effort against the Nazis. Chamberlain, as he himself recognises, is not cut out to be a war leader. 'Holy Fox' Halifax, 'Slippery Sam' Hoare and Simon are all heavily tainted by appeasement. Wood, though efficient and with acute political antennae, is seen as merely a protégé of Chamberlain's. Chatfield, despite his grand-sounding title, has little political clout, and Hankey, while a great civil servant, is virtually unknown to the general public. As regards Hore-Belisha, many of his cabinet colleagues and the military 'top brass' think him 'publicity mad' and lacking in substance. His Jewish ancestry also tells against him in the mildly anti-semitic atmosphere of the British Establishment.

Churchill towers over them all. Today has proved that he has been consistently right in his warnings about Hitler's aggressive designs. He is seen by many as the man who will put both backbone in his colleagues and much-needed drive into the nation's war effort.

5.00pm, *PARIS SOIR* OFFICE, PARIS
Editor Pierre Lazareff writes in his diary, 'This time it's definite. We're in. We're at war. No wild enthusiasm. There's a job to be done; that's all. As our men leave to join their regiments they can be heard to say, "We've got to put an end to this."'

Just as in Britain, Lazareff recalls that the French 'have been told for months now, that "on the very first day of the war, there will be raids on all the big cities . . . and Paris will be destroyed within a few minutes". A number of citizens have left Paris, but not many. Parisians stroll around with their gas masks slung over their shoulders. Every once in a while, they look up into the sky, but there is no trace of panic. Life goes on.'

4.00pm (5.00pm), BERLIN

At the British Embassy all telephone lines are now cut. Sir Nevile and his staff's only contact is now through the United States Embassy which is now looking after British interests in Germany as the 'Protecting Power'. In Britain, the Swiss Legation is doing the same for Germany. Outside the Adlon Hotel newsboys are giving away an extra edition of the *Deutsche Allegemeine Zeitung* to passers-by. Its headlines read:

BRITISH ULTIMATUM TURNED DOWN
ENGLAND DECLARES A STATE OF WAR WITH GERMANY
BRITISH NOTE DEMANDS WITHDRAWAL OF OUR TROOPS
   IN THE EAST
THE FUEHRER LEAVING FOR THE FRONT TODAY
GERMAN MEMORANDUM PROVES ENGLAND'S GUILT

4.00pm (5.00pm), FRIEDERICHSTRASSE STATION

William and Margaret Joyce see that newspaper extras announcing Britain's declaration of war are being given away by newsboys under the bridge outside the station. The Joyces join Berliners scrambling for copies. On their faces, Joyce sees no sign of anger or hatred. They just look at each other as if the incredible has just happened.

4.00pm (5.00pm), BERLIN

Life correspondent William Bayles is holding an impromptu drinks party for some other Americans. They celebrate war, Bayle wryly notes, 'with more complete abandon than we had ever celebrated a diplomatic peace'. They soon polish off a case of champagne.

4.00pm (5.00pm), UNITED STATES EMBASSY, BERLIN

Embassy clerk William Russell notes down some of the rumours flying round the German capital this afternoon:

France will not take part in the war.

Russia has given an ultimatum to England.

The first Italian divisions are already pouring through the Brenner Pass into Germany.

Von Papen is in Paris to negotiate.

The German and French armies on either side of the Rhine River are fraternizing with each other and have refused to fight.

It is said that Saarbruecken has been shelled by the French and has been destroyed stone by stone.

None of them turns out to be true.

4.30pm, FRENCH GENERAL HEADQUARTERS, CHÂTEAU DE VINCENNES

French commander-in-chief General Maurice Gamelin sends out secret instructions to France's armed forces: 'our ultimatum expires at 5pm today unless the Germans accept it. But to act in accord with the British Air Force we have decided not to commence operations until tomorrow morning at 5am.'

4.30pm, BROADCASTING HOUSE

Chief Announcer Stuart Hibberd takes a break from reading news bulletins. He goes to Regent's Park for a breath of fresh air. In the park, Hibberd, who fought at Gallipoli in the last war, looks up to a sky seemingly full of barrage balloons. On the ground he sees an RAF lorry that is securing one of these 'monster fish', Hibberd also notices there is a large earth-pin nearby. Dozens of civilians, both men and women, are hard at work, filling sandbags to protect the RAF balloon crew. Pleased to see this sign of national solidarity, Hibberd makes his way back to Langham Place. He has to be on hand for the King's broadcast at 6.00pm.

5.30pm (6.30pm), FRENCH EMBASSY, WARSAW

At the Frascati Palace, which houses the French Embassy, Ambassador Noël hears, with considerable relief, that his country is now at war with the Third Reich. The mood and size of the crowd outside has diminished since the euphoria of the morning's announcement of the British declaration. But there is still a large number of Poles outside cheering, and Noël hears snatches of 'La Marseillaise' being sung. Colonel Beck now arrives, but his chauffeur finds it difficult to get through the crush of demonstrators outside the embassy's gates. Beck eventually makes it through. He presents to Noël, with whom he has not enjoyed the best of relations, Poland's thanks to France for honouring her obligations. The two men have to meet in a small salon on the ground floor of the ornate embassy. The larger reception rooms are being cleared of paintings, furniture and other valuable objects to save them from destruction or damage in air raids. Noël escorts Beck to his car. The French ambassador is surprised that the Colonel is being given such a rapturous reception by the crowd. Until only recently Beck had never gone out into the streets of the capital without a strong escort, his car driven at a high speed. Today he is being acclaimed as the man of the hour.

4.55pm, PARIS

The French ultimatum is about to expire and France will soon be at war with Germany. A rumour is circulating around the French capital that Chamberlain and Daladier decided that Britain should be the first to declare war because people in both France and Poland were by no means sure that she would fight.

6.00pm (7.00pm), FRENCH EMBASSY, WARSAW

Now that Beck has gone, Ambassador Noël sets out to make a symbolic gesture towards Franco-Polish solidarity. He is driven across Warsaw to Pilsudski Square to the Tomb of Poland's Unknown

227

Warrior. In front of the tomb is a statue of Polish Prince Joseph Poniatowski, a marshal of France who died in 1813, fighting in Napoleon's ranks. This afternoon, Poles have showered the French embassy with bouquets of flowers. Now Noël lays some of them at the tomb of the Polish Unknown Warrior of the Great War. He also places a wreath at the foot of the Poniatowski statue. In the twilight the ambassador's gesture is seen by a few passers-by. They appreciate the gesture and call out, '*Vive La France.*'

5.00pm, PARIS
The French ultimatum to Germany expires and France is now at war with Germany. Just as in Berlin today, there are no scenes of patriotic fervour in the French capital this afternoon comparable to that of 1914. Then the crowds shouted *A Berlin!* (To Berlin!), and threatened to cut off the Kaiser's moustache. Today, on the café terraces and boulevards, the slogan is the more resigned *Il faut en finir* (We've got a put to stop it). Geoffrey Cox, driving down the Boulevard Montmartre in fellow reporter Alan Moorehead's Ford V8, notices that the crowds are as thick as on a normal Sunday. But their faces are tense, and their steps more hurried today. Suddenly the car splutters and stops. The two men have to get out and push it. In the middle of a stream of impatient horn-blaring traffic Cox quickly glances at his wristwatch. It is just after five o' clock. France too is now at war.

5.00pm, TATE GALLERY, MILLBANK
Director John Rothenstein finishes working. The Tate was closed to the public eleven days ago at midday on 24 August, and the greater part of the Gallery's collection has now been safely evacuated. While it was being packed up ready to go, Rothenstein received an unexpected visit from the King. He cheerfully tells the Tate's director, 'I thought I'd have a look at them before they go, although if it weren't for those labels of yours, I wouldn't know one from another. Would you?'

Rothenstein now returns home to find Colonial Secretary Malcolm MacDonald's car outside the house. MacDonald himself is asleep on the sofa. He has come, tired out, from Parliament. He tells Rothenstein, 'You see, I've nothing to do. My resignation, like those of the rest of the Ministers, is in the Prime Minister's hands. Only the Service Ministers are at their desks.' With no notion of whether or not he is still in the Cabinet, MacDonald sits down with the Rothensteins to listen to the King's broadcast at 6.00pm.

6.00pm, BUCKINGHAM PALACE, LONDON

King George VI broadcasts to the peoples of Britain, the Empire and Commonwealth from his study at Buckingham Palace. The King is wearing the uniform of an Admiral of the Fleet. He has resolved not to wear civilian clothes in public again until victory has been won. Queen Elizabeth is listening in another room of the Palace as her husband begins to speak:

In this grave hour, perhaps the most fateful in our history, I send to every household of my peoples, both home and overseas, this message, spoken with the same depth of feeling for each one of you as if I were able to cross your threshold and speak to you myself.

For the second time in the lives of most of us we are at war. Over and over again we have tried to find a peaceful way out of the differences between ourselves and those who are now our enemies. But it has been in vain. We have been forced into a conflict. For we are called, with our allies, to meet the challenge of a principle which, if it were to prevail, would be fatal to any civilised order in the world.

It is the principle which permits a State, in the selfish pursuit of power, to disregard its treaties and its solemn pledges: which sanctions the use of force, or threat of force, against the sovereignty and independence of other States. Such a principle, stripped of all disguise, is surely the mere primitive doctrine that might is right; and if this principle were established throughout the world, the freedom of our own country and of the whole British Commonwealth of Nations would be in danger. But far more than this – the peoples of the world would be kept in the bondage of fear, and all hopes of settled peace and security of justice and liberty among nations would be ended.

This is the ultimate issue which confronts us. For the sake of all that we ourselves hold dear, and of the world's order and peace, it is unthinkable that we should refuse to meet the challenge.

It is to this high purpose that I now call my people at home and my peoples across the seas, who will make our cause their own. I ask them to stand calm, firm and united in this time of trial. The task will be hard. There may be dark days ahead, and war can no longer be confined to the battlefield. But we can only do the right as we see the right, and reverently commit our cause to God. If one and all we keep resolutely faithful to it, ready for whatever service or sacrifice it may demand, then, with God's help, we shall prevail.

May He bless and keep us all.

Listening to the King while on duty at Broadcasting House, BBC Chief Announcer Stuart Hibberd thinks the broadcast 'magnificent'. James Agate recognises that although, for the King, the broadcast 'is obviously a great strain . . . he comes through it nobly'. Florence Speed considers the King's 'voice is more assured' and that he spoke well.

Others are much more critical. Left-wing intellectual and poet Stephen Spender dubbed 'The Rupert Brooke of the Depression', writes in his diary: 'The King broadcast a speech . . . which was badly spoken, enough, I should have thought to finish the Royal Family in this country. It was a great mistake. He should never be allowed to say more than twenty words. After this his voice has the effect of a very spasmodic and often interrupted tape machine. It produces an effect of colourless monotony, except that after a very slow and drawn out passage sometimes the words are all jumbled together at the end of a sentence. First of all one tries to

Britain's three Chiefs of Staff in September 1939 (left to right): *General Sir Edmund Ironside (Chief of the Imperial General Staff); Air Chief Marshal Sir Cyril Newall (Chief of the Air Staff) and Admiral of the Fleet Sir Dudley Pound (First Sea Lord and Chief of the Naval Staff).*

King George VI broadcasts to the Empire from Buckingham Palace, 6.00pm, 3 September 1939. A public announcement was made that each household in the United Kingdom would receive a copy of the King's speech. In the event, the project was abandoned on the King's initiative, as it would have cost £35,000 and required 250 tons of paper.

listen to what he is saying. Then one forgets this and starts sympathizing with him in his difficulties. Then one wants to smash the radio.'

6.00pm, JERSEY, CHANNEL ISLANDS
Norman Scarlyn Wilson has spent the afternoon sunbathing and swimming. He is now in the lounge of his hotel to hear the King's broadcast. With him are the other guests. There are two Royal Army Medical Corps ex-colonels who constantly try and cap each other's army stories; a young honeymoon couple who only arrived, like Wilson, just three days ago, and a blind man with his nurse. There is also a Boer War sapper colonel, long since retired. He constantly talks of De Wet and Botha, of Ladysmith and Mafeking, names that now seem fantastically remote. Wilson admires the King's 'simple, natural touch' and contrasts it with 'the torrents of insults and menaces, of the furious, hysterical babblings hurled across the ether by the raucous, demoniac voice of the Fuehrer'. When the King finishes, Wilson and the others all stand, as they did this morning, for the National Anthem. The honeymoon couple surreptitiously hold hands.

6.00pm (7.00pm), MADRID
Spanish dictator General Francisco Franco broadcasts an appeal to the warring nations to get them to localise the conflict. He tells them, 'The more the conflict is extended the more the germ of future wars is sown. In these circumstances, I appeal to the common sense and responsibility of the rulers of the nations in order to direct the efforts of all toward the localization of the present conflict.'

6.00pm (8.00pm), BANJA LUKA, YUGOSLAVIA
Julian Amery, son of former Conservative cabinet minister and anti-appeaser Leopold, is on his way to Belgrade. His car has got a Union Jack tied to the mudguard and this has attracted a small crowd.

One of the crowd is a student who can speak a little English. He tells Amery that Radio Belgrade has earlier announced that Britain and France are at war with Germany. Banja Luka is only an hour or so from Sarajevo. Amery reflects how appropriate it is to learn of the outbreak of the Second World War so near to where Gavrilo Princip fired the fatal shots that lead to the First World War.

6.15pm, BROADCASTING HOUSE

Following the King's broadcast, the BBC announcer reads out the new government appointments which Chamberlain decided upon this afternoon. In addition to the composition of the War Cabinet, it is announced that two First World War ministries are to be reconstituted. The former Ministry of Blockade now becomes the Ministry of Economic Warfare with Tory MP Ronald Cross as minister. Its task is to bring about the systematic disorganisation of the Nazi economy. The second revived ministry is that of Information. In 1918, it was headed by the dynamic press baron Lord Beaverbrook. No such colourful personality is to head the ministry this time. Instead, Chamberlain has picked Lord Macmillan, one of the judicial members of the House of Lords and an authority on international law, to become minister. His ministry is going to handle all Government press news, censorship, and propaganda to Nazi Germany and the neutrals.

Resting at home, tired-out Foreign Office official Oliver Harvey listens to the radio announce the new government appointments. He is delighted that his old boss Anthony Eden is back in office as Dominions Secretary and that Churchill is First Lord of the Admiralty. 'Best news I could have had,' writes Harvey in his diary tonight.

6.15pm, HMS *ARK ROYAL*, NORTH SEA

On the wardroom radio Guy Griffiths and his brother officers are listening to the news of the new Government appointments. Churchill's appointment as First Lord of the Admiralty is announced and there is an instantaneous roar of delight in the wardroom. Cheering breaks out all over the carrier as the news spreads. At last, thinks Griffiths, the Navy has got the man it wants to lead them.

6.30pm, BRACKNELL, BERKSHIRE
Pacifist schoolmaster Arnold Monk-Jones agonisingly writes to his fiancée Eileen Bellerby, a science teacher at Cheltenham Ladies College, 'It seems the worst is happening. It was a horrible sensation listening to Chamberlain this morning . . . I incline to adopt the position, in regard to myself, of refusing military service. I am fully convinced that universal pacifism, say in this country, would have prevented war; and therefore the more pacifists there are, the better for the future state of the world. The counter-consideration that troubles me is this: once we are at war avoidable tho' it may have been by pacifism in the past, ought we not to work for victory of our side, as being slightly less bad of the two? If my pacifism now increases the chance of a German victory, is it sound? Or is a British victory now less important than keeping alive the pacifist outlook?'

6.30pm (7.30pm), BERLIN
The German home service radio broadcasts the text of a speech that Reichsfuehrer SS Heinrich Himmler has given today. It ends with the words, 'The Fuehrer expects every man to do *more* than his duty. God commands, and Heil Hitler!'

6.45pm (7.45pm), BERLIN
On the radio the German home service is playing Beethoven's Fourth Symphony when the music stops, and a proclamation by Hitler is read by an announcer:

England has for centuries pursued the aim of rendering the peoples of Europe defenceless against the British policy of world conquest by proclaiming a balance of power, in which England claimed the right to attack on threadbare pretexts and destroy that European state which at that moment seemed most dangerous.

Thus at one time she fought the world power of Spain, later the Dutch, then the French, and, since the year 1871, the Germans.

We ourselves have been the witnesses of the policy of encirclement which has been carried on by England against Germany since before the war.

Just as the German nation had begun, under its National Socialist leadership, to recover from the frightful consequences of the Versailles *Diktat*, and threatened to survive the crisis, British encirclement immediately began once more.

The British war inciters spread the lie before the war, that the battle was only against the House of Hohenzollern or German militarism, that they had no designs on German colonies, that they had no intention of taking the German mercantile fleet.

They then oppressed the German people under the Versailles *Diktat*. The faithful fulfilment of this *Diktat* would have sooner or later exterminated 20,000,000 Germans.

I undertook to mobilise the resistance of the German nation against this and to assure work and bread for them. I have many times offered England and the English people the understanding and friendship of the German people. I have always been repelled.

I had for years been aware that the aim of these war inciters had for long been to take Germany by surprise at a favourable opportunity.

I am more fully determined than ever to beat back this attack. Germany shall not again capitulate. There is no sense in sacrificing one life after another and submitting to an even worse Versailles *Diktat*.

We have never been a nation of slaves, and will not be one in the future.

Whatever Germans in the past had to sacrifice for the existence of our Reich they shall not be greater than those which we are prepared to make today.

235

This resolve is an inexorable one. It necessitates the most thorough measures and imposes on us one law above all others:

If the soldier is fighting at the front no one shall profit by the war. If a soldier falls at the front no one at home shall evade his duty.

As long as the German people was united it has never been conquered. It was the lack of unity that led to collapse.

Whoever offend against this unity need expect nothing else than the annihilation as an enemy of the nation.

If our people fulfils its highest duty in this sense then God will help us, Who has always bestowed His mercy on him who was determined to help himself.

6.30pm (7.30pm), GERMAN-POLISH BORDER

Wilhelm Prueller and his company are stood down. Their expected attack will not now take place this evening. Prueller is hungry and thirsty as he hasn't eaten or drunk since this morning, but his unit have got a pig with them. They intend to kill and eat it once they have captured Poland's ancient capital, Krakow. In the meantime rumours are flying around the encampment. 'If the war isn't over by midnight,' Prueller writes, 'Russia and Latvia will attack. That will be a decisive move.' Before turning in, he writes of his wife and child in his diary, 'but I am still alive today, and so are you and Lore. All of us!'

7.00pm, U-30, ATLANTIC OCEAN

Lemp is on the submarine's bridge as a Force 4 wind is whipping up the waves around the U-30. Suddenly, the U-boat commander sees something to the starboard of the submarine. He calls his artillery officer Leutnant Hans-Peter Hinsch to the bridge. The two men see the silhouette of an approaching big ship. Lemp wonders if she is one of the British armed merchant cruisers that U-boat chief Karl Doenitz has warned his commanders to be on the lookout for them.

7.15pm (9.15pm), GERMANY EMBASSY, MOSCOW
Ambassador Count Friederich-Werner von der Schulenberg has
just received a telegram from von Ribbentrop. Its instructions
read: 'Very Urgent ! Exclusively for the Ambassador! Strictly secret!
For Chief of Mission or his representative personally. Top secret.
To be decoded by himself. Strictest secrecy!' Von der Schulenberg,
like so many top German diplomats, is no Nazi. He now sets
about decoding his foreign minister's message. The ambassador
sees that it contains an invitation for the Russians to invade Poland.
He is told to 'discuss this at once with Molotov and see if the
Soviet Union does not consider it desirable to move against Polish
forces . . .'

7.15pm, *U-30*, ATLANTIC OCEAN
Lemp orders the submarine to dive, and the klaxon sounds 'battle
stations'. He is still unsure about the identity of the approaching
ship, but thinks it suspicious that she is showing no lights even
though dusk is now falling. With his adrenaline flowing, Lemp
weighs up the pros and cons of the situation. He decides to attack.

7.30pm, US EMBASSY, PARIS
Hubert Earle, who is helping out at the US Embassy, goes out to
dinner at the Café de la Paix with two other embassy employees.
They find the café a gloomy place this evening. There are no menus,
merely a typewritten list with a small selection, mainly egg dishes
and no meat on offer. The café is full of servicemen but not many
civilians. Most of the waiters are elderly men as the young ones
are already in uniform. The only young one on duty is an Italian
who is delighted that he will not have to fight.

7.30pm, SS *ATHENIA*, ATLANTIC OCEAN
Captain James Cook joins the first-class passengers for dinner
tonight, the first time since the *Athenia* has sailed. Most of the

diners regard this as a good omen. At the Captain's table are Sir Richard and Lady Lake, a former Lieutenant-Governor of Saskatchewan and his wife. Young actress Pax Walker-Fryett, who has been appearing at Worthing's Connaught Theatre this summer season, and is now on her way to Hollywood, is also having dinner. Pax has seen the notice that Captain Cook has had put up saying that war was declared at 11.00am this morning. Now as she takes her seat at the table she notices that the ship appears to be zigzagging and that a strict blackout is in force. Pax has been told that the ship is completely unarmed. At her table is a veteran of the last war who still suffers from the effects of poison gas. Pax and her dining companions ask him, 'What do you think? Do you think that we're likely to get attacked going to America or Canada? What do you think our chances are?'

7.38pm, SS *ATHENIA*, ATLANTIC OCEAN
On deck a group of children are entertaining some of the other passengers. They have just started to sing this summer's big hit 'South of the Border, Down Mexico Way'.

7.38pm, *U-30*, ATLANTIC OCEAN
Lemp gives the order to fire the torpedoes, 1,600 yards from the *Athenia*.

7.39pm, SS *ATHENIA*, ATLANTIC OCEAN
The Great War veteran at Pax Walker-Fryett's table is reassuring. He is just telling Pax and the others, 'Oh no, they'll wait till the ship comes back with armaments on before they do anything', when Lemp's torpedo crashes into the liner's side. In the dining room everything seems to rise up, and the diners too are involuntarily forced to their feet. The electricity goes off and everything is in complete darkness. Pax has the sensation of the liner starting to roll over and the tableware, china, cutlery, chairs and passengers

all end up in a heap on one side of the dining room. The *Athenia* then seems to straighten up. Pax and the others get up and start stumbling about. Pax feels a hot trickle down her leg and suddenly realises that she is bleeding from a cut knee. Some of the waiters in their white mess jackets now get the passengers to form a chain behind them. They then wind their way up to the ship's deck. To Pax's surprise, it still seems like daylight up on deck.

As the lights go out, Claud Barrie, one of the bedroom stewards and a soldier in the last war, thinks he can smell cordite. But a mate of his tells him, 'The swine has hit us.' The two men run to the alleyways to warn their passengers and then go 'up on deck in time to see the periscope of a submarine disappear'. Another crew member John M'Ewan at first can hardly see through the smoke, but it soon clears a little and M'Ewan makes out the U-boat breaking the surface. To M'Ewan's shocked surprise it turns its deck gun on the stricken liner. Captain James Cook reckons that the U-boat is aiming to destroy the *Athenia*'s wireless equipment to prevent it from sending out distress signals.

7.40pm, *U-30*, ATLANTIC OCEAN

Two of the *U-30*'s torpedoes have missed the *Athenia* completely. Another is faulty and is stuck in its tube. But the fourth has found its mark. It has exploded in the *Athenia*'s No. 5 hold and against the engine-room bulkhead. Its impact has claimed the first victims of the war in the west. German Jewish refugee Edith Lustig is blown overboard by the force of the torpedo's explosion. She is never seen again. Ten-year-old Margaret Hayworth, returning home to Canada with her mother and sister, is killed by a metal splinter when No. 5 hold is hit. In the liner's third-class accommodation, nine-year-old Daniel Wilkes sees his mother die when the wall of their cabin collapses on her as she lies ill in bed. Daniel manages to wriggle free from the wreckage and, clinging to a chair, floats out into the passageway.

7.45pm, Wireless Room, SS *Athenia*, Atlantic Ocean
Chief Radio Officer Don is ordered by Captain Cook to send out an SOS signal in naval code. For a quarter of an hour, and working on his own in the liner's large wireless room, Don finally gets through to the nearest coast station at Valentia. His message reads:

'athenia torpedoed – 5.42 north, 14.05 west'

Captain Cook comes on the speaking tube again and tells Don to send the signal '*en clair*' as well as in code. Don does so and almost immediately he gets a response. It is from the 5,000-ton Norwegian freighter *Knute Nelson*, which is only about forty miles away. After acknowledging, the Norwegian's radio officer signals Don back:

the old man doesn't believe you've been torpedoed – but he's coming to your assistance anyway.

7.51pm (8.51pm), German Embassy, Rome
A personal message from Hitler to Mussolini is just coming through on the wire. Hitler thanks his fellow dictator for his last attempt at mediation, but tells him, 'It would have been impossible to allow blood which was being sacrificed there [Poland] to be squandered by diplomatic intrigue.' Hitler accepts that Italy, just as in 1914, is going to remain neutral, at least for the time being. But he warns his fellow dictator, 'If National Socialist Germany were to be destroyed by the Western Democracies, Fascist Italy also would face a hard future.'

7.55pm (8.55pm), Anhalter Station, Berlin
Hitler arrives to board his train *Amerika* for the Eastern Front. The specially armoured train consists of fifteen carriages and has two steam engines to haul it. Hitler's own carriage is made up of a bedroom, bathroom, office and a combined dining-conference room

which is large enough to accommodate twelve people. Over 200 members of the Fuehrer's staff occupy the remaining carriages. There are also anti-aircraft gun wagons at the front and rear of the train. The train pulls out on its way to Gross-Born in Pomerania, where Fuehrer Headquarters is to be located. Hitler calls in Heinz Linge, his personal servant. He tells Linge that in future he intends to have an even more Spartan diet than hitherto. 'You will see to it,' the Fuehrer instructs Linge, 'that I have only what the ordinary people of Germany can have. It is my duty to set an example.' Hitler is also giving up watching feature films for the duration of the conflict.

8.00pm, 'VILLA VOLPONE', SOUTH HAMPSTEAD
James Agate observes that the setting sun is turning the barrage balloons to golden asteroids.

8.15pm, U-30, ATLANTIC OCEAN
Lemp gives the order to surface. From the conning tower, crew member Adolf Schmidt can quite clearly see the stricken *Athenia*. It is listing heavily and he sees 'much commotion on the torpedoed ship' as the liner's lifeboats are launched. While Schmidt watches the scene on the liner, his captain is handed a transcription of one of Chief Radio Officer Don's distress signals. With a jolt, Lemp realises that instead of an armed merchant cruiser, he has torpedoed an unarmed passenger liner. He turns to Leutnant Hinsch and exclaims, 'What a mess!'

8.30pm, PARIS
Chamberlain's French opposite number, Edouard Daladier, whose actual title is President of the Council of Ministers, has hurried from the Chamber of Deputies back to the Ministry of National Defence to deliver a broadcast to the nation. Daladier knows war at first hand. He served in the infantry throughout the Great War, rose to the rank of captain, was twice wounded and decorated with

241

the Croix de Guerre and the Legion of Honour. A musical programme from evacuated Strasbourg is faded out, and, after a brief introduction, Daladier speaks to the French people and the men of France's armed forces:

Since daybreak on 1st September, Poland has been the victim of the most brutal and most cynical of aggressions. Her frontiers have been violated. Her cities are being bombed. Her army is heroically resisting the invader. The responsibility for the blood being shed falls entirely upon Hitler's government. The fate of peace was in Hitler's hands. He chose war. France and England have made countless efforts to safeguard peace. This very morning they made a further urgent intervention in Berlin in order to address the German Government with a last appeal to reason and a request to stop hostilities and open peaceful negotiations.

Germany met us with a refusal. She had already refused to reply to all men of goodwill who recently raised their voices in favour of the peace of the world. She therefore desires the destruction of Poland so as to be able to dominate Europe quickly and to enslave France. In rising against the most frightful of tyrannies, in honouring our word, we fight to defend our soil, our homes, our liberties. I am conscious of having worked unremittingly against war until this minute. I greet with emotion and affection our young soldiers, who now go forth to perform the sacred task which we ourselves performed before them. They can have full confidence in their chiefs, who are worthy of those who have previously led France to victory.

The cause of France is identical with that of righteousness. It is the cause of all peaceful and free nations. It will be victorious. Men and women of France! We are waging war because it has been thrust upon us. Every one of us is at his post, on the soil of France, that land of liberty where respect for human dignity finds one of its last refuges. You will all co-operate, with a profound feeling of union and brotherhood, for the salvation of the country. *Vive La France!*

8.30pm (9.30pm), FOREIGN MINISTER'S RESIDENCE, WARSAW
At the request of Colonel Beck, American ambassador Biddle arrives
to hear a report on the events of today. Beck begins by telling the
US envoy that he and his associates are 'profoundly appreciative
of France's and Britain's honouring their respective alliances with
Poland'. The Colonel then gives Biddle the latest official information on German air attacks. Yesterday, twenty-seven towns and
cities were bombed, while today, Deblin, Torun, Poznan, Krakow
and Plock have been the Luftwaffe's principal targets. So far, 1,500
civilians have been killed or seriously injured in the bombing. Beck
claims that the Poles have brought down sixty-four German planes in
the last three days for a loss of eleven Polish aircraft. In conclusion,
the Colonel tells Biddle that his government is transmitting a
vigorous protest to The Hague. It will list all of the Luftwaffe's
violations of the Polish-German Agreement of 2 September, which
is supposed to limit aerial bombardments to only military objectives.
As Biddle leaves the Foreign Ministry and walks through the fore-
court, he notices that the Poles are already packing up their archives
ready for evacuation.

9.00pm, BROADCASTING HOUSE
The BBC German Service broadcasts a message from Chamberlain
to the German people.

German people!
    Your country and mine are now at war. Your Government has
bombed and invaded the free and independent state of Poland which
this country is honour bound to defend. Because your troops were
not withdrawn in response to the Note which the British Government addressed to the German Government, war has followed.
    With the horrors of war we are familiar. God knows this country
has done everything possible to prevent the calamity. But now that the
invasion of Poland by Germany has taken place, it has become inevitable.

You are told by your Government that you are fighting because Poland rejected your Leader's offer and resorted to force. What are the facts? The so-called 'offer' was made to the Polish Ambassador in Berlin on Thursday evening, two hours before the announcement by your Government that it had been 'rejected'. So far from having been rejected, there had been no time even to consider it. Your Government had previously demanded that a Polish representative should be sent to Berlin within twenty-four hours to conclude an agreement. At that time the sixteen points subsequently put forward had not even been communicated to the Polish Government. The Polish representative was expected to arrive and within a fixed time to sign an agreement which he had not even seen. This is not negotiation. This is a *diktat*. To such methods no self-respecting and powerful State should assent. Negotiations on a free and equal basis might have well settled the matter in dispute.

You may ask why Great Britain is concerned. We are concerned because we gave our word of honour to defend Poland against aggression. Why did we feel it necessary to pledge ourselves to defend this Eastern Power when our interests lie in the west, and when your Leader has said he has no interest in the west?

The answer is – and I regret to say it – that nobody in this country any longer places any trust in your Leader's word.

He gave his word that he would respect the Locarno Treaty; he broke it. He gave his word that he neither wished nor intended to annex Austria; he broke it. He declared that he would not incorporate the Czechs in the Reich; he did so. He gave his word after Munich that he had no further territorial demands to make in Europe; he broke it. He gave his word that he wanted no Polish Provinces; he broke it. He has sworn to you for years that he was the mortal enemy of Bolshevism; he is now its ally. Can you wonder his word is for us not worth the paper it is written on?

The German-Soviet Pact was a cynical *volte face* designed to shatter the Peace Front against aggression. This gamble failed. The Peace

Front stands firm. Your Leader is now sacrificing you, the German people, to the still more monstrous gamble of a war, to extricate himself from the impossible position into which he has led himself and you. In this war we are not fighting against you, the German people, for whom we have no bitter feelings, but against a tyrannous and forsworn regime, which has betrayed not only its own people, but the whole of western civilisation and all that we hold dear.

May God defend the right!

9.00pm (10.00pm), Gracie Fields's Villa, Capri

Gracie Fields, Britain's most popular entertainer, is still recovering from a serious operation for cancer. This morning, she and her partner, film director Monty Banks, listened to Chamberlain's broadcast. Now she looks out towards Naples where there is a blackout tonight. But Gracie is thinking that Britain is also in darkness. She wants to be there, 'doing something'. Monty senses what Gracie is thinking, 'You want to go back and get into it, don't you?' he asks her. 'I must,' Gracie replies. With that, Monty goes off to start their packing.

9.15pm, Wireless Room, SS Athenia, Atlantic Ocean

Chief Radio Officer Don is still steadily sending out SOS messages. As he tries to contact other rescue vessels, only two of the *Athenia*'s lifeboats remain to be launched. Assembled by one of them, in a scene reminiscent of the sinking of the *Titanic* twenty-seven years ago, the waiting passengers are singing 'Nearer My God to Thee' and 'Abide with Me.' But now, Don has managed to get through to two other ships. One is the American freighter *City of Flint*. The other is a luxury yacht, the *Southern Cross*, owned by Swedish millionaire businessman Axel Wenner-Gren. He is the founder of the Electrolux Company and an acquaintance of Hermann Goering. Brilliantly lit with its blue and yellow Swedish flag illuminated by an arc-light, the *Southern Cross* answers Don's signal at 9.22pm. Four minutes later, the *City of Flint* does the same, and in another signal promises Don that it 'would reach the given position in ten hours'.

9.15pm, BROADCASTING HOUSE

It is now the turn of Labour's acting leader Arthur Greenwood to take his place at the BBC microphone and speak for the Opposition. He has already won high praise for his forthright speech in the Commons last night. He now tells his listeners:

> We are at war because the British people are united and steadfast in their conviction that there are cherished possessions of mankind which are worth defending, for without them life is empty. We believe in liberty, through which alone the mind and soul of the peoples of the world can find free expression. All peoples, whether they be great powers or small nations, have a right to live in security and independence, without threats or menaces, or the use of force. If we do not overthrow the forces of Dictatorship now, our turn will come sooner or later.
>
> We deny the right of any power to commit acts of brigandage or to seek to attain its ends by means of force or the threat of force. We believe there is no kind of dispute between nations which cannot be settled by peaceful methods, if the will is present . . .
>
> This is a bitter hour for us all. It is a bitter hour for the Labour Party, which has always regarded peace with freedom as the greatest blessing of mankind. Those for whom I can especially speak are fighting for a world in which henceforth law shall rule instead of force. We do not want increased power for Britain in the world. We want no new lands. We do not want to destroy the German people, whose scholars, writers, musicians, democratic leaders and others have made such noble contributions to European civilisation which Hitler seeks to destroy.

We want – having paid an incalculable price – when the air raid sirens have been silenced and the war is ended, to make a new start to build a world where peace will be eternal, and where the arts of peace may flourish for the enjoyment of the whole of mankind . . .

9.15pm, EALING FIRE STATION, WEST LONDON

Elsie Warren cuts herself a few sandwiches and then sets off to the fire station for an all-night shift or 'vigil', as she thinks of it. Elsie hates the blackout and thinks it terrible now at night when you can hardly see a foot ahead of you.

9.30pm, BROADCASTING HOUSE

Liberal leader Sir Archibald Sinclair now comes to speak on behalf of his party. He tells his listeners, 'What is at stake in this great conflict is your right and mine, and the rights of other plain and ordinary people like us in this and other countries, to life, liberty and the pursuit of happiness. Let us in that cause, like the authors of the American Declaration of Independence, with a firm reliance on the protection of Divine Providence, mutually pledge to each other our lives, our fortunes and our sacred honour.'

9.30pm, JERSEY, CHANNEL ISLANDS

Norman Scarlyn Wilson and the other guests listen to the broadcasts by Greenwood and Sinclair. Wilson is particularly struck by the vision and courage of Greenwood's speech. He reflects on how on such occasions some politicians 'can unerringly find just those words that best express what is in our hearts'. But it is the two Royal Army Medical Corps colonels who, in Wilson's view, sum up the whole 'position with commendable brevity'.

'Well, *he's* asked for it,' says one, as the other limps slowly across the room. In the doorway he turns. 'Yes,' he gruffly replies, 'and *he'll* get it.' There is no need to name any names.

9.30pm, SS *CITY OF FLINT*, ATLANTIC OCEAN

Captain Joseph L. Gainard has called a meeting of his passengers. He tells them: 'Ladies and gentlemen, we are changing our course – the *Athenia* has just been torpedoed. I've been torpedoed three times myself and I can't stand by and see people kicking about in the water. That's all.' Only minutes after Captain Gainard's speech, his passengers, many of them American academics and college students, start helping the crew to prepare the ship to receive the *Athenia*'s survivors. Gainard cannot quite believe his eyes when he sees what is happening, but concedes that his passengers are 'a swell bunch'.

9.45pm (10.45pm), FOREIGN MINISTRY, WARSAW

Foreign press correspondents have been called together to hear some important news from the government's press spokesmen. They tell the journalists that units of the famed Polish cavalry have carried the war back into German territory, crossing into East Prussia north of Treuburg. The heartening news is wired back to London and the late editions of the *Daily Express* carry the headline, 'Poles Invade East Prussia'.

10.00pm, US EMBASSY, PARIS

Hubert Earle and a colleague leave the embassy and stumble through the darkness to Harry's Bar, the only place in the French capital where American hamburgers and hot dogs are to be got. On the way, Earle is stopped by a policeman because he is not carrying a regulation gas mask. The *flic* allows him to go on only after Earle assures him that his mask is at the embassy. He'll go and retrieve it and promises to keep it with him at all times in the future. Arriving at Harry's Bar, Earle and his companion find the place in uproar. It is jammed with American students and tourists, many of them blind drunk. The dance floor is crowded with dancers giving a riotous performance of 'The Big Apple'. Earle and his colleague get into conversation with a young couple at the next table, which is jammed up against their own. Totally oblivious to the war, the couple are already celebrating their marriage tomorrow. The bride-to-be is a student from Milwaukee and her groom comes from San Francisco. They met in Germany, and only just managed to get out before the frontier closed. Earle's colleague questions them about conditions in the Reich. He doesn't get very far with his questioning. The couple aren't interested in anything except their marriage, and their only worry is that the war might interfere with it. They do tell him, however, that the German people they met certainly didn't want war. Indeed, they were very depressed about the prospect of it.

10.00pm, EALING FIRE STATION, WEST LONDON
Auxiliary Firewoman Elsie Warren and the rest of her shift arrive and are given their orders for the night. Elsie and the others are all feeling rather miserable, but the District Fire Officer 'is bubbling over with fun'. He keeps them all laughing with his fund of jokes and wisecracks.

10.00pm, SS *ATHENIA*, ATLANTIC OCEAN
Chief Officer Barnet Copland reports to Captain Cook that all passengers are off the ship. In the wireless room Chief Radio Officer Don is sending off his last signals. He tells the *Knute Nelson* that 'we are now abandoning ship'. He gets the simple reply, 'Good luck.' In lifeboat No. 6, eighty-year-old Sir Richard Lake gallantly insists on taking his turn at the oars.

10.00pm (11.00pm), WESTERPLATTE
Captain Franciszek Dabrowski signals Warsaw that the garrison is still holding out. This afternoon the Luftwaffe again attacked the fort. The planes dropped fifty or sixty bombs, but were driven off by machine-gun fire.

10.00pm, Ministry of War, Paris

The first French war communiqué is issued. It reads simply: 'Operations have begun, involving the entire land, naval and air forces.' It is released now so that it will make the morning papers' later editions. Some of their first editions are already out. An editorial in *Le Petit Parisien* tells its readers:

> Hitler has remained deaf to the last warnings of the British and French governments as he has to suggestions from Rome. Perhaps he imagined that once more his audacity could drive back justice and reason. Already, millions and millions of human beings pronounce the name of Hitler with a holy horror. If he wanted that 'honour' he has it and will continue to have it. Mr Chamberlain was right to say that today was a sad day for him. As he said, with a sort of heroism, all that he believed in and everything for which he worked has fallen into ruins. Today is also sad for all of us who, with him and our own leaders, have made superhuman efforts to spare mankind from the terrible struggle which is beginning. Mr Chamberlain has nothing to reproach himself with, and neither have we.

10.00pm, Daily Express Building, Fleet Street, London

The presses are rolling off hundreds of thousand of copies of Britain's largest-selling daily newspaper. In his William Hickey column Tom Driberg writes, 'Now I suppose we must just set to and win. Some of us have, in a sense, been at war since January 1933, when paganism and persecution became officially OK in Germany; but we can't sit back and say, "I told you so". We're all in it.'

10.00pm (11.00pm), Berlin

The German High Command issues a communiqué on today's fighting. It states that German troops have captured the city of Czestochowa, the site of Poland's holy shrine of the Black Madonna, and have also reached and crossed the River Vistula (Weichsel).

And the Luftwaffe, it claims, shot down seven Polish planes and one balloon over Warsaw with no loss to themselves.

10.00pm (11.00pm), STEGLITZ, BERLIN
Dedicated anti-Nazi resister Ruth Andreas-Friederich, on hearing the High Command communiqué, writes in her journal, 'state of war between England and Germany ... France is also at war with us. Yet neither Frenchmen nor Englishmen are marching across our frontiers. Why don't they, too, cross some river or other, and put an end to the madness of war before the best blood of all nations has been drained?'

10.30pm, GERMAN EMBASSY, RUE DE LILLE, PARIS
130 members of the German Embassy staff, their families and other 'protected' personnel are waiting to leave on the first leg of their repatriation back to Germany. There is a strong police guard outside the embassy building tonight, but there have been no hostile demonstrations against the embassy by Parisians all day.

10.30pm, THE ADMIRALTY, WHITEHALL, LONDON
A message from Malin Head is received in the Admiralty's wireless room: 'Important Important Admiral Rosyth Intercept 2059 jamming near SSSS SSSS Athenia GFDM torpedoed position 56 44 14 05'.

10.30pm, BROADCASTING HOUSE
The Home Service announces that General Lord Gort is to command the British Expeditionary on the Continent, and General Sir Edmund Ironside is taking over as Chief of the Imperial General Staff.

11.00pm, WICK, SCOTLAND
The *Daily Express*'s Northern Scotland correspondent telephones the passenger manager of the Donaldson Line, W.B. Fleming. He

tells Fleming, 'I've heard that the *Athenia*'s been torpedoed. Can you confirm it?' A stunned Fleming sets about trying to do so.

11.00pm, GARE DES INVALIDES, PARIS
The German Chargé d'Affaires, Herr Brauer, arrives at the station and takes his leave of Messieurs Loze, Director of Protocol at the Quai d' Orsay, and Langeron, Prefect of Police. The German diplomatic party board the first-class coaches, which are guarded by French security police, and the train sets off for Switzerland just after 11pm.

11.00pm (12pm midnight), BERLIN
The Armed Forces High Command issues another communiqué. It covers all the operations in Poland today, and claims that the Polish incursion into East Prussia has been beaten back. The communiqué tersely ends, 'there were no hostilities on the Western Front'.

11.00pm, POLISH EMBASSY, LONDON
Count Raczynski receives a telephone call from Churchill, who tells the ambassador: 'From today I am First Lord of the Admiralty. If you should need me, I am at your disposal at any time.'

11.00pm, BUCKINGHAM PALACE, LONDON
King George VI has decided to follow the example of his father and keep a daily diary. Tonight he writes:

At the outbreak of war at midnight of 4th–5th August 1914, I was a midshipman, keeping the middle watch on the bridge of HMS *Collingwood* somewhere in the North Sea. I was eighteen years of age.

In the Grand Fleet everyone was pleased that it had come at last. We had been trained in the belief that War between Germany & this country had to come one day & when it did come we thought we were prepared for it. We were not prepared for what we found a modern war really was, & those of us who had been through the Great War never wanted another.

Today we are at war again, & I am no longer a midshipman in the Royal Navy . . .

11.00pm, SS *ATHENIA*, ATLANTIC OCEAN
Captain Cook changes into civilian clothes. During the last war the Germans used to take ships' masters prisoner, and Cook wants to avoid the same thing happening to him. But in the rush he leaves his pipe in the uniform jacket.

11.45–3.00am, Putney
'Home about 11.45 very tired and fell into a lovely sleep only to be awaked [*sic*] at three o'clock by the air-raid warning! All downstairs yawning heavily to sit in the hall, nothing happened and after a little while the all clear enabled us to get to bed again. The first day of war! How long will this diary be by the time in type – the last day of war?' (Vivienne Hall)

11.56pm, THE ADMIRALTY, WHITEHALL, LONDON
Another signal about the *Athenia* is picked up in the wireless room:

IMPORTANT ADMIRAL ROSYTH INTERCEPT 2207 JAMMING NEAR THE ATHENIA GFDM 1400 PASSENGERS SOME STILL ABOARD SINKING FAST BEARING 291 APPROX.

4 September

12.00 midnight, POLAND
'Sunday today, the first in enemy territory. Splendid weather. Yesterday we did twenty-five kilometres . . . All the villages in our

rear have been burned to the ground. The streets are littered with corpses and dead horses. Working parties are digging mass graves; the corpses are piled on lorries, brought to the pits and thrown in – a strange sight.

'The war is frightful, you see nothing all day long but burnt out houses. Each house must be smoked out, there's nothing else to be done with the Pollacks.

'The remaining inhabitants are the worst. Yesterday, a German officer was chatting with some woman from the village, and when he turned round to drink some water from the fountain, he received a blow in the back from one of the women which killed him.

'After crossing the Warte, a quick Sunday dip was had, but soon we received orders to get ready to move off. Many of my comrades were not yet fully clothed, and so they had no choice other than to get changed in the trucks.

'Women and children stood in front of their burnt out houses and collected together the last of their belongings, most of which are already burnt.' (Corporal Wilhelm Krey, 13th Artillery Observation Battery, German Army)

12.00–1.00am, GERMANY

Three Whitley bombers from 51 Squadron, and seven from 58 Squadron, RAF, are over Hamburg, Bremen and nine cities in the Ruhr. They are not on a bombing mission, but are dropping a total of 5.4 million propaganda leaflets. The leaflets tell any German brave or foolhardy enough to pick one up why Britain has gone to war:

WARNING: A MESSAGE FROM GREAT BRITAIN

German Men and Women: The Government of the Reich have, with cold deliberation, forced war upon Great Britain. They have done so knowing it must involve mankind in a calamity worse than that of 1914. The assurances of peaceful intentions the Fuehrer gave to you and the world in April have proved as worthless as his words at the Sportpalast last September, when he said: 'We have no more territorial claims to make in Europe.'

Never has a government ordered subjects to their death with less excuse. This war is utterly unnecessary. Germany was in no way threatened or deprived of justice.

Was she not allowed to re-enter the Rhineland, to achieve the *Anschluss*, and to take back the Sudeten Germans in peace? Neither we nor any other nation would have sought to limit her advances as long as she did not violate independent non-German peoples.

Every German ambition – just as others – might have been satisfied through friendly negotiation.

President Roosevelt offered you both peace with honour and the prospect of prosperity. Instead your rulers have condemned you to the massacres, miseries and privations of a war they cannot ever hope to win.

It is not us, but you who have been deceived. For years their iron censorship has kept from you truths that even uncivilized peoples know. It has imprisoned your minds in, as it were, a concentration camp. Otherwise they would not have dared to misrepresent the combination of peaceful peoples to secure peace as hostile encirclement.

We had no enmity against you, the German people.

The censorship has also concealed from you that you have not the means to sustain protracted warfare. Despite crushing taxation, you are on the verge of bankruptcy.

Our resources and those of our Allies, in men, arms and supplies are immense. We are too strong to be broken by blows and we could wear you down inexorably.

You, the German people, can, if you will it, insist on peace at any time. We also desire peace, and are prepared to conclude it with any peace-loving Government in Germany.

12.00 midnight, SS *ATHENIA*, ATLANTIC OCEAN
As promised the *Knute Nelson* arrives to help rescue the liner's survivors. Some of the Jewish refugees in the lifeboats panic. They think that the Norwegian freighter is actually the crack German liner, the *Bremen*. One family even throw their passports into the sea, and resolve to pass themselves off as Swiss citizens if the rescue vessel turns out to be German.

12.00 midnight, 'VILLA VOLPONE', SOUTH HAMPSTEAD
As the first day of war draws to a close, James Agate jots downs his impressions of the day: 'So far as I can judge in my suburb, which I have not left to-day, the people are taking the war with extraordinary calmness. In one matter I confess that I have been utterly wrong. I expected every road leading out of London to be cluttered up and impassable. Actually, not only has there been no exodus, but the traffic has been less than on an ordinary Sunday ... The BBC has been exemplary all day, dispensing music not too heavy and not too light. Homely stuff, with many familiar airs and ballads, things like "Sally in Our Alley", which at this juncture are strangely moving.'

12.00 midnight, BROADCASTING HOUSE
The BBC Home Service makes its final announcement of the day. From tomorrow pigs cannot be sold for slaughter over a price of thirteen shillings (65p), dead weight. 'The Londonderry Air' is played and the BBC goes off the air until 7.00am.

12.05am, WIRELESS ROOM, HMS *VANQUISHER*
An urgent message is received from 'C in C Western Approaches'. It reads:

IMMEDIATE PROCEED TO SS 'ATHENIA' SINKING IN POSITION 56 42 NORTH 14 05 WEST.

12.56am, WIRELESS ROOM, HMS VIVACIOUS

The destroyer leader gets a signal from Western Approaches:

IMMEDIATE HMS 'VANQUISHER' PROCEEDING TO BRITISH SHIP 'ATHENIA' SINKING IN POSITION 56 42 NORTH 14 05 WEST. DETAIL ONE OF YOUR DIVISIONS TO ACCOMPANY HER. ACKNOWLEDGE.

1.00am, PARIS

Temporary US diplomat Hubert Earle makes his way home from Harry's Bar. Tonight he enjoys an unbroken sleep and the luxury of staying in bed late for the first time in three weeks.

2.30am, US EMBASSY, GROSVENOR SQUARE, LONDON

Ambassador Joseph Kennedy is in the country. He is woken up by his private secretary James Seymour, who is phoning from the embassy with news of the *Athenia*'s sinking. Kennedy gets dressed quickly, returns to London, and issues orders to his staff to find out the names of all American citizens who are on board the liner. He telegraphs the State Department in Washington:

REPORT STEAMSHIP 'ATHENIA' OF DONALDSON LINE TORPEDOED 200 MILES WEST MALIN HEAD WITH 1400 PASSENGERS ABOARD. SOS RECEIVED. SHIP SINKING FAST.

2.30am, SS ATHENIA, ATLANTIC OCEAN

Axel Wenner Gren's *Southern Cross* now arrives to help in the rescue of the *Athenia*'s passengers and crew. The yacht's crew have got hot drinks prepared and have laid out warm clothes for the survivors. One of those survivors is Nicole, the ten-month-old daughter of German Jewish film director Ernst Lubitsch, a Hollywood exile from Nazi Germany. Nicole and her nurse Consuela Stroheimer have just had a lucky escape. Their lifeboat capsized, and with fifty others they were flung into sea. Somehow Consuela has managed to keep little Nicole's head above water for an hour, but they and 378 others are now safe on board and enjoying piping hot soup. Nearby, the *Knute Nelson* has so far lifted 430 survivors and her capacity is now stretched almost to the limit. Captain Carl Johan Anderssen was making for Panama, but now, with so many people on board and with only limited food supplies, Anderssen decides to make for the nearest port – Galway, in neutral Eire – instead.

2.45am, EALING FIRE STATION, WEST LONDON

The District Fire Officer is still keeping up a barrage of comic stories and would-be witticisms in order to entertain Elsie Warren and the other girls. 'Look girls,' he says, shining his torch on an old sack, 'I've found a pillow case!' Elsie starts writing a poem about the AFS and is just finishing the penultimate line when one of the others says urgently, 'Listen.' It's the air-raid siren sounding the Alert, and Elsie has never seen such a scramble in all her life. The switchboard operator receives the signal code for 'raid is on', which she immediately sends to the fire sub-stations. Elsie and the others dash over to the Fire Chief's office and each takes over a telephone extension. None of them is feeling 'any too good expecting a raid any minute'. One of Elsie's older colleagues who had been in the last war keeps repeating, 'I don't care what you say, I've got great faith in our Spitfire planes.' Elsie's supervisor Miss Harrison only went upstairs half an hour ago to try and get some sleep. Now she's had a 'rude awakening,' and the girls all laugh as she blearily peers round the door in her pyjamas and asks 'Everyone correct?'

2.50am, TEDDINGTON

'Raid warning at 10 to 3am. Went down to hall (after saying we wouldn't) and sat until the "All Clear". Royal Air Force distributed thirteen tons of six million leaflets in north-western German towns telling G[erman] people we were at war and why. These leaflets!' (Helena Mott)

Following the torpedoing of the SS Athenia on 3 September 1939, a number of survivors were landed at Galway, where they received assistance from the Irish Army.

3.00am (9.00pm), THE WHITE HOUSE, WASHINGTON DC

President Franklin Delano Roosevelt delivers a nationwide message to the American people. When the First World War broke out in 1914, Roosevelt's predecessor President Woodrow Wilson told Americans that they must be neutral 'in fact as well as name' and 'impartial in thought as well as in action'. This evening Roosevelt has a different message for his fellow countrymen: 'This nation will remain a neutral nation, but I cannot ask that every American remain neutral in thought as well. Even a neutral has a right to take account of the facts. Even a neutral cannot be asked to close his mind or his conscience.'

Without naming names, FDR makes it clear with whom his own sympathies lay, just the same as they did in 1914, when he was Wilson's Assistant Secretary of the Navy:

> Some things we do know. Most of us in the United States believe in spiritual values. Most of us, regardless of what church we belong to, believe in the spirit of the New Testament – a great teaching which opposes itself to the use of force, of armed force, of marching armies and falling bombs. The overwhelming masses of our people seek peace – peace at home, and the kind of peace in other lands which will not jeopardize peace at home.

The President finishes the broadcast on a reassuring note for his millions of listeners:

> I have said not once, but many times that I have seen war and that I hate war. I say that again and again. I hope the United States will keep out of this war. I believe it will. And I give you assurances that every effort of your government will be directed towards that end. As long it remains within my power to prevent it, there will be no blackout of peace in the United States.

3.00am, 10 Downing Street

Just as President Roosevelt is beginning his radio speech, the sirens sound again in London. Led by the half-dressed Prime Minister, with Mrs Chamberlain in a dressing gown with her hair down her back, the staff make their way to the basement of Number 10. There, PPS Alec Douglas-Home observes that he and the others are all in various stages of undress. Not so the new Minister without Portfolio and member of the War Cabinet, Lord Hankey. To Douglas-Home's astonishment, he arrives 'in the shelter fully dressed with a rolled-up umbrella and bowler hat!'

3.00am, Cambridge

It is a blazing moonlight night as the sirens begin to wail. The Koenigsbergers, their landlady and her ten-year-old daughter scramble out of their beds and huddle under the stairs. Like so many others in Britain today, the landlady has yet to master how to black-out the windows properly. The Koenigsbergers are afraid that the light showing is going to attract German bombers. Outside the city on her farm, Trainee Land Girl No. 9600 E.M. Barraud can hear the sirens in Cambridge. In the village, air-raid wardens are cycling round, blowing their whistles in warning. For what seems like hours, but is probably only about twenty minutes, the Koenigsbergers await the 'All Clear'. As it sounds they vow to organise the house's blackout themselves. They decide too that it is better to stay in bed and risk the bombs rather than shiver under the stairs.

3.00am, Huddersfield

George and Marjorie Gothard are fast asleep in bed when the air-raid warning sounds. They finally got to bed at about 10.30pm, both of them really tired out. Marjorie is in a deep sleep as George wakes her and tells her that an air raid is on. Marjorie sits up in bed really frightened, as all the sirens seem to be going. She puts on her slippers and then a leather coat over her nightie. She then dashes upstairs for George Junior and Guy. George is close behind and they find some coats to wrap the boys up in. George then climbs through their bedroom window and lights a candle in their makeshift air-raid shelter. Next, they take the boys in, telling them that it is just a rehearsal. But actually neither of their sons is at all frightened. With the boys now safe, Marjorie fetches the family's pet dogs 'Vera', 'Demon' and 'Cara' into the shelter. Some neighbours also soon arrive, and Marjorie is pleased to see that, 'apart from a little palpitation', everyone is 'very calm and collected'. The 'All Clear' now sounds and the Gothards go back to their bedroom. The boys are going to stay in their bed with them for the rest of the night. Marjorie makes them all a cup of tea. She then tries to get back to sleep, but fails even to doze off.

3.45am, Ealing Fire Station, West London
Elsie Warren's shift receives the 'All Clear' message with a collective sigh of great relief. They put the kettle on and have several pots of tea and a few more laughs. They are all looking forward to finishing their stint at 6.00am.

4.30am, SS *Athenia*, Atlantic Ocean
Two Royal Navy destroyers HMS *Electra* and *Escort* have arrived to take part in the rescue. A third destroyer, HMS *Fame*, is on its way and should arrive in about an hour and a half.

6.00am, Ealing Fire Station, West London
At the end of her shift, Elsie Warren leaves the fire station. 'The weather is great' on this, the first full day of the Second World War. Elsie thinks to herself, 'It seems a shame that a war is on.'

6 September

WORTHING

Resumé of the week

'It has been impossible to write daily for the last week as life has suddenly become very difficult under wartime conditions. Very few people felt this terrible blow would fall and right up to Sunday morning there was the glimmer of hope. On Friday the Germans "crossed the frontiers to resist the Poles" and the newspapers immediately declared "war begins". Everyone's spirits sank but rose again when Mr Chamberlain gave Hitler one more chance in a message sent on Saturday with a time limit up at eleven o'clock on the Sunday morning . . . two air-raid warnings already – one on Sunday morning about 11.35 (twenty minutes after the declaration of war) . . . I must try to write this daily now but so far I have not blacked out my bedroom window – blow! That's where I do my reading and writing.' (Joan Strange)

The German war flag is raised over the ruins of Westerplatte, 7 September 1939. In describing the bombardment of the garrison, a German reporter wrote, 'It seems as if all the fire and lightning of hell has been let loose.'

CHAPTER 5

The Fall of Poland

As Britain and France finally honoured their pledges to Poland, Hitler's forces successfully pressed on with the invasion. Two invading army groups, comprising of fifty-two divisions and totalling 1,516,000 men, launched a double pincer movement from the south and the north. They were supported by 897 bombers and 426 fighter planes of the Luftwaffe. No declaration of war had been made. But in his Reichstag speech of 1 September justifying the invasion, Hitler had claimed that regular Polish troops had invaded German territory the previous evening. This was an allusion to the faked incidents at the Gleiwitz radio station and the Hochlinden customs post.

From the start of the campaign, the Poles found themselves faced by an enemy who had crushing superiority in aircraft, tanks, guns and men. But the Poles fought bravely, as even Hitler acknowledged in a speech at Danzig, and no more so than at Westerplatte, near the city-port. There a company of 180 men under Major Henryk Sucharski and Captain Franciszek Dabrowski held out for six days and nights against attacks by land and air, and from bombardment

'So it is now our job to free the Polish people from all this wretchedness and, under our leadership, to make it into one of the happiest nations on earth.' An SS non-commissioned officer interrogates Polish civilians.

'Cowards, cowards, they are! You can hardly get them to fight a decent fight. But they are very good at murdering!' SS men interrogate Polish prisoners of war, Zelechov, mid-September 1939.

by the old battleship *Schleswig-Holstein*'s eleven-inch guns. From Warsaw, Polish commander-in-chief Marshal Smigly-Rydz wired them, 'Soldiers of Westerplatte fight! You are fighting the fight of Poland. Poland watches your gallant struggle with pride. Fight for Poland to the last man.'

After the Poles were forced to surrender due to lack of ammunition, the Germans took a party of foreign correspondents to Westerplatte. Jack Raleigh of the *Chicago Tribune* saw that, 'Bombs had fallen everywhere . . . the main buildings were total wrecks.' One large pillbox which had received a direct hit still contained the charred remains of a Polish Army cook, who had been preparing a meal as the bomb fell. Raleigh saw 'bits of his uniform had embedded themselves in the cement around him. Blackened flesh rotted in the half darkness . . .' It was, the journalist noted, 'one of the most gruesome sights I saw during the whole Polish campaign'.

In some places the Poles achieved local successes. But by Sunday, 17 September, the Corridor had been overrun, Polish forces in the River Vistula bend overcome, and the Germans had advanced to the River Bug. On that same day, the Red Army crossed Poland's eastern frontier on its mission of 'liberation'. Poland's position was now absolutely hopeless, To avoid capture, the now-discredited government of Colonel Beck and Marshal Smigly-Rydz fled to Roumania, where they were interned.

On 1 October, Austrian Nazi Wilhelm Prueller wrote in his diary: 'Smigly-Rydz has declared that the Polish Army is now defeated. He could have made this silly observation on 1st September! For it was a joke to fight against us with horse-drawn wagons. I've seen only very few trucks or tanks in the Polish Army, and aeroplanes only at the beginning. And with their weapons they can't compare with us at all. If their hand grenades were distributed to their whole army, it would mean two hand grenades for thirty-five men! Or take the company which took us prisoner: they had one MG! It was ridiculous!'

Polish civilians forced to flee the burning town of Govorovo, 9 September 1939. During the campaign fifty-five towns and 476 villages were deliberately burnt down by the Germans, and 714 mass executions took place, in which 16,336 Poles were murdered.

'Here we can destroy all the Jews at one stroke.' Elderly Jews forced to clear up the rubble in the destroyed village of Piatek. On 13 September, fifty Poles, including seven Jews, were murdered by the Wehrmacht.

Warsaw had held out until 27 September when, after severe bombing and shelling, the city was forced to capitulate. Teenagers Wlodzimierz and Zbigniew Leon hid in a cellar under the family shop at Szpitalna Street. Their apartment had received a direct hit from an artillery shell, which had blown it to pieces. In the streets of the capital, Wlodzimierz saw the corpses of soldiers, civilians and horses lying where they had fallen. The Leon brothers, like most Poles, had been confident that Britain and France, by declaring war, would come to Poland's aid. Optimistic but false rumours abounded about the RAF bombing Hamburg into ruins, and the French piercing the Siegfried Line. But no aid from the Western Allies was forthcoming. Wlodzimierz Leon and his brother, like the majority of Poles, were over-confident in their own army. This was reflected in the boast that Polish cavalrymen would be tethering their horses in Berlin's Tiergarten within a few weeks. They were also completely unaware of the strength of Hitler's armed forces and unprepared for the tactics of *Blitzkrieg*.

After the city's surrender, *Picture Post* wrote that 'the defence of Warsaw is the first epic of this war'. The leading hero of that defence was City President, or Lord Mayor, Stefan Starzynski, who made many inspirational radio broadcasts during the siege. In them he both rallied his fellow citizens, and also called on world opinion. In his 'Appeal to the Civilized World' on 19 September, Starzynski, or 'Stefan the Stubborn' as he was nicknamed, declared: 'These Polish men, women and children are not dying in vain, but they are dying not only for the freedom of their own country, but for the freedom of Europe. We know that our friends want to help us and will help us. Our lives may be in danger now, but our souls are undisturbed. We shall fight to the last man if we have to go down fighting. We shall stand at our post imbued with holy faith in our ultimate victory even in this dark hour. The day will come.'

After Warsaw's surrender, Starzynski remained in office for four weeks, before being arrested by the Germans at the end of October 1939 and sent to Dachau concentration camp.

A few days after the city's capitulation, Hitler held a victory parade in Warsaw. About to mount the saluting stand, the Fuehrer was greeted by General Walther von Reichenau with the words, '*Mein Fuehrer! Ich gebe Warschau!*' ('My Fuehrer! I give you Warsaw!'). One of the only two American reporters present, Jack Raleigh, noted how Hitler 'unceasingly saluted file after file of grey clad men', during the three-hour-long parade. 'As they clumped past', observed the newsman, Hitler would, 'catch the eye of one or two men in each rank . . . I, being just beyond, saw the effect his glances had on the soldiers. The men's faces fairly beamed . . . the power the man displayed even at a distance of twenty yards . . . was amazing. He seemed automatically to instil courage, loyalty, and an immense pride.'

Driving back to Warsaw airport after that display of German military might, Raleigh came face to face with the reality of the effects of *Blitzkrieg* on Poland's capital. In the space of one block he saw three women who had been driven mad by the bombing and shelling. 'No one paid any attention to them as they wandered aimlessly up and down the bread queues giggling hysterically and slavering.' A little further on, Raleigh saw a ragged teenage boy, his cheeks 'smudged by great gobs of encrusted dirt riveted by streams of tears', standing by the kerb. Raleigh then saw how 'suddenly he wrapped both arms about his chest and began sobbing pitiably. He did not cry as a child – rather as a lost soul, eyes wide open, flooded with tears, and great gasping sobs shaking his body. In a final paroxysm he sank to the gutter – where he lay, racking coughs and sighs shaking his small body. None of the passers-by gave him a second look.'

At the airport, Raleigh and his fellow correspondents were each in turn introduced to Hitler. He then told them: 'Gentlemen, you have seen for yourself what criminal folly it was to try and defend

After the fall of Warsaw, the Germans opened soup kitchens to feed the capital's hungry civilian population. The soup kitchens were filmed in order to demonstrate to the world the so-called generosity of the German occupiers. In fact, Warsaw's municipal authorities were presented with a bill for the food distributed.

this city. The defence collapsed after only two days of intensive effort. I only wish that certain statesmen in other countries who seem to want to turn all Europe into a second Warsaw could have the opportunity to see, as you have, the real meaning of war!'

With that, the Fuehrer saluted and made for his plane to fly back to Berlin and deliver his 'peace offer' speech to the Reichstag. Raleigh found himself 'burning with the injustice' at Hitler's words. But they obviously struck a chord with *Picture Post* reader J.E. Lake of Winchmore Hill, who wrote to the magazine, 'You show pictures of suffering citizens of Warsaw and slang Hitlerism. But you do not point out that Hitler warned Warsaw, and that Warsaw could have surrendered when it liked. It was the Poles' fault that they were bombed so mercilessly. The "heroic" resistance was futile. They could not possibly win. They were throwing away their own lives.'

To which the magazine gave the tart response, 'So if *we* fight on for justice and freedom in face of a pirate's threat, it will be *our* fault if we suffer? And are there not times when a man *must* "throw away" his life?'

Organised Polish resistance continued at some places until 5/6 October, and even after that, guerrilla warfare under Major Henryk 'Hubal' Dobrzanski went on sporadically until the spring of 1940. Many thousands of Polish servicemen managed to escape to France, where a government-in-exile under General Wladyslaw Sikorski was established at Angers.

Poland itself was divided up between Germany and Russia in a treaty signed in Moscow by von Ribbentrop and Molotov on 29 September. Poland's western provinces were annexed to the Greater German Reich, while a General Government of Occupied Polish Territories was set up with Nazi lawyer Hans Frank at its head. Russia received nearly 200,000 square kilometres of Polish territory, including the oilfields of Galicia. In both parts of occupied Poland, her conquerors brutally set about trying to wipe out any

IWM HU 87205

A Red Army soldier guarding a Polish Air Force PWS 26 biplane trainer at Porubanek Airfield, Wilno. At the time of the German invasion, the Polish Air Force had 392 serviceable warplanes to the Luftwaffe's 1941.

IWM HU 5512

'England! This is your work!' was the slogan on this anti-British poster that the Germans plastered throughout Warsaw. A contemporary account claimed that a nine-year-old boy, Staś Kempiński, tore down one of the posters at the corner of Trembacka and Krakowskie Przedmieście streets. He was shot on the spot by a German patrol.

traces of Polish national identity. 'East and west the prisoners rolled away into slavery', many never to return.

In Warsaw, the Germans put up posters depicting a wounded Polish soldier blaming Chamberlain for the destruction of the capital with the caption 'England, this is your work'. On 3 November 1939, two women, widow Eugenia Wlodarz and student Elzbieta Zahorska were sentenced to death and shot for tearing down copies of the posters. As she faced the firing squad, Elzbieta defiantly shouted out to them in German the first line of the Polish national anthem, '*Noch ist Polen nicht verloren*!' ('Poland Is Not Yet Lost!')

CHAPTER 6

The War in the Air

While Poland was being crushed, Britain and France failed to render their ally any real practical assistance. A Royal Air Force reconnaissance flight over the German fleet on 3 September 1939 was followed the next day by an attack on the ships by fifteen Blenheim and fourteen Wellington bombers. The raid was not a success. Five bombers from each force failed to find targets in the low-cloud conditions. The remaining Blenheims carried out low-level attacks on the pocket battleship *Admiral Scheer* and the cruiser *Emden* in Wilhelmshaven. At least three bombs landed on the *Admiral Scheer*, but they failed to explode. The *Emden* was damaged when a Blenheim crashed on it, one of the five lost in the raid. While little damage was done to the German warships that day, bombs were dropped on the neutral Danish town of Ejsberg, 110 miles north of the target area, killing two civilians.

No. 9 Squadron lost two Wellingtons during the raid. One of them was No. L 4275, shot down either by anti-aircraft fire or a German fighter over Brunsbuettel at the mouth of the Kiel Canal. In its crew were two young Aircraftsmen 2nd Class; twenty-year-old

Kenneth Day from Essex and twenty-two-year-old Londoner George Brocking. Day's body was recovered from the sea ten days later, and he was buried with full military honours by the Germans in Cuxhaven cemetery. Brocking's body was never found, and he is commemorated on the Commonwealth War Graves Commission Air Forces Memorial at Runnymede. Both men were ground crew who had volunteered as air gunners. They were also pre-war, and now non-active, members of Sir Oswald Mosley's British Union of Fascists. On 16 July, Mosley had held a large anti-war rally at Earls Court. Six weeks later, on the day Poland was invaded, Mosley issued a message to all members of the British Union. In it, Sir Oswald declared:

'To our members my message is plain and clear. Our country is involved in war. Therefore I ask you to do nothing to injure our country or to help any other Power. Our members should do what the law requires of them, and if they are members of any of the Forces or Services of the Crown, they should obey their orders, and in every particular, obey the rules of their service.'

As they took off on their first and last operational flight over Germany, it is doubtful if Brocking and Day had had the opportunity of reading that part of their leader's message. Nor Mosley's reminder that 'Nearly twenty-five years ago when I was barely eighteen years of age, I was flying over the German lines in the last war.'

After the Kiel Raid, RAF Bomber Command operations were mainly directed at dropping propaganda leaflets over Germany. Already on the first night of the war, nearly six million leaflets had been dropped over Hamburg, Germany's second-largest city, Bremen and the Ruhr industrial belt. This 'confetti war' soon became the source of numerous jokes. One of the first to appear in print was featured in the Peterborough column of the *Daily Telegraph*:

The pilot of one of our 'leaflet' planes reported back to headquarters two hours before he was due. His astonished C.O. asked for an explanation.

'Well, Sir,' the young officer replied, 'I flew over enemy territory as instructed and tipped out the parcels over the side.'

'Do you mean you dropped them out still roped in bundles?' said the C.O. in an anxious voice.

'Yes, Sir.'

'Good God, man, you might have killed somebody!'

Another joke told of the 'leaflet' plane that arrived back many hours overdue. When asked why he had taken so long, the pilot told his C.O. that to ensure safe delivery, he had posted each leaflet through the letter box. While a 'naval' version went:

Lieutenant-Commander reports to the Captain on the bridge of a
     destroyer: 'The ship's engines have stopped, sir.'
Captain: 'I know. There's an enemy U-boat about.'
Lieutenant-Commander: 'Are you going to depth-charge her, sir?'
Captain: 'No, I'm sending down a diver with leaflets.'

But not everybody saw it as a joke. Churchill was characteristically contemptuous of such methods of waging war, later recalling, 'We contented ourselves with dropping pamphlets to rouse the Germans to a higher morality.' Noël Coward, working in Paris on a propaganda liaison job with the French, wrote a memorandum on the subject. In it he said that if it was the policy of His Majesty's Government to bore the Germans to death he didn't think we had enough time. 'For this,' Coward recalled, 'I was reprimanded.'

Despite the official reason that the 'leaflet' raids were giving aircrew valuable training, many RAF officers and men were sceptical as to their usefulness. Quite a few shared the view of future Bomber Command chief Arthur Harris that the leaflets were only going to augment Germany's supplies of lavatory paper for the duration. But the height of official farce over the leaflets was reached when the 'ace' American foreign correspondent John Gunther asked at the Ministry of Information to see a copy of a leaflet. MP Harold Nicolson recorded the exchange in his diary on 14 September:

'The request was refused. He asked why. The answer was, "We are not allowed to disclose information which might be of value to the enemy." When Gunther pointed out that two [sic] million of these leaflets had been dropped over Germany, the man blinked and said, "Yes, something must be wrong there."'

At Westminster, there were many who shared Churchill's view that it was nothing short of a disgrace that while our Polish ally's cities, towns and villages were being ruthlessly bombed and machine-gunned, all the RAF appeared to be doing was dropping leaflets. Air attacks in the west on German airfields and communications would at least relieve some pressure on the Poles. Conservative MP Edward Spears tackled the Secretary of State for Air Sir Kingsley Wood directly on the subject. There was a heated exchange between the two men. The air minister begged Spears on grounds of national security not to raise the subject in the House. Spears reluctantly agreed.

Fellow Conservative MP Leopold Amery also went to see Sir Kingsley to urge him to take more offensive action. Amery, one of the senior statesmen of the party, but who had been out of office since 1929, suggested to the air minister that the RAF attack the Black Forest with incendiary bombs. The vast wooded area was full of arms dumps and other war supplies, so it was a legitimate military target. Moreover, as it had been a very dry summer, the wood would burn very easily. But, Amery argued, it would have to be done quickly before the autumn rains came. Sir Kingsley, who unlike Spears and Amery had not served during the First World War, and whose previous portfolios had been Health and the Post Office, flatly turned down the suggestion, 'with some asperity'.

Airmen loading propaganda leaflets to be dropped over Germany, into a Whitley bomber. Public reaction to the RAF's leaflet raids was mixed. Comments ranged from the contemptuous 'fighting with bloody pamphlets' to the gentler 'I'm glad they dropped them pamphlets instead of bombs.'

'You can leave it to our great little air minister. He will lead the RAF on to winged victory.' During a visit to the RAF units in France in October 1939, Sir Kingsley Wood, Secretary of State for Air, is photographed on a converted Paris bus.

'Are you aware it is private property?' he asked the combative Amery. 'Why, you will be asking me to bomb Essen next!'

'It takes a lot to turn an appeaser into a belligerent,' was Spears's acidic verdict when told of the interview by Amery.

But the reports that Wood and his War Cabinet colleagues were getting were hardly reassuring. On 6 September they received news of what became known as 'The Battle of Barking Creek':

'Air raid warning (red) was received at 0640 on 6th and later unconfirmed reports of twenty-eight hostile aircraft near Hornchurch. RDF (radar) and observer reports indicated a massed attack on London and the Thames Estuary. Fighters were sent to intercept. Hurricane fighters were engaged by our own guns. Spitfires then attacked Hurricanes. Two Hurricanes were shot down by Spitfires and one Spitfire crashed . . . British submarine 'Seahorse', returning from patrol, was attacked and damaged by an Anson aircraft . . .'

There were genuine German air raids on Britain during the first months of what was soon to become known as the 'Phoney War'. But they too were confined to attacks on British warships rather than land targets. The first came on Monday, 16 October. Royal Navy ships were attacked in the Firth of Forth near Edinburgh. Peter Walker, Provost of South Queensferry, witnessed the raid from his house, just two miles away from the scene of the action:

'I heard a terrific explosion, and saw a great waterspout rising from the river into the air. A bomb was released and I could plainly see it fall. More 'planes came over. A terrible hail of shells went up from the anti-aircraft batteries. It seemed as if the raiding aircraft reeled. Then they seemed to recover. Numbers of bombs fell – but all dropped into the water. It seemed impossible that the 'planes could live in the barrage of shrapnel put up by the anti-aircraft guns. A shot struck one 'plane and I saw part of the machine fall into the Firth.'

Its crew were picked up by John Dickson's fishing vessel *Day Spring*. His son, John Junior, helped with the rescue:

A Heinkel He IIIH bomber brought down at Long Newton Farm, Humbie, near Edinburgh, 28 October 1939. Of the four-man crew, two died and two were captured. A London clerk was overheard to say, 'I hope they don't start getting very fierce, just yet. I don't feel like being bombed: I'd be ever so scared if they did come.'

'We threw ropes to the crew of the sinking 'plane, and when we hauled them on board we discovered that they were all three wounded. They told us that another member of the crew had gone down with the 'plane. They were all young chaps. The man who appeared to be the senior had a bad eye injury. Another had been shot in the ribs and we stretched him out on the deck. The third man had been shot in the arm and it was broken. The three men were very grateful for being rescued, and the leader, who spoke English fairly well, took a gold signet ring from his finger and gave it to my father ... "This is a ring for saving me," he said.'

The next day, the naval base at Scapa Flow was the target, and sporadic raids continued throughout the rest of the year. Casualties were negligible but as 1939 closed Major-General Charles Foulkes, an authority on civil defence and gas warfare, warned:

'Of course, we must not assume that air raids are not a very real source of danger to this country. But public attention was, for a long time, confined to how they might be endured rather than how they might be met and defeated – an attitude which is not in harmony with the spirit that the nation has shown in its past history.'

CHAPTER 7

The War on Land

On land, the Allied effort was not much more successful or indeed warlike than that in the air. The first units of the British Expeditionary Force started crossing over to France on 4 September, but the main effort began six days later. In five weeks, 158,000 men and their equipment were transported across the Channel without a single casualty, as war minister Leslie Hore-Belisha proudly announced to the Commons on 11 October. Their transports were covered with confident graffiti: 'Look out Adolf, here we come!', 'Berlin or Burst!' But, unlike their predecessors of 1914, 'The New Contemptibles', as the press dubbed them, did not immediately get to grips with the enemy. In fact it was not until 9 December that the first British soldier was killed in action. In his (illegal) diary entry for that day, Second Lieutenant Alec Pope of 1st Battalion, The King's Own Shropshire Light Infantry, wrote:

'A quiet day. Saturday night our fighting patrol ran into its own booby trap and were bombed and fired on by our ambush party. One man killed and five wounded. Max took out a Rescue Party through "D" Company lines and I acted as Covering Party. My covering patrol left out by mistake – reported "missing" – but we all fetched up safely . . .'

The man killed was twenty-seven-year-old regular soldier Corporal Thomas Priday, the son of Allen Priday and his wife Elizabeth of Redmarley in Gloucestershire. Priday's funeral at Luttange Communal Cemetery was an Anglo-French occasion, with a French honour guard and the local corps commander present. Such occasions were seen as necessary to shore up the military *Entente Cordiale,* and to counteract German propaganda, which was forever harping on that Britain would fight to the last Frenchmen. The day before Corporal Priday was killed, Alec Pope had picked up a German propaganda leaflet shaped like an autumn leaf. Its message in French read:

'Autumn. The leaves fall. We shall also fall. Leaves fall because God so wishes it. But we fall because the English wish it. Next spring no one will remember either the dead leaves or the soldiers who are killed. Life will pass on over our graves.'

These leaflets and the propaganda broadcasts of French fascist Paul Ferdonnet, 'The Traitor of Stuttgart', undoubtedly had their effect on sapping morale among the *poilus* that autumn. Not that General Gamelin's forces were doing much fighting themselves. A secret military convention concluded with the Poles in May 1939 had agreed that 'from the moment the bulk of the German forces marched against Poland, France would launch an offensive against Germany, putting in all her available forces from the fifteenth day after mobilisation'. Even before that date, Gamelin had agreed to both the French *Armée de l'Air* launching air attacks and land forces undertaking, 'a series of offensive actions against limited objectives'.

But despite desperate entreaties from the beleaguered Poles, Gamelin limited his action in September to the so-called 'Saar Offensive'. Only nine divisions out of the eighty-five on France's north-eastern front were involved, and there was no Allied air

The two Allied commanders-in-chief, Lord Gort VC (left) with General Maurice Gamelin, photographed in October 1939.

Men of the British Expeditionary Force disembarking in France, September 1939. The first fighting troops started to land on 10 September. To the consternation of the British censor, Daily Express *reporter Geoffrey Cox broke the news two days later. This led to the seizure of the edition which featured Cox's story.*

French troops in a captured German village during Gamelin's Saar 'offensive' on the Western Front. 'More than half of our active divisions on the north-east front are engaged in combat. Beyond our frontier the Germans are opposing us with a vigorous resistance.'

activity apart from a few reconnaissance flights over the Siegfried Line. But in both the French and British media the 'offensive' was presented in a grossly exaggerated terms. The press and newsreels were full of images of French troops 'triumphantly' advancing through German villages towards the Siegfried Line. *The Times* claimed that French forces were in occupation of 100,000 acres of German territory, which sounded a considerable achievement. In reality, it was just about twenty-one square miles.

Back in Huddersfield, Marjorie Gothard wrote in her diary on 15 September: 'French troops have cut off Saarbrucken and dominate communications with the German interior. High points all round the town are held by the French. It is now certain that Saarbrucken will fall to the French and enable the army to proceed straight to the main forts of the Siegfried Line.'

The next day, she noted that the 'news' was even better: 'The French have seized dozens of German villages, their grip is tightening like a vice around Saarbrucken, the fall of which is considered imminent.'

But even as Marjorie was writing up her diary, Gamelin had already decided to call off the 'offensive'. In a letter to the Polish military attaché, he had made extravagant claims about its success. 'We know,' he untruthfully told the Pole, 'we are holding down before us a considerable part of the German air force.' Furthermore, 'prisoners indicate the Germans are reinforcing their battle-front with large new formations'. In reality, not a single German soldier, tank, or plane was diverted from Poland to reinforce the Western Front. The French began to withdraw the bulk of their troops from the 'conquered' territory on 30 September. It was done much to the annoyance of Premier Daladier who feared 'the reaction of public opinion not only in France, but throughout the world'. The withdrawal was completed on 4 October, with only a light screening of French troops left in position. Ten days later, Gamelin, convinced that the Germans were about to launch a major attack, issued a rousing order of the day. It was worthy of Napoleon himself:

'Soldiers of France! At any moment a battle may begin on which the fate of the country will once more in our history depend. The nation and the whole world have their eyes fixed upon you. Steel your hearts! Make the best use of your weapons! Remember the Marne and Verdun!'

Two days later, on 16 October, the Germans duly attacked, but only in company or battalion strength. By evening the next day, at the cost of 198 casualties, they had regained every one of those 100,000 acres.

For the rest of the autumn and winter, the French and British settled down to a defensive war on the Western Front, with routine patrols and very limited local attacks. The newspapers were full of photographs of VIPs visiting the BEF and 'human interest' stories about Gort's men, and how they were furthering the *Entente Cordiale*. Typical was that of one in December when British Bren gun carriers hauled a French wine merchant's van out of a ditch. 'So again,' the caption read, 'the soldiers of 1939 are giving practical proof that the alliance has something more than military significance.' To those who complained about the lack of action, came a stern warning in a broadcast from Major-General Sir Ernest Swinton:

'The war is not being run to provide news. And when I hear people complaining about the lack of news from France and talking about "All Quiet on the Western Front", I say "Thank God that there *is* no news of battles; thank God that the commanders have learned something from 1914–1918, and that the Allied troops are not going to be thrown in haste, without due preparation, against a stone wall, or rather, a steel and concrete maze, bristling with every sort of gun."'

A return to trench warfare? Scottish troops reinforcing a trench in France, November 1939.

'You have been chosen to go into action as the vanguard of the British Army ... The enemy awaits your arrival with expectancy. The opportunity is yours to maintain and enhance the glorious traditions inscribed on your colours.' Men of the Gloucestershire Regiment use their Bren gun carriers to rescue a French wine merchant's delivery van from a ditch.

CHAPTER 8

The War at Sea

Only at sea did the Allies, and especially Britain's Royal Navy, actually seem to be getting to real grips with the enemy. The sinking of the SS *Athenia* by *U-30*, with the loss of 112 lives, including twenty-eight Americans and Canadians, was only the first in a series of sinkings by U-boats during the war's first months. But under Churchill's bellicose leadership, the Royal Navy was hitting back. Just as in 1914, so again in 1939, Churchill was reluctant just to sit back and let naval matters take their course. First priority was to try and intercept the crack 51,000-ton North German-Lloyd liner *Bremen*, which was on its way back from America.

Evert Post, a Dutch member of the liner's crew, told the Amsterdam newspaper *Het Volk*: 'After we left New York on 30th August we went at top speed. During the night we carried no lights, and no one was allowed even to light cigarettes on deck. In daytime all hands were in the lifeboats with pots of paint and long brushes, painting the hull a greyish colour. No radio reports were sent out.

'On 3rd September Captain Ahrens called everybody into the saloon and told us war had broken out. "I swear solemnly," he said, "that the English won't get me alive, nor my ship. I prefer to sink her." The crew answered with "Hochs" and gave the Nazi salute. Next day the captain again called us together again and said, "Between England and Iceland where we are now, British warships are watching every ten miles. We are in a lion's den."

'Every day lifeboat drill was held. The forepart of the ship was evacuated, in case we ran into a mine. Everywhere on deck were set barrels of petrol, to be set on fire if a British warship came near. Everyone wore his best clothes, as we would not have been able to take any baggage into the boats with us. No one slept or undressed.'

Eventually, on 6 September, the *Bremen* reached the Soviet port of Murmansk after a voyage of 4,750 miles. And in Berlin, a rumour was soon going the rounds that Hitler had offered the *Bremen* to the Russians in exchange for 100 submarines.

Churchill, intensely annoyed at missing the *Bremen*, then ordered the establishment of battle groups to seek out and sink the underseas enemy. On 14 September, one such group, led by aircraft carrier HMS *Ark Royal*, was attacked by the U-39. The U-boat fired its torpedoes at the carrier, but all missed. *Ark Royal*'s destroyer escorts then launched an immediate counter-attack on the submarine and sank her – the first U-boat to be sunk in the Second World War. Three days later, the Germans got their revenge when *U-29* sank the aircraft carrier HMS *Courageous*, while on patrol off the Bristol Channel. Sixteen-year-old Boy Seaman John Desmond Wells from Seaton, Devon, was reading in his hammock when the torpedo struck. The explosion momentarily stunned him:

'After groping about I managed to get to the upper deck. Many men were running about but there was no panic. I slid down a blister [a form of protection on the ship's side], to within six feet of the water and stayed there for ten minutes. Other men did the same. It was apparent that the ship was sinking, her bows being nearly under water. I jumped clear and swam in the direction of a destroyer which was standing about a mile off. There were also two other destroyers and two merchant vessels.'

While in the water awaiting rescue, John and the other men sang 'Roll Out the Barrel'.

Naval writer eighteen-year-old Tom Hughes from St Anne's, Lancashire, was in the water for nearly three hours before being rescued:

'As for myself, I just swam and swam. Those three hours in the water seemed much longer. I must pay tribute to the handling of the destroyer that saved us. She was so navigated that the swell created by her progress helped us to swim towards her.

'As I got fairly near her a fellow swam alongside me and said, "Help me." I gripped him by the hair and when a man off the destroyer caught me to pull me aboard I was still hanging on. That chap's long absence from the barber's saved his life.'

The carrier's escort destroyers immediately set about trying to locate and sink the U-boat, which ironically enough had been about to return to Wilhelmshaven because of fuel shortage, when she sighted the *Courageous*. Her skipper, Kapitänleutnant Otto Schuhart, having fired off his last three torpedoes, thought, 'The noise of the depth charges was enormous, it was the worst we heard, but we kept our heads because we were sure to have had a great success. The next day we heard by English radio that we had sunk the carrier *Courageous* and we were very proud of our success ... but we were well trained for this task and we had only done our duty.'

Forty-nine-year-old Captain William T. Makeig-Jones went down with his ship, together with over 500 members of the crew. Civil servant and poet Humbert Wolfe penned a tribute to them:

FOR THE LOST OF HMS COURAGEOUS

You have given all.

Fate has no more to ask.

But we, for whom you died, Do here renew

Our sacred promise to complete the task

For the love of England – and because of you.

A month later on 14 October, an even more spectacular success was achieved by Germany's U-boat arm. Kapitänleutnant Gunther Prien in the *U-47* sank the battleship HMS *Royal Oak* at anchor at the Scapa Flow naval base.

Eighteen-year-old Vincent Marchant of Doncaster was asleep in his hammock when the *Royal Oak* was hit at 12.58am:

'I ran to the upper deck to see what happened. There was a second explosion twenty minutes later, followed by a third and then a fourth. By that time the ship was tilting. She was sinking rapidly. Remembering what had happened on the *Courageous* and the lesson that taught us, I stripped myself of all my clothing and, tying my safety belt around my waist dived into the water. Searchlights were playing over the surface and I could see hundreds of heads bobbing around.

'Great volumes of oil started to belch up to the surface. My eyes started to smart and the faces of all the men swimming in the water turned a greasy black. I was caught by a searchlight for several minutes and saw two of my pals swimming alongside me. Later, however, they had cramp and disappeared . . . I swam and swam for I don't know how long, but I must have gone about a mile and a half when I felt a rock under me. I scarcely remember what happened after that. It was like a nightmare.'

14 October was the birthday of Paymaster-Lieutenant Harrison from Glasgow:

'I was in the mess at two minutes to one when I heard a minor explosion. I was just about to open a parcel from my wife – a

Lieutenants Fritz-Julius Lemp of the U-30 *and Otto Schuhart of the*
U-29 exchange greetings at the Wilhelmshaven U-boat base. Lemp was
responsible for sinking SS Athenia *on 3 September, and Schuhart had sunk*
HMS Courageous *on 17 September 1939.*

A dramatic photograph of HMS Courageous *sinking after being torpedoed by*
U-29, off the south-west coast of Ireland. On hearing the news Churchill said,
'We can't expect to carry on a war like this without that sort of thing
happening from time to time. I have seen lots of it before.'

birthday present – but I replaced the string and went up on deck. Three minutes after I left the mess there was a violent explosion. I was pitched forward. Then there came another explosion. I joined a queue and was making to go overboard on the portside when there came a fourth explosion. I managed to get to a canvas life-boat, but after I clung to it for a while another poor fellow arrived almost exhausted. I hoisted him into my grip on the boat and swam away. A piece of wreckage came along and I used it for a swimming support. Later I bumped into a log, and with wood support under both arms I swam to a drifter and was taken aboard. It was lucky birthday for me.'

The loss of the *Royal Oak* at Scapa Flow came as a great shock to a nation which since Nelson's time had taken the Royal Navy's supremacy, indeed invincibility, for granted.

Florence Speed's reaction was typical, 'As I left the station the posters said "Royal Oak sunk". My heart sank.' Up and down the country, Mass Observation diarists and observers recorded a welter of emotions on the battleship's loss:

'Terrible news about the 'Royal Oak'. My mind flies to Bob, in the Navy. Hope like Hell nothing happens to him.'

'. . . terrible, when you come to think of it. That's when you begin to realize what a war means. Nearly a thousand dead . . .'

'. . . three captured U-boats are nothing, compared to the loss of a boat like that.'

'First there was that aircraft carrier, and now this: we don't seem to be having a very easy time of it.'

'. . . a shame. All those men dying for nothing, like that. We might as well make peace and be done with it.'

'. . . so I said, and I say it again now, once they admit one defeat, you don't know how many defeats they're hiding from us. Them papers only say what they're told.'

'. . . we frankly can't afford it. A boat like that costs more than ten German U-boats; we simply can't afford it.'

'Terrible thing. Terrible. We simply aren't giving them our best. If we wanted to, we could smash them to bits in two minutes. There's something wrong with the organization at the top.'

While the British people were coming to terms with the ship's loss, Prien was able to escape undetected back to Germany. There he received a hero's welcome and the Knight's Cross from Hitler. Four days after his exploit, Prien and his crew were paraded before the international press corps in Berlin. William Shirer was present when 'Captain Prien, commander of the submarine, came tripping into our afternoon press conference at the Propaganda Ministry this afternoon, followed by his crew – boys of eighteen, nineteen, twenty. Prien is thirty, clean-cut, cocky, a fanatical Nazi, and obviously capable. Introduced by Hitler's press chief, Dr Dietrich, who kept cursing the English and calling Churchill a liar, Prien told us little of how he did it. He said he had no trouble getting past the boom protecting the bay. I got the impression, though he said nothing to justify it, that he must have followed a British craft, perhaps a mine-sweeper, into the base. British negligence must have been something terrific.'

A view shared by Albert Hirst in the *Daily Express* newsroom, who jotted in his diary the same day, 'There is a devil of a row at the Admiralty about it. While all praise is given to the submarine crew the feeling is that it ought never to have happened. No U-boat got through the barrier in Jellicoe's time although he hadn't the help of the so-called wonderful submarine detecting apparatus.'

When two of his colleagues thought that someone would be shot 'over this job', Hirst was scornful. 'I disagreed with them to the extent of saying that whoever was responsible would probably be promoted to the House of Lords . . .'

While the controversy over the sinking of the *Royal Oak* still continued in Britain, attention there and throughout the world now centred on another vessel. This was the American freighter *City of*

Flint, which under the command of Captain James H. Gainard, had helped to rescue survivors of the SS *Athenia* on the first day of the war. Sailing from New York to Britain on 3 October, the *City of Flint* was stopped six days later by the German pocket battleship *Deutschland*, which put a heavily armed prize crew under Lieutenant Hans Hussbach on board. Hussbach told Captain Gainard and his crew, 'We are proceeding as a prize to Germany. You will obey your own captain. My soldiers will obey me. Attend to the safety of the ship. If you interfere, I'll put you in boats and sink the ship.'

The Germans painted out all American insignia as the freighter made its way to the Norwegian port of Tromso. It arrived on 21 October, but neutral Norway, citing a royal decree of May 1938 forbidding captured ships to be taken to Norwegian ports, refused her entry. She then sailed to Murmansk, the port the *Bremen* had made for the previous month. Sailing back from there to Norway at the beginning of November, the *City of Flint*'s command was handed back to Captain Gainard, and Lieutenant Pussbach and his men were interned. Although a storm in the diplomatic tea cup, the *City of Flint* episode did much to swing both US public opinion and Congress towards favouring the repeal of the Neutrality Act, which could only benefit the Allies. For, as Elsie Warren recorded in her diary, 'Only England can take advantage of this as she's *Queen* of the *Sea*.'

*   *   *

Back on 19 September in his speech at Danzig, Hitler had spoken of a mysterious secret weapon that Germany possessed. Many, thinking it a bluff on the Nazi leader's part, laughed it off. At the Finsbury Park Empire, comedian Max Miller came on the stage with his gas-mask cardboard box. He asked the audience, 'Do you know what I've got in here? I've got Hitler's mystery weapon.' He then opened the box and, to roars of laughter, took out a German sausage. But it ceased to be a joking matter when, on 19 November, the press reported the sinking of the Dutch liner *Simon Bolivar* in the North Sea with the loss of eighty-three lives. This was the first of a whole series of sinkings, including that of the destroyer HMS *Gipsy*, attributed to the German's new weapon, the magnetic mine.

This 'latest abomination of German savagery' caused a tide of indignation in the press and even the usually restrained BBC called it 'murder'. The *Daily Express* agreed: 'Of course the German act is murder. Bloody murder. It is not war at all. Not even the new type of the war.' While the *Sunday Graphic* urged, 'Let us get on with the job of beating up the enemy that is doing his best to destroy us as well as peace and liberty.'

But many now found it hard to work themselves up into a lather over this latest manifestation of 'Nazi wickedness'. An anonymous Mass Observer noted in his diary on 23 November: 'Have not noticed any symptoms of shock over Hitler's new secret weapon – alleged magnetic mines and mines dropped from planes – these things appear to be cynically accepted.'

But the reality of the mine campaign was ghastly enough. On the *Simon Bolivar*, Dr William Besson lost his wife, four-year-old daughter and six-year-old son. He drifted for four hours in the water with a broken spine and a shattered right arm after trying vainly to save his son. 'I was thrown high into the air by the explosion as the ship struck the first mine. I smashed my spine and my arm as I landed on the deck. The ship's boat we clambered into capsized and I was thrown into the water. Clinging to the wreckage I drifted for four hours. Then I saw a rope trailing from the side of a British destroyer. I caught hold of it with my teeth and clung to it. Then using my teeth and my good arm I gradually hauled myself up. I was too weak to shout for help.'

Dutch shorthand writer Ella Lieutenant told a reporter, 'I have had some training as a nurse, and helped the ship's surgeon Dr Ebes, to tend to the injured. One was a child of seven months who was held down by a heavy plank of wood. There was so much oil over everything that we could not get a grip on the wood, and it was some time before we could ease the child's suffering. The child's parents were both dead.'

Three days later HMS *Gipsy* was sunk. Lieutenant J.A.J. Dennis on HMS *Griffin* saw how 'she blew up with an almighty bang and a flash of light. She broke in two right between the funnels.' Dennis recalled, 'We spent a dismal few hours trying to pick up survivors in the dark ... Mingled with the cries of drowning men was the mournful tolling of the channel bell buoy. A fitting requiem for the first of our flotilla to go.'

More fortunate were the passengers and crew of the Japanese liner *Terukuni Maru*, who were all saved when she was mined the same day. Helen Swailes from Aberdare, the wife of a Royal Navy chief petty officer, gave her account of the sinking to the *Daily Express*:

'I was pacing the deck with my dog Nutty, thinking that if we were struck I was at least safe on the upper deck, when there was a shattering explosion in the forward part of the ship. Nutty jumped and yapped with excitement. We were immediately ordered to our stations. There was no panic whatsoever. The oldest British passenger on board, Mrs Huntley, aged seventy, was magnificent. To all passengers she said, "We must remain calm." While she was waiting to enter the lifeboat she carefully adjusted her hair ... Nutty was the first to leap into the lifeboat. We were under the care of a Japanese coxswain. I shall never forget that man's behaviour. Although blood was streaming down his face, he gave all orders quietly and calmly. Within a few minutes we were taken on board a drifter. The crew gave us rum and coffee. Nutty wagged his tail in delight when he was given some meat.'

By the end of the month, nearly 800 magnetic mines had been laid by surface vessels, U-boats and aircraft. Priority was now being given to counteract the 'mine menace'. Fortunately, one air-dropped

King George VI decorates Lieutenant Commander John D.G. Ouvry with a Distinguished Service Order for his part in the recovery of the first intact magnetic mine. Churchill wrote at this time, 'when a sudden emergency, like this magnetic mine stunt, arises it is natural that everyone who has any knowledge or authority in the matter should come together, and that a move should be got on in every direction'.

mine was recovered at Shoeburyness. Lieutenant Commander John Ouvry was dispatched immediately to examine it, 'and when we got there, there was a black cylindrical thing with horns on its nose stuck in the mud, and very horrid it looked!' By an amazing stroke of luck, Ouvry found the mine's safety pin, and he and his team were able both to render the mine safe and find out its secrets. For 'skill and bravery of the highest order', Ouvry and four others were decorated by the King on 19 December.

No posthumous decoration went to Captain Edward Coverley Kennedy, commander of the armed merchant cruiser HMS *Rawalpindi*, sunk on 23 November in an unequal combat with the German battlecruisers *Scharnhorst* and *Gneisenau*. Newly-wed twenty-one-year-old ship's steward Harry Fleming had had only five days' honeymoon before going to sea on the *Rawalpindi*. One of only twenty-eight survivors to reach home, Harry told a reporter:

'The Nazis, I estimate, came to within 200 or 300 yards of us and fired at point blank range. One of our gunners scored three direct hits before his gun jammed. When he turned round to call on his mates for assistance he found them lying around him dead . . . Many men were walking or sitting about with severe wounds, refusing to go to the surgeons who were attending to the totally disabled. I saw one man with his arm and shoulder torn off calmly sitting on a locker smoking. When a burst of flame enveloped him he was too weak to get out of its way.'

Harry was given a hero's welcome when he returned home to Seabright Street, Bethnal Green on 29 November. He was saved when, as the whole ship blazed from stem to stern, he 'was thrown into the sea trying to launch one of the boats. Four of us scrambled on to an overturned lifeboat, but gradually one by one the others fell off. Flattened myself against the hull, and when I was picked up unconscious the cold and sea had frozen my body to the shape of the hull. One of my rescuers said they had a job to drag me off the boat, so firmly had I fixed myself rigid with cold.'

Another survivor, Royston Ledbetter of Stoke-on-Trent, tried to save his brother Jack, whose gun crew had been put out of action in another part of the ship. Royston put a lifebelt round his brother and took him to the boat deck: 'I left him there to search for a friend. I had no clear recollection of what happened after that, but I did not see either my brother or our friend again. As the ship was sinking I saw a half submerged lifeboat about seventy yards away from the ship. Although, I could only swim a few strokes I jumped into the water and somehow or the other got to the boat.'

Royston and the others in the boat were eventually picked up by SS *Chitral*. Kennedy's taking on the two German capital ships was inevitably compared to Sir Richard Grenville and the *Revenge* at the time of the Armada. Many thought that Kennedy should have received the Victoria Cross for the action as 'it was an epic fight in the finest naval traditions'. A view echoed by an anonymous survivor: 'Against terrific fire from two enemy warships the poor old *Rawalpindi* had no chance at all. Soon the whole ship was in flames. Yet our men fought their guns to the very last as though they were on manoeuvres. They were great – every man of them. Maybe some people think that the British Navy tradition is some kind of fairy story. Now, that I have watched the Navy fight, I know better. The tradition of the British Navy is something far greater than can be imagined by anyone who has never seen the Navy in action.'

But the Navy was not just taking punishment, it was giving it out as well. And only three weeks after the *Rawalpindi* action, came a naval victory which, as Churchill said, 'in a dark, cold winter, warmed the cockles of the British heart'.

The pocket battleship *Admiral Graf Spee* under the command of Captain Hans Langsdoff had left Wilhelmshaven to take up battle stations in the South Atlantic a few days before war was declared. On receiving orders allowing for attacks on Allied mercantile shipping, Langsdorff began to sink British merchantmen in the South

Hitler, in the presence of Grand Admiral Erich Raeder, Commander-in-Chief of the German Navy, decorates Lieutenant Guenther Prien with the Knight's Cross of the Iron Cross for the sinking of HMS Royal Oak *at Scapa Flow, 14 October 1939.*

Some of the twenty-seven survivors of HMS Rawalpindi *captured by the Germans under escort to a prisoner-of-war camp. The* Rawalpindi *had been sunk in an action with the two German battlecruisers,* Scharnhorst *and* Gneisenau, *23 November 1939.*

Atlantic and Indian Oceans. Nine ships were sunk by the *Graf Spee* before it developed engine trouble. Langsdorff then decided to head for the busy shipping lanes of South America before making for home. And it was off the mouth of the River Plate on 13 December that Langsdorff encountered a British force of three cruisers, HMS *Exeter*, *Ajax* and the New Zealand-manned *Achilles*.

Their commander Commodore Henry Harwood decided to split his forces and engage in battle. The eight-inch-gun *Exeter* was to draw the *Graf Spee*'s fire while the other two cruisers were to get in close enough to attack the German with torpedoes. Langsdorff, thinking that the British ships were just destroyers, ignored his instructions not to engage enemy warships, and went on the attack. On board the *Graf Spee* were twenty-three captains and officers of the merchant ships that she had sunk. Captain Charles Dove of the *Africa Shell* heard the order to man action stations sounded then: 'I and my colleagues were locked up on the mess deck. The *Graf Spee* opened fire and the *Exeter* immediately replied. According to our reckoning the *Graf Spee* was hit at least sixteen times. We played cards, including bridge, throughout the battle. One shell exploded near us, and we kept splinters of it as souvenirs.'

During the course of the battle *Exeter* was badly damaged, receiving over forty hits by shells three times the weight of those with which she could reply. Her forward gun turrets were put out of action, and her one remaining gun could only be fired by hand; sixty-four of the cruiser's complement were killed and over twenty seriously injured; second-in-command Commander Robert R. Graham had fifteen pieces of shell splinter in his body. The dead were committed to the deep by the ship's padre, the Reverend 'Bish' Grove, but there were insufficient Union Jacks to go round and some of the men were shrouded in blankets. In a bizarre contrast to the death and destruction all around, at the height of the battle the ship's canary laid an egg. When it hatched out, the chick was raffled for sixpenny (3p) tickets, which raised £8 for the relatives of those killed in action. It was inevitably named 'Graf Spee'. And *Exeter*'s cat Splinters survived the battle unscathed.

Eighteen-year-old Seaman Tom Surkitt from Cambridge was the youngest sailor on board: 'For two hours I sat behind my gun handing out cordite for all I was worth. Altogether we fired ninety-four rounds. We doubled our "action ration" of biscuits and bully beef as we piled into the *Graf Spee*. After what seemed an age we got the "Cease Fire" signal. I climbed out of the turret into the sunshine, and I saw the havoc that had been done to our dear old ship. I saw the bodies of pals who hadn't been as lucky as me laid in rows on the deck. I recognised two special pals lying there among them. That was a bad moment. Then I began to realise the magnificent victory we had gained. I felt proud of *Exeter* and everybody in it.'

The *Ajax* was badly hit, too. Only two of her eight guns were able to fire and she had lost her radio aerials when the topmast was hit. But morale remained high. Nineteen-year-old Able Seaman Lancelot Jacques said that he and his gun crew 'didn't bother at all', when told that their opponent was the *Graf Spee*, and another gun crew kept their spirits up by singing 'Roll Out the Barrel' and other songs during lulls in the battle. Able Seaman Robert Macey gained the Distinguished Service Medal (DSM) for his action in charge of a shell room. He 'set a fine example of cheerful and good hard work', ensuring that there were no delays in supplying ammunition to the turret which was able to fire the greatest number of rounds at the *Graf Spee*.

Early in the action in the New Zealand-manned *Achilles*, shell splinters struck the gun-director tower, killing three men and wounding two others. Another DSM was awarded to Boy Seaman Allan Dorset for behaving 'with exemplary coolness despite the carnage around him'. During the action, Petty Officers William Headon and Alfred Maycock, together with Able Seaman Henry Gould, managed to keep up an accurate output of over 200 broadsides. They achieved this despite being faced with large alterations of course as the cruiser manoeuvred at full speed. For this they too all received the DSM. So too did Chief Stoker Job Wain, for acting as 'an inspiration and a help to all' and keeping things in the boiler room going with 'the highest efficiency' throughout the battle.

On the burning and badly listing *Exeter*, Harwood weighed up whether or not to break off the action. 'We might just as well be bombarding her with bloody snowballs,' one of his officers heard him say in frustration. But almost at that very moment, to the Commodore's great surprise, the British ships saw the *Graf Spee* put up a smokescreen and head westwards, making for the port of Montevideo in neutral Uruguay. The British ships shadowed her until late that evening when, at about 10.30pm, the *Graf Spee* anchored off the Uruguayan capital. The British captives were now released. A German officer remarked to Captain Dove, 'You fellows have been prisoners here for quite a while. Now it looks as if it's our turn.' Before leaving the *Graf Spee*, Dove was called to the bridge. There, Langsdorff told him, 'Your cruisers made a very gallant fight. When people fight like that, all personal enmity is lost. Those British are hard.'

The *Graf Spee*, Harwood's frustrated remark notwithstanding, had received serious damage too: thirty-six of her crew were dead and over sixty badly wounded. Langsdorff was not sure that his ship could make it back to Germany without having essential repairs done immediately. But under international law, his ship would only be allowed to remain in the neutral port for a fixed time limit. Harwood was determined to try and prevent her from leaving before British reinforcements could be brought up. Guile, deception and diplomatic persuasion by the resourceful and energetic British Minister Eugen Millington-Drake were all brought into play. Naval attaché Captain Henry McCall arranged that a bogus order for fuel oil was leaked to the Germans, and Langsdorff was fooled into thinking that the oil was intended for strong reinforcements that had joined Harwood.

On 17 December, with the time limit nearing expiry and reports that the *Graf Spee* was about to sail, the sea front at Montevideo was packed with expectant crowds. That evening, just before 6.20pm, the *Graf Spee* steamed from the harbour, and many now expected to witness a spectacular naval battle. But just three miles out, the pocket battleship stopped, and tugs and small boats were seen to be taking off crew members. Then suddenly at 7.50pm, smoke began to pour from the ship and 'with a blaze of light and ear-splitting boom', it blew up. An eyewitness noted how, 'At that moment the sun was just sinking below the horizon, flooding the sky in which small grey clouds floated lazily, a brilliant blood red. It was a perfect Wagnerian setting for this amazing Hitlerian drama.' And Captain Henry Daniel, the *Daily Telegraph*'s special correspondent, saw how 'sheets of flame spread over the tranquil sea as the oil from the bunkers of the riven ship came to the surface and caught fire. Dense clouds of smoke rose in the air, and soon the wreck was a blazing inferno from stem to stern. It was the end of the tragedy.'

Rather than risk the British getting hold of the *Graf Spee* and its equipment, including an early form of radar, Langsdorff had scuttled his ship. Torpedoes had been primed to explode in the ammunition magazines after the skeleton crew had been taken off. Three days later Langsdorff, whom his British prisoners all acknowledged as 'a real gentleman', shot himself in his Buenos Aires hotel room. He was wrapped, it was rumoured, in the old Imperial flag and 'not the Swastika of Hitler'. In his letter of farewell he wrote, 'I am quite happy to pay with my life for any possible reflection on the honour of the flag.' He was buried the next day with full naval honours. His funeral was attended by Captain Charles Pottinger of the SS *Ashlea*, as the representative of the *Graf Spee*'s captives, whom Langsdorff had treated so chivalrously. Captain Pottinger recalled that Langsdorff had once told him, 'he was proud to say that not a single British life had been lost by his exploits'.

In Britain, Langsdorff's suicide featured prominently in the diaries and reports sent to Mass Observation. On hearing of the Captain's death, a Tyneside housewife wrote, '5pm – Oh! I could weep, feel that I have lost a friend – Captain of the "Graf Spee". The world has lost another brave man, and Hitler and Co. live . . . that Captain of the "Graf Spee"! – I cannot forget him . . . Queer there are people in this world I feel are my special pals tho' I know them not.' But comments recorded in an Ipswich workshop were much more mixed:

'Can't see how he died for the Fatherland.'

'It shows that there are some decent men in the German Navy.'

'He was a good chap. Treated his prisoners well.'

'Lot of tripe sharing the fate of his ship.'

'He was bloody well told to do it.'

In Germany, the loss of the *Graf Spee* plunged the Nazi leadership into gloom. Goering was outraged by the scuttling of the ship, while Goebbels wrote in his diary that the ship's loss 'tears at the heart'. The morale of the German Navy was further eroded by a 'deeply saddened' Hitler. He changed the name of *Graf Spee*'s sister ship from *Deutschland* to *Luetzow*, for fear that a ship bearing the name 'Germany' might share the same fate.

The Battle of the River Plate was hailed as a triumph both in Britain and throughout the world by Britain's friends. To Washington, Churchill dispatched details of the 'brilliant sea fight' to an appreciative and approving President Roosevelt. And in a special edition on the battle, *Picture Post* waxed both eloquent and prophetic:

'Violent, insolent, intolerant in success. Bitter and sullen in defeat. Such is the ideal the Nazis have tried to force upon the world. To Nazi Germany the destruction of the *Graf Spee* is more than a naval disaster. It is a symbol, foreshadowing the collapse of a whole regime – a regime founded upon hatred and the denial of every human right.'

Photograph showing the scuttling of the Admiral Graf Spee. *In Churchill's words, 'thus ended the first surface challenge to British trade on the oceans'.*

Captain Hans Langsdorff, the commander of the pocket battleship Admiral Graf Spee. *In his suicide note, Langsdorff wrote, 'I alone bear the responsibility for scuttling the pocket battleship "Admiral Graf Spee". I am happy to pay with my life for any possible reflection on the honour of the flag. I shall face my fate with firm faith in the cause and the future of the nation and of my Fuehrer.'*

CHAPTER 9

The Empire at War

September–December 1939

The British Government's pre-war policy of appeasement was partly dictated by uncertainty as to whether it would receive support from the self-governing 'white' Dominions in the event of war. During the Great War, they had raised nearly one and a half million men to serve overseas, a tenth of whom had died. Distinct national identities had been forged by Australians and New Zealanders at Gallipoli, and at Vimy Ridge by the Canadians. They had all gained a fierce reputation in battle among friend and foe alike.

But in the late 1930s, it was by no means certain that Australian sheep farmers or Canadian lumberjacks would go to war, 'because of a quarrel in a far away country between people of whom we know nothing'. In the event, Hitler's tearing-up of the Munich Agreement and his occupation of Prague did much to rally public opinion in the Dominions to Britain's cause. There was a now-general, if reluctant, acceptance that Hitler's aggressive designs had to be opposed and, if necessary, by force. And the vast majority of the Dominions' populations, particularly in Australia and New Zealand, regarded Britain as their 'mother country'. As Melbourne

'We Australians have no doubt, as you have no doubt, that this war will be won and that the future of humanity will yet be made secure.' Australian airmen arrived in Britain on Boxing Day to serve with RAF Coastal Command.

dress designer Patricia Penrose put it, 'The lion has roared, the cubs are with you.'

On 3 September, Australia and New Zealand declared war on Germany as soon as Britain's declaration had been confirmed. In his radio address, Australian premier Robert Menzies, unconsciously echoing a Nazi slogan, declared, 'there is unity in the Empire ranks – one King, one flag, one cause. We stand with Britain.' And Labour Party leader John Curtin gave his assurance that 'the Australian Labour Party can be relied upon to do the right thing for the defence of Australia and the integrity of the British Commonwealth of Nations'.

In New Zealand, dying Prime Minister Michael Savage announced, 'We range ourselves without fear beside Britain.' And in a broadcast, his deputy Peter Fraser promised New Zealand's fullest cooperation. Already, plans were being drawn up to raise and send an expeditionary force overseas as volunteers rushed to enlist. And in London, over 600 young New Zealanders resident in Britain registered at the High Commission for military service.

In Canada, Prime Minister William Mackenzie King also spoke over the radio that Sunday. Earlier in the summer he had told Lord Maugham, the British Lord Chancellor, 'Owing to the attitude of certain of his colleagues, it was not possible for him to make any further announcement of Canada's attitude until war has broken out, but that Canada would be in it with us.' Now, referring to the King's broadcast, in which he had appealed to all his subjects to make this their own fight to destroy once and for all the doctrine that might is right, the premier declared, 'Canada has already answered that call.' Mackenzie King went on to tell the Canadian people that parliament was going to be recalled immediately, and that war measures were already being put into operation. 'There is no home in Canada,' Mackenzie King declared, 'and no man, woman or child whose life is not bound up with this struggle.'

Four days later, in a special session of the Canadian parliament, the Governor-General Lord Tweedsmuir, better known as novelist John Buchan, asked for the provision of war expenditure to be made. And on 10 September, there came the formal announcement that 'His Majesty's Dominion of Canada was in a state of war with the German Reich.' In his war speech to parliament, Mackenzie King reminded his listeners that 'Canada's liberties came from those men in England and France who never hesitated to lay down their lives when their freedom was threatened.'

Just over three months later, on 17 December, the first contingent of Canadian troops arrived in Britain. They were greeted at Greenock by Dominions Secretary Anthony Eden and Canadian High Commissioner Vincent Massey. The Canadians' arrival had been kept secret, 'till the troops and ships were clear and safe from German bombings, and even the people of the port knew nothing'. But soon word got round that 'the Canadians were here, cheering wildly and waving their rifles above their heads, their bugle band blowing like mad. The sailors on the little warship at the pier cheered them as they passed.' Singing 'Pack Up Your Troubles', the Canadians, 'thick-set, open-faced boys in the same battle-kit that the British Army wears', were given a warm welcome by the VIPs and the small crowd that had assembled. As the men disembarked, their commander, Major-General Andrew McNaughton, issued a stirring order of the day in which he reminded his men: 'The people of Canada have reposed in us their trust to defend the cause of justice and liberty against oppression and aggression.'

In the Union of South Africa, where only the white population had any say in matters, the position was not so clear-cut. There were real doubts in Pretoria and London as to whether the Dominion would go to war at Britain's side. The large Boer, or Dutch-speaking, population remained hostile or at least antipathetic to Britain. Elements of it were highly sympathetic towards Nazi Germany and especially its racial policies. In the First World War there had been a Boer rebellion, and there were fears that this might happen again.

'In India the present, like the last, war has found us eager and ready to play our part. Our eagerness is the greater through the justice of our cause.' The first Indian Army contingents arrived in France to join the BEF, late December 1939.

'The arrival of the first Canadian Division in the United Kingdom – safe and sound every one of them – can be marked up as another fine achievement by Britain's fighting forces in this war.' The scene at Greenock, 17 December 1939. One Canadian soldier was heard to say, 'Mr Hitler: nuts to you.'

The Prime Minister General James Hertzog and some members of his cabinet were in favour of South Africa remaining neutral. In this, he was opposed by General Jan Smuts. Smuts had fought against the British in the Boer War of 1899–1902, but had since become a great believer in the idea and ideals of the British Empire and Commonwealth. Smuts had considerable backing in the country. Typical of that support was an editorial in the *Cape Town Independent*: 'By proclaiming an attitude of neutrality we shall be defying the elementary fact that the liberty of South Africa is dependent on the liberty of England.'

With the support of the Labour and Dominion parties, Smuts defeated Hertzog and replaced him as prime minister. On 6 September, South Africa declared war against Germany, with Smuts stating that his country had taken 'a stand for the defence of freedom'.

Three months later, on 2 December, the Dominion's forces achieved a notable success. Planes of the South African Defence Force intercepted the German liner *Watussi*, which had slipped out from Lorenço Marques in neutral Portuguese East Africa (now Maputo in Mozambique) on 23 November. Ordered to heave to by the 'planes, Captain Stamer of the *Watussi* gave the order to scuttle his ship. The passengers' quarters were set on fire, the sea cocks opened and the order to abandon ship given. Stamer later told a Reuters reporter:

'When the aeroplane ordered me to recall the boats or take the consequences it was too late to turn back as the ship was blazing below decks. In any case, I would not turn back as I was determined that my ship should not be captured.'

Stamer, his 196 passengers and crew were picked up by the British cruiser HMS *Sussex*. He told Reuters: 'We could not have been better treated by the Royal Navy. The captain gave me a much-needed drink and the passengers were given coffee and food. My crew also received every attention.'

315

Ironically enough, the planes that had intercepted the 9500-ton vessel were German-built Junkers Ju 86 airliners that had been converted over to military use.

The smaller countries of the Empire and Commonwealth all rallied around Britain. On 4 September, Queen Salote of Tonga put all her island kingdom's resources at Britain's disposal. The next day, the Legislative Council of Malta and the State Council of Ceylon re-affirmed their loyalty and offered wholehearted support. That same day the Bahamas declared their allegiance, while, on 6 September, the High Commissioner for Basutoland, Bechuanaland and Swazi-land telegraphed to London a loyal resolution on behalf of the Swazi nations. And 'native chiefs' in Nigeria and North Rhodesia declared their loyalty the following week, as did British Honduras, Trinidad and Barbados.

In many of the colonies, voluntary funds, usually for the Red Cross or British war charities, were established. By the end of 1939, the Malayan Patriotic Fund had reached £100,000, including a generous donation from Singapore's Chinese rickshaw owners. From Sierra Leone came a cheque for £758 11s 0d (£758.55p) for the Red Cross. And to celebrate the New Year, the Sultan of Lahej, in the Aden protectorate, sent 13,500 rupees as his contribution to the Empire's war chest.

Some colonies went perhaps a little too far in their identification with the Motherland's war effort. Major-General Charles Foulkes, Britain's leading exponent of chemical warfare during the First World War, for example, thought it 'an absurdity . . . that . . . in the Gambia, our West African colony . . . sacks used for packing ground nuts are being used for sand-bag protection and intensive training is being carried out in (gas) decontamination'.

But as the rest of the Empire rallied round the 'Motherland', it was India, 'the jewel in the crown', that remained the great imponderable. During the Great War, 680,000 Indians had fought overseas for Britain. Over 62,000 had died. Now, on 3 September,

THE EMPIRE AT WAR

the Viceroy, Lord Linlithgow announced, without consulting any of the country's political leaders, that India was at war. And although he declared that 'Nothing could be more significant than the unanimity of approach of all in India – princes, leaders, great political parties, the ordinary man and woman – or of their political contributions, and offers of personal service which have reached me from the princes and people of India', the reality was somewhat different.

Gandhi acknowledged Britain's 'moral strength' compared to the Nazis and denounced their aggression against Poland. But, he and the All-Indian Congress Party with its six million members still demanded India's independence. Their cause suffered a great setback in October when the Viceroy decided to postpone any further measures towards giving India Dominion status until after the war. As a result, Congress withdrew its cooperation from the war effort. This was condemned by Moslem leaders in India and by the Government in London, where it was hinted that coercion might have to be applied.

Despite the tangled political and religious situation, many Indians still did rally to Britain's cause. By the end of 1939, mule companies of the Indian Army Service Corps had arrived in France to join the British Expeditionary Force on the Western Front. And in Britain, the Indian Auxillary Military Pioneer Corps was formed 'for Indian subjects who wish to join the fighting forces'. 'The response', the press proudly announced, 'has been excellent. Indian students and graduates of British universities are among the recruits.' Two of the latter, P.B. Mathur of Cambridge and R.P. Swamy of London, were photographed for the papers in their quarters. Also pictured was an Indian cook, 'preparing a curry which would be far too hot for most Europeans' taste'. And as the year ended, it was announced that India had delivered over 910,000,000 sandbags for Britain's Air Raid Precautions.

Of the countries that made up the British Empire and Commonwealth in 1939, only Eire, or the Irish Free State as it was sometimes still called, was not at war with Germany. The night before Hitler invaded Poland, the Irish Prime Minister Eamon de Valera had been in touch with Chamberlain concerning Eire's status in the event of war. De Valera informed the Prime Minister that Dr Hempel, the German Minister in Dublin, had told him that, if war broke out, 'Germany was anxious to respect the neutrality of Eire.' Chamberlain reported to the Cabinet, 'Mr de Valera had replied that his policy was to maintain the neutrality of Eire but he had, it was understood, added that Eire would not, of course, tolerate any German activities, including propaganda, on Eire soil.'

In the discussion that followed, Dominions Secretary Sir Thomas Inskip told his cabinet colleagues 'that it been contemplated that we should ask Eire at the least to break off diplomatic relations with Germany, if we became involved in war'. But Sir Thomas also told ministers that Dublin's representative in London had 'informed him that he thought that in a week Eire would come in on our side as a result of attacks on shipping'. In the event, neither of these actions occurred. The Germans maintained their legation in Dublin at 58 Northumberland Road, while William Warnock remained Eire's chargé d'affaires in Berlin. And despite the sinking of the *Athenia* and other vessels, de Valera's government remained steadfastly neutral.

Eire even refused to consider returning to the Royal Navy the use of the three Irish ports that Britain had handed back under the terms of an agreement made in May 1938. The loss of the ports was a major blow to the Royal Navy in its protection of Atlantic convoys, 'and the resultant toll in ships and lives was to be cruel and hard to bear'. As those same convoys were bringing supplies to Eire, there was naturally enough a lot of resentment and ill-feeling, especially in the Royal Navy, towards Dublin's policy of neutrality. Anthony Eden who, as Dominions Secretary, had the responsibility for dealing with the de Valera government, noted, 'Small wonder that the seizure of the ports by force should have been considered by the Cabinet in October 1939, and only abandoned with reluctance by Mr Churchill, as First Lord of the Admiralty.'

The First Lord was also concerned about the 'possible succouring of U-boats by Irish malcontents in West of Ireland inlets . . . If they throw bombs in London,' Churchill asked First Sea Lord Admiral Sir Dudley Pound, 'why should they not supply fuel to U-boats?' But even Churchill, in a very rare moment of self-doubt, had to admit, 'the question of Eirish neutrality raises political issues which have not yet been faced, and which the First Lord is not certain that he can solve'.

CHAPTER 10

The Beer Hall Bomb

8 November 1939

On 8 November, as in every year since coming to power in 1933, Hitler was in Munich to commemorate the abortive 1923 Beer Hall Putsch. Because of the war, the commemoration ceremonies had been scaled down. But, as always, Hitler delivered a speech that night in the Buergerbraukeller, where the 1923 Putsch had begun. The tone of the speech was violently anti-British. 'For 300 years,' the Fuehrer told his audience of Nazi Party veterans, 'Britain has conquered people after people. Now she is satisfied; now there must be peace.' But, Hitler rhetorically asked his audience, 'Has ever an enemy been deceived in a more infamous manner than the German people by British statesmen during the last twenty years?'

Hitler's annual address usually lasted from around 8.30pm to ten o'clock. But this year, he began his speech at 8.10pm and finished less than hour later at 9.07pm. Usually too he would spend time chatting with 'Old Fighters' from days of the 'struggle for power', but this time he left immediately after his speech to catch the 9.31pm train back to Berlin. Back in the beer hall, according to an eyewitness account broadcast two days later:

'About 100 "Old Fighters" were in the hall, and I myself was about a yard away from the door. Suddenly there was a flash overhead and a sudden pressure forced me out of the door. Almost immediately afterwards came a thunderous sound, and then everything was over before we could think what had happened. The air was so full of dust we could neither see nor breathe. We held our handkerchiefs over our mouths and got into fresh air. When the dust settled, we went back and found that the ceiling had fallen in. There were about fifty "Old Fighters" in the hall uninjured, and we set about rescue work. It was dangerous work because at any moment more of the ceiling might have fallen in. We worked for some time getting out the injured and dead.'

The final death toll was eight, with a further sixty-three injured, sixteen of them badly. Among the injured was schoolteacher Fritz Braun, the sixty-year-old father of Hitler's mistress.

The explosion was the work of just one man, Georg Elser, a thirty-six-year-old joiner from Koenigsbroon in Wuerttemberg. Before the Nazis came to power, Elser had supported the German Communist Party and joined its Red Front Fighters' League. But he was not really interested in Communist ideology, rather in improving the conditions of the working class. Under Hitler, Elser believed, those conditions had badly deteriorated. To improve them, and to prevent the war which he was sure the Nazis were planning, Elser decided that his only recourse was to eliminate Hitler and the other Nazi leaders. Knowing that they would all be at the Beer Hall Putsch commemoration in November, Elser started his planning in April 1939. He stole explosives from his workplace and reconnoitred the beer hall on visits to Munich.

From August until November, Elser hid over thirty times in the Buergerbraukeller, painstakingly preparing to install his bomb in a pillar behind the podium from where Hitler would deliver his speech. He even lined the cavity of the pillar with tin to prevent any hollow sound in case anyone tapped on the pillar or damaged the bomb

'The entire world knew that England, whose statesmen had made the annihilation of "Hitlerism" a war aim, was the perpetrator of this vile crime.' In Gestapo custody Georg Elser, the would-be assassin, gives his account of the attempt on Hitler's life.

'A man must have luck,' Hitler said when told of the bomb attempt on his life at the annual commemoration of the 1923 Beer Hall Putsch at the Buergerbraukeller, 8 November 1939. The bomb went off thirteen minutes after he finished his speech.

mechanism when the swastika decorations were nailed up. He installed and set the bomb on 6 November, and made one last visit the next night before leaving Munich for the safety of Switzerland.

But he was caught near a customs post near Constance, trying to cross the border illegally, and was still under arrest there when his bomb went off. It was only some hours later that his captors, searching the contents of Elser's pockets and finding a postcard of the beer hall, began to put two and two together. He confessed on 14 November, and gave a full account of the assassination attempt and his reasons for trying to kill Hitler. He was then taken to Sachsenhausen concentration camp where he was given privileged prisoner status while the Nazis debated on his fate.

Hitler, who regarded his escape as the work of 'Providence', learnt of the attempt as his train passed through Nuremberg. Goebbels was with Hitler when he received the news:

'At first the Fuehrer thinks this must be a mistake. I check with Berlin, and the entire report is correct . . . An assassination attempt, doubtless cooked up in London and probably carried out by Bavarian separatists . . . The Fuehrer and the rest of us have escaped death by a miracle . . . He stands under the protection of the Almighty. He will die only when his mission has been fulfilled.'

In Duluth, Elsie Warren noted in her diary, 'Hitler gave a speech to-night in a cellar of a beer-garden. A time-bomb exploded twenty minutes after the speech injuring a number of people and killing about five. It is thought that Hess, a high German official was killed. (Sad to announce that later we were informed as to his safety.)'

While at the *Daily Express*, Albert Hird thought the bomb attempt a cynical ploy on the part of the Nazis themselves: 'no one doubts that they put it there themselves, probably with the threefold idea of getting rid of old enemies; as a prelude for an attack on the monarchists who seem to be getting pretty powerful, and as a means of rallying the nation to Hitler. Time will show.'

In Germany itself, anti-Nazis shared Elsie's disappointment at

'The morning news told us about the bomb that missed Hitler by twenty minutes. What a hell of a shame it didn't get him!' Rescue workers during the aftermath of the assassination attempt at the Buergerbraukeller.

the failure of Elser's bomb. A member of Ruth Andreas-Friederich's resistance group said, 'Boy, if it had worked, we'd all be dead drunk under the table by now.' And another complained, 'What good are infernal machines to us if they don't explode when they should?' While a Berlin milkman felt that 'Germany was cursed with the worst luck of any nation on earth.' But this was the minority view. A report on public opinion compiled by Himmler's security service concluded:

'The attempted assassination in Munich has strengthened the people's feeling of solidarity ... Love for the Fuehrer has grown even stronger and the attitude towards the war has become more positive in many circles as a result.'

CHAPTER 11

The Venlo Incident

9 November 1939

Only hours after Elser's failed assassination attempt at Munich, the Nazi Party newspaper *Voelkischer Beobachter* was blaming the British for planting the bomb:

'There is no question that the English Secret Service had a hand in this outrage. But this time the British gentry have mistaken their man. The gloves are now off with the enemies of the state in Germany who fatuously expect to carry on their criminal activities in the pay of the Secret Service. The gloves are off, with German thoroughness.'

In order to give substance to the claim, Himmler ordered one of his subordinates, Walter Schellenberg, to cross into neutral Holland. There he was to kidnap two British intelligence officers with whom he had been in contact. For the past month or so, the twenty-nine-year-old Schellenberg, posing as anti-Nazi 'Major Schaemmel', had been meeting with Captain Sigismund Payne Best and Major R.H. Stevens to discuss the overthrow of the Nazi regime. Schellenberg had told the men that he represented a group of German generals anxious both to rid Germany of Hitler and to

'Our number is up, Best.' Major Richard Stevens (left) *and Captain Sigismund Payne-Best in captivity. The original German caption claimed that both men were 'leading agents in the British Secret Service [and were] arrested on the Dutch frontier as they tried to contact the German opposition'.*

conclude peace with the Allies. Best and Stevens swallowed Schellenberg's story, as did London. Schellenberg was even given a radio set to transmit further intelligence.

The three men had last met on 7 November in the Café Backus at Venlo, on the German-Dutch border. There they had agreed that the two British agents would meet with a German general the next day to begin definitive negotiations. That meeting was then put off until the afternoon of the 9th. At 4pm Best and Stevens punctually arrived at the café, only to be kidnapped by a group of SS men under Alfred Naujocks, who had led the bogus attack at Gleiwitz radio station back at the end of August. In the ensuing exchange of fire, Lieutenant Dirk Klop, a Dutch intelligence officer who had accompanied the two British agents at their meetings with Schellenberg, was mortally wounded. Best, Stevens and the dying Klop were thrown, Schellenberg said, 'like bundles of hay' into a car, and driven across the border into Germany.

The next day, with rumours of the German attack on Holland in the air, Elsie Warren jotted down in her diary a version of the kidnapping going the rounds: 'There was an incident on the German-Dutch frontier. A party of Nazis started a shooting affair. Six Dutchmen were kidnapped, one killed. A Dutch car was also taken into Germany. Both Belgium and Holland stand by. They are prepared for any move Hitler might make to invade their land.'

Hitler had indeed intended to invade both countries on 12 November, using as an excuse an entirely bogus French military incursion into Belgium. But on 7 November, he postponed the date of the attack. This was the first of fourteen postponements by Hitler that autumn and winter, the weather usually being given as the reason. But Elsie Warren heard another reason: 'it is said that German officials refuse to invade Holland'. Moreover, 'Holland says that although she is prepared for the worst she has no immediate fear of invasion from Germany.' This view was comfortingly endorsed by *The War Illustrated*: 'and many a worthy Hollander, listening to the radio and sipping his schnapps, must have wondered what all the pother was about. After all, how many times was Holland on the eve of invasion in the last war?'

A partial explanation of 'all the pother' on the Dutch-German border came on 21 November, when Himmler announced that his security service had 'solved' the mystery of the Buergerbraukeller assassination attempt. It was done, he proclaimed, at the instigation of the infamous British secret service, two of whose chiefs 'had been arrested on the Dutch-Frontier' the day after the bomb attempt. The German press played the story up for all it was worth with photographs of Best and Stevens juxtaposed in the newspapers with one of Elser. Like him, both British agents were incarcerated as privileged prisoners in Sachsenhausen, pending a show trial.

In the meantime, the Café Backus at Venlo had become a focal point for the world press. Geoffrey Cox of the *Daily Express* went to the café to interview the waitress who had witnessed the kidnapping. Cox thought the café very exposed and throughout the interview kept a wary eye on the nearby German border guards. He was left alone, but his colleague Ralph Izzard of the *Daily Mail* had a narrow escape. Izzard and a Dutch newspaperman were interviewing the waitress when German troops surrounded the café. Izzard hid in the lavatory, ready to ditch his British passport down the pan should they find him. But the waitress argued with the Germans persuasively that only the Dutch journalist was present, and they left without searching the café.

CHAPTER 12

The War on the Home Front

As the war entered its third month, middle-aged spinster Jessie Rex of Hornsey, North London, wrote a letter to young relatives in America. They had written to her asking how Britain at war was faring. 'We are carrying on as usual,' she told them, 'the shops are open in much the usual way . . . occasionally there was a shortage, viz; sugar, but only a temporary affair for a few days.' But Miss Rex, like everyone in Britain, found the blackout hard to bear: 'The blackout still needs a bit of getting used to . . . I have been out though, but take a torch . . . I am really nervous of stepping off a kerb without knowing it.'

Mass Observation polls taken during the war's first months showed that the blackout was the top grievance among both men and women of all ages. A fifty-year-old housewife told an observer: 'I've just barked my shins on a bicycle in the lane. It's so dark. Old Hitler's got a lot to answer for.' While a twenty-five-year-old man told him, 'This blackout is a bloody nuisance. I wish old Hitler and his gang would drown themselves.' A sentiment echoed by an anonymous diarist after the failed Munich bomb attempt on Hitler:

'I think this black-out's awful. I haven't been out in the dark once. I don't mind saying I'm frightened.' A South London pedestrian takes precautions when crossing the road in the blackout, 8 September 1939.

'What a hell of a shame it didn't get him . . . we should have done our Christmas shopping from lighted windows but for that bastard stepping off the platform twenty minutes too soon.'

Florence Speed in Brixton, on the other hand, thought that 'the nights are like country nights now, with a velvety darkness which is lovely'. Her own house was 'draped with black. The fanlight & upper landing windows permanently so, & and the electric bulbs have black shades – very sombre & funereal.' Her neighbours were much less punctilious about their blackout, as she noted in her diary on 9 September: 'About mid-night, an ARP warden shouted to the people next door to darken their back windows. There was loud hammering and banging as the curtains were nailed down to the window frames, while the "lady" of the house stood in the garden & bawled instructions. This is their third warning – they are a sleep-shattering family! Only some of them alas! have evacuated.'

Traffic accidents soared in the blackout: 4,133 persons, including 2,657 pedestrians, lost their lives on Britain's roads during the four months of 1939. The figure for the corresponding period in 1938 had been 2,494. There were many alarmist stories too about the increase of crime in the blackout. The *Daily Telegraph* on 13 November reported the battering-to-death in Stepney of thirty-seven-year-old dock labourer Charles Lawrence: 'It is possible that police officers passed the body when they went to the assistance of Mrs Emily Murty, a middle-aged women, who was attacked in a street near by and beaten over the head . . .'

In actual fact, crime decreased. In September and October 1939 the Metropolitan Police recorded 12,283 indictable offences. For the same months in 1938, the figure had been 16,023. Only the theft of bicycles had increased. But the fear remained, and a London landlady was heard to say, 'I'm not going out in all that. At one time I used to enjoy getting the 44 bus to Piccadilly, listening to the band, and coming home at ten. But not now. I've never been out after dark since the black-out, and I don't want to.'

In Blackpool, a forty-year-old insurance manager complained with pent-up frustration, 'Had a nice night last night. Tommy bloody Handley on the wireless again; read every book in the house. Too dark to walk to the library, bus every forty-five minutes, next one too late for the pictures. "Freedom is in peril," they're telling me!'

Morals in the blackout were cause for concern too. A Mass Observer reported, 'I have heard of two or three cases where young men have boasted of intercourse in a shop doorway on the fringe of passing crowds, screened by another couple who were waiting to perform the same adventure. It has been done in a spirit of daring, but it is described as being perfectly easy and rather thrilling.'

At the Finsbury Park Empire, the flamboyant and risqué music-hall comedian Max Miller joked, 'I bet nobody'll bump into me in the blackout. Do you like these black nights, ducky, do you like 'em lady? No, no – they're nice, ain't they, ducky? I don't care, I don't care how dark it is – I don't care, I like it. All dark and no petrol – I don't want any petrol. I didn't ask for any. I don't. Before the war I used to take 'em out in the country – it's any doorway now!'

The authorities remained both unrepentant and unresponsive to public grousing over the blackout. Anyone breaking it was liable to be punished. The Lord Mayor, aldermen and citizens of Plymouth were collectively fined £2 for not properly blacking out the city's Guildhall. Similarly, a Bexley Heath aquarist had to pay a fine of £1 for failing to screen the heating lamp in his fish tank. And a man in Bridgend was fined ten shillings (50p) for striking matches in the street as he tried to look for his false teeth. Mrs Ann Fleming of Renfrew was fined £3 when her six-month-old child had a fit in the middle of the night. In dashing to the child's room she let a light be exposed for one minute. Mrs Fleming's appeal went all the way up to Lord Advocate of Scotland before the fine was eventually revoked.

Mr Albert Batchelor was driving his car near Great Missenden, Buckinghamshire, when the radiator burst and washed the black paint off his lamps. For this accidental breach of the regulations, he was fined 15s (75p). At Worthing Police Court in Sussex on Armistice Day, Inspector Wright told magistrates that when he called on ninety-one-year-old Fanny Smith to tell her that she was showing a light, she had replied, 'I thought it was all over.' When asked a further question by Wright, Miss Smith told the inspector, 'I thought the Germans had something better to do.' She was fined ten shillings (50p).

Some solutions for beating the blackout were quite simple but ingenious, to say the least. Mr A. Collet of Between-Towns Road, Cowley, Oxford told *Picture Post*, 'We've solved the black-out problem, or at least part of it. My pal and I have over a mile's walk home every night … when our first torches ran out, it was a bit of a job, I can tell you. We soon got to know where the lamp-posts lay, and even the kerb at the crossroads. But it was the people – every few yards we had collisions. Then we got an idea. We started to whistle. Now we have no collisions. People hear us coming and step out the way – and by the time we get home, we've quite whistled away those black-out blues.'

Churchill, in a note circulated to his cabinet colleagues on 20 November, suggested that a 'sensible' modification of the blackout be made. This was agreed upon, and in time for Christmas, 'amenity lighting' was introduced. This was the equivalent to the light of a candle about seventy feet away; 500–1,500 times less bright than the pre-war lights of London.

Those in the civilian army of Air Raid Precautions responsible for enforcing the blackout, especially air-raid wardens with their cry 'Put that light out!', soon became targets for the public's pent-up fury and frustration. A thirty-seven-year-old female civil servant told an observer from Mass Observation: 'I loathe every warden, and would like to murder them.'

'It's not very nice to get out of a warm bed and creep down into those things.' Alan Suter and his sister Doris enter the family Anderson shelter at 44 Edgeworth Road, Eltham, south-east London.

A Bradford navvy was of the opinion that 'Three quid a week's too much for just playing cards and such-like for them buggers. They conscript t'lads, don't they, for t'army? Well, I'd conscript old 'uns for ARP, and they'd get army pay. And if they say they've homes to keep and they've themselves to feed, I'd make them live in barracks.' And a typist in Northumberland thought, 'Most of the ARP workers seem to be having a cushy time. I wonder if they couldn't have some work to do and be summoned at short notice if there's an air raid.'

This attitude, a not uncommon one, led an exasperated fifty-year-old warden to tell Mass Observation, 'I've a good mind to chuck it all up. If there had been an air raid we would all be public heroes. As it is, we're called wasters and slackers.'

Florence Speed, whose brother Fred was a warden, was of the same opinion. 'The Press are complaining that the blackout is *too* effective. Had real air raids followed the warnings since Sunday [3 September] – they might not be so keen to get London lightened.'

And once again, the inimitable Max Miller had a topical joke ready to hand, telling the audience at the Finsbury Park Empire, 'I'm an ARP warden. Last night I had fun. I went out and saw a light in a lady's room. I shouted up, I said, "Put that light out!" She said, "What?" I said, "Put that light out!" She said, "You come and put it out, you left it on!" You've got to be careful, haven't you?'

One item of air-raid personal protection that everybody had was a gas mask. Most people assumed that the Germans would use, sooner rather than later, poison gas bombs in air raids on British towns and cities, and thirty-eight million gas masks, or respirators as they were officially designated, had been distributed at the height of the Sudeten Crisis the previous September. This measure had prompted a parody of the current hit tune by Joe Loss and his band, 'Gonna Lock My Heart and Throw Away the Key'.

Since then, young children's coloured 'Mickey Mouse' gas masks, designed 'to make them less repellent to their wearers', and gas helmets for babies and infants had also been issued. During the first days of the war, everybody, at least in London, seemed to be carrying gas masks in their cardboard boxes. On 6 September, Mass Observation did a spot check of passers-by on Westminster Bridge to see how many were carrying gas masks: 71 per cent of men and 76 per cent of women had their masks with them. But a similar survey in Bolton on the same day showed that only 14 per cent of men and 41 per cent of women were with masks. Many government and civic offices, commercial firms and other organisations refused admittance to their premises to those without gas masks. A paragraph in the press reported, 'The Reading Room of the British Museum was never very easy to enter. Today not only must one have a reader's ticket, but no person will be admitted unless he carries a gas-mask.'

The civic authorities of the Royal Borough of Kingston upon Thames were particularly gas-conscious. The town's mayor, Sir Edward Scarles, was photographed in the press wearing his mayoral robes, chain of office and a Civilian Duty gas mask. Presiding over Kingston Police Court, Sir Edward asked all those present to wear their gas masks for five minutes in order to get used to them. The press also reported, 'At Kingston-upon-Thames people queue up daily at the entrance to the gas chamber, opened for the purpose of letting them test the efficiency of their respirators. It was stated that people arrived somewhat nervously but left full of confidence.'

When the sirens had sounded after Chamberlain's broadcast, many, like the lady quoted in the *Topical Times*, thought that they were heralding a gas attack: 'she had been informed that the best way to prevent gas poisoning was to fill your bath full of cold water, wrap yourself in a blanket, put on your gas mask, and jump into the bath. This she had done, and waited for the All Clear ...

*'I fell over some sandbags in town yesterday and dropped my handbag.
I couldn't see a thing.' The HMV store on Oxford Street defiantly proclaims
'business as usual' despite its own protective sandbags.*

*A group of adults and children line up to test the efficiency of their gas masks.
'Children took to their masks far more readily than anyone, and went on
carrying them after their parents had given them up.' Nicknames for the masks
included 'Dicky-bird', 'Canary', 'Nose-bag' and even ''Itler'.*

it caused a good laugh. She said, "It was the first cold bath I ever had, and it took a war to make me do it."'

To prevent such future misunderstandings, the new Ministry of Home Security issued a little jingle to aid the public in identifying the types of alarm:

> *Wavering sound:*
> *Go to ground:*
> *Steady blast:*
> *Raiders past:*
> *If rattles you hear:*
> *Gas you must fear:*
> *But if handbells you hear:*
> *Then all is clear.*

This did not stop some Britons from taking their gas drill over-seriously. In exasperation, Mrs S. Smith of Stafford Road, Cannock wrote to *Picture Post* about her two daughters, 'Often during the last fortnight, they have slept in their gas masks from 10pm till 8am. Will it harm them? Please print this . . . it might shame my girls into a little more sense.'

In its 30 September issue, the magazine replied with the warning, 'Not getting usual air will harm them, Reader Smith. But more harm will be done to the gas masks. They should be kept carefully until really needed.'

But not everybody was careful with their masks. Within a few months over 20,000 had been left in London's buses, trams and tube trains. Tens of thousands more had been handed in to police stations or lost-property offices throughout the country. As often as not they had little more in the way of identification than a pencilled 'Mum' or 'Dad' on the cardboard boxes.

Gradually, as autumn turned into winter, and the threat of air raids seemed to recede, more and more people began to leave their masks at home. But not before, 'a burning problem on the home front', as *Picture Post*, tongue in cheek, described it, was solved. In a letter to *The Times*, Mrs Peggy Pollard of St Mawes in Cornwall came up with the answer to what bearded men should do about gas masks: 'Four curling-pins may be bought and the beard tightly rolled up in these and tucked under the chin. The gas mask is then drawn over the face, beard and all, and is perfectly airtight. This discovery has been the means of preserving my husband's magnificent beard, and I submit it to you in the hope that it may save others.'

If the blackout was the principal grievance among Britons in late 1939, then the rise in prices was not far behind. On 27 September, the same day that Warsaw surrendered, Chancellor of the Exchequer Sir John Simon introduced Britain's first wartime budget. Income tax went up two shillings (10p) in the pound to 7s.6d (38p). Surtax and Estate Duty both went up sharply, at 60 per cent. An Excess Profits tax was imposed and duties raised on beer, spirits, wines, sugar and tobacco. Sir John, even at the best of times not the most popular of cabinet ministers, budgeted for £2,000,000,000, nearly three times more than £700,000,000 in his last peacetime budget five months before. The new taxes still left a gap of £938,000,000 between expenditure and revenue, which was to be met by borrowing.

Reaction to Sir John's measures varied. Britain's leading economist, John Maynard Keynes wrote in *The Times*, 'What strikes me about this Budget is the utter futility of the old imposts to solve the problem, even when pushed to the limits of endurance.' A leader writer in the same paper commented, 'The House found nothing imaginative enough in the Budget to arouse its enthusiasm, or constructive enough to command its respect.' While the *Daily Express* took a characteristically down-to-earth stance: 'The Chancellor overdoes it. Sir John is going to work with a meat-axe. He would have done better to take a slice now and another one later.'

Ordinary citizens, by and large, took things philosophically.

'Fancy, the income tax 7/6d in the £', wrote Jessie Rex to her young relatives in the USA, 'money will be scare now'. Gladys Cox of West Hampstead thought the Budget 'a bitter pill, and it remains to be seen what its effect will be on the life (and soul) of the nation'. But Albert Hird of the *Daily Express*, thinking of the wasted years of the Depression, believed 'that even the most bigoted Tory now would pray to heaven for the young men and women we might have had had they devoted a few millions of the country's money to putting the people in the distressed areas to work instead of half starving them.'

Two days after the Budget, on 29 September, all over Britain, householders were completing National Register forms. The next day, an army of 65,000 enumerators under the direction of Sir Sylvanus Vivian, the Registrar General, were at work collecting the forms and issuing identity cards. All went very smoothly, though few of Sir Sylvanus's volunteers could have been as fortunate as John Rider of Birmingham. During the course of his rounds to collect the forms and issue the cards, he received no less than one packet of twenty-four cigarettes and thirty loose ones, seven books, twelve cups of tea, one eating pear, five glasses of beer, one glass of 'pop' and two pounds of tomatoes.

Once collected, the forms served both as a register for national service and for food rationing. On 8 November, Jessie Rex wrote to her relations in America that she had just received her ration book that day. But it was not for another two months before the first foodstuffs were rationed in Britain. When, on 1 November, Minister of Food William Morrison had announced that food was to be rationed, it brought forth a storm of protest. *Picture Post* thought it 'the most unpopular Government decision since the war began'. The *Daily Mail*'s comment was highly indignant and typical of press reaction: 'Your butter is going to be rationed next month. It would be scarcely possible – even if Dr Goebbels were asked to help – to devise a more harmful piece of propaganda for Great

Britain. Our enemy's butter ration has just been increased from 3ozs to just under 4ozs. Perhaps because Goering's phrase, "guns or butter" has given butter a symbolical significance. But mighty Britain, Mistress of the Seas, heart of a great Empire, proud of her wealth and resources? Her citizens are shortly to get just 4ozs of butter a week. There is no good reason to excuse Mr Morrison, the Minister of Food, for this stupid decision.'

In more sober language, *The Economist* agreed: 'The methods adopted by the Ministry of Food, first to oppose rationing, and secondly to find reasons for postponement, have run the whole gamut of plausibility and ingenuity and are now verging on the fantastic.'

But if the press, and in particular Lord Beaverbrook's *Daily Express*, waxed indignant, the general public were not so hostile to the idea of rationing. A Liverpool housewife told Mass Observation, 'I wish to goodness they would introduce rationing. At last I would be able to go into a shop and get what I was allowed. As it is I've got to beg for certain commodities and make up large orders before asking for what I want particularly – sugar, for instance – and then they turn around and say they haven't any, and if you go in the next day and ask, they're quite snooty, because you don't buy anything else. This constant scrounging is getting on my nerves.'

Many believed that rationing would bring fair shares for all and stop profiteering. A Dorking cleaner thought that the 'Price of food at the local grocer is scandalously high. And I'm sure he's profiteering. He complains he'll be ruined by the war. I hope he will. *I* shan't register with a man who charges so high and has such poor supplies.'

Shopkeepers suspected of profiteering came in for a good deal of abuse, as one Mass Observer overheard: 'Profiteers! Money-grabbers! We know who reap the benefit in times like these. Blinking profiteers, that's what you are! Sucking money from the poor!' And he concluded his report on 'Grocery in War': 'On one point grocer and customer are at accord. A hundred times a day the sentiment is expressed on both sides of the counter, *"I'll be glad when they start rationing. It'll put an end to all this."'*

This view was borne out by polls that Mass Observation and the British Institute of Public Opinion undertook after the food minister had made his announcement. The BIPO poll showed that 60 per cent of those questioned thought rationing was Necessary, 28 per cent said Unnecessary, while 12 per cent said Don't Know. Mass Observation's poll produced similar figures in favour of rationing.

In Germany, rationing had begun a week before the war, although some foodstuffs, such as butter, had been virtually rationed for years. Clothes and soap were rationed, too. Many in Britain saw this as a sign of German weakness, and during the first months of the 'Phoney War' there was much wishful thinking regarding Germany's imminent economic collapse. But as the year came to a close, an article in *The War Illustrated* warned that while 'Surely it is obvious, we argue, that if rationing has been carried to such lengths in Germany so early in the struggle, the front of our enemies must already be cracking ... But, Germany's rationing may be a sign not of weakness, not even of undue shortage, but of the determination to employ the available supplies to the best advantage, and so husband the resources that victory may be won.'

It was Britain's 2,360,000 private-car and motorcycle owners who were the first to experience rationing, when, on 22 September, petrol was rationed. Even before rationing was introduced, brands like Shell and ESSO had been replaced by 'pool', a blended petrol reckoned to be better in quality to some cheaper peacetime blends. It cost 1s.6d (7p) a gallon, which soon went up after the Budget to 1s.8d (8p). Rationing and the increased cost of petrol and fuel was another major cause of complaint when Mass Observation conducted its poll in November. With the basic petrol ration, few motorists had enough fuel to do more than 200 miles a month. Many private cars disappeared from the roads, while some were converted over to gas propulsion.

'The Good Old Horse Comes Back' read one magazine headline in October. 'Horses,' it reported, 'which for many years had been slowly disappearing from the London streets, had a remarkable "comeback" when rationing took effect.' On 27 September, Minister of Transport Euan Wallace announced that the ban on horses using certain thoroughfares in the capital was now being lifted in view of petrol rationing and the resultant reduction of motor vehicles on London streets. A tradesman in Westwood, Thanet, solved the problem of carrying on making deliveries by hitching a horse to his car. In the country too, the article concluded, 'many a pony and trap and dog-cart were once more on the roads after being regarded for years only as lumber'. Just as British motorists were coming to terms with petrol rationing, a news item appeared in the press which put things into perspective. A Warsaw banker, desperate to leave the besieged capital had, it was claimed, paid £2,300 for just twelve gallons of petrol.

Fourth on the list of the British public's war grumbles and grievances was evacuation. It was one that would dominate the press and public debate throughout the last four months of 1939. 'The Children's Trek To Safety: A Triumph of British Civilian Organisation' had been one paper's headline at the start of the Government's evacuation scheme. Altogether, 659,527 evacuees from the London area and 1,220,581 from the provincial urban areas had been evacuated between orders going out on Thursday, 31 August and Monday, 4 September. The majority of those evacuated (1,134,235) were schoolchildren accompanied by their teachers. But there were other groups also deemed vulnerable to air attack who were evacuated. These included young children with their mothers, expectant mothers, blind and physically handicapped adults. In the London County Council area, schoolchildren had taken part in a rehearsal on 28 August, while some had even actually been evacuated during the Sudeten Crisis the previous year. The evacuees went by train, bus and even boat. A number of

London's distinctive 'Green Line' buses had been specially converted to take hospital patients. The Government had agreed to pay the evacuees' hosts ten shillings (50p) a week for the one child, or 8s.6d (43p) each for more than one, £1.1s.0d (£1.05p) for a teacher or helper, 5s (25p) for a mother and 3s (15p) for each child with her.

At first all appeared to go smoothly. An anonymous welfare worker on the scheme was much quoted: 'I maintain that it was a miracle of organization and not a simple transmigration. For two days, I was the humblest worker in the thick of it, and I take my hat off successively to the L.C.C., the Board of Education, the Ministry of Health, the teachers, the railways, the transport companies, and the organized workers. And finally, the biggest and longest hat-raising of all to the British mothers and to the children.'

And the newspapers were full of photographs that seemed to back up his words. For as a later and cooler appraisal of the scheme put it, 'The daily press of that period did much to spread the story of the successful venture. Boys and girls who had never seen farm-life before provided good material for the Press photographer. He was able to snap groups of happy children racing down the village lane when the lunch-bell rang, or setting out on a blackberrying expedition, or watching one of their number emulating Henry Cotton on the golf course . . .'

But very soon the first rumblings of trouble and discontent began to be heard. On 15 September, *The Times* summed up the situation: 'It is not surprising that the House of Commons was impelled last night to discuss the problems of evacuation. Certain troubles and grievances were bound to follow the dispersal of nearly a million and a half town-dwellers, mostly children and women, into the country and other places of safety. None of the complaints put forward in our correspondence columns has been trivial or unreasonable. Collectively, however, they are serious and even more widespread than the published letters have indicated. The Ministries of Health and Education have, in communications to the local

Hospital patients as well as children were evacuated from London and other vulnerable towns and cities at the beginning of September 1939. Many left in specially adapted ambulance trains.

authorities, recognized the necessity for remedial measures, and are stirring up the authorities to helpful and sympathetic action, and assuring them of Treasury assistance.'

Minister of Health Walter Elliot, who had previously 'twice broadcast on his Department's wonderful performance', now had to admit that there was cause for complaint. He told MPs that 'tact, tolerance, and understanding, as well as administrative enterprise and ingenuity will be required' to sort the problems out. But his voice was soon drowned out in a veritable whirlpool of evacuation 'atrocity' stories. On the war's first day, Evelyn Waugh recorded in his diary that 'Mr Page [a neighbour] has a destitute woman, pregnant, with four children in his stable loft. We took them a bed and some clothes. The woman was sitting at a table in tears, Page ineffectually trying to put wire round the railings to keep the children, which the mother won't control, from falling through them. Little groups of children are hanging round the village looking very bored and lost . . .' Five days later, he noted, 'The discontent among the evacuees has increased. Seven families left the village amid general satisfaction. Those who remain spend their leisure scattering waste paper round my gates.'

Now the press was full of similar stories, and worse. Typical was that of a letter from a John Marshall that *Picture Post* published on 28 October: 'I'm sick of you and your sweet little refugees [*sic*]. Perhaps this story will make you sit up. Some friends of ours had seven lousy little Birmingham brats parked on them. These friends were farmers and kept poultry. Going into a coop where turkeys were kept, they found the little brats had cut the heads off thirteen turkeys. For fun! This story is perfectly true. I'd rather have a savage from Fiji than a child from Birmingham.'

But *Picture Post* was not sympathetic: 'It won't make us – or anyone else – sit up unless we believe it. Come forward with your own address and details. If true we'll print them. If not we'll forward you a savage from Fiji.'

347

Evacuation caused such a great disruption to the British education system that on 28 October 1939 Earl de la Warr, President of the Board of Education, said, 'We cannot afford as a nation to let three-quarters of a million grow up as little barbarians, and the government have not the slightest intention of doing so.'

Mass Observation was inundated with stories similar to John Marshall's. Two Blackpool landladies were quoted as saying, 'If you say two words to them they turn around and swear at you. I've seen a lot of dogs with better manners.'

'Carve their initials on the sideboard. Wrote all over the wall. Eat their food on the floor. Broke half the china.'

But it was not just the evacuees' hosts who had cause for complaint or who could recount 'atrocity' stories. The wife of a Romford hairdresser, evacuated at the beginning of the war with her children, recounted her experiences to an observer from Mass Observation: 'They had to share a verminous bedroom with a young married woman and her baby. The window was broken and the door loose, and before long everyone in the room had influenza. The baby developed whooping cough and kept the rest of them awake at night. The younger child of the hairdresser's wife caught some sort of vermin in her hair and had to have it cut off. The landlord and landlady were drunkards and beat their children.

'The woman couldn't stand it any longer and came home. Observer met her in the street, and she said, "I'd rather be bombed to bits than go back again. Not at any price will I leave my home again. It's taught me a lesson."'

Another mother complained, 'My boy is sharing a bed, single, with an improperly washed coalman.'

To establish the truth was nigh on impossible, as a schoolteacher evacuated to Brighton found out: 'The first week of evacuation was unbearable. The rumours of lousy, dirty, ill-behaved children bandied about Brighton were exasperating. We knew that 90 per cent of the children were well behaved and happy. But the only stories regaled to me were of the horrors of the wild London children.'

The majority of complaints that Mass Observation received about evacuation concerned 'dirty, diseased or ill-mannered children'. Bedwetting was a particular problem and one of the major faults found with evacuee children, 'regardless of the fact that it is a form of nervousness . . . brought on under the unaccustomed conditions of evacuation'. But with a little sympathy and understanding it was relatively easy to cure: 'Edna, seven, the eldest, wet her bed every night, but didn't last night, a result of being given a sweet instead of lemonade at night.'

Much of the trouble, however, was due to social and class differences, as a Mass Observer from Bexhill-on-Sea reported: 'The main problems between evacuees and hosts arise from mixing up families on different social levels. One case which struck me was of a woman putting a parcel of fish and chips on her host's polished table.'

With the debate on evacuation still waging fiercely in Parliament and the press, *Picture Post*, in its edition of 18 November, sought to present a more balanced view. It pointed out that mistakes had occurred, 'but to carry out a social revolution such as this in four days without a hitch would be a miracle'. Moreover, 'without denying faults, without defending anyone, it must be acknowledged that the whole country rallied amazingly to pull the scheme through'. Where difficulties had arisen it was because 'never before have town and country been thrown so closely together, or rich and poor found themselves in such intimate contact'. And to remedy this, 'understanding and patience is needed on both sides'.

Even before the article appeared, parents had started to bring their children back to the towns and cities. *Picture Post* sternly warned against it: 'they have deliberately taken their children back to danger. The fact that raids did not come in the first weeks of war is no reason for false security. Devastating air-raids may be very near.'

Concluding its survey, the magazine admitted, 'the present scheme has its weaknesses. But one fact remains – evacuation is essential. Somehow, between us all, we have got to make it work.'

But there was another and a much brighter side to the evacuation coin. Queen Elizabeth, on one of her visits to evacuated families, called on Mrs Bridge, the wife of an electrical engineer in the Royal Navy. At her home in Birdham, near Chichester, Mrs Bridge had

Queen Elizabeth visits evacuated children 'somewhere in Sussex', 8 November 1939. The Queen later sent a personal message of appreciation to those who had taken in evacuees: 'By your sympathy you have earned the gratitude of those to whom you have shown hospitality, & by your readiness to serve you have helped the State in a work of great value.'

eighteen children to look after, seven of her own and eleven evacuees. She began her day at 5am, cooking eighteen breakfasts of porridge. Then she sent the children to school, where they got lunch. Every other evening each child had a hot bath. The children did their homework in one room, and played games in another. 'A wonderful woman', was the Queen's comment.

And among the thousands of letters that *Picture Post* received on the subject there was one from Mrs E.A. Hemming of Great King Street, Hockley, Birmingham, who wrote, 'My son, just six years old, has been evacuated to Monmouth, South Wales. I went to see him on Sunday, and I can't really express my gratitude and how much I appreciate the kindness shown to him and myself in the wonderful way in which we were welcomed. I didn't think there was so much kindness in this world. If you could see the smiling faces in Monmouth, it would do you a world of good.'

And a middle-aged couple in Kettering told the magazine that they had always wanted children, and now, at last they had them: 'They scream and race about the place and yesterday the little girl was sick on the drawing room carpet. But that's what we have always wanted. Thank God for our little evacuees!'

Fear of devastating air raids brought about the mass slaughter of domestic animals in the first few days of the war. Some estimates put the number of animals destroyed at 2,000,000, but the Royal Society for the Prevention of Cruelty to Animals (RSPCA) calculated that around 200,000 dogs had been put down. In the East End of London there was a 'secret burial-ground' near excavations for a Tube extension. According to the *Sunday Express*, 80,000 animal carcasses were buried there in one night. As well as the danger from air raids, many animal lovers had their pets put down because they feared there would be no food for them anyway. Thousands of others claimed that there had been a Government announcement ordering the compulsory destruction of cats and dogs. For those pets retained by their owners, the People's Dispensary for

Sick Animals (PDSA) offered gas-proof kennels at £4 each, while gas masks for dogs retailed at £9 a time. In London's Hyde Park, the Air Raid Precautions Animals Committee put up a large number of white posts, with leads and chains, for dog owners to attach their pets before going down into the park's trench shelters.

Writing to the *Topical Times*, Mr E.J. Foster of 2 Hazel Avenue, North Shields came up with his own solution to the problem of how to protect pets in gas attacks, earning himself five shillings (25p) in the process: 'In wartime, a grand way to stop pet birds (budgies, canaries &c) from being gassed is to wrap a wet towel around the cage and so exclude all poison gas. Another way is to put the cage in the bathroom and close all windows and door. Then turn on the hot taps and so fill the room with steam. The steam keeps away all gas which may seep in.'

London Zoo evacuated some of its animals, including the elephants and pandas, to Whipsnade. Others, especially the whole collection of poisonous and constrictor snakes and black-widow spiders, were given a lethal dose of chloroform by their keepers. The aquarium, which if it had been hit by bombs would have released 200,000 gallons of water, was emptied and used as a storehouse for newsprint and paper. During air-raid alerts that autumn and winter, posses of keepers at London Zoo and at the Scottish Zoological Park at Edinburgh were armed with Lee Enfield rifles with instructions to shoot any larger flesh-eating animals which might escape in the bombing and be a danger to the public.

But some animals were in danger themselves, as the *Daily Express* reported on 23 October:

WATCH YOUR CATS – THIEVES ARE BUSY
Watch your cats. Thieves have been busy in London since the war began stealing them – especially Persians.

An animal welfare authority said yesterday that the thefts appear to be organized. There is a shortage of cat pelts in the fur trade.

THESE ANIMALS
ARE
DANGEROUS

A monkey family proud of the sandbag defences in front of the cage at London Zoo. Larger animals had been evacuated to Whipsnade, and after the Zoo reopened on 15 September 1939, its Californian sea lions were sent 'on loan to the National Zoo Park, Washington, for the duration of the war'.

A month later a Hampstead cleaner had heard the rumour: 'You know what they're doing with all them cats what vanishes? They use the skins for lining British Warms [overcoats], and they boil the fat down for margarine or something. They do say there is cats in pies.'

A month before Armistice Day, *Picture Post* published a letter from Mrs Stelfex of Broadoaks Road, Flixton, Manchester: 'The Cenotaph here is desolate and flowerless. Men hurry by and do not raise their hats. What is going to happen on 11 November this year? To have the usual two minutes silence in honour of those who died in the Great War would be a paradox when lives are still being given in the same cause ... Yet we can't just forget our 1914–1918 heroes.'

Picture Post answered Mrs Stelfex: 'There will be no service at the Cenotaph this year, in all probability, because crowding together into a public place is forbidden in war-time. Question of silence is still being considered. There is no danger of the men of 1914–1918 being forgotten.'

Officially, there was no two minutes' silence on Armistice Day 1939 but on the first stroke of 11am, traffic came to a voluntary standstill and passers-by stood bare-headed until two minutes had elapsed. At the Cenotaph, wreaths were laid on behalf of the King and Queen, followed by the chiefs of staff, Admiral Sir Dudley Pound, General Sir Edmund Ironside and Air Chief Marshal Sir Cyril Newall on behalf of the fighting forces. Then, a French *matelot* and a Polish staff officer laid wreaths on behalf of Britain's allies. To mark the anniversary, King George and President Lebrun exchanged telegrams. And in Paris, the Grenadier Guards took part in France's commemoration of the Armistice at the tomb of the Unknown Warrior at the Arc de Triomphe.

Picture Post wrote eloquently of the scene in Whitehall: 'all through day, a crowd of men and women stand around the wreath-laden Cenotaph ... In the grey November light, with their sombre clothes and gas-mask cases, they look pathetic, almost like ghosts from another age. Some come to lay flowers, some come to look at the wreaths, some come to stand for a moment and think about the men who died – the men whose sons are fighting in a new war now.'

That same day Queen Elizabeth broadcast to the women of Britain and the Empire: 'War has at all times called for the fortitude of women. Even in other days, when it was an affair of the fighting forces only, wives and mothers at home suffered constant anxiety for their dear ones and too often the misery of bereavement . . . Now this has all changed, for we, no less than men, have real and vital work to do . . . All this, I know, has meant sacrifice, and I would say to those who are feeling the strain: Be assured that in carrying on your home duties and meeting all those worries cheerfully you are giving real service to your country. You are taking your part in keeping the home front, which will have dangers of its own, stable and strong . . .'

CHAPTER 13

Wartime Entertainment

In Britain, as soon as war was declared, all places of entertainment were closed down. This was done on the orders of the Home Office, 'until the scale of attack is judged'. This draconian measure prompted a characteristically blistering attack from George Bernard Shaw in *The Times* on 5 September. He described it as a 'masterstroke of unimaginative stupidity'. He further put forward the novel suggestion that 'all actors, variety artists, musicians and entertainers of all sorts should be exempted from every form of service except their own all-important professional one'.

While not daring to go that far, on 9 September, the Government did sanction the reopening, until 10pm, of all theatres and cinemas in areas deemed not to be in immediate danger of attack. Two weeks later, permission was given for entertainment venues to open in 'vulnerable areas'. They too were to shut at 10pm, except in the West End, where a curfew was to operate at 6pm. This proviso lasted until the beginning of December.

At the Victoria Palace, the musical *Me and My Girl*, starring Lupino Lane and Teddie St Denis, was one of the first shows to reopen. It featured 'The Lambeth Walk' and before the war had already chalked up 1,062 performances. The first new musical show opened in October. Entitled *The Little Dog Laughed*, it starred the Crazy Gang and ran for 461 performances; 1,500 troops were invited to the Palladium for the dress rehearsal of the show, which had a cast of eighty, twenty-four tons of scenery, nearly five tons of properties and three tons of costumes. At the show's start, a topical note was introduced, 'with a sudden drone of bombers diving on the stalls and a copious shower of pamphlets giving a general low-down on the Nazi leaders'.

Punch's critic was highly complimentary: 'Mr George Black's aim has been to take the mind of his vast public off the war for a couple of hours, and in this he certainly succeeds ... what a relief it is to come in out of the dreary black-out to such a scene of cheer and gaiety! It is worth every one of the preceding collisions with a dozen lamp posts and a hundred bulky and detestable strangers.'

The show featured two early wartime hit songs, both sung and later recorded by the Crazy Gang's Bud Flanagan and Chesney Allen. The first was 'F D R Jones', written the previous year by Harold Rome for an American political revue *Sing Out the News*. The other was 'Run, Rabbit, Run' by Noel Gay, composer of the 'The Lambeth Walk'. Legend had it that the song referred to the German air raid on the Shetland Islands when 'Careful inspection of the area involved in the raid revealed the corpse of one rabbit who, there is reason to believe, died as a result of enemy action.'

A month later, the revue *Black Velvet*, starring Churchill's son-in-law Vic Oliver, opened at the Hippodrome. It too pleased *Punch*'s critic: 'It makes no notable contribution to the arts, but is very much what is wanted. Gay from the outset, it has a generous number of good turns and is constantly brightened by the personality of Vic Oliver.' Appearing with the Austrian-born Oliver were Alice Lloyd, 'who gives an excellent imitation of her ever-to-be-lamented

'Doing the Lambeth Walk, Oi!' Men of the Royal Air Force join Lupino Lane and the rest of the cast of Me and My Girl *at the Victoria Palace. The show was one of the first to reopen after the outbreak of war.*

The King and Queen at a performance of George Black's review Black Velvet *at the London Hippodrome, 27 November 1939. 'This is a good evening's fun, thanks mostly to Vic Oliver' wrote a critic in* Punch.

sister Marie', xylophonist Teddy Brown and Pat Kirkwood, who sang two Cole Porter standards, 'Most Gentlemen Don't Like Love' and 'My Heart Belongs to Daddy'. The show received the royal seal of approval when the King and Queen and the Dukes and Duchesses of Gloucester and Kent made an informal visit on 27 November.

J.B. Priestley's *Music at Night* at the Westminster Theatre was the first serious new play to open in wartime London. *Punch*'s critic was usually disdainful of theatrical first nights, 'because commonly the audience is more anxious to have its features registered by the society papers than to allow the curtain to be rung up'. But, he conceded, after 'six weeks of play-starvation', the opening of *Music at Night* was quite different: 'Gripping gas masks and torches, and mostly glad in day clothes, the audience surged under the dim blue bulbs in the hall hungrily on into its seats as if the play was all that mattered and there was not a moment to be wasted in getting at it.'

Florence Speed went to see the play just after it opened: 'It was interesting and original in its setting, but hardly ideal for wartime. It is played in some darkness with only the individual players spotlighted. It's the story of several people's reaction to Music and their varying thoughts as they listen ... Each in his thoughts criticize the others, then they think of their childhood, are visited by the ghosts of their dead ... and banal finish, come down to whiskies and soda. The first two acts held you but the third I'm afraid was too highbrow for me and a little dreary.'

Gradually other plays such as *Dear Octopus*, *The Importance of Being Earnest* and Emlyn Williams's *The Corn Is Green* began to reopen. By Christmas, thirty London theatres, of which twenty-three were in the West End, were 'welcoming crowded audiences ... the queues have been lengthened as the promised Christmas leave began to operate, and husbands, brothers, sweethearts came back from France eager for charm and jollity'.

Outside of London, the provincial theatres were also doing good business. By December, there were reckoned to be over eighty touring companies putting on serious drama, comedies, musicals and revues, together with about thirty resident repertory companies. Gifted amateurs also did their bit, as when society photographer Cecil Beaton and friends staged their own pantomime, *Heil Cinderella*, for the troops. Putting on a pantomime was, Beaton thought, 'like running a war and I cannot think that Hitler feels more unnerved and responsible than I now do . . . The Russians bomb Finland and it matters less to us because we have to still find a Dandini.'

One of the most popular features of Beaton's pantomime, as it toured army camps around Salisbury Plain, was the community singing of some of the first wartime hits, including a parody of 'Run, Rabbit, Run', popularised by Arthur Askey. The revised lyrics substituted 'Adolf', Goering and Goebbels in the refrain. As Mass Observation noted, with the outbreak of war, Britain's music business, centred on London's Denmark Street – 'Tin Pan Alley' – 'reacted immediately and sensationally'. The hits of the summer like 'South of the Border' and 'Little Sir Echo' gave way to a spate of war-related songs. One of the first and certainly the most popular was Jimmy Kennedy and Michael Carr's 'We're Gonna Hang Out the Washing on the Siegfried Line'. Its inspiration was a cartoon by St John Cooper in the *Daily Express* where 'Young Bert', writing home to his mother, says, 'I'm sending you the Siegfried Line to hang your washing on.' By Christmas, the song's sheet-music sales had reached 300,000.

But in Germany, the *Daily Telegraph* reported on 6 October: 'The incorrigible flippancy of the new British war song "We're Gonna Hang Out the Washing on the Siegfried Line" has given great offence . . . Indignant references have been made to it in the German propaganda wireless broadcasts in English. The statement by the BBC that the song was written by men of anti-aircraft units is said, by the German wireless, to be obviously untrue. "This is not a soldiers' song, because soldiers do not brag," it was stated. "It was not written in the soldiers' camps, but by the Jewish scribes of the BBC. The Englishmen's washing will be very dirty before they come anywhere near the Siegfried Line."'

Almost as popular was Ross Parker and Hughie Charles's 'There'll Always Be an England' which sold 200,000 copies at one shilling (5p) each. Gracie Fields's 'Wish Me Luck as You Wave Me Goodbye' from the film *Shipyard Sally* was a perfect song for wartime partings, and was sung with equal enthusiasm both by evacuees and the men of the British Expeditionary Force off to France. And her 'I'm Sending a Letter to Santa Claus' ('to send back my daddy to me') was a big success at Christmas.

The same theme of separation and reunion was a popular one that autumn with songwriters turning out such titles as 'Goodbye Sally', 'It Won't Be Long', 'We Won't Be Long Out There' and Ivor Novello's sentimental and nostalgic 'We'll Remember', which he co-wrote with *Daily Mail* journalist Collie Knot and which failed spectacularly to match the huge success of his 1914 song '(Keep the Home Fires Burning) Till the Boys Come Home'. Much more popular was Michael Carr's 'Somewhere in France With You'.

In France too, there was a similar glut of topical and patriotic war songs. Maurice Chevalier's 'Ça Fait D'Excellents Français' ('All This Makes Fine Frenchmen') was, an American journalist thought, 'a complete portrait of France's democratic army'. While his 'Paris sera toujours Paris' was a light-hearted catalogue of the changes that war had brought to the French capital; gas masks, petrol rationing, sandbags and the blackout. The *Entente Cordiale* was celebrated with such tunes as 'Bonjour Tommy' and 'Tommy and the French Girl'. Ray Ventura and his band had big hits with both a musical tribute to Britain's Prime Minister, 'La Chamberlaine' (The Umbrella Polka), and their own version of 'We're Gonna Hang Out the Washing on the Siegfried Line'.

In Germany, as in Britain and France, there were war songs in circulation that autumn. 'Erika' was a great favourite with the troops, but it was 'Wir Fahren gegen Engelland' ('We Are Sailing against England'), that received immense official plugging. But even Dr Goebbels, when writing about war songs, had to admit the relative weakness of Germany when it came to producing such tunes. In any case, most Germans preferred songs without a war theme, like the huge hit 'Bel Ami'. Amazingly popular too that autumn was band leader and accordionist Willi Glahé's version of a 1934 Czech tune, now retitled 'Rosamunde'. It enjoyed equal popularity in Britain, where it was one of Churchill's favourites, under the title 'Roll Out the Barrel'.

In Britain, most songs on topical wartime themes enjoyed only a transient popularity. The blackout inspired no less than five hit tunes, including 'Till the Lights of London Shine Again', 'They Can't Blackout the Moon' and Tommie Connor's 'The Blackout Stroll'. The services came in for their share of topical tunes with such titles as 'Lords of the Air', 'Oh, Ain't It Grand to Be in the Navy?', 'Wings over the Navy' and 'Reckless Jeff of the RAF'. But the most unlikely tune that autumn to achieve popularity was dance-band leader Harry Roy's 'God Bless You, Mr Chamberlain', the lyrics of which referred to the Prime Minister's 1938 flights to Germany and his famous umbrella. Roy wrote to 10 Downing Street to seek the Prime Minister's permission to publish the song, and 'in reply Mr Chamberlain said he had no objection to the lyric'.

As the year drew to a close, Mass Observation undertook a survey of current song releases:

43 per cent were war songs

49 per cent plain love songs (many actually written or prereleased before the war)

2 per cent were ballads

2 per cent were comic

A music publisher told Mass Observation: 'Generally speaking the people go back pretty much to normal songs. The ordinary sentimental ballad type will lead. A song like – what shall I say? – like "We'll Meet Again", a song we're putting out now – that sort of sentiment. To you – no doubt – and even to us it is just emotionalism, but the public like it . . .'

But as the year ended, and despite the best efforts of Tin Pan Alley, the press was still asking, 'Where are our marching songs? Can we not do better than "Roll Out the Barrel"?'

For more-serious-music lovers, there were the National Gallery lunchtime concerts, where 'every day from Monday to Friday, you can hear world-famous artists . . . for one shilling (5p) a time'. The idea for the concerts came from pianist Myra Hess. When war broke out she initially thought of giving up music and going into some form of war work. But then she realised that 'now of all times was the moment when her music was needed'. Cheap lunch-hour concerts, which would avoid the problem of the blackout, at a shilling a time seemed to be the answer. The money raised would go to the Musicians' Benevolent Fund.

The National Gallery, with most of its paintings now removed to safety, seemed to be the ideal location for the concerts. Director Sir Kenneth Clark was approached and he welcomed the idea. He agreed to the concerts being held in the dome hall of the National Gallery, where the old Italian masters had hung before they were evacuated to Wales. The Home Office gave permission for the concerts to take place, and HM Customs and Excise exempted them from entertainment tax. Within the space of a fortnight, the first programmes had been drawn up. Myra Hess herself gave the first concert and played Beethoven's 'Appassionata' and her own arrangement of Bach's 'Jesu Joy of Man's Desiring'. Sir Kenneth confessed that 'in common with half the audience, I was in tears. This is what we had all been waiting for – an assertion of eternal values.'

'The compère of the Entente Cordiale'. Maurice Chevalier at Arras, 12 November 1939, before an Anglo-French audience which included Dominions Secretary Anthony Eden, Lord Gort and the Duke of Gloucester.

'It was left to the initiative of a single woman, Myra Hess, to pierce the black-out by producing her own concerts and peopling the central hall of the National Gallery with humans instead of evacuated masterpieces.' Her audiences were enthusiastic:

   Wife, thirty-five: 'Terribly exciting!'

   Officer, forty: 'Yes, such fun! We must come tomorrow. A lovely programme
      – Bach.'

Myra Hess was delighted at the public's response: 'It has been the greatest experience of my life. We thought we might get perhaps 300 people. But as many as a thousand try to find a place. They even sit on the marble floor – and we have to turn scores away.' The Queen came, and soon the idea of lunchtime concerts caught on all over Britain.

During the First World War, it was not until February 1915 that any attempt was made to provide entertainment for the troops. But in September 1939, under the forceful leadership of theatre and film director Basil Dean, the Entertainments National Service Association (ENSA), quickly came into being. Only a week after the declaration of war, ENSA gave its first concert, starring Frances Day, at Old Dene Camp, Camberley. By the end of the year, from its headquarters at the Theatre Royal, Drury Lane, ENSA had sent out concert parties that had entertained nearly a million soldiers, sailors and airmen.

The first ENSA concerts in France were given at Douai and Arras on 15 November. Both shows starred Gracie Fields, the then 'reigning queen of British show business'. She was only just recovering from a serious operation and appeared against her doctor's orders. She told Dean before going on, 'my knees wobble a bit. Hope I won't disappoint you.' Walking on to the stage, she was greeted with such a barrage of applause from the troops that even the hard-bitten Dean caught himself gulping back some tears. Overcome by this emotional display: 'Gracie made a supreme effort to steady herself. Putting her fingers in her mouth and whistling shrilly, she shouted: "Now then, lads, no muckin' about!" With this touch of Lancashire vernacular the emotional atmosphere dissolved into laughter.'

A few days after Gracie's concert, the King and Queen paid an informal visit to the Theatre Royal, Drury Lane to inspect ENSA headquarters and to see some of the some of the stars like James Mason, Willy Hay, Binnie Hale and Jack Hylton's band rehearsing.

'Our Gracie'. Gracie Fields performs at a concert for the men of the BEF 'somewhere in France'. Of the concert Gracie said, 'Most of the boys were like old friends. They'd seen me in the halls or heard me on the radio and I suppose I was part of the life they left behind. The songs I sang . . . were the ones they'd whistled on the way to work.'

'Who pays for all of this?' the King asked Dean.

'NAAFI, sir,' Dean replied.

'Good,' said the King, 'stick to it, they've plenty of money.'

Cinemas, like all other places of entertainment, had been closed on Government orders at the outbreak of war. Only the Pier Cinema at the Welsh seaside resort of Aberystwyth, defied the order until specifically instructed to close by the Home Office on 7 September. Permission for all cinemas to reopen was announced on the BBC nine o'clock news on 15 September. The Granada Group gave orders that all its cinemas were now to fly the Union Jack instead of the house flag, and that there should be bright lights and jolly music in their foyers to offset the gloomy blackout outside. At the Granada, Welling on the first Sunday night reopening under blackout conditions: 'The queues stampeded when the swing doors were thrown back; they made a blind rush towards the lights, sweeping the doorman aside, but in the foyer the habitual discipline of the ordinary citizen reasserted itself and they came to an orderly halt at the pay-box.'

As cinema audiences began to return, 'conscientiously clutching their gas masks', there was little except the newsreels and an occasional Government short information film to remind them that Britain was at war. Naturally enough, at first nearly all the films shown were peacetime productions. From British studios came *Goodbye Mr Chips*, starring Robert Donat and Greer Garson; *The Four Feathers* with Ralph Richardson and John Clements; and Hitchcock's *Jamaica Inn*, featuring Charles Laughton. Only *Q Planes*, a spy thriller starring Laurence Olivier, had anything remotely topical in its plot. Hollywood productions in cinemas that autumn included: John Wayne in *Stagecoach*, Fred Astaire and Ginger Rogers in *The Story of Vernon and Irene Castle*, and Clark Gable and Norma Shearer in *Idiot's Delight*.

At the outbreak of war, production in British film studios stopped abruptly. Alexander Korda was just finishing his spectacular

The Thief of Baghdad, while Carol Reed was in the middle of directing the gritty mining drama *The Stars Look Down*. At the Gainsborough Studios in Islington, Arthur Askey was working on a film version of his hit radio show *Band Waggon* when production ceased. After three weeks, Askey was told that filming would re-start, but this time at the Lime Grove Studios at Shepherd's Bush. As quite a few of the actors and crew had already been called up, Askey had to reshoot several scenes. He ruefully reflected that 'after fifteen years' struggle to get my name in lights, came the black-out!'

In November, the first British 'war' film was released. It was Korda's *The Lion Has Wings*, starring Ralph Richardson and Merle Oberon, and it had as its centrepiece the Kiel Raid of 4 September. The Nazis got hold of a print and showed it to foreign correspondents in Berlin. William Shirer noted in his diary: 'at the Propaganda Ministry we were shown the English propaganda film "The Lion Has Wings". Even making allowances for the fact that it was turned out last fall, I thought it very bad. Supercilious. Silly.'

Gracie Fields's *Shipyard Sally*, which featured her huge hit 'Wish Me Luck as You Wave Me Goodbye', had come out the month before, and so had the First World War espionage drama *The Spy in Black*, starring the German émigré Conrad Veidt and Valerie Hobson. October also saw a less-than-successful film version of Lupino Lane's smash stage hit *Me And My Girl*, that included 'The Lambeth Walk'. But it still enjoyed huge audiences as did most other films that autumn and early winter.

Venturing out to 'the pictures' in the blackout was fraught with many hazards: 'cinemas were swallowed up in the prevailing blackness, and even regular patrons, who had navigated unconsciously twice a week for years ... found that going to the cinema was now something of an adventure'. But masses of cinemagoers in the first four months of the war still went, reflecting the craving for 'entertainment for entertainment's sake. People were jumpy; they sought emotional release and did not care whether they laughed or cried.'

For those not wishing to brave the blackout there was always the wireless. On 1 September, the BBC had merged the National Programme with its eight regional programmes to form the Home Service. The broadcasting day now began at 7.00am and continued right through until midnight. Before the war, and by agreement with the newspapers, the first news bulletin would not have been broadcast until 6.00pm. Now there were frequent news bulletins, but, in most British homes, it was the nine o'clock news that became the focal point of the broadcasting day. During the war's first week, the BBC regarded itself as principally a news and information service, with bulletins every hour, on the hour. In between, it broadcast a succession of official Government announcements punctuated by gramophone records and 'for some mysterious patriotic reason endless programmes of "Sandy Macpherson at the Organ"'. An irate listener-in wrote to the BBC: 'I could be reconciled to an air raid, if in the course of it a bomb would fall on Sandy Macpherson and his ever-lasting organ, preferably while he was playing his signature tune.'

Apart from Chamberlain's and the King's broadcasts, the radio highlight on 3 September itself was the first instalment of J.B. Priestley's *Let The People Sing*. Read by the author, it was the first novel to be written specifically for radio, and its title provided Evelyn 'Boo' Laye with a hit song that winter.

In expectation of massive air raids on London, the BBC had dispersed its various departments around the country to safe areas. The Drama Department was evacuated to Wood Norton Hall, near Evesham, while the Variety Department went to Bristol. Here, the Clifton Parish Hall became the BBC's 'Garrison Theatre', broadcasts from which starred Jack 'Mind-My-Bike' Warner.

The BBC's Television Service, which had been operating from the Alexandra Palace since November 1936, went off the air at midday on 1 September in the middle of a Mickey Mouse cartoon being transmitted from Radiolympia. There were several reasons offered for the shutdown. The official one was that it freed skilled technicians to work on sound radio. It was also said that the cost of operating the service in relation to the number of television-set owners (20,000, and almost all in the London area) was too high to justify keeping the service going in wartime. And it was claimed that television's short-range transmissions could help guide German bombers to their targets. The BBC was fairly unapologetic about closing the service down:

'It has been pointed out to us that nobody said a word in the *Radio Times* about the passing of television. That is quite true, but so many things were passing, too, on that ominous week-end at the beginning of September, that television was at least not singled out for neglect. As a matter of fact we ourselves as viewers miss television as much as anyone could.'

This gave scant comfort to television owners, some of whom had paid as much as £40 for their twelve-inch screen sets. Nor to the sixteen firms manufacturing television sets, 15,000 of which now had to be scrapped. In Germany, the television service, transmitting programmes from studios under the Berlin Olympic Stadium, continued until 1944.

After two or three weeks, during which the expected German aerial onslaught failed to materialise, the BBC reverted to broadcasting entertainment programmes. One of the first to go back on the air at 8.15pm on Saturday, 16 September was *Band Waggon* starring Arthur 'Big Hearted' Askey and Richard 'Stinker' Murdoch. First broadcast in January 1938, *Band Waggon*, had been a huge success, turning Askey into a star almost overnight. The show's catchphrases:

'Hello playmates!'

'You silly little man'

'Ah, happy days'

'It isn't the people who make the most noise who do the most work'

'Don't be filthy'

'Doesn't it make you want to spit?'

'What would you do, chums?'

and particularly Askey's 'Aythangyow', were heard everywhere. But by the time *Band Waggon*'s third and final series finished on 25 November, its popularity was already being overtaken by a new comedy programme.

ITMA had first gone out on the air on 12 July 1939. The show's title, *It's That Man Again*, had originally been a newspaper head-line referring to Hitler. It now referred to Tommy Handley, a variety comedian, who, like Askey, came from Liverpool. The first series, which ran until 30 August, was not a great success, partly because its format was too much like *Band Waggon*. Nevertheless, a second series was sanctioned by the BBC Variety Department and the first programme went out on 19 September. In a swipe at wartime restrictions and the much-abused Ministry of Information, Handley was cast as the Minister of Aggravation and Mysteries at the Office of the Twerps:

'Good evening, Great Britain. As Minister of Aggravation it is my duty tonight on the umpteenth day of the war against depres-sion to explain to you that I have 700 further restrictions to impose on you. Here in the heart of the country I have been able to think out some of the most irritating regulations you've ever heard of.'

This poking fun at wartime bureaucracy and restrictions certainly touched a chord with the listening public, and very soon *ITMA* was attracting a huge audience. In the second programme, the German spy Funf appeared. Like all *ITMA* characters, he had his own catchphrase – 'this is Funf speaking'. Funf was played by Jack

Train, who produced the spy's voice by speaking sideways into a glass. He also played the civil servant Fusspot, whose catchphrase, 'Most irregular!', was almost as much imitated. ITMA's second series ran for twenty weeks with a Boxing Day special, 'Funf and Games for Everyone'.

But it was not just comedy programmes that attracted huge audiences that autumn and winter. An estimated one out of every three adults in Britain tuned into the fortnightly series on the history of the Nazi Party, *The Shadow of the Swastika*, 'the biggest event of the winter's broadcasting'. First broadcast on 9 November, the anniversary of Hitler's Beer Hall Putsch, the series featured actor Marius Goring as Hitler and Alan Wheatley as Dr Goebbels; Leo Genn was the narrator. The BBC assured its listeners 'that every care has been taken to base the programmes on ascertained facts', but it was noted, 'some listeners, particularly older women, refuse to listen, saying that the programmes frighten them'.

In Germany itself it was forbidden to listen to the BBC or indeed any foreign broadcasts. Explaining the reason why, Dr Goebbels said in an interview, 'We don't let our people listen to foreign broadcasts; the English do. Why should we permit our people to be disturbed by foreign propaganda? Of course we broadcast in English, and the English people are legally permitted to listen in. I understand lots of them do.'

CHAPTER 14

Lord Haw Haw

On 14 September 1939, Jonah Barrington, radio critic of the *Daily Express*, wrote in his column: 'A gent I'd like to meet is moaning periodically from Zeesen (the German radio station beaming overseas broadcasts). He speaks English of the haw-haw damit-get-out-of-my-way variety, and his strong suit is gentlemanly indignation.'

Four days later, Barrington expanded on this: 'Jonah Barrington listening at the "Daily Express" short wave station in Surrey to the war on radio, introduces "Lord Haw Haw" . . . from his accent and personality I imagine him with a receding chin, a questing nose, thin yellow hair brushed back, a vacant eye, a gardenia in his button hole. Rather like P.G. Wodehouse's Bertie Wooster.'

In Berlin on that same day, thirty-three-year-old William Joyce received a contract as a newsreader on the German Radio Corporation. Anybody less like Bertie Wooster would be hard to imagine, but in the weeks to come, by a 'single-minded determination, ruthless ambition and sheer application', Joyce became "Lord Haw Haw": the English Voice of Germany'.

Joyce had been born in New York on 24 April 1906 to natural-ised American citizens. In 1909, the Joyce family returned to their native Ireland. As staunch supporters of the British cause, when Ireland was partitioned in 1922, the Joyces thought it prudent to move to England. It was not long before the ultra-patriotic William developed a taste for extreme right-wing politics, joining the British Fascists when only seventeen. Ten years later, Joyce joined Sir Oswald Mosley's British Union of Fascists and within a short time became Deputy Leader. In public Joyce called Sir Oswald 'the greatest Englishman I have ever known', but in private was scathing of him, 'Mosley was hopeless. He was the worst leader of what should have been the best cause in the world.' In 1937, matters came to a head, and Mosley dismissed his deputy. Joyce founded his own National Socialist League which, with its violently antisemitic and pro-Nazi programme, attracted only a tiny membership.

On 24 August 1939, with war imminent, Joyce decided, 'England was going to war. I felt that if, for perfect reasons of conscience, I could not fight for her, I must give her up forever.' Accordingly, and with his second wife Margaret, he set out for Berlin. Anxious to play his own small part in Hitler's 'sacred struggle to free the world', Joyce applied for a job at the German Radio Corporation. His initial voice test did not go well, but an engineer thought that Joyce's voice had potential, and he first spoke over the air on 11 September, receiving a contract a week later.

Obviously the Lord Haw Haw that Barrington heard that week could not have been Joyce. It was most probably Wolff Mittler, a German 'playboy of the first order', who used to sign off his broad-casts with 'Hearty Cheerios!' to his listeners. But it was Joyce who soon established his own claim on the title. In this he was aided by the British public's enormous interest in the broadcasts. This was undoubtedly because 'in no other war had the British enjoyed the novelty of being cajoled and hectored by renegades in their own sitting rooms', but also by the relative lack of war news. And it

'Jairmany calling, Jairmany calling.' William Joyce, Lord Haw Haw, at the microphone. 'I think that, secretly, we are rather terrified by the appalling things he says. The cool way he tells us of the decline of democracy and so on. I hate it; it frightens me. Am I alone in this? Nobody has confessed as much to me.'

was not long before Lord Haw Haw became the 'Number One Radio Personality of the War', and the major topic of conversation. In the press too, items about him filled the correspondence columns. There was endless speculation about Haw Haw's social origins, education and accent. In Berlin, Dr Goebbels, gratified at the size of the British audience for Joyce's broadcasts, told an American correspondent:

'Can you imagine what is one of the chief discussions about it across the Channel? It is, whether our German [sic] announcer has an Oxford or Cambridge accent! In my opinion, when a people in the midst of a life-and-death struggle indulge in such frivolous arguments, it doesn't look well for them.'

Many found the whole idea of treason by radio repugnant. 'What can have induced an Englishman, if he is an Englishman, to behave in such a sickening renegade manner?' asked Mr A.R. Thomas of Bournemouth in *News Review* on 19 October. But a Mr Heath, quoted in *Illustrated* of 4 November, thought that 'Lord Haw Haw was funnier than anything that the BBC ever put on.' This was a view shared by a Canadian listener whose letter appeared in *London Calling* three weeks later: 'Whenever we are short of entertainment we tune in to that comedian. We often wonder whether he knows what a lot of laughter he causes.'

But it was not always laughter that Joyce's broadcasts engendered. That Christmas, a Mass Observation correspondent asked an aunt, 'a very patriotic Conservative woman', what she thought of Lord Haw Haw. He was surprised at her response: "Oh I don't listen to him now. I am not going to be frightened by him. And it's no use calling what he says rubbish, because there's never smoke without fire!" And,' he added, '*she* thinks that everything in Germany's bad.'

Another Mass Observation correspondent was of the opinion: 'I think that, secretly, we are rather terrified by the appalling things he says. The cool way he tells of us of the decline of democracy and so on. I hate it; it frightens me. Am I alone in this? Nobody has confessed as much to me.'

There was no shortage of advice on how to combat the effectiveness of Lord Haw Haw's broadcasts. In the 25 November issue of *Picture Post*, Mr A.E. Waugh of Sheffield offered his solution: 'My part in the radio war. I put on the radio to listen to the Hamburg announcer, he is so amusing. When he has done, my daughter and I give him the Raspberry. Only sorry he can't hear what we say.' In the same magazine, Londoner Mr C.N. Edge suggested, 'Could the BBC therefore be persuaded to give each night immediately after Haw-Haw's talk, a ten minute "Spot The Errors" item on the "Inspector Hornleigh" principle, with a run through of Haw-Haw's speech, and then STOP. The announcer pointing out the errors or mis-statement.'

This suggestion had already been the subject of at least two memoranda at the BBC, where Sir Stephen Tallents had been told by the Countess of Harrowby: 'My hostess's servants listen in to Haw-Haw, and one of them remarked the other day there was probably something in what he said ... thousands of people like those maids listen to him daily and find themselves influenced by his malicious lies.'

Others when listening to Joyce took the view of an RAF airmen: 'He talks a lot of cock and 75 per cent of his statements are either lies or propaganda, but occasionally he hits the nail on the head, it's then that he makes you think. You wonder whether a lot of his statements are true.' And a woman librarian said, 'We nearly always turn him on at 9.15 to try and glean some news that the Ministry of Information withholds from us. It is interesting to get the BBC's views and the German wireless's accounts of the same aerial engagements. Between the frantic eulogies of the BBC and the sneers of the German wireless one achieves something like the truth.'

As the year ended, the BBC and Ministry of Information were still agonising on how best to deal with Lord Haw Haw. One idea was to put leading show-business personalities like Arthur Askey, Gracie Fields or George Formby on the BBC at the same time that Lord Haw Haw was broadcasting from Hamburg. Like them, he was now a distinct personality in his own right, even featuring in advertisements like one for Smith's Electric Clocks, 'Don't risk missing Haw-Haw. Get a clock that shows the right time always, unquestionably.' At the Holborn Empire that month, impresario George Black put on a revue entitled *Haw Haw*, starring Max Miller. To Black, 'the thought of Haw-Haw's regimented voice having the slightest connection with the endearing, confidential vulgarities of Miller had a delicious fantasy about it.' And two other music-hall comedians, the Western Brothers, had a hit with their song 'Lord Haw Haw the Humbug of Hamburg'.

CHAPTER 15

The Winter War

Russia Invades Finland: 30 November 1939

Following his occupation of eastern Poland, Stalin set about consolidating his sphere of influence in the Baltic, assigned to him under the terms of the secret protocols of the Molotov-Ribbentrop pact. The Soviet dictator was still deeply suspicious of his new 'ally', and wished to gain as much buffer territory between him and Hitler as possible. So-called mutual assistance pacts were signed with the small Baltic states of Estonia, Latvia and Lithuania, all of which were forced to agree to Soviet demands for military bases on their territory.

From Finland, Stalin required a similar agreement, and the Finns sent veteran statesman J.K. Paasikivi to Moscow to negotiate the Soviet demands with the Kremlin. There, Paasikivi found that the Russians wanted a mutual assistance pact, the occupation of the southern part of the Karelian Isthmus, the leasing of the port of Hango as a naval and air base, the cession of islands in the Baltic, and the leasing of the Rybachi Peninsula on which was Petsamo, Finland's only ice-free port. In return the Russians offered 2,134 square miles of Soviet Karelia, considered by the Finns as worthless.

Negotiations between the two sides, in which Stalin himself played a considerable part, eventually broke down. The Finns mobilised their forces, under Field Marshal Carl Gustav Mannerheim, along the frontier and waited for the inevitable.

On 26 November, the Soviets fabricated a border incident, and four days later, after severing diplomatic relations but without a declaration of war, launched an all-out attack on Finland. Soviet bombers raided Helsinki, and the Finnish capital was soon experiencing what Warsaw had gone through in September. A British United Press correspondent graphically described it:

'When the first bomb was dropped I was thrown to the floor. All the windows of the hotel were shattered. Being none the worse for my fall, I telephoned the City Exchange in order to get a trunk call. The telephone girl was still at her post and quite coolly got me my number. I counted at least a dozen bombs, two of which were huge and shattered windows over a radius of about half a mile. Incendiary bombs were dropped, evidently aimed at the airport. They went wide and started several fires in the centre of the city. The heavy bombs were presumably for the railway station, but a motor bus got the worst of one and a number of people in it were killed. There was pandemonium from continuous anti-aircraft gun fire . . . The raid had come practically without warning. The first bombs dropped barely one minute after the sirens were sounded. There was no panic, but many people appeared too dazed to make for the cellars and stood stupefied, staring up into the sky. City transport was paralysed. In one area, the fire department took charge, and the firemen began digging in the debris to recover bodies . . . The darkness, which came down at 4pm, was broken by winking flashlights of citizens picking their way through the rubble, and by the glare from burning buildings where rescue work was still going on.'

In a political blunder of the first magnitude, the Soviets set up, at the border village of Terijoki, a puppet government under the

Finland's commander-in-chief, Field Marshal Carl Gustav Mannerheim. Meeting the Field Marshal in 1938, Lady Diana Cooper wrote, 'the great Field-Marshal Mannerheim was there. He made Finland and is treated half-royal, half-Godhead. He looks fifty and is said to dye his hair . . . and he is only seventy-two. He is an old Russian Imperialist (that I find irresistible) and says in French "pardon".'

veteran Finnish Communist exile Otto Kuusinen. This only served to unite the Finnish people even more behind the new legitimate government of Rysto Ryti, former Governor of the Bank of Finland, who reaffirmed Finland's will to resist. Seventy-two-year-old aristocrat Mannerheim issued a stirring Order of the Day to his men, calling on them to 'fulfil their duty even under death. We fight for our homes, our faith, our fatherland.'

The Soviet invasion was deplored by statesmen throughout the world. President Roosevelt said how 'all peace-loving peoples . . . will unanimously condemn this new resort to military force . . .' And in the Commons, Chamberlain stated that his government 'deeply regret this attack on a small independent nation, which must result in fresh suffering and loss of life to innocent people'. Ordinary people shared their governments' disgust at the Soviet action. On 4 December, Auxiliary Firewoman Elsie Warren wrote in her diary, 'Russia is still bombing Finnish towns. The town [*sic*] of Helsinki is suffering the most. Stalin made as if to be friendly with the Finns; even wishing them "Good Luck!" The Finnish women and children returned to their homes after having been evacuated thinking that all was well. Suddenly without warning and refusing to negotiate on the matter Russia invaded Finland. She rained bombs from the air on towns killing helpless women and children. The rest of the world were disgusted.'

Evacuee schoolteacher Arnold Monk Jones writing to his wife Eileen from Berkshire thought too that 'It's a nasty business about Finland.' But he told her that a colleague thought the Soviet invasion was 'partly justifiable as a defensive measure by Russia to close a gap thro' which she was invaded after the last war, against a possible or probable attack on her by the Western Powers'. Monk Jones gloomily concluded, 'I wouldn't put it beyond Chamberlain to try and organise an anti-Russian war.'

But this was a decidedly minority view. Most people expected Finland to be overwhelmed in a matter of days. But, as one headline

IWM HU 102734

Members of the Finnish air-raid precautions organisation keep watch for Soviet bombers over Helsinki, Christmas 1939. 'But they are unusually alert, these remaining Finns. It's a peculiar alertness that comes to life under death-dealing skies.'

put it, 'Finland's Heroic Resistance Surprises the World.' The Finns had built a defensive line across the narrow strip of land, south of Lake Ladoga, which provided the principal route into southern Finland from the Soviet Union. It was called the Mannerheim Line, in honour of their commander-in-chief. It resembled more the trench fortifications of the First World War than the Maginot or Siegfried Lines. But in the early weeks of what came to be known as the Winter War, it withstood massive Soviet infantry assaults supported by tanks and guns.

Very soon in the homes of armchair strategists throughout Britain, maps of Finland began to replace those of the Western Front. And Gort and Gamelin seemed to be in serious danger of being over-shadowed by Mannerheim and his Northern Army commander General Martii Wallenius, 'a great general and a fine man'. It was to Wallenius's command that *Daily Express* war correspondent Geoffrey Cox went in mid-December to report on Finnish successes on the northern front. He sent back to his paper a graphic account of the battlefield above the Arctic Circle:

'I stood today among the bodies of a Russian column struck on the flank by the Finns. To make this attack the Finns marched all night through the woods on skis. For more than a mile both sides of the narrow snow covered roads were choked with lorries, some smashed, some whole with the carcasses of horses, overturned carts, masses of clothing, rifles and foodstuffs. Amid this at every turn lay the crumpled figures of the dead. This was where a supply column ... had been trapped. The Finns waited in pits by the roadside to fire into them practically at point blank range. But the main battle-field was half a mile back. There strewn across the road lying on the stunted pine trees were bodies in their drab Soviet khaki with peaked caps carrying the red star in front. There too were Finns in their white capes and grey fur caps fallen in the attack. They were easily identifiable. Their comrades had always covered their faces, sometimes with a cloth, sometimes just with a pine brush.'

Contrary to some reports that were being received in Britain about the Red Army's dismal performance, Cox came across grim scenes that testified to the bravery of the ordinary Russian soldier: 'In one place a small group of Soviet soldiers lay around a machine gun. They had fought to the end, for Finnish losses in the snow ahead were heavy . . . In a small clearing were a dozen Soviet guns. Their horses were dead in their traces fifty yards behind. The men were piled around a gun wheel. There had been hand-to-hand fighting, for many of the dead had died from bayonet wounds. This battle had lasted for forty-eight hours.'

Further up the roadside Cox encountered a single Soviet prisoner guarded by two Finns, 'grey with exhaustion. He had been wandering in the woods for two days.' Later the same day, Cox was driven across a frozen river to see another smashed Red Army column, which looked 'at first sight . . . like a great junk heap'. Masses of Soviet equipment lay about, and there too were the bodies of Russian and Finnish soldiers who had died in the ambush. As Finnish peasants and soldiers loaded the dead into a large van, Cox reflected, 'It seemed impossible in the winter afternoon silence, with the sky a soft gold behind the pine trees, to think what this battle meant, to realize how many of these people had been husbands, lovers, sons and fathers.'

New Zealander Cox had arrived in Finland on the first day of the war. He soon developed a real affection and admiration for the people, and wrote that when looking at the dead, 'I could feel more easily about the Finns, because I lived among them and am surrounded every day by these men in grey uniforms. But the Russians I do not know as individuals. Then suddenly I saw lying in a pile of telephone material a broken plaster doll. It had come from a small suitcase in which was a child's pair of gym shoes and some woollen clothes. It was not hard to realize how they came there. A Russian soldier, thinking of his child, had picked them up in some evacuated Finnish village. He had probably looked forward

Finnish ski troops pass through a small town on their way to the front. The winter of 1939/40 was one of the harshest since records had begun in 1828, and temperatures of –30°F were not uncommon. The Russians labelled both the dangers of the extreme cold and the snow-camouflaged Finnish troops as 'The White Death' (Belaya Smert).

to the day when he would go back to his village and his child. Now the doll and clothes lay there in the snow.'

Finnish successes, such as those Cox witnessed, won the admiration and support of virtually every civilised country from the most corrupt South American dictatorship to Finland's ultra-democratic Scandinavian neighbours. And the Finns made every effort to capitalise on this sympathy, because, as a Finnish diplomat told foreign correspondents as the war entered its third week, 'Plenty of sympathy has been dealt out, but Finland must have more than sympathy.'

CHAPTER 16

Christmas and the End of the Year

As December got underway, an advertisement for the Christmas number of the *Strand* magazine summed up the feelings of most Britons after nearly four months of the 'Bore War':

'Do you mind if we forget you for a few hours, Mr Hitler? Let's ignore that man for a few hours. Let's get back to the sane, sensible things in life like plum puddings and crackers and the Christmas number of the "Strand" – old friends that we can trust – the spirits of Christmas past and Christmas still to come. Let's get back to Yule logs and Heath Robinson and P.G. Wodehouse – for a few hours at any rate with the "Strand" Christmas number.'

For many, Christmas 1939 was going to be comparatively normal. Rationing was on the horizon, but food was still plentiful in the shops. An advertisement for Stork margarine in *Picture Post* confidently informed readers: 'War-time cooking isn't going to be such a problem after all! For you can get Stork again – *as much Stork as ever you need*. So now it will be no trouble to make your Christmas cakes, puddings and pastry as light and delicious as Stork always makes them. And remember, Stork-made things are more digestible – more nourishing, too. Both are especially important in these times. Be sure to use Stork for all your Christmas cooking.'

Women's Own magazine featured a recommendation for producing a complete Christmas dinner of 'clear soup, roast turkey with chestnut and forcemeat stuffing, bread sauce, baked potatoes and Brussels sprouts or celery, Christmas pudding or mince pies'. It also carried recipes for making marzipan holly and fruits, trifle and shortbread. Its rival, *Women's Pictorial*, thought, 'One of the best things about Christmas is all the lovely things we have to eat – a greedy thought perhaps, but I think that is one that most people have. Why we don't have plum puddings, turkey and mince pies at other times of the year I don't know.'

Such thoughts of culinary extravagance were, however, frowned upon by the Ministry of Food. Just before Christmas, its Parliamentary Secretary Alan Lennox-Boyd suggested that those families who normally treated themselves to a ham at Christmas should, in view of the imminence of rationing, forgo it this year. Such advice went down badly when, the very next day, the public read in their newspapers that the Lord Mayor of London had attended a dinner at Frascati's restaurant. The menu, which was supposed to consist of dishes unlikely to be rationed, comprised: Whitstable oysters, bortsch soup, fillets of sole, kirsch punch, wings of chicken with a puree of mushrooms, comice pear cooked in vanilla syrup, vanilla ice and cheese savoury with chopped almonds on toast, dressed with pickled walnuts. At the same time there was a massive advertising campaign to popularise French food and drinks. In its 23 December issue, *The Economist* devoted three full pages of advertisements to boosting British Allies' wines, liqueurs and foodstuffs. Wines from Alsace were highly recommended for cocktails, 'at any time of the day', while no meal could be complete without a French cheese and a French wine with which to wash it down.

Chancellor of the Exchequer Sir John Simon's Budget back at the end of September had raised the price of a pint by 1d a pint,

1s.6d (8p) on a bottle of whisky and 1d on a packet of cigarettes. But despite these increases, newspapers and magazines were full of advertisements both for alcoholic Christmas cheer and tobacco products. In one, *Band Waggon* stars Askey and Murdoch boosted the restorative properties of Martini Vermouth, 'to make it a *Merry Xmas, Playmates!*':

'Challenge the blackout by opening a bottle of Martini, nature's gayest health-giving wine ... Martini Vermouth is an economical drink even in these hard times, so open a bottle tonight and close the doors against "wartime nerves," and don't forget to order your supply of Sweet and Dry for a Merry Christmas.'

And, in another, Father Christmas, wearing a steel helmet, 'advised' readers, 'Since parties find black-outs a bit of a blow .. . I'm taking them MOUSSEC wherever I go!' For those households which found it difficult to splash out seven shillings (35p) on a bottle of sparkling Moussec, there was always Stone's Ginger Wine – 'You'll Glow In the Blackout' – at a more modest 3s.3d (16p). And for 'housewives who win praises rare when preparing Christmas fare', there was always 'Point' British Sherry from Vine Products at Kingston, Surrey, at a modest 2s.6d (13p) a bottle.

Cigarette smokers and their friends were urged to 'Give them all Craven A this Xmas ... because these famous Cork-Tipped cigarettes are so fresh, cool-smooth to the throat. You can be certain you are a choosing a gift which will be thoroughly appreciated if you send all your friends Craven A this Christmas. Made specially to prevent sore throats.' And for those wishing to imitate the First Lord of the Admiralty in their smoking habits: 'Make it a Mannikin Xmas: a case of Manikin Cigars is the ideal gift that suits *your* purse and *his* pocket. He'll enjoy their Mild Havana Flavour. You can send sixty Mannikins to the boys in France for 7/6d [38p].'

As Christmas approached, the public were being bombarded with conflicting advice from Government ministers as to whether they should spend or save this year. President of the Board of Trade

Oliver Stanley saw no harm in a little seasonal spending on Christmas gifts. But, in a ministerial broadcast, Chancellor Sir John Simon strongly recommended that money should not be wasted on presents. Only if everybody saved, Sir John said, could prices be kept down. In the event, most people spent much the same as normal. Traditional Christmas gifts like Yardley soaps and perfumes, 'lovely things, priced to suit everyone from 2/6d [13p] to 45/- [£2.25] await your choice at any good chemist or store', were as popular as ever.

Books were popular gifts, 'to beat the blackout', and a number of celebrities were asked to recommend their Christmas favourite reading. Arthur Askey chose Arnold Bennett's *Imperial Palace*, while Gracie Fields opted for John Galsworthy's *The Forsyte Saga*. Tommy Handley recommended *The Diary of a Nobody* by George and Weedon Grossmith. Vic Oliver, when asked, replied rather pompously, 'I have no time for books. When I don't work in the theatre, I entertain the troops.' Mrs Chamberlain recommended Collingwood and Myers's *Roman Britain*. The Prime Minister himself received a Christmas gift of a walking stick in the form of a rolled-up umbrella, carved out of elm wood with a pocket knife by an eighty-six-year-old Suffolk shepherd.

For those on a tighter budget there were always gramophone records at two shillings (10p) each. Decca Records, proudly claiming it was keeping 'the flag flying with entertainment for the troops & the home . . . as in 1914 so in 1939', featured the Ambrose, Jack Payne and Lew Stone bands in its December advertisements. Adelaide Hall's recordings of 'Deep Purple' and 'Solitude' were also included as was Tommy Handley's novelty number, 'Hints on Blow-Outs for Black-Outs'.

For children, there was no shortage of toys in the shops at Christmas in 1939. Teddy bears, 'made in finest quality gold-coloured or white mohair plush' and ranging from 10 inches to 26¼ inches in height sold from 2s.3d (11p) to 22s.6d (£1.13). Dolls' houses could be had for 10s.11d (55p), while deluxe ones sold for 75s (£3.75). For boys, a Hornby No. 1 Special Passenger Train Set cost 33/6d (£1.68), and Meccano sets ranged in price from 3/3d (16p) to 22/6d (£1.13). But besides traditional Christmas presents, there were many others that had taken on a more warlike aspect; clockwork balloon barrages, model tanks, Bren gun carriers and searchlights at 4/11d (25p). A F.R.O.G. Interceptor Fighter retailed at 5s (25p) and an Astra mobile anti-aircraft gun at 6/6d (33p). Girls' dolls were still readily available, but now with smart-looking gas-mask carriers slung across their shoulders. And there were miniature uniforms for Red Cross nurses, pilot officers and naval officers selling at 5/11d (30p). Topical board games in the shops included the popular novelist Dennis Wheatley's 'Invasion: a thrilling battle of wits in which players have as their playing pieces the armed forces of the Navy, Army and Air Force. Complete with map, 160 playing pieces, dice and shaker', which sold for 7/6d (38p). Even cheaper was 'The Dover Patrol. Great Game of Naval Tactics' at 4/6d (23p) and the picture puzzle 'Soldiers of the King', which retailed at five shillings (25p).

But for many families in Britain even that sum was beyond their means. Two days before Christmas, *Picture Post* highlighted the plight of the family of forty-nine-year-old John Warrington of Clarissa Street, Hagerston, East London. Married with eleven children, Mr Harrington had had a number of labouring jobs in the Thirties, before losing the last one when war broke out. He was one of the 1,270,000 registered unemployed in Britain that December. As Mr Harrington had served during the First World War, he rejoined the Army, only to be discharged after two months because of a weak chest. 'Now, with Christmas in sight, he is without a job once more.' Mrs Warrington told the magazine, 'I would be pleased if he could get something. People think because I send my children out in decent clothes, we don't need anything. But the two flats we live in cost us £1 a week in rent alone.' Although 'the children are healthy and gay', the article concluded, 'when war came it took away their father's job. It lessened their mother's housekeeping money. But it didn't take away their appetites. And whether their father gets a job or not, they will at least still have their appetites at Christmas.'

Whatever their circumstances, the highlight of Christmas Day 1939 for many people in Britain and the Empire was the King's broadcast that afternoon. Since coming to the throne in December 1936, King George VI had not followed the practice of his father in delivering an annual Christmas broadcast. Because of his stammer, broadcasting, indeed any form of public speaking, was an ordeal that the King dutifully but agonisingly endured. But, with the same sense of duty with which he assumed the kingship after the Abdication, he and his advisers decided that he should broadcast to his peoples on Christmas Day 1939. While the text of the broadcast was being prepared, a clipping from *The Times* was sent to Buckingham Palace. It contained some words found written on a postcard in the desk of a recently deceased doctor in Bristol. His daughters had used the words on homemade greeting cards, one of which was sent to Mrs J.C.M. Allen of Clifton. Mrs Allen, thinking the words appropriate to the current war situation passed them on in turn to *The Times*.

Broadcasting on Christmas Day began at 7.00am with the programme *Christmas Greetings – A Sackful of Stories, Verses and Records*. The Christmas Day morning service at 10.55am came from the Chapel Royal at St James's Palace. That was followed by half an hour of music from the Foden's Motor Works Band. At 1.35pm there was a programme of national and popular songs in the programme *The Soldier Sings*. Then at 2.15pm came *The Empire's Greeting*. The *Radio Times*, in advertising the programme, had described how, 'On Christmas Day . . . when most people at home will be nearing the end of their Christmas dinners, the sound of Christmas bells will ring out from all the home and overseas transmitters of the BBC. Across the five continents and seven seas

London will be calling, sending Christmas greeting throughout the world.'

The programme featured messages from a Royal Navy destroyer, from men of the BEF out in France and from an RAF 'plane. From the West Country came a message from a farmer and his wife who had two London evacuee children as guests at their Christmas table. A Welsh male voice choir followed and then there were link-ups with Scotland, Northern Ireland and Northumbria. Messages from the Empire came next; a Newfoundland fisherman, a Canadian pilot, a New Zealand farmer, a dressmaker in Sydney, a Malayan naval rating, an Indian Army officer, and lastly a member of Cape Town's Coastal Defence Service. The programme ended with a shepherd in the Cotswolds passing on the Empire's greetings to the King-Emperor.

Then, just after three in the afternoon, the King himself, in a 'hesitant, upper class, un-dramatic voice', began a nine minute broadcast to his subjects in Britain and the Empire:

> The festival which we know as Christmas is above all the festival of peace and of the home. Among all free peoples the love of peace is profound, for this alone gives security to the home.
>
> But true peace is in the hearts of men, and it is the tragedy of this time that there are powerful countries whose whole direction and policy are based on aggression and the suppression of all that we hold dear for mankind.
>
> It is this that has stirred our peoples and given them a unity unknown in any previous war. We feel in our hearts that we are fighting against wickedness, and this conviction will give us strength from day to day to persevere until victory is assured.
>
> At home we are, as it were, taking the strain for what may lie ahead of us, resolved and confident. We look with pride and thankfulness on the never-failing courage and devotion of the Royal Navy upon which, throughout the last four months, has burst the storm of ruthless and unceasing war.

And when I speak of our Navy today, I mean all the men of our Empire who go down to the sea in ships, the Mercantile Marine, the minesweepers, the trawlers and drifters, from senior officers to the last boy who has joined up. To every one in this great fleet I send a message of gratitude and greeting, from myself as from all my peoples.

The same message I send to the gallant Air Force, which, in co-operation with the Navy is our sure shield of defence. They are daily adding laurels to those that their fathers won.

I would send a special word of greeting to the armies of the Empire, to those who have come from afar, and in particular to the British Expeditionary Force.

Their task is hard. They are waiting, and waiting is a trial of nerve and discipline. But I know that when the moment comes for action they will prove themselves worthy of the highest traditions of their great Service.

And to all who are preparing themselves to serve their country, on sea or land or in the air, I send my greeting at this time. The men and women of our far-flung Empire, working in their several vocations, with the one same aim, all are members of the great family of nations which are prepared to sacrifice everything that freedom of spirit may be saved to the world.

A new year is at hand. We cannot tell what it will bring. If it brings peace, how thankful we shall all be. If it brings us continued struggle we shall remain undaunted.

In the meantime, I feel that we might all find a message of encouragement in the lines which, in my closing words, I would like to say to you.

'I said to the man who stood at the gate of the year: "Give me a light that I may tread safely into the unknown."

'And he replied, "Go out into the darkness, and put your hand into the hand of God. That shall be to you better than light, and safer than a known way."'

May the Almighty hand guide and uphold us all.

Advance copies of the speech had been sent to newspaper offices and there was a veritable stampede in Fleet Street to trace the author of the quotation. From America and the Dominions came cables requesting the same information. When asked, John Masefield, the Poet Laureate, thought that the lines had the ring of G.K. Chesterton about them. Other poetry experts thought that they might have come from the pen of John Bunyan or of Thomas à Kempis. But it was not until midnight on Christmas Day that the BBC was in a position to give the definitive answer. The author was sixty-four-year-old Miss Minnie Louise Haskins.

Miss Haskins, by this time retired, had been a lecturer at the London School of Economics. In December 1939, she was living in Crowborough, Sussex and had actually not heard the King's broadcast that afternoon. She had, however, heard a BBC summary of it later that evening and thought that the opening words were 'oddly familiar'. Only when the quotation was finished did she recall that over thirty years before she had written something very similar in a slim book of verse entitled *The Desert*. It had been privately printed in 1908 and sold in aid of missionary work in India.

Within a few days of the King's broadcast, and despite objections from members of the clergy that St John's Gospel and John Bunyan had phrased it better, Miss Haskins found herself a celebrity. She was interviewed by the press and for the newsreels, and her book of verse was promptly republished.

The rest of the day's broadcasting included a competition in which 'soldiers in France will join in a parlour game with their parents in a BBC studio at home'. The inevitable Sandy Macpherson had a half-an-hour slot at 5.00pm, followed by 'Hullo, Mum', a link-up between evacuees in a Gloucestershire village and their parents in Stepney. A soldiers' service from France was broadcast at 6.20pm and then came 'A Radio Christmas Party: comedians, Christmas songs, musical games, and join-in listening in to other parties elsewhere ... a pill-box fort near the front line, an Army concert from one of the bases in France, a children's hospital ward, and a wartime edition of *Flying High* from an RAF hangar'.

Gracie Fields appeared at 9.15pm in an ENSA concert from 'somewhere in France' and then there was *A Christmas Cabaret* with Jack Hylton and his Band and Cyril Fletcher. After the news at midnight, the day's broadcasting closed down at 12.15am. Boxing Day's radio highlights included steeplechasing from Windsor, football between Sheffield Wednesday and Chesterfield and a live broadcast of the London Coliseum's pantomime *Cinderella*. 'In view of all that,' the *Radio Times* proudly trumpeted, 'who cares for the blackout? Who cares if it snows?'

If in 1939 the secular aspects of Christmas predominated, the religious element was by no means forgotten nor neglected. Striking an optimistic note, Archbishop of York William Temple reminded readers of *Picture Post* that: 'On Christmas morning German Christians, French Christians, Polish Christians, Finnish Christians, British Christians, Russian Christians – let us never forget the heroic multitude of Russian Christians – nor the Japanese and Chinese who in the Name of the Christ are all this time making the unity which will unite their nations as friends in days to come ...'

In an accompanying picture essay, the magazine published two photographs of villagers at Oberammergau at a Christmas service. It reminded readers that 'for six years, directly and indirectly, the Nazis have been trying to destroy Christianity in Germany'. But it was confident that 'these men and women in the village of the world-famous Passion Play will outlive the concentration camp, the swastika, the Gestapo'.

In his Christmas Day broadcast, the King had spoken of 'the great family of nations' that made up the British Empire and Commonwealth. Only a week before, the first Canadian troops had arrived in Britain. Now, on Boxing Day, a contingent of Australian airmen arrived to serve with the Royal Air Force's Coastal

Command. In a message to them, Australian air minister J.V. Fairbairn said, 'A great responsibility rests upon you as members of the First Australian Air Force squadron to come on active service in this country. You will be comrades in a great and just campaign with the men of the RAF, and Australia is confident that you will play your part in whatever spheres you may be called upon to serve.'

And the next day it was announced that the first Indian Army mule companies had joined Lord Gort's British Expeditionary Force in France. There had been fairly generous Christmas leave allowances for the British Expeditionary Force, but comedian Jack Warner raised a laugh on the BBC's *Garrison Theatre* when reading a letter from his 'Bruvver Syd' out in France: 'PS: I thought I was coming home on leave this weekend, but Lord Gort thought different!'

Among those, like Syd, unable to get back for Christmas was Rifleman William Smedmore. Writing to his sixty-four-year-old mother at the family home in Glamorgan Street, Pimlico, William told her: 'We are in good billets here. But not as good as last Christmas, at home with you. I'll be home next year without fail.'

For those servicemen stationed around Britain and unable to make it home for Christmas, Mr and Mrs F. Maguire of 74 Lynette Avenue, Clapham had come with a novel idea. Writing to *Picture Post* a month before Christmas, they had asked the magazine: 'If you can find us some eight to a dozen chaps (we are quite indifferent as to who or what they are) we would be glad if they would be our guests for Christmas dinner and a slice off the pudding! The only conditions attached are that they make themselves at home and help us to make the party go with a sing-song afterwards.'

'We can find you a dozen with the greatest pleasure,' the magazine replied. 'We can find you a thousand if you want them. We will find soldiers or groups of soldiers, for any other readers who feel generous.'

If Britain's Christmas, brightened by the River Plate victory and with ample food, drink and presents available, was a reasonably normal one, Germany's was a much more austere and depressing one. Unlike in Britain, both food and clothes rationing were firmly in place, but special concessions were made for the holidays. There was a slight raising of the food ration for the whole month and a special Christmas bonus. Not that they amounted to much. In practice it worked out at an extra egg, one-eighth of a pound of butter, the same amount of ersatz honey, a little chocolate candy and about two ounces of sweets per person. The sugar ration was also increased. On the clothing front, men were allowed a tie, and women, a pair of stockings, without having to surrender any of their precious coupons.

In Berlin's huge department stores and shops there was very little that customers could actually buy without special permission. The stores themselves had done their best to put on a festive front. The giant AWAG department store (formerly the Jewish-owned Wertheim's), had spent lavishly on a children's fairyland display in the main foyer, with animated animals, dwarfs, elves and fairies waving wands. But there was little worth having on sale. All the children's toys had gone a fortnight before Christmas, and none had been made since the outbreak of war. And in desperation, another store, the famous KaDeWe was reduced to selling Easter rabbits as its stock of other Christmas cuddly toys had sold out. Only the AWAG's book and record departments were well stocked, and even then in the latter, one had to hand over an old record before one could buy a new one. Just before Christmas, on coming out of the store, a Berliner remarked, 'I've been going in there every day for the past week and can't find anything that is not either purchasable only by permission of the government or totally foolish to give.'

Nor did the war news give many Germans cause for satisfaction. The scuttling of the *Graf Spee* off Montevideo came as a great shock to the public, as the action off the River Plate had been depicted as a German victory. And many believed that the claim of thirty-four RAF bombers shot down next day over Heligoland was 'eyewash' by Dr Goebbels to get them to forget the less-than-heroic end of the pocket battleship.

Dr Goebbels himself was much exercised at two major rail accidents in which over 200 died. He also fumed in his diary that 'Berlin "society" is still celebrating merrily as if the war had nothing to do with them. The dregs! To the rubbish heap with them!' The awful weather over Christmas – snow, rain, frost and sleet ice – did little to improve the propaganda minister's temper. He spent the holidays reading a Somerset Maugham novel, which only went to confirm his belief in the 'inner rottenness of English society'. And, 'sterile and idiotic' was Goebbels's withering and snide judgement on the King's Christmas Day broadcast. In his own Christmas message to the German people, Goebbels had told them:

'This is a "war Christmas" celebrated by a determined people . . . with that profound faith which is always a prerequisite of victory . . . Although peace is the real meaning of Christmas, we shall talk peace only after victory.'

While Dr Goebbels was spending Christmas with his family, Hitler was inspecting his troops on the Western Front. On 23 December he visited a reconnaissance squadron of the Luftwaffe and then the infantry regiment *Grossdeutschland*. He finished the day by participating in the Christmas celebrations of his own bodyguard unit *SS Leibstandarte Adolf Hitler*, giving the men an address on the 'meaning of the present struggle'. On Christmas Eve, he visited *flak* units and after again addressing the men was presented with a hand-carved German eagle, but without, it was noted, the swastika. In the afternoon, Hitler visited the *Hauptkampflinie* (main front line) and then tank and armaments factories in the Saarbruecken area. Afterwards, and for the first time since 1918, the Fuehrer found himself on French soil near Spichern, in a section abandoned by Gamelin's men back in October. Christmas Day was spent with a

IWM HU 40080

'In the afternoon Christmas celebration . . . many children present . . . they are very sweet and charming, the public are in good fettle despite all their troubles, my speech is greeted with great applause and there is great delight when Father Christmas arrives.' Dr Goebbels, 23 December 1939.

IWM HU 40088

'Midday with the Fuehrer. He tells me about his Christmas trip to the West Wall, which impressed him deeply. The mood at the front could not be better. The troops were beside themselves with joy. The Fuehrer's visit came as a complete surprise to them.' Dr Goebbels, 28 December 1939.

Luftwaffe fighter unit and the reconstituted List Infantry Regiment in which he had served during the Great War. The German press made great play with the fact that the Fuehrer, in contrast to Chamberlain, Daladier, Churchill, Eden and Co., was among his fighting men at Christmas.

Unlike Berlin, Christmas in *drôle de guerre* Paris was almost pre-war, like Britain's. There was no shortage of turkeys, oysters, foie gras or champagne, according to journalist Alexander Werth. Twice over the holidays, Werth visited a night club where chanteuse Lucienne Boyer entertained an audience of 'lots of young men in uniform, and young women, drinking champagne, and also fat bald podgy people', whom the journalist took to be war profiteers. The uncrowned king and queen of French show business, Maurice Chevalier and Josephine Baker, alternated each night at the Casino de Paris, while other music halls, theatres and cinemas did a roaring trade. For children, the shops on the *grands boulevards* had plenty of toys and presents in stock. At Lancel's, on the Boulevard Raspail, one could buy terracotta Aberdeen terriers raising a hind leg over a copy of Hitler's *Mein Kampf*. And, 'to keep our soldiers warm' in the Maginot Line, quite a few stores were offering tarred paper vests.

The newspapers and journals were full of officially inspired optimism, with stories of 'poor old Fritz' shivering away in the waterlogged Siegfried Line. Victory was taken for granted. Germany, already rationed, would sooner rather than later succumb to the Allied blockade. Meanwhile, writing in the December 1939 issue of *Les Annales de la Guerre*, Captain Georges Montgredien dwelt longingly and lovingly on the French Army's own food-and-drink situation: 'Midday everything is ready. There is a hors d'oeuvres, meat, vegetables and dessert . . . The messing officer reads out the menu, wishes everyone *bon appetit* and gives the signal for the regimental tune to be struck up.'

Montgredien noted that when it came to aperitifs, his commanding officer was 'very strict'. Only the *poilus* in the advance posts were to get Pernod, the rest had to make do with the lower-alcoholic-content St Raphaël. The Captain finished his idyllic account with the telling sentence, 'Provided the enemy's artillery lets us alone and provided there is a bit of sun, one can, for a moment, forget the war and think it all a picnic.'

But there was no 'picnic'or Christmas truce at sea in 1939. Just as its crew members were having drinks before their Christmas dinner, the London steamer SS *Stanholme* hit a mine that had been laid by the *U-33* at the beginning of November. She sank within five minutes. The ships' boats were smashed by the explosion, but two of the crew managed to lower a raft. For about a quarter of an hour, they rowed round where the *Stanholme* had gone down, picking up survivors. But soon the raft itself started to sink, and it was the only the timely arrival of a lifeboat from a Norwegian ship that saved the eleven survivors of the sinking. One of them was the wife of the chief engineer, forty-two-year-old Percy Jenvey:

'The captain had poured us out drinks in his cabin and wished us all Merry Christmas, when a terrible explosion occurred which threw us to the floor. We rushed on deck as the vessel began to heel over, and a second explosion shook us. My husband ran to the lifebelts, put one over my head and threw me into the water. That was the last I saw of him, for he went down with the ship.'

Neither did Christmas bring any respite to the fighting in Finland. Helsinki experienced several air-raid warnings on Christmas Day as Soviet bombers attempted to raid the capital. They did not get through to the city centre, but around thirty bombs were dropped in the suburbs. Over forty other places, including the cities of Viborg, Tampere and Turku, were bombed, and Viborg was also subjected to long-range bombardment. Elsie Warren noted admiringly in her diary, 'The Finns are still fighting bravely . . . Russians have been found frozen to death inside tanks. Helsinki was bombed on Xmas Day. The occupants spent from ten to three in air raid shelters.'

Paris, December 1939: 'Christmas draws near and the poultry merchants have a grand show of the traditional turkeys.'

'From somewhere in France, I wish all ranks of our forces throughout the world – navy and army and RAF – a happy Christmas and a bright New Year. Do remember, everyone at home, that we are happy and contented, and don't forget, when we come home, to roll out the barrel.' Men of the BEF at their Christmas dinner.

In German-occupied Poland, the Christmas holidays brought no relief from the Nazi terror. During a tavern brawl in the village of Wawer, near Warsaw, on 26 December, a couple of local criminals shot two German non-commissioned officers. That night, as soon as the news reached the German police authorities in Warsaw, reprisals were ordered. Under the command of Police Major Friederich Wilhelm Wenzel, men of *Polizei-Regiment Warschau* were sent to Wawer and the neighbouring suburb of Anin to undertake a special 'pacification' operation. 120 men between the ages of sixteen and seventy were rounded up. Among the men arrested were workmen, artisans, shopkeepers, office workers, a journalist and a retired Polish Army officer. The majority were Poles, but Jews and one Russian were also included in the number. When the men were 'dragged out of their beds, none of them had the slightest idea of what had happened in the restaurant . . . All of them were charged with actions not of their commission. Their only offence was that they happened to be in the area covered by the raid.' In fact, as well as permanent residents of the two villages, there were a number of men arrested who were just visiting their families or friends over the Christmas holidays.

Wenzel, with his immediate superior Lieutenant-Colonel of Police Max Daume present, presided over the mockery of a trial and sentenced 114 of the men to death. Antoni Bartoszek, the proprietor, had already been hung above the door of his tavern. The rest of the men were taken off to be machine-gunned to death on a piece of open ground. One of them managed to get away unhurt, while another seven, although wounded, were also able to escape. One of those executed, forty-year-old Warsaw bank official Daniel Gering, was of German descent. Three times he was given the chance to save himself, but each time told his captors, 'I am Pole.' This only served to infuriate the Nazis more, and before he was killed, Gering was treated with particular brutality. 'They beat him to pulp,' recalled one eyewitness, Janina Przedlacka, who lost both her husband and a son: 'I was left by myself, aching and desolate, stricken in a way that no human words can express.'

As the year drew to a close, the Allies issued their casualty figures. Three British soldiers and 1,135 French had been killed in action. In the air, the British had suffered 438 fatalities, and forty-two French airmen had died. At sea, the Royal Navy had lost 2,070 men, while French losses amounted to 256 men. A total of 2,511 British servicemen had been killed since 3 September, while French losses totalled 1,433. But heavy as these losses were, they bore no comparison to those of 1914. Then, between August and December 1914, the first BEF had lost 17,164 dead, 19,918 prisoner and 55,689 wounded. And in 1914, over a million Frenchmen had been killed, wounded or taken prisoner. Nor were casualty figures anything like the death toll from the earthquake that struck Anatolia in neutral Turkey. Elsie Warren recorded in her diary on 29 December, 'a report from Turkey says that an earthquake took place yesterday. There are over 30,000 dead.' In a few minutes whole towns were wiped out and vast areas of the region devastated. Cold, fire and famine added to the death toll and the suffering.

In London as the New Year approached, and despite the blackout, many were anxious to have as a good time as possible, CBS radio correspondent Ed Murrow told his listeners in America: 'There are more dance bands playing in the West End now than in the months before peace went underground. Any establishments where we could eat in those old days now engaged small orchestras. Customers want to dance. Places like the Embassy Club, Quaglino's, the Paradise and the Café de Paris are jammed every night. People come early and stay late ... practically no-one wears formal evening dress. That's a change from pre-war days.'

On New Year's Eve itself, at the Savoy Hotel there were no less than three cabarets that night and, at midnight, trumpeters of the Life Guards to sound in the New Year. Similar jollifications were to be found at the Berkeley. For those on more modest incomes, the Strand and Regent Palace Hotels and Lyons Corner Houses still offered 'gala entertainment', with celebratory 'Zebra' cocktails at 2s.6d (13p) a time.

Because of the blackout and the Control of Noises (Defence) Order which forbade the sounding of sirens, factory hooters, whistles, or noisy rattles, the New Year was ushered in on a relatively quiet note. In London's Piccadilly Circus, there was a chorus of ironic cheers as somebody in the crowd illegally shone their torch on a clock face at midnight. In the booking hall of the Circus's Underground Station, a crowd of youngsters wearing paper hats welcomed in 1940 with the singing of 'Knees Up, Mother Brown'.

First Lord of the Admiralty Winston Churchill saw the New Year in at a party given by cabinet colleague President of the Board of Trade Oliver Stanley and his wife Maureen. Their house at 58 Romney Street, Westminster, was filled to overflowing and an accordion-player went the rounds playing all the latest popular tunes. Churchill joined in with gusto the singing of a particular favourite of his 'Run, Rabbit, Run'. American foreign correspondent Virginia Cowles was a fellow guest: 'when the clock struck twelve a solemnity fell over the group. Mr Churchill took Freda Casa Maury and me either side of him; we all joined hands in a circle and sang Auld Lang Syne'.

Virginia, who was about to leave London to cover the war in Finland, sensed that uppermost in everybody's mind was what 1940 would bring. None more so than the First Lord of the Admiralty, for 'when Mr Churchill sang out the old year, he seemed deeply moved, as though he had a premonition that a few months later he would be asked to guide the British Empire through the most critical days it had ever faced'.

EPILOGUE

What happened to the people in this book?

James Agate remained a prolific writer and critic until his death in 1947. Among his theatrical discoveries was the talented young Donald Sinden.

Ruth Andreas-Friederich, operating a resistance group in Berlin, survived the Nazi regime and after the war went to live in Munich, where she married. She committed suicide in September 1977, aged seventy-six, and was honoured as Righteous Amongst Nations by Yad Vashem.

Edward Beattie, of the American news agency United Press, covered the war in Europe before being taken prisoner by the Germans in September 1944. He was released by the Red Army in April 1945. He wrote of his experiences in two books, *Passport to War* and *Diary of a Kriegie*.

Jozef Beck, after Poland's defeat, was interned in Roumania. He wrote an account of his foreign policy entitled *Final Report* and died, still an internee, in June 1944.

Anthony Wedgwood Benn served in the Royal Air Force during the latter part of the Second World War. He became a Member of Parliament in November 1950 at the age of twenty-five. He succeeded his father as Viscount Stansgate but renounced his title in 1963. Benn held a number of ministerial posts in the governments of Harold Wilson and James Callaghan. He retired as an MP in 2001.

Anthony Drexel Biddle Jr became United States Ambassador to the Polish Government in Exile in 1939 in France, and later to all the governments in exile in London from 1941. He resigned his diplomatic post to join the United States Army. In 1961 President John F. Kennedy made him ambassador to Spain but he died shortly and suddenly after the appointment was made.

Georges Bonnet was moved from the Foreign Ministry to become Minister of Justice a fortnight after war was declared. Along with Daladier, he lost office in March 1940 and spent the rest of his long life writing justifications for his policy in 1938/1939. He died in June 1973.

Nellie Carver worked at the Central Telegraph Office for the rest of the war, and on her retirement edited a news bulletin for former members of the CTO. She died in 1970 and her diaries came to the Imperial War Museum in 1989.

Neville Chamberlain remained Prime Minister until 10 May 1940. He became Lord President of the Council in Churchill's first cabinet and was a loyal supporter of the new premier. Diagnosed with bowel cancer, Chamberlain retired from office on 3 October 1940 and died on 9 November at his country home near Reading.

Moyra Charlton served with the First Aid Nursing Yeomanry and then the Auxiliary Territorial Service before joining the WRNS in

December 1942. She later married and lived on the Isle of Skye. She deposited transcripts of her diaries with the Imperial War Museum in 1988 and died at the age of eighty-two in November 2000.

Maurice Chevalier remained in France after the 1940 defeat and was unfairly accused of collaboration with the Germans. After a short spell in the doldrums his career picked up again. Following his appearance in the 1958 film *Gigi* he was awarded an Honorary Academy Award. He died in January 1972.

Count Galeazzo Ciano remained Italian foreign minister until February 1943 when he became ambassador to the Vatican. He voted against his father-in-law, Mussolini, in the Fascist Grand Council meeting which led to the *Duce's* overthrow in July 1943. Tried at Verona for 'treason', under pressure from the Nazis he was executed there on 11 January 1944, bravely facing the firing squad.

Kenneth Clark, in addition to his duties at the National Gallery, headed the Films Division of the Ministry of Information. He also encouraged official war art through the War Artists Advisory Committee. Many of the works of art produced as a result are now at the Imperial War Museum. Clark's most famous post-war achievement was the television series *Civilisation*. He died in 1983 aged eighty.

Alfred Duff Cooper, unlike Churchill and Eden, was not offered office in September 1939. He became Minister of Information in May 1940, but was not a success. Sent to the Far East in Autumn 1941, he was unfairly associated with the debacle of the fall of Singapore the following year. In 1944 he was made ambassador to France, a post in which he excelled. Dogged by ill health, he died on 1 January 1954.

Robert Coulondre was repatriated back to France and performed a number of diplomatic tasks during the 'Phoney War'. Unemployed during the Vichy regime, his last official role was as a representative on negotiations dealing with reparations in 1945. He published his memoirs, entitled *From Stalin to Hitler*, in 1950 and died in March 1959.

Noël Coward was tireless in entertaining servicemen and -women throughout the rest of the war. Denied a job in the Secret Service, he went on to produce one of the war's finest films, *In Which We Serve*, based on the early war career of his friend, Lord Louis Mountbatten. Coward was knighted in 1970 and died in March 1973.

Virginia Cowles reported on the fighting in Finland and on a number of other fronts, as well as in Britain. In 1945 she married Aidan Crawley. She authored a number of bestselling historical biographies, including *The Kaiser* in 1963. Twenty years later she was killed in a car crash in France, aged seventy-three.

Geoffrey Cox, *Daily Express* correspondent in Paris, had a distinguished post-war career which included editorship of Independent Television News from 1956 to 1968, during which time he founded *News at Ten*. He died in April 2008.

Edouard Daladier fell from power in March 1940. He was imprisoned by both the Vichy regime and by the Nazis. Returning to France after the war, he continued to play a part in politics but never again held ministerial office. He died in October 1970.

Hugh Dalton served in Churchill's wartime coalition as Minister of Economic Warfare and President of the Board of Trade. When Labour came to power in July 1945, Dalton expected to be made foreign secretary, but instead Prime Minister Attlee made him Chancellor of the Exchequer. Forced to resign over a Budget leak, Dalton remained a grandee of the Labour Party until his death in 1962.

Sefton Delmer escaped from Poland and covered the war in France before becoming the outstanding head of British black propaganda to Germany from 1941 to 1945. He resumed his newspaper career after the war and wrote two volumes of memoirs, *Trail Sinister* and *Black Boomerang*. He died in September 1979.

Alec Douglas-Home was very ill during the Second World War, which prevented him from taking an active role. He lost his seat in the 1945 election but was elected again in 1950. He was a member of the Churchill, Eden and Macmillan administrations and was foreign secretary between 1950 and 1963 when he became Prime Minister. He lost the 1964 election to Harold Wilson but regained office as foreign secretary in June 1970 in the Heath government. He returned to the House of Lords in 1975 and died in October 1995.

Tom Driberg continued writing the 'William Hickey' column in the *Daily Express*, but in 1942 was elected as an independent to Parliament in a sensational by-election at Maldon in Essex. He joined the Labour Party, eventually becoming its chairman. Ennobled in 1975 as Lord Bradwell, he died the following year. A memoir of his rackety private life, *Ruling Passions*, was published posthumously.

Anthony Eden became war minister in May 1940 and foreign secretary again in December. In that post he helped to curb some of Churchill's wilder ideas and was very much the Prime Minister's heir apparent. Eventually succeeding Churchill in 1955, Eden's own administration will be for ever associated with the Suez Crisis of 1956. Due to a breakdown in health, Eden resigned in January 1957 and died almost exactly twenty years later in January 1977.

Georg Elser remained in Nazi concentration camps until almost the end of the war. The Nazis hoped to use him in a show trial to prove that the British Secret Service had been responsible for his attempt to kill Hitler. In the event, the trial did not take place and

Elser was murdered in Dachau concentration camp on 9 April 1945. Elser is now regarded as a hero of the German resistance and in 2003 appeared on a commemorative stamp.

General Maurice Gamelin was dismissed on 18 May 1940 by Daladier's successor Paul Reynaud. Like Daladier he was imprisoned by Vichy and the Germans, but survived the war to write a three-volume defence of his career entitled *Servir.*

Dr Josef Goebbels, overshadowed during the early years of German military successes, came into his own as the war went against Germany. Preaching a radical approach to fighting a 'total war', Goebbels was the only one of the Nazi leaders to visit and encourage Germans in their bombed towns and cities. His propaganda was partly responsible for keeping the Germans fighting after all hope of victory had disappeared. After poisoning their six children, Goebbels and his wife Magda committed suicide on 1 May 1945.

Hermann Goering was lauded and promoted for the Luftwaffe's early successes. He had, however, fallen into virtual disgrace by 1943 because of defeat in the Battle of Britain, failure to supply to Stalingrad and the inability to defend the Reich against the Anglo-American strategic bombing offensive. Dismissed by Hitler at the war's end, Goering put up a spirited defence at the Nuremberg Trial. Sentenced to death, he cheated the hangman by committing suicide the night before his execution.

Marjorie Gothard wrote her war diary up until June 1940. Her husband George documented the family war and immediate post-war history in a number of colour home movies which were donated to the Imperial War Museum by George and Marjorie's sons in 2005.

Arthur Greenwood joined Churchill's coalition government in May 1940 as Minister without Portfolio with a seat in the War Cabinet.

Although Churchill called him 'a wise counsellor of high courage and a good and helpful friend', Greenwood's drinking problem meant that he was less effective than he might have been. A member of Attlee's post-war Labour government, Greenwood was forced out of office in 1947 and died seven years later in June 1954.

Lord Halifax continued as foreign secretary in Churchill's first cabinet until December 1940, when he was appointed British Ambassador in Washington. Initially unpopular in the United States, Halifax gained the confidence of the Roosevelt administration and surprising popularity among ordinary Americans. He helped Lord Keynes in the negotiations of the American loan before retiring in 1946. He died in December 1959.

Vivienne Hall kept her diary for the rest of the war. She remained unmarried and died in 1985.

Oliver Harvey served in the Paris Embassy until the fall of France when, after a short spell at the Ministry of Information, he returned to the Foreign Office as Private Secretary to Eden. He succeeded Duff Cooper at the Paris Embassy in 1947, retired from the Foreign Office in 1951 and died in 1968.

Sir Nevile Henderson returned to Britain via Holland after the declaration of war. He wrote and published an account of his twenty-eight months as ambassador to Germany, entitled *Failure of a Mission*. The original manuscript had to be seriously pruned by the Foreign Office, as sections of it were deemed to be too sympathetic to the Nazis as a whole and to Goering in particular. It also showed up the vacillations in British policy. Sir Nevile retired, served in the Home Guard and died of cancer of the throat in December 1942.

Stuart Hibberd continued as chief announcer at the BBC until his retirement in 1951, but carried on broadcasting until 1964. Having fought there in 1915, he was an enthusiastic member of the Gallipoli Association until his death in 1983.

Adolf Hitler continued on a path of military conquest. In 1940 he invaded Denmark, Norway, the Low Countries and France. The following year he attacked Yugoslavia and Greece, before turning on his erstwhile ally Stalin. Defeat at Stalingrad in 1943 heralded the beginning of the end for the Nazi regime. An attempt to assassinate Hitler in July 1944 failed, and he retained control and commanded loyalty right up until his suicide in Berlin on 30 April 1945.

Clare Hollingworth, who witnessed the opening shots of the Second World War in Katowice, covered the rest of the conflict as a war correspondent in the Balkans and the Middle East. After 1945 she became one of Britain's most distinguished foreign and defence correspondents, only finally retiring at the beginning of the twenty-first century.

Leslie Hore-Belisha left the War Office in January 1940, the victim of a plot involving the generals and Buckingham Palace. Chamberlain offered him the Board of Trade, but he turned it down and returned to the back benches. He was a persistent critic of the Government during the remainder of the war, but was brought back as Minister of National Insurance in Churchill's caretaker administration between May and July 1945. Defeated in the July 1945 general election, Hore-Belisha never held office again. He was ennobled in 1954 and died suddenly in February 1957 while making a speech in Paris.

Max Jordan became the Head of Religious Broadcasting for NBC, but returned to Europe to cover the last months of the war, and while in Switzerland scooped news of the Japanese decision to surrender. He took holy orders as a Benedictine priest and died in November 1977, aged eighty-three.

William Joyce, aka **Lord Haw Haw,** made his last broadcast from Hamburg on 30 April 1945. A month later he was captured by two British officers while in hiding near the Danish border. He was brought back to England, tried for treason and sentenced to death. Appeals for clemency were turned down and Joyce was hanged at Wandsworth Prison on 3 January 1946.

William Lyon MacKenzie King was Prime Minister of Canada from 1935 until 1948 – the longest-serving Commonwealth premier. Under his administration, Canada built up the third-largest Allied navy and fourth-largest Allied air force during the Second World War. He died in July 1950.

Wilhelm Krey served throughout the Polish campaign, where he was personally responsible for the persecution and murder of at least one Jew. His later wartime service and what became of him is not known.

Zbigniew Leon and his brother both survived the German occupation of Poland and were members of the Polish Home Army. They both live in Warsaw today.

Vera Lynn, through her morale-boosting radio broadcasts and personal appearances both on the home and fighting fronts, earned the title 'Forces Sweetheart'. She was made a Dame of the British Empire in 1975 and retired in 1995. At the age of ninety-two Dame Vera is still an active supporter of service charities.

Patrick Maitland of *The Times* served as a war correspondent until 1943, when he joined the Foreign Office. He served as Conservative MP between 1951 and 1959 and succeeded his brother as the seventeenth Earl of Lauderdale in 1968.

Marshal Carl Gustaf Mannerheim commanded Finland's forces in the Continuation War against Russia, 1941–44. In August 1944 he became the President of Finland and successfully negotiated his country's withdrawal from the war. He retired to Switzerland in 1946 and died there in January 1951.

Robert Menzies remained Prime Minister of Australia until August 1941. He became premier again in 1949 and served until 1966. On Churchill's death, Menzies inherited his mantle as the 'grand old man of the Commonwealth'. He died in May 1976.

Unity Mitford returned from Germany via Switzerland and France in January 1940. The *Daily Express* offered her father, Lord Redesdale, £5,000 for her exclusive story. This was turned down. Unity spent the rest of the war in isolation, still talking of her admiration for the Fuehrer. She died in 1948 through the long-term effect of her suicide attempt.

Helena Mott moved from Teddington, Middlesex to Greenwich in 1946, and continued to write her diary almost up until her death in 1951. It was donated to the Imperial War Museum in 1997.

Benito Mussolini declared war on the Allies in June 1940. The course of Italy's war was disastrous and Mussolini was toppled from power in July 1943. Rescued by the Germans, he was set up by them as the puppet ruler of Northern Italy, the so-called 'Italian Social Republic' of Salo. He and his mistress, Clara Petacci, were shot by partisans on 28 April 1945.

Wilhelm Prueller fought in France and Russia, was wounded and commissioned as an officer. He remained an unrepentant Nazi right to the end of Hitler's regime and beyond. The manuscripts of his diaries came to light in October 1959. His own subsequent fate remains unknown.

Count Edward Raczynski remained Polish Ambassador in London, and later served as foreign minister in General Sikorski's government. At the end of the war, Raczynski stayed in Britain and became President of the Polish Government in Exile. He died in July 1993, eighteen months after his third marriage at the age of 100.

John McCutcheon Raleigh returned to the United States in 1940. After Pearl Harbor, he covered the war in the Far East for the Columbia Broadcasting System, and wrote an account entitled *Pacific Blackout*. From 1943 he spent the rest of the war as a broadcaster on Minneapolis local radio.

Joachim von Ribbentrop, despite his ignorance and stupidity, remained Hitler's foreign minister right up until the end of the Third Reich, although Hitler dropped him in his last will and testament. Von Ribbentrop's influence and power declined throughout the war, but his involvement in the 'Final Solution of the Jewish Problem' – the Holocaust – ensured his inclusion as a major war criminal at the Nuremberg Trial. At Nuremberg he cut a pathetic figure, still in awe of Hitler's personality. After Goering's suicide, von Ribbentrop was the first to mount the gallows on 16 October 1946.

William Russell returned to the United States in 1940. He wrote an account of his time in the German capital, *Berlin Embassy*, which was published in Britain by Michael Joseph in 1940, and reissued in 2004.

Michael Joseph Savage, terminally ill when war broke out, died in March 1940. He was succeeded as premier by Peter Fraser, who remained in office until 1949. Fraser died a year after leaving office, in December 1950.

Dr Paul Schmidt continued to interpret for Hitler for the duration of the war, including at meetings with General Franco and Marshal Pétain. Despite his association with Hitler, Schmidt only joined the Nazi Party in 1943. After the war, he stood unsuccessfully for the West German Parliament, before becoming principal of the

Institute of Linguisitics and Translation in Munich. Schmidt died in April 1970.

John Simon remained as Chancellor until Churchill became prime minister in May 1940. Surprisingly, given his track record on appeasement, Churchill retained Simon in the Government, but in the decorative post of Lord Chancellor. Simon wrote a bland volume of memoirs entitled *Retrospect* and died in 1954 at the end of his eightieth year.

Jan Christiaan Smuts continued as South African Prime Minister until 1948. Churchill consulted him on almost all major decisions and it was even suggested that, should Churchill become incapacitated, Smuts would take over as Prime Minister of Great Britain. He was made a British field marshal in 1941. Smuts died in September 1950.

Florence Speed spent the rest of the Second World War with her brother and sister at their house in Vassall Road, SW9. She continued to keep a diary, which was donated to the Imperial War Museum after her death in 1979.

Richard Stevens and **Sigismund Payne-Best** were incarcerated in Nazi concentration camps until liberated in 1945. After the war they were accused of providing the Nazis with detailed information on British Secret Intelligence Service personnel in western Europe. Stevens went on to translate a number of books dealing with the period of the Third Reich and died in 1965. Payne-Best was declared bankrupt and for a long time tried, in the end successfully, to obtain compensation from the West German government for the time spent in concentration camps. He died in 1978.

Joan Strange remained a physiotherapist living at Langton Road, Worthing, Sussex. She died in 1994 at the age of ninety-one, having lived to see her Second World War diary published.

Gwyneth Thomas worked at both Highgate and Lewisham hospitals for the remainder of the war. She retired to Poole, Dorset, and gave her wartime diary to the Imperial War Museum in 1985.

Elsie Warren continued to work with the Auxiliary and then National Fire Service for the rest of the war. She donated her Second World War diary, her Defence Medal and a number of photographs to the Imperial War Museum in 1985.

Evelyn Waugh had a chequered career during the war, serving with the Royal Marines, the Commandos and the Royal Horse Guards. In 1942, he published *Put Out More Flags*, a brilliant satire of the 'Phoney War' period. In 1944, he was given special leave to write *Brideshead Revisited*, before going to Yugoslavia to act as liaison officer with Marshal Tito's partisans. Much of Waugh's wartime experiences are reflected in his *Sword of Honour* trilogy, which was televised in 2001 with Daniel Craig in the lead role. Waugh died on Easter Sunday, 1966.

Ernst von Weizsacker continued as State Secretary in the German Foreign Office under von Ribbentrop until 1943, when he became ambassador to the Vatican. Tried at Nuremberg at the Wilhelmstrasse Trial, he was given a prison sentence but was released early. He died in 1951. Weizsacker's son Richard was President of the German Federal Republic from 1984 to 1994.

Alexander Werth, *Manchester Guardian* correspondent in Paris, went on to cover the war in the Soviet Union in 1941 and wrote a bestselling book entitled *Russia at War*. He continued his career as a foreign correspondent after the war and also held academic posts. He died in March 1969.

ACKNOWLEDGEMENTS

Firstly, I would like to express my gratitude to Lord Bragg for taking time off in a very busy schedule to write the foreword to this book, and for his very generous comments about it. I would also like to take this opportunity to thank the team of the ITV documentary *Outbreak*, which Lord Bragg masterminded, edited and narrated, and on which I was the historical consultant. They are: Executive Producer, Matt Cain; Director, Martina Hall; Researchers, Alexandra Lowe and Stephanie Pochet; Film Researcher, Peter Scott; Production Manager, Siobhan Kiernan; and Film Editor, Steve Scales.

Secondly, I would like to thank at Virgin Books, Ed Faulkner, Davina Russell and Kelly Falconer for all their help, advice and encouragement in the production of this book. Special thanks go to Martin Noble, who has done a marvellous job of the editing of the book.

As my colleagues at the Imperial War Museum must be sick and tired of hearing me say, 'wars are won with high morale, good communications and dedicated teamwork'. This book has been very much the product of the latter and I hope has encompassed the other two as well. I am very grateful to all friends and colleagues throughout the Museum for their help, advice and interest in the preparation of this book. I would especially like to thank the following:

Department of Documents
Emma Goodrum
Tony Richards
Simon Robbins
Sabrina Rowlett
Rod Suddaby

Exhibitions
Alison Brown
Sarah Gilbert
Rebecca Wakeford
Laura Whalley

Film Department
Toby Haggith
Matt Lee

Photograph Archive
Richard Bayford
Glyn Biesty
Ian Carter
Damon Cleary
Laura Clouting
Dave Parry
Ian Proctor

Museum Services
Elizabeth Bowers
Madeleine James

Laura McKechan
Diana Morley
Abigail Ratcliffe
Victoria Smith

Sound Archive
Margaret Brooks
Richard Hughes
Richard McDonough

Thanks are also due to Laurence Burley, Ann Carter, Paul Cornish, John Delaney, Philip Dutton, Brad King, Emily Macarthur, Andrew McDonnell and Jane Rosen.

Lastly, it gives me immense satisfaction to acknowledge all the help, support and encouragement that I have had from my own colleagues in the Research and Information Department at the Imperial War Museum. Nick Hewitt willingly gave me the benefit of his immense knowledge of naval warfare for the chapter on the War at Sea, as well as shrewd advice on other sections of the book. I am most grateful to him. Sarah Batsford's contribution to the book has been, at all times, 'above and beyond the call of duty'. Her extensive researches in the IWM's collecting departments yielded much in the way of valuable source material that I might otherwise have overlooked. In so many other ways, Sarah's enthusiasm, support and practical assistance in the book's preparation have proved invaluable, and I owe her a great debt of thanks. Finally, since the book's inception, James Taylor has once again proved to be all that a friend and colleague should be, and it is to him that I dedicate *Outbreak*.

Terry Charman
Imperial War Museum
May 2009

BIBLIOGRAPHY

Agate, James, *Ego 4: Yet More of the Autobiography of James Agate,* George G. Harrap & Co. Ltd., London, 1940.

Allingham, Margery, *The Oaken Heart,* Michael Joseph Ltd, London, 1941.

Anderson, Verily, *Spam Tomorrow,* Rupert Hart-Davis, London, 1956.

Andreas-Friedrich, Ruth, *Berlin Underground: 1938–1945,* Henry Holt & Co., New York, 1947.

Aster, Sidney, *1939: The Making of the Second World War,* André Deutsch, London, 1973.

Avon, The Rt Hon. The Earl of, *The Eden Memoirs: The Reckoning,* Cassell, London, 1965.

Ball, Adrian, *The Last Day of the Old World,* Doubleday & Co., Inc., New York, 1963.

Bannister, Sybil, *I Lived under Hitler: An Englishwoman's Story,* Rockliff, London, 1957.

Barnes, Derek Gilpin, *Cloud Cover: Recollections of an Intelligence Officer,* Rich & Cowan, London, 1949.

Barraud, E. M., *Set My Hand upon the Plough,* Littlebury & Co. Ltd, Worcester, 1946.

Bartlett, Dorothy A., *Nurse in War*, P.R. Macmillan Ltd, London, 1961.

Bartoszewski, Władysław, *Warsaw Death Ring 1939–1944*, Interpress, Warsaw, 1968.

Baxter, Beverley, *Men, Martyrs and Mountebanks: Beverley Baxter's Inner Story of Personalities and Events behind the War*, Hutchinson & Co. Ltd, London, 1940.

Bayles, William D., *Postmarked Berlin*, Jarrolds, London, 1942.

Beardmore, George, *Civilians at War: Journals 1938–1946*, John Murray, 1984.

Beattie, Edward W., *Passport to War*, Peter Davies, London, 1943.

Bethell, Nicholas, *The War Hitler Won: September 1939*, Allen Lane, The Penguin Press, 1972.

Bielenberg, Christabel, *The Past Is Myself* Chatto & Windus, London, 1969.

Bois, Elie J., *Truth on the Tragedy of France*, Hodder & Stoughton Ltd, London, 1940.

Bonnet, Georges, *Quai d'Orsay*, Times Press, Anthony Gibbs & Phillips, Isle of Man, 1965.

Boothby, Robert, *I Fight to Live*, Victor Gollancz Ltd, London, 1947.

Boyce, Robert and Maiolo, Joseph A., *The Origins of World War Two: The Debate Continues*, Palgrave Macmillan, 2003.

Briggs, Asa, *The War of Words*, Oxford University Press, London, 1970.

Bright Astley, Joan, *The Inner Circle: A View of War at the Top*, Hutchinson, London, 1971.

Broad, Richard and Fleming, Suzie, *Nella Last's War: A Mother's Diary 1939–45*, Falling Wall Press, 1981

Bullitt, Orville H., *For the President: Personal and Secret: Correspondence between Franklin D. Roosevelt and William C. Bullitt*, André Deutsch, London, 1972.

Butler, Ewan, *Amateur Agent*, George G. Harrap & Co. Ltd, London, 1963.

Butler, Lord, The *Art of the Possible: The Memoirs of Lord Butler*, Hamish Hamilton, London, 1971.

Cannistraro, Philip V., Wynot Jr, Edward D. and Kovaleff, Theodore P. (eds), *Poland and the Coming of the Second World War: The Diplomatic Papers of A J Drexel Biddle, Jr., United States Ambassador to Poland, 1937–1939*, Ohio State University, Columbus, 1976.

Carley, Michael Jabara, *1939: The Alliance That Never Was and the Coming of World War II*, Ivan R. Dee, Chicago, 1999.

Christiansen, Arthur, *Headlines All My Life*, Heinemann, London, 1961.

Churchill, Randolph S., *Into Battle: Speeches by the Right Hon. Winston S. Churchill P.C., M.P.*, Cassell & Co. Ltd, London, 1941.

Churchill, Winston S., *The Second World War, Volume I: The Gathering Storm*, Cassell & Co. Ltd, London, 1948.

Clark, Kenneth, *Another Part of the Wood: A Self-Portrait*, John Murray, London, 1979.

Coats, Peter, *Of Generals and Gardens: The Autobiography of Peter Coats*, Weidenfeld & Nicolson, London, 1976.

Colville, John, *The Fringes of Power: Downing Street Diaries 1939–1955*, Hodder & Stoughton, London, 1985.

Connell, Daniel, *The War at Home: Australia 1939–1949*, Australia Broadcasting Corporation, Crows Nest, NSW, 1988.

Cooper, Diana, *The Light of Common Day*, Rupert Hart Davis, London, 1959.

Cooper, Duff, *Old Men Forget: The Autobiography of Duff Cooper*, Rupert Hart-Davis, London, 1954.

Cosgrave, Patrick, *Churchill at War: Volume I: Alone 1939–40*, Collins, London, 1974.

Coward, Noël, *Future Indefinite*, William Heinemann Ltd, London, 1954.

Cowles, Virginia, *Looking for Trouble*, Hamish Hamilton, London, 1940.

Cox, Geoffrey, *Countdown to War: A Personal Memoir of Europe 1938–1940*, William Kimber, London, 1988.

Cox, Geoffrey, *The Red Army Moves*, Victor Gollancz, London, 1941.

Crampsey, Bob, *The Young Civilian: A Glasgow Wartime Boyhood*, Mainstream Publishing, 1987.

Cudahy, John, *The Armies March: A Personal Report*, Charles Scribner's Sons, New York, 1941.

Davie, Michael (ed.), *The Diaries of Evelyn Waugh*, Weidenfeld & Nicolson, London, 1976.

Delmar, Sefton, *Trail Sinister: An Autobiography. Volume 1*, Secker & Warburg, London, 1961.

Deuel, Wallace, *People Under Hitler*, Lindsay Drummond, London, 1942.

Dolin, Anton, *Autobiography*, Oldbourne, London, 1960.

Donnelly, Peter (ed.), *Mrs Milburn's Diaries: An Englishwoman's Day-to-Day Reflections 1939–1945*, Harrap, London, 1979.

Douglas, Roy, *1939: A Retrospect Forty Years After*, Archon Books, Connecticut, 1983.

Earle, Hubert P., *Blackout: The Human Side of Europe's March to War*, J.B. Lippincott Co., Philadelphia, 1939.

Ellis, L.F., *The War in France and Flanders 1939–1940*, Her Majesty's Stationery Office, London, 1953.

Elliston, H.B., *Finland Fights*, George G. Harrap & Co. Ltd, London, 1940.

Fields, Gracie, *Sing as We Go: The Autobiography of Gracie Fields*, Frederick Muller Ltd, London, 1960.

Fleming, Nicholas, *August 1939: The Last Days of Peace*, Peter Davies, London, 1979.

Foreign Office, *The British War Blue Book*, Farrar & Rinehart, New York, 1939.

Gilbert, Martin, *Finest Hour: Winston S. Churchill 1939–1941*, Heinemann, London, 1990.

Gilbert, Martin, *Prophet of Truth: Winston S. Churchill 1922–1939*, Minerva, London, 1990.

Goldsmith, John (ed.), *Stephen Spender: Journals 1939–1983*, Faber & Faber, London, 1985.

Haining, Peter, *The Day War Broke Out*, W.H. Allen, London, 1989.

Hammerton, John, *The Second Great War: A Standard History, Volume 1*, The Amalgamated Press Ltd, London, 1939–1940.

Hammerton, John, *The Second Great War: A Standard History, Volume 2*, The Amalgamated Press Ltd, London, 1940.

Hammerton, John, *The War Illustrated: Complete Record of the Conflict by Land and Sea and in the Air, Volume 1*, The Amalgamated Press Ltd, London, 1939–1940.

Hammerton, John, *The War Illustrated: Complete Record of the Conflict by Land and Sea and in the Air, Volume 2*, The Amalgamated Press Ltd, London, 1940.

Harrisson, Tom and Madge, Charles, *War Begins at Home: by Mass Observation*, Chatto & Windus, London, 1940.

Harvey, John (ed.), *The Diplomatic Diaries of Oliver Harvey 1937–1940*, Collins, London, 1970.

Hehn, Paul N., *A Low Dishonest Decade: The Great Powers, Eastern Europe and the Economic Origins of World War II, 1930–1941*, Continuum, New York/London, 2002.

Henderson, Sir Nevile, *Failure of a Mission: Berlin 1937–1939*, Hodder & Stoughton Ltd, London, 1940.

Hibberd, Stuart, *This Is London . . .*, MacDonald & Evans, London, 1950.

Hollingworth, Clare, *The Three Weeks' War*, Duckworth, London, 1940.

Home, Lord, *The Way the Wind Blows: An Autobiography*, Collins, London, 1976.

Hutching, Megan (ed.), *Last Line of Defence: New Zealanders Remember the War at Home*, HarperCollins, Auckland, 2007.

Jacob, Naomi, *Me – In Wartime*, Hutchinson & Co. Ltd, London, 1941.

James, Robert, Rhodes (ed.), *Chips: The Diaries of Sir Henry Channon*, Weidenfeld & Nicolson, London, 1967.

Jesse, F. Tennyson and Harwood, H.M., *London Front: Letters Written to America (August 1939–July 1940)*, Constable & Co Ltd, London, 1940.

Johnson, B.S. (ed.), *The Evacuees,* Victor Gollancz, London, 1968.

Jordan, Max, *Beyond All Fronts: A Bystander's Notes on This Thirty Years War*, The Bruch Publishing Co., Milwaukee, 1944.

Kee, Robert, *The World We Left Behind: A Chronicle of the Year 1939,* Weidenfeld & Nicolson, London, 1984.

Lazareff, Pierre, *Deadline: The Behind-the-Scenes Story of the Last Decade in France*, Random House, New York, 1942.

Lehmann, John, *I Am My Brother: Autobiography 2,* Longmans, 1960.

Longmate, Norman, *How We Lived Then: A History of Everyday Life during the Second World War,* Arrow Books, London, 1973.

Lukacs, John, *The Last European War: September 1939/December 1941,* Routledge & Kegan Paul, London and Henley, 1976.

Mackenzie, Compton, *My Life and Times 1939–1946,* Chatto & Windus, London, 1969.

Maitland, Patrick, *European Dateline,* Adelphi, London, 1946.

Mass Observation, *Britain,* Penguin Books, Middlesex, 1938.

Mass Observation, *The Pub and the People: A Worktown Study,* Victor Gollancz, London, 1943.

Middlebrook, Martin and Everitt, Chris, *The Bomber Command War Diaries: An Operational Reference Book, 1939–1945,* Viking, Middlesex, 1985.

Minney, R.J., *The Private Papers of Hore-Belisha,* Collins, London, 1960.

Mosley, Leonard, *On Borrowed Time: How World War II Began,* Weidenfeld & Nicolson, London, 1969.

Muggeridge, Malcolm (ed.), *Ciano's Diary,* William Heinemann Ltd, London, 1947.

Niven, David, *The Moon's a Balloon: Reminiscences,* Coronet Books, London, 1973.

Panter-Downes, Mollie, *London War Notes 1939–1945*, Longman, 1971.

Penglase, Joanna and Horner, David, *When the War Came to*

Australia: Memories of the Second World War, Allen & Unwin, St Leonards, NSW, 1992.

Picture Post, Volumes 4,5 & 6, Hulton Press, London, 1939–1940.

Polish Ministry of Information, *The German Invasion of Poland: Polish Black Book*, Hutchinson & Co. Ltd, London and Melbourne, 1941.

Powell, Anthony, *To Keep the Ball Rolling: The Memoirs of Anthony Powell, Volume III: Faces in My Time*, The Quality Book Club, London, 1980.

Raczynski, Edward, *In Allied London*, Weidenfeld & Nicolson, London, 1962.

Raleigh, John McCutcheon, *Behind the Nazi Front*, George G. Harrap & Co. Ltd, London, 1941.

Ramsey, Winston G. (ed.), *The Blitz, Then and Now*, Battle of Britain Prints International Ltd, London, 1987.

Reynaud, Paul, *In the Thick of the Fight 1930–1945*, Cassell & Co. Ltd, London, 1955.

Robbins Landon, H.C. and Leitner, Sebastian, *Wilhelm Prüller: Diary of a German Soldier*, Faber & Faber, London, 1963.

Roberts, Cecil, *Sunshine and Shadow: Being the Fourth Book of an Autobiography 1930–1946*, Hodder & Stoughton, London, 1972.

Rossino, Alexander B., *Hitler Strikes Poland: Blitzkrieg, Ideology, and Atrocity*, University Press of Kansas, Kansas, 2003.

Rothenstein, John, *Brave Day Hideous Night: Autobiography 1939–1965 (I)*, Hamish Hamilton, London, 1966.

Russell, William, *Berlin Embassy*, E.P. Dutton & Co. Inc., New York, 1941.

Salter, Cedric, *Flight From Poland*, Faber & Faber Ltd, London, 1940.

Schmidt, Paul, *Hitler's Interpreter*, William Heinemann Ltd, London, 1951.

Seth, Ronald, *The Day War Broke Out: The Story of the 3rd September 1939*, Neville Spearman Ltd, London, 1963.

Sewell, J.E., *Mirror of Britain*, Hodder & Stoughton, London, 1941.

Sheridan, Dorothy, *Among You Taking Notes ... The Wartime Diary of Naomi Mitchison 1939–1945*, Victor Gollancz Ltd, London, 1985.

Shirer, William L., *Berlin Diary: The Journal of a Foreign Correspondent 1934–1941*, Alfred A Knopf, New York, 1941.

Shirer, William L., *The Collapse of the Third Republic: An Inquiry into the Fall of France in 1940*, Pan Books Ltd, London, 1972.

Shirer, William L., *This is Berlin: A Narrative History: 1938-40*, Hutchinson, London, 1999.

Spier, Eugen, *The Protecting Power*, Skeffington & Son Ltd, London, 1951.

St John, Robert, *Foreign Correspondent*, Hutchinson, London, 1961.

Struther, Jan, *Women of Britain: Letters from England*, Harcourt, Brace & Co., New York, 1941.

Thorne, Christopher, *The Approach of War, 1938–1939*, Macmillan, London, 1967.

Turner, E.S., *The Phoney War on the Home Front*, Michael Joseph, London, 1961.

Von Hassell, Ulrich, *The Von Hassell Diaries: 1938–1944*, Hamish Hamilton, London, 1948.

Wacław, Jedrzejewicz ed., *Diplomat in Paris 1936–1939: Papers and Memoirs of Juliusz Łukasiewicz, Ambassador of Poland*, Columbia University Press, London 1970.

Watt, Donald Cameron, *How War Came: The Immediate Origins of the Second World War, 1938–1939*, Heinemann, London, 1989.

Weymouth, Anthony, *A Psychologist's War-Time Diary*, Longmans, Green & Co., London, 1940.

Wilson, Norman Scarlyn, *A United People Goes to War*, Hodder & Stoughton, London, 1939.

Winn, Godfrey, *The Infirm Glory: Volume 2, The Growing Years*, Pan Book Ltd, London, 1967.

Wyndham, Joan, *Love Lessons: A Wartime Diary*, Heinemann, London, 1986.

List of unpublished sources

For anybody researching and writing on the two world wars and other conflicts since 1914, the Imperial War Museum's Department of Documents is a treasure trove of unpublished diaries and letters. In writing *Outbreak*, I set myself the task of recording what people actually wrote and said at the time, rather than what people remember today of 1939. This task was greatly assisted by the fact that the Department had such a wealth of material from 1939.

The following collections have been the most useful in the preparation of the book. I was especially struck by the fact that so much excellent material was to be found in the diaries of ordinary people at home, the majority of whom were women, going through an extraordinary time. I am most grateful to them, and to their families, for their kind and generous permission to use and quote from them.

Name	IWM Department of Documents Catalogue Number
Mott Miss H P L	97/14/3
Gothard Mrs M	06/26/1
Carver Miss N V	90/16/1
Charlton Miss M	88/13/2
Thomas Miss G	90/30/1
Speed Miss F M	86/45/2
Strange Miss J C	96/13/2
Hall Miss V	DS/MISC/88 & 84/35/1A
Warren Miss E	87/14/1
Pope Major A A K	99/18/1
Rex Miss J M	87/14/1
Monk-Jones, Mr and Mrs A	Con Shelf & 01/50/1
Cox Mrs G	PP/MCR/C41
Lockwood F T	96/52/1
Paine N A	89/3/1
Hird A F	61/113/1
The R Wiley Collection of Second World War memories	Misc 258/1-3 (3511)

The Museum's Sound Archive is likewise a veritable goldmine for historians and researchers. It was fascinating to go through the collection hearing the sounds and voices of 1939. Because of the parameters I set myself, I have not included, in most cases, people's recorded interviews in which they give their recollections of 1939, but the following were most useful:

Name	IWM Sound Archive Catalogue Number	
Schuhart, Otto	2358	Recorded 1960
Young, Walter	9405	Recorded 1986
Chilton, Thomas	27345	Recorded 2004
Fryett Walker, Pax	27335	Recorded 2004
Ouvry, John	9260	Recorded 1986
Lewis, Roger	8782	Recorded 1976
Richards, Brooks	9970	Recorded 1987
Hall, John	25935	Recorded 2003

INDEX